Insurance Law Handbook

Fifth Edition

Insurance Law Handbook

Fifth edition

by

Noleen John

Charlie Weston-Simons

Laura Hodgson

Bloomsbury Professional

LONDON • DUBLIN • EDINBURGH • NEW YORK • NEW DELHI • SYDNEY

BLOOMSBURY PROFESSIONAL
Bloomsbury Publishing Plc

50 Bedford Square, London, WC1B 3DP, UK
1385 Broadway, New York, NY 10018, USA
29 Earlsfort Terrace, Dublin 2, Ireland

First published in Great Britain 2022

British Library Cataloguing-in-Publication Data

A catalogue record for this book is available from the British Library.

ISBN: PB: 978-1-52651-591-9
ISBN: Epub: 978-1-52651-593-3
ISBN: Epdf: 978-1-52651-592-6

Typeset by Evolution Design & Digital Ltd (Kent)
Printed and bound by CPI Group (UK) Ltd, Croydon, CR0 4YY

To find out more about our authors and books visit www.bloomsburyprofessional.com. Here you will find extracts, author information, details of forthcoming events and the option to sign up for our newsletters

Preface

This fifth edition marks the continued development of Professor Robert Merkin's original work and seeks to maintain his aim of providing a concise and practical statement of insurance law for the benefit of both practitioners and students of the subject.

We have provided an overview of how the essential principles of insurance law and, where relevant, insurance regulation apply to the major lines of insurance business. The impact of the UK leaving the EU is not considered in depth, but is referred to where it helps the reader to understand a change in the treatment of insurance companies or policyholders.

This new edition of the book is organised into six parts – a structure which we hope will enable the reader to gain a sound and joined-up understanding of the subject. First, it looks first at the legal principles relevant to the creation of insurance contracts. Second, it considers the various parties that may be involved in the creation and operation of an insurance contract and how they go about their business. Third, it considers the legal principles applicable to the making of claims. Fourth, it looks at the question of how insurance contract disputes can be resolved. Fifth, it looks at the various types of insurance that are available in the market, from motor insurance to cyber insurance; this part also includes a chapter on reinsurance. Finally, the sixth part considers the regulatory environment in which both insurers and insurance intermediaries operate (in particular, when selling insurance products) and insurance business transfers under the Financial Services and Markets Act 2000.

Among the legal and regulatory developments which are covered in this new edition are the impact of the Consumer Insurance (Disclosure and Representations) Act 2012 and the Insurance Act 2015 – both of which made significant changes to the assured's duty of utmost good-faith disclosure; the impact of the Insurance Distribution Directive on the design and sale of insurance products; and the development of cyber and comprehensive crime insurance.

We hope that the reader will find this revised work continues to satisfy the criteria originally set down by Professor Merkin – namely, to provide the reader with a basic understanding of insurance law in an easy-to-follow, logical format.

This book is based on our understanding of the laws of England and Wales on 30 September 2021. Nothing in this book represents advice in relation to any person or situation. Any views expressed by the authors are personal views and should not be regarded as the views of Norton Rose Fulbright LLP.

Finally, we would like to thank our colleagues who have helped in updating and editing this book, including in particular David Bartlett, Ben Hilary, Simon Baker, Amy Teece and Angus Graham-Watson.

Noleen John
Charlie Weston-Simons
Laura Hodgson
Norton Rose Fulbright LLP

London
December 2021

Table of Contents

Table of Cases

C

D

E

H

I

J

M

S

T

Table of Statutes

Table of Statutory Instruments

Table of Directives

Table of Treaties and Conventions

Part 1

The Insurance Contract

Chapter 1

Contract of insurance

- General definition of 'insurance'
- Contract formation
- Formation of a contract at Lloyd's
- The policy

GENERAL DEFINITION OF 'INSURANCE'

1.01 It is important to define 'insurance', for a variety of reasons. Firstly, some legal requirements apply only to insurance contracts. For example, a non-consumer insured's duty of fair presentation applies only to insurance contracts. Secondly, legislation – particularly tax legislation – lays down special rules for insurance contracts. Thirdly, and perhaps most significantly, there is comprehensive statutory regulation of the insurance industry, including the carrying on of insurance business in the UK (see **Chapter 42**). However, these statutory provisions do not define the term 'contract of insurance' on which such regulation is based.

As there is no statutory definition of a 'contract of insurance', it is still necessary to rely on the common law definition. A frequently quoted definition of 'insurance' (but not necessarily an exhaustive one) is that of Channell J in *Prudential Insurance Company v Inland Revenue Comrs* [1904] 2 KB 658. In that case, three elements of insurance were identified:

(a) It is a contract whereby, for some consideration (generally, but not necessarily, for periodic payments called premiums), the insured secures some benefit on the occurrence of an event;

(b) The event must be uncertain as to whether it will happen or not; or if the event will happen, there must be uncertainty as to when; and

(c) The event must be adverse to the insured, in that he possesses an insurable interest (see **Chapter 4**) in the subject matter insured.

Premiums

1.02 In most forms of insurance, the insured pays a sum – identified as the 'premium' – to the insurer. A premium is a payment, buying cover for a specified period (often one year). If the insurer's premium income is insufficient to cover losses, the insurer cannot generally seek a further payment from the insured during the policy year. This position should be contrasted with that under mutual insurance, where the member of the mutual insurer (the insured) may be required to pay additional calls to the insurer during the currency of the policy.

Premiums generally take the form of money payments. However, there is no rule of law which prevents an insurance premium from constituting part of a wider payment – for example, the membership fee of a society providing benefits other than insurance (*Nelson v Board of Trade* [1901] 65 JP 487 concerned a retailer promising pensions in order to promote the sale of tea). Combined payments are less common than was once the case. However, in recent years, certain markets have developed ways of offering discounts/refunds based on the behaviour of the policyholder and data collected in connection with the risk (eg, black boxes and apps used for motor insurance). Consideration for the insurance may also be provided in a form other than money – for example, the provision of services.

The benefit payable to the insured

1.03 The insurer's primary obligation is usually to provide a payment to an insured on the occurrence of a specified event. However, in policies on property, the insurer will generally reserve the right to repair damage or to replace destroyed items. Equally, there is no reason why payment cannot be in the form of services to the insured, such as the provision of transport (*Department of Trade and Industry v St Christopher Motorists Association Ltd* [1974] 1 WLR 99 was a case involving insurance which provided a driver where the insured was unable to drive his vehicle). To that extent, payment can be in a form other than money, as long as it is measurable in monetary terms.

The insured must, however, be entitled to some benefit under the policy. If the insurer has a discretion, but not an obligation, to make payment upon application by the insured, the contract is not one of insurance. This may be so even if the evidence demonstrates that the 'insurer' always exercises its option to make payment (*Medical Defence Union Ltd v Department of Trade* [1980] Ch 82).

Uncertain events

1.04 Insurance is against contingencies and not certainties. The insured cannot insure against events which have taken place; neither can he insure against certain events. There must always be an element of uncertainty. In the case of indemnity insurance (eg, fire, theft), the uncertainty is whether there will be a loss at all. In the case of contingency insurance (the principal example of which in modern insurance is life assurance), the uncertainty relates not to the event, but rather to the date at which it might occur (*Gould v Curtis (Surveyor of Taxes)* [1913] 3 KB 84).

CONTRACT FORMATION

1.05 The common law permits insurance contracts to be made orally, but there are statutory inroads into this principle which effectively require various insurance contracts to be in writing. One notable example is s 22 of the Marine Insurance Act 1906, which provides that a contract of marine insurance is not admissible in evidence unless embodied in a policy.

The negotiations leading up to a contract of insurance are often found in the proposal form, the cover note and the policy document itself. In relation to Lloyd's policies, the proposal form can in effect be replaced by a slip, and a binding contract is concluded as soon as the slip is executed by the underwriter.

The offer

1.06 Generally speaking, the offer is made by the insured to the insurer, by means of a proposal form or other application. For example, the insurer may have written to the insured directly inviting him to complete the proposal form for consideration or the invitation may have come through an advertisement ('invitation to treat'). In these circumstances, the offer emanates from the insured, who either completes the proposal form himself or has it completed on his behalf by the broker. If the proposal form is filled out on the insured's behalf, the insured is nonetheless responsible for ensuring that the answers on the proposal form are accurate and complete.

Any counter-proposal made by the insurer puts the onus back on the insured to accept the counter-offer (and thus a contract is made at that stage) or to make a further counter-proposal.

The proposal form

1.07 Once completed, the proposal form can be looked at as an offer to accept insurance by the insured. The offer made by the insured will be made open for acceptance by the insurer for a specified time or, if none is specified, for a reasonable time. It is open to the proposer to withdraw his offer to take insurance at any time before it is accepted by the insurer (see *Dickinson v Dodds* (1875-76) LR 2 Ch D 463).

'Basis of the contract' clauses

1.08 Under the current law, representations and information provided in the proposal form cannot form part of the contract of insurance without clear provisions to that effect.

Prior to the implementation of the Consumer Insurance (Disclosure and Representations) Act 2012 and the Insurance Act 2015, it was common practice for insurers to include a 'basis of the contract' clause in policies. A 'basis of the contract' clause converted all statements made by the insured in the proposal form into warranties under the policy. Following consultation by the Law Commission, 'basis of the contract' clauses were prohibited by s 6 of the Consumer Insurance (Disclosure and Representations) Act 2012 for consumer insurance and s 9 of the Insurance Act 2015 for non-consumer insurance. Any warranties in insurance contracts must now be specifically identified as part of the contract.

The cover note

1.09 On receipt of the completed proposal, the insurer is, of course, allowed time to consider the proposal and a cover note can provide temporary cover in the interim, cover being fully effective from the date of issue of the cover note. Alternatively, the grant of temporary cover is frequently conditional upon the completion by the insured of the proposal form for full cover. The use of cover notes is common in personal lines insurance – for example, household and motor – and is particularly convenient for risks which are subject to compulsory insurance, such as motor.

Cover notes may be issued by insurers themselves or by brokers authorised by insurers under binding authorities. If the latter, the broker will be in possession of blank cover notes printed in common form which he will fill out and issue on behalf of the insurer, thereby binding the insurer (*Mackie v European Insurance Society* (1869) 21 LT 102). Alternatively, the company may send a cover note to the broker for the broker to sign and issue to the insured. In these circumstances, the broker has no general authority to grant cover. Temporary cover could also be given orally by the broker or the insurer (*Stockton v Mason [1978]* 2 Lloyd's Rep 430).

If a policy is subsequently issued, the cover note ceases to have any effect. It is usual for the cover note to remain in force for a fixed period of time – generally a maximum of 30 days or so – but the insurer can give notice to terminate the cover note at any time during that period.

If the cover note obliges the insurer to notify the insured if his proposal is rejected, the cover note will remain in force until the insurer takes this step (*Hawke v Niagara District Mutual Fire Insurance Co* (1876) 23 Gr 139).

If the cover note provides that the insurer, as well as notifying the insured of the rejection of the proposal, must repay any deposit paid, the insurer must ensure that it fully discharges its obligations. In the case of *Grant v Reliance Insurance Company* (1879) 44 UCR 229, it was held that the insurance was not terminated unless the insurer complied with the term to give ten days' notice of its intention to terminate the insurance and also with the term to repay the premium (this would be the pro rata return of the premium based upon the number of days the insurer was on risk). If the terms of the cover note provide either that the insurer must intimate its acceptance of the proposal or that it is not bound until a policy is issued, then cover will cease at the end of the period specified in the cover note, unless such a term has been complied with. Insurers should take care to ensure that the cover note clearly states the precise period for which they are on risk.

The cover note is a binding contract of insurance and will bind the insurer exactly as if a full policy had been issued. If the insurer decides it is not prepared to accept the risk, it will still be liable for any claim arising prior to the cover note expiring or being cancelled.

Most cover notes provide that the cover provided is that contained in the insurer's standard form of policy. In the event that a loss occurs during the period before the policy is issued, the insured may have some difficulty in knowing precisely what formalities he must meet in order to make a claim. In *Coleman's Depositories Ltd and Life & Health Assurance Association's Arbitration, Re* [1907] 2 KB 798, the insured employer under a employers' liability insurance cover note failed to give immediate notice to the insurer of an injury sustained during the period of the cover note, contrary to the terms of the insurer's standard policy wording. The policy had not been issued to the insured at this point. The insurer repudiated liability on the grounds (among others) that the employer had not given immediate notice in accordance with the policy conditions. The injured workman died on 15 March 1905, having been injured on 2 January 1905, the insurer only being notified the day before his death. The Court of Appeal held, by a majority, that the requirements for immediate notice did not defeat the claim as:

(a) it was impossible for the employer to comply with a policy term of which it had no knowledge; and

(b) because the claim arose before the employer had knowledge of the notice provision, the true inference was that the condition was never imposed on the employer.

If the cover note does not incorporate the terms of the policy, the insurer will need to demonstrate that the insured was aware of the terms and conditions of the policy or had the means of becoming aware of the terms; or that the insured had actually agreed the terms and conditions of cover.

During the period of the cover note, it is open to both the insured and the insurer to decline to continue with the insurance after expiry of the cover note. If cover is to continue, the note will usually be replaced by a policy.

The acceptance

1.10 No particular form of acceptance is required and the offer can be accepted by the insurer in a number of ways – for example:

(a) the insurer may notify the insured of its acceptance (orally or in writing); or

(b) acceptance may be implied from conduct including:

  (i) the execution of the policy;

  (ii) where the insured has tendered and the insurer has accepted the premium; or

  (iii) where the premium has been demanded or the policy has been issued.

Whatever means of acceptance is used, the insurer's acceptance must be unconditional for a binding contract to come into effect and, according to general contract law principles, the insurer's silence cannot amount to acceptance (unless, of course, there has been a previous agreement that silence is to be regarded as consent). However, the law on this point may be different in other countries, where the insurer can find itself on risk if it has failed to respond to the proposal within a reasonable period.

The insurer's 'acceptance' may be conditional. If the insurer's acceptance is on different terms from the offer, the acceptance is itself a counter-offer (*Canning v Farquhar* (1886) 16 LR QBD 727).

Generally speaking, acceptance must be communicated to the offeror for the contract to be concluded. However, if, for example, the insured sends his proposal to the insurer by post, he impliedly authorises the insurer to use the same means of communication and thus the insurer's acceptance is effective when the letter is posted, notwithstanding that it may never be received by the insured, and the contract is in force.

The making of the contract is not necessarily the same thing as the commencement of the risk, as the insurer will commonly refuse to allow cover to commence until the first premium has been paid or some other formality has been completed (eg, the issue of a policy). The distinction between the making of the contract and the commencement of the risk is of importance mainly in relation to the insured's duty to take reasonable care not to make a misrepresentation (for consumer insurance contracts) or of fair presentation (for non-consumer insurance contracts) (see **Chapter 6**). These duties (although not the general duty of utmost good faith) come to an end when the contract is made, and not at any later date at which the risk commences, so that a change of circumstances prior to the commencement of the risk need not be notified to the insurer, unless the policy states otherwise.

An applicant for insurance is deemed to have applied for a policy issued on the insurer's standard terms, whether or not the applicant knows of those terms (*General Accident Insurance Corporation v Cronk* [1901] 45 Sol Jo 261, 17 TLR 233). Consequently, once the contract is made, the insured cannot dispute what the terms of the policy are even though he has not received a copy of the policy. However, this does not necessarily mean that any term included will be enforceable. Enforceability may be affected by, for consumer contracts, the Consumer Rights Act 2015 and the Financial Conduct Authority's (FCA) Principles and rules relating to treating customers fairly. The FCA rules also specify appropriate pre-contractual disclosure of key terms in insurance contracts (see **Chapter 43**). Also, where the matter falls within the jurisdiction of the Financial Ombudsman Service, it will be determined on the basis of fairness; and the ombudsman has previously ruled that an insurer cannot rely upon policy terms which, although standard, are unusual and onerous, unless they have been brought specifically to the insured's attention prior to the making of the contract – a principle derived from the common law (*Interfoto Picture Library v Stiletto Visual Programmes* [1989] QB 433).

If the insurer, having received a proposal, wishes to vary its standard policy terms or charge a premium other than at the rate originally quoted, the insurer's response to the proposer is treated as a counter-offer which must be accepted by the proposer before a contract can come into being. This was held to be the case in *Canning v Farquhar* (referred to above), in which a proposal for life insurance was replied to by the insurer with a quotation for the premium and a statement that the policy would come into effect when the premium was paid. The proposer died four days before the premium was tendered by his administrator. The Court of Appeal held that the insurer was not liable; the insurer had, by its reply, made a counter-offer which required acceptance, and acceptance was not possible after the proposer had died.

Intention to create legal relations

1.11 It is usually self-evident that the parties to the insurance contract intend to create legal relations, any problems with this aspect of the law of contract usually being confined to non-commercial contracts.

Consideration

1.12 In order for the insurance contract to be enforceable, the insured must have given something of value to the insurer for the contractual promise. This aspect is also unlikely to cause any practical problems, as the premium is normally the consideration under an insurance contract. It is usually the obligation to pay the premium, rather than actual payment of the premium, that is required.

FORMATION OF A CONTRACT AT LLOYD'S

The slip

1.13 Insurance is placed at Lloyd's by means of a slip. The slip contains a summary of the essential features of the proposed cover. The broker prepares the slip on behalf of his client, the insured, and takes it round the Lloyd's market. Contracts can also be concluded electronically.

In *Balfour v Beaumont* [1984] 1 Lloyd's Rep 272; (1984) 81 LSG 197, Webster J described the slip as 'a document prepared by a broker, setting out a proposal to be made to an underwriter which when accepted by the underwriter becomes binding on him'. The broker drafts the slip in accordance with the instructions received from his client. As the slip is designed to be concise, it is in abbreviated form and thus commonly refers to standard market clauses by description, showing any appropriate deletions or alternatives contemplated to a standard form of wording. This should now reflect the Market Reform Contract (MRC) (Open Market) Guidelines, which also include a pro forma line slip (see **1.15**).

If the underwriter wants to accept the business, it will usually initial ('scratch') and/or stamp the slip indicating the percentage of the risk it is prepared to write. Contracts may, however, be executed in a number of ways and the MRC (Open Market) Implementation Guide (31 March 2021) advises that use of a 'Mode of Execution Clause' is advisable in order to clarify how the risk has been bound, and how the MRC format can be amended. The standard clause envisages execution in any one or a combination of methods, including:

(a) electronic signature technology employing computer software and a digital signature or digitiser pen pad to capture a person's handwritten signature in such a manner that the signature is unique to the person signing, is under the sole control of the person signing, is capable of verification to authenticate the signature and is linked to the document signed in such a manner that if the data is changed, such signature is invalidated;

(b) a unique authorisation provided via a secure electronic trading platform

(c) a timed and dated authorisation provided via an electronic message/ system;

(d) an exchange of facsimile/scanned copies showing the original written ink signature of paper documents; or

(e) an original written ink signature of paper documents (or a true representation of a signature, such as a rubber stamp).

On executing the slip, the underwriter is contractually bound. The broker continues to present the risk to the market until it has been fully subscribed or, perhaps more usually, oversubscribed (with the amount of each subscription being later 'signed down').

It is possible that the broker will ask an underwriter for a 'pencilled line', which is understood to be a 'promised' line. The underwriter is committed to take the promised line when the broker returns with a finalised slip. In *General Accident, Fire and Life Assurance Corporation v Tanter, The Zephyr [1985] 2 Lloyd's Rep 529*, the judge recognised this market practice: 'a promised line is, by practice of the market, of the same effect as if it was written on the slip itself. It gives both parties the right to have that promised line written on the slip.' The situation is different where the broker uses a 'quotation slip' to test the market to ascertain likely insurance support and current rates. Unless a promised line is requested, the fact that the underwriter has indicated on the slip the terms and the rate is seen merely as a non-binding quotation.

An account of the way business is placed at Lloyd's can also be found in *General Reinsurance Corporation v Forsakringsaktiebolaget Fennia Patria* [1983] QB 856, [1983] 2 Lloyd's Rep 287 (see **Chapter 11**).

It is possible that an underwriter may want to amend one or more of the terms of the slip before putting down its line. In the *General Reinsurance* case referred to above, the Court of Appeal recognised this possibility. Kerr LJ stated: 'where an underwriter varies the terms of the slip with the consent of the broker before writing his line, this would accordingly constitute a counter-offer which is accepted by the broker on behalf of his client.'

Contract certainty and confidence

1.14 In December 2004, the Financial Services Authority challenged the London Market to devise a solution to what it characterised as a 'deal now, detail later' culture – that is, that the precise wording of an insurance contract was often not agreed at the time the parties committed themselves to that contract; and that the end client did not receive evidence of cover until after the business was on risk. In the worst cases, litigation had occurred without the terms and conditions of the contract having been agreed and without the client ever having received a copy of the contract.

The challenge related to the whole UK general insurance industry. The London Market set a series of targets for itself to demonstrate that it was seriously pursuing a market solution to this issue.

In June 2007, a consolidated Contract Certainty Code of Practice was published. This was the first publication ever to apply to the entire UK insurance industry – subscription and non-subscription; commercial and retail. The Code (Principles and Guidance) was updated in October 2012 to reflect changes in regulatory structures and to tidy up minor inconsistencies. A further review was undertaken in 2018, which confirmed that the guidance was still relevant and current. It was therefore re-published in September 2018 without any substantive changes to the principles, guidance or model checklist material.

Lloyd's also issued guidance in relation to the processes to be followed in checking contract documentation.

Market Reform Contract Open Market Contract

1.15 As part of the move to contract certainty, the London insurance market was the subject of a Market Reform Programme over a number of years, which was designed to increase efficiency in placing business, processing claims and settling accounts.

The first significant reform achievement was the introduction and adoption as a standard of the London Market Principles (LMP) Slip. The LMP slip was introduced in October 2001 and was mandated by the Lloyd's Franchise Board for business incepting from 2 January 2004. This ensured a common format and content to the way that business was introduced to the market and represented a significant cultural change. This was followed by the introduction of the Market Reform Slip in June 2006, building on the LMP Slip and further increasing the efficiency of the placement process by providing an enhanced standard for introducing business to London. In June 2007, this was replaced by the MRC – the name change reflecting the fact that the document presented by the broker to underwriters is that which forms the contract of insurance which became mandatory for the London Market on 1 November 2007.

Version 2.1 of the MRC (Open Market) Guidance (which includes the layout and form of the standard contract) became the required standard for new and renewal business from 1 August 2021. It applies to the following:

(a) all firm quote and firm order open market insurance and reinsurance business placed by London Market brokers;

(b) all marine open cargo covers and declarations attaching thereto. 'Marine open cargo covers' are defined as those risks where the insured has acquired, or is expected to acquire, an insurable interest in each declaration bound;

(c) declarations or off-slips attaching to line slips, where the use of the MRC (Lineslip Declarations) is not appropriate; and

(d) applicable declarations of limited binding authority agreements, where the coverholder, broker and insurers agree that it is appropriate.

It does not apply to:

(a) binding authority agreements and line slips which have their own separate London Market guidelines;

(b) contracts that fall within the 'Market Reform Exempt – Client Requirement' category (ie, the client has expressed a preference to use a London placing document in a different format) – although the guidance is that it would be preferable to comply as far as possible; or

(c) contracts relating to motor, personal lines or term life insurance business which are not processed by DXC.

The current Lloyd's mandate governing the use of the MRC is incorporated into the Underwriting Byelaw and documented in Chapter 1 – Section 4 Franchisees' commitments – Service Standards 3A.

1.16 *Contract of insurance*

The benefits of the MRC contract are that a standard layout:

(a) makes it easier for insurers to assimilate the information;

(b) makes subsequent processes more efficient (eg, the creation of contract documentation); and

(c) promotes compatibility of information which will enable mapping to the ACORD Reinsurance & Large Commercial 'Placement' XML message Contract Certainty Principles.

The MRC is made up of the following sections:

(a) Risk Details – details of the risk/contract involved (eg, insured, type, coverage, conditions).

(b) Information – free text additional information.

(c) Security Details – includes reinsurer's liability; order hereon; basis of written lines; basis of signed lines; signing provisions; insurer(s)/reinsurer(s) 'stamp' details. These indicate each insurer(s) share of the risk and their reference(s).

(d) Subscription Agreement – this establishes the rules to be followed for the processing and administration of post-placement amendments and transactions.

(e) Fiscal and Regulatory – fiscal and regulatory issues specific to the insurers involved in the risk.

(f) Broker Remuneration & Deductions – information relating to brokerage, fees and deductions from premium.

The requirement to comply with the guidelines set down for the MRC applies.

THE POLICY

1.16 Insurance policies issued by insurance companies or Lloyd's will vary as to their form and contents, especially for consumer contracts, and should be drafted with care.

Insurers' policies

1.17 Insurers will generally use their own standard forms of policy wording, which will also vary according to the type of insurance. The old-style narrative policies are generally a thing of the past and today are only of academic interest. Rather than adopting the narrative style, modern policies are 'scheduled' policies. The various parts of the policy will be in clearly defined sections which are identical within a class of business, except for that part of the policy called the 'schedule', which will list all information particular to that individual risk. Scheduled policies are convenient for insurers, allowing them to keep on file a copy of the master policy and individual schedules.

Lloyd's policies

1.18 Following completion of the slip, if a policy is to be issued, this will be drawn up. Where this happens, the wording supersedes the slip, although this does not affect the insured's duty of disclosure, which ceases when the slip is executed. Section 21 of the Marine Insurance Act 1906 provides:

> 'A contract of marine insurance is deemed to be concluded when the proposal of the assured is accepted by the insurer, whether the policy be then issued or not; and, for the purpose of showing when the proposal was accepted, reference may be made to the slip or covering note or other customary memorandum of the contract …'

Where there is an apparent inconsistency between the wording of the slip and the subsequent policy, the court may refer to both documents in an attempt to reconcile the terms (*HIH Casualty & General Insurance Ltd v New Hampshire Insurance* Co [2001] 2 Lloyd's Rep 161).

Today, policy wordings are often not drawn up, and the slip remains of paramount importance in embodying the terms of the contract.

Lloyd's policies will be in a standard form and will deal with the same matters as any other policy. However, points worthy of note are the premium and underwriters' liability. In relation to the premium, the policy will usually acknowledge that this has been paid, which means that the insured can enforce the policy even if the premium has not in fact been paid. Underwriters' liability is several, not joint or joint and several. This means that underwriters' liability is restricted to the amount of their line. Properly analysed, therefore, the insured has entered into a number of separate contracts with each individual underwriter.

If Lloyd's is only writing part of a risk and the insured also has insurance with one or more insurers, the Lloyd's policy will usually include a clause referring to the other policy and may provide that the Lloyd's policy is subject to the same conditions as the insurer's policy.

Policy conditions can be classified into two types: express conditions and implied conditions. Express conditions will vary according to the type of insurance cover. Generally, express conditions will include what constitutes notice to the insurer, cancellation, contribution, any arbitration or court jurisdiction clause, adjustment of premium and claims procedure. Implied conditions will include matters such as the existence of an insurable interest and the existence and identity of the subject matter. Express and implied conditions can be further categorised into conditions precedent to the policy, conditions subsequent to the policy and conditions precedent to liability (see **Chapter 2**).

Chapter 2

Terms in insurance contracts

- Classification of terms
- Construction of terms

CLASSIFICATION OF TERMS

Warranties

2.01 A 'warranty' in insurance law has a different meaning from a 'warranty' in the general law of contract.

In insurance law, a 'warranty' is typically a promissory term where the insured promises either that a particular state of affairs exists at a particular point in time – usually at inception (a present warranty); or that a particular state of affairs will exist over a period of time – usually over the period of the insurance policy (a continuing warranty).

The law in relation to warranties in insurance policies has been substantially amended by the Consumer Insurance (Representations and Disclosures) Act 2012 and the Insurance Act 2015. This section explains changes made by those Acts on certain terms in insurance contracts (eg, warranties) (for more information on the changes made see **Chapter 6**). The law on warranties both pre and post-amendment is described below.

Pre-amendment

Prior to the Consumer Insurance (Representations and Disclosures) Act 2012 and the Insurance Act 2015 coming into force, warranties in insurance contracts were required to be strictly and literally complied with. A breach of warranty automatically terminated the contract, notwithstanding that the loss had no connection with the breach (or that the breach had been remedied before the time of loss). An insurer was not required to make any decision or exercise any option to repudiate or avoid the contract of insurance following the breach of a warranty.

Section 33 of the Marine Insurance Act 1906 defined a 'promissory warranty' as a term 'by which the insured undertakes that some particular thing shall or shall not be done, or that some conditions shall be fulfilled, or whereby he affirms or negatives the existence of a particular state of facts …'. It was clear from s 34(3) of the Marine Insurance Act 1906 that 'breach of warranty may be waived by the insurer'. This had been taken to suggest that an election on the part of the insurer was required to avoid an insurance contract in the event of breach of warranty, notwithstanding that s 33(3) of the Marine Insurance Act 1906 provided that if a warranty is not 'exactly complied with', then 'subject to any express provision in the policy the insurer is discharged from liability as from the date of breach of warranty, but without prejudice to any liability incurred by him before that date'.

In *Bank of Nova Scotia v Hellenic Mutual War Risks Association* [1992] 1 AC 233, the House of Lords held that the wording of s 33(3) was clear. Discharge of the insurer from liability was automatic upon breach of warranty and was not dependent upon any decision by the insurer to treat the contract of insurance as at an end. Although that case concerned a contract of marine insurance, the same principle applied to non-marine contracts of insurance.

The mere fact that a term is labelled a 'warranty' will not always mean that it will be treated as such by the court. As warranties were terms with a draconian nature, the courts often tried to limit their operation. If there was any ambiguity in the wording, the court would try to restrict the application of a warranty (*Printpak v AGF Insurance Ltd* [1999] 1 All ER (Comm) 466). The courts were also very reluctant to find that a warranty was a continuing warranty unless the wording was very clear indeed (*Hussain v Brown* [1996] 1 Lloyd's Rep 627).

Post-amendment

Section 6 of the 2012 Act and s 9 of the 2015 Act prohibit 'basis of the contract' clauses (eg, which converted all statements in a proposal form into warranties) in both consumer and non-consumer insurances (see **Chapter 1**). Sections 10 and 11 of the 2015 Act also significantly amended the consequences of a breach of a warranty for consumer and non-consumer insurance policies.

Section 10 abolished the strict rule that a breach of a warranty results in the entire discharge of an insurer's liability under a policy. Instead, an insurer will have no liability in respect of loss that occurs or which is attributable to the breach of a specific warranty. If a warranty ceases to be applicable due to a change in circumstances, compliance with the warranty is rendered unlawful or the insurer waives the breach of warranty, the insurer will have no right to avoid liability for a claim.

Section 11 applies in addition to s 10 and provides that an insurer cannot rely on the breach of a term (other than a term which defines the entire risk) to exclude, limit or discharge its liability for loss if the breach could not have increased the risk of the loss that actually occurred. For example, if the policyholder of a home insurance policy fails to install a fire alarm in breach of his policy, an insurer cannot rely on the breach to avoid liability for a claim due to flood damage.

As s 11 does not apply to terms that define the risk as a whole, it is not intended to apply to a failure of the claim to fall within the cover set out in the insuring clauses or to exclusions to cover.

The Insurance Act 2015 does provide the ability for the parties to non-consumer contracts to 'contract out' of specific requirements of the Act (see **6.24**). Accordingly, parties to non-consumer insurance policies may agree to dis-apply the requirements of ss 10 and 11 of the 2015 Act. However, the right to contract out does not apply to consumer insurance or to the prohibition of 'basis of the contract' clauses.

Conditions precedent

2.02 There is some confusion in the law as to the difference between a warranty and a condition precedent. Whereas a 'warranty' is a term where the insured promises that a particular state of affairs exists or will exist, a 'condition precedent' *to the insurance* is a condition or state of affairs that must be fulfilled before the insurance contract comes into existence. At the other end of the scale, a 'condition precedent' *to liability to meet a particular claim* is a condition or state of affairs which must be met before the insurer has a liability to deal with a particular claim made under the policy. With conditions precedent, it is technically for the insured to prove that the condition has been met which would entitle him to make a valid claim under the contract of insurance. If there is breach of a condition precedent *to the insurance*, then the insurer will probably never come on risk. If there is breach of a condition precedent *to liability to meet a claim*, then the insurer is still on risk, but not in respect of the relevant claim.

For consumer contracts, use of the term 'condition precedent' is difficult (eg, on grounds of fairness) and would need to be explained in a transparent and prominent way. In practice, it is not normally used. For commercial insureds, if used, conditions precedent will be subject to s 11 of the 2015 Act. For example, *conditions precedent to liability* will need to be relevant to (eg, they would have increased the risk of) the loss sustained by the insured. In practice, it may therefore be better for the insurer to build the relevant requirement into the scope of the cover provided. Care is also required in relation to reinsurance where Solvency II requirements for certainty of risk transfer can prevent acceptance of conditions, such as conditions precedent which are outside of the cedant's control.

Exclusion clauses

2.03 It is also necessary to distinguish between warranties and exclusion clauses. Both types of clause have the effect of limiting the cover provided by the insurer, but they operate in different ways.

If a warranty is broken, cover is automatically terminated; but if an exclusion clause operates, cover simply does not apply. For example, in an 'all risks' policy (which insures property against 'all risks'), the insurer's liability under the policy may be limited by an exclusion clause which states:

> 'This policy will not cover:
>
> War risks, any consequence of war, invasion, acts of foreign enemies, hostilities (whether war be declared or not), civil war, rebellion, revolution, insurrection, military or usurped power.'

The insurer's liability under the policy does not automatically terminate in the event of war, but the insured risks are limited so that they do not include damage which occurs to the property as a result of war.

Exclusions may be express or implied. Express exclusions will be terms of the insurance contract. It is sometimes possible to argue that there is an implied exclusion in the insurance contract on the basis of limits inherent in the usual meaning of the cover written by the contract of insurance. For example, an 'all risks' policy does not cover loss caused by inevitable deterioration.

Mere conditions

2.04 Where a term of the policy is not a warranty, a condition precedent or an exclusion clause, it will be a mere condition. Breach of a mere condition by the insured will give rise to an action in damages by the insurer against the insured. The amount of damages will be proportionate to the prejudice caused to the insurer as a result of the breach. That said, it is unusual for insurers to sue insureds for damages.

Innominate terms

2.05 An 'innominate' (or 'intermediate') term in an insurance contract is a term which is not a warranty, a condition precedent or a mere condition as described above. With these terms, the consequences of any particular breach by the insured cannot be laid down in advance, but will depend on the nature and gravity of the particular breach. In *Alfred McAlpine plc v BAI (Run-Off) Ltd* [2000] 1 Lloyd's Rep 437, the court had to consider the nature of a condition in the insurance policy which required the insured to give notice of any occurrence which might give rise to a claim under the policy 'in writing with full details as soon as possible'. The insurer argued that the clause was a condition precedent; whereas the court held that it was not. The Court of Appeal held that the notice clause was an innominate term and breach thereof, however serious, would be unlikely to permit the insurer to repudiate the whole contract of insurance. Following the decisions in *Friends Provident Life & Pensions Ltd v Sirius International* [2005] EWCA Civ 601 and *King v Brandywine Reinsurance Co (UK) Ltd* [2004] Lloyd's Rep IR 554, it has been confirmed that the breach of a claims notification clause (which is not in the nature of a condition precedent) will result only in the insurer being able to claim damages.

CONSTRUCTION OF TERMS

2.06 The courts have developed various rules of construction to assist in the process of interpretation of written contracts; non-consumer contracts of insurance are no different from commercial contracts in this respect and are subject to the same principles of interpretation.

The intention of the parties must prevail

2.07 The most basic principle of interpretation is that the court must interpret the contract so as to give effect to the parties' intention. Nothing is relevant to the interpretation of a written contract unless it was known to or reasonably capable of being known to both parties at the time the contract was made (see *New Hampshire Insurance Co Ltd v MGN Ltd* [1996] 5 Re LR 103). This intention is to be gathered from the written language of the contract of insurance, including all documents which may be incorporated into that contract. An undisclosed intention held by one of the parties to the contract is not admissible in evidence for the purposes of interpretation. In addition, particular clauses in the policy will not be looked at in isolation; it is the policy as a whole which will be considered.

Words should be given their ordinary and natural meaning

2.08 There is a rebuttable presumption that the words of a written contract should be construed according to their ordinary and natural meaning, since the parties to the contract must be taken to have intended, as reasonable people, to have used the words and phrases in their commonly understood and accepted sense (see *Yorke v Yorkshire Insurance Co Ltd* [1918] 1 KB 662, per McCardie J). If the ordinary meaning of the word has already been judicially established, the courts will have regard to this earlier interpretation under the doctrine of precedent (see *Reardon Smith Line Ltd v Yngvar Hansen-Tangen* [1976] 1 WLR 989). The court will generally give effect to the ordinary and natural meaning of the language used by the parties, provided that the language is clear and unambiguous – even if, with the benefit of hindsight, such an interpretation is unfortunate. The court will not rewrite a contract to create a better deal for the parties.

Technical or trade meaning

2.09 There are some circumstances, however, in which the court may not construe the words used by the parties according to their ordinary and natural meaning. This occurs where the words used in the contract are words which frequently have a highly technical or trade meaning. If a word has acquired a technical meaning in the usage of a particular trade or business, the court will assume that the parties intended it to receive that customary meaning. In *Price & Co v A1 Ships' Small Damage Insurance Association, Ltd* (1889) LR 22 QBD 580, the Master of the Rolls held that the word 'average' used in the context of marine insurance was clearly a technical expression whose meaning had been well established.

Similarly, a word or phrase which has a recognised technical meaning in law will be given that meaning. For example, the word 'dishonest', which often appears in insurance policies, is construed in accordance with its definition in s 2(1) of the Theft Act 1968; although the courts have gone on to consider the standard of dishonesty to be applied in civil cases in *Royal Brunei Airlines v Phillip Tan Kok Ming* [1995] AC 378 and *Abbey National plc v Solicitors Indemnity Fund* [1997] PNLR 306 as more akin to not acting as an honest person would act in the circumstances and could usually be equated with conscious impropriety.

Meaning may be limited by the context

2.10 The meaning of a word is to be construed with reference to its context, and its ordinary meaning may be restricted by that context. This rule was stated by Farwell LJ in *Yangtsze Insurance Association v Indemnity Mutual Marine Assurance Co* [1908] 2 KB 504. The Master of the Rolls, in *Arbuthnott v Fagan: Deeny v Gooda Walker Ltd* [1996] LRLR135, also confirmed this: 'the courts will never construe words in a vacuum. To a greater or lesser extent, depending on the subject matter, they would wish to be informed of what may variously be described as the context, the background, the factual matrix.'

Surrounding words

2.11 This rule of construction is a particular application of the general principle that the primary meaning of words may be affected by their context. The construction of words can be affected by their immediate environment or surrounding words within the contract.

The *eiusdem generis* rule provides that where specification of particular things is followed by general words, the general words are to be limited to matters *eiusdem generis* (ie, of the same kind) with those specifically mentioned. In an insuring clause, there may be a specific list of insured perils which is followed by more general words such as 'all other perils'. Here, the general words will be construed to be limited to matters of the same kind as those specifically mentioned.

This rule does not, however, always apply. For example, where the preceding words do not contain a specification of particulars, but rather a description of a complete genus, later general words will not be construed as being limited by the genus of the particular thing. In *Sun Fire Office v Hart* (1889) LR 14 App Cas 98, a fire insurance policy had a condition empowering the insurer to terminate the policy if it should wish to do so for various specified reasons or 'from any other cause whatsoever'. The words 'from any other cause whatsoever' were not construed by the court as limited to the type of reasons specified earlier in the policy, but as allowing the insurer the option of terminating the policy at will.

There is a rule that words may be limited by proximity where the meaning of one word within a list of words is limited by proximity to other words. For example, in *Young v Sun Alliance and London Insurance Ltd* [1976] 3 All ER 561, the Court of Appeal held that a policy which provided cover against damage for 'storm, tempest or flood' did not apply to a claim for damage where three inches of water seeped into the insured's bathroom from an underground spring. The word 'flood' was held in this case to be treated as being limited by its proximity to 'storm' and 'tempest', and in this context a 'flood' was 'something large, sudden and temporary, not naturally there …'. In *Rohan Investments Ltd v Cunningham* [1999] Lloyd's Rep IR 190, the Court of Appeal upheld the insured's claim under the 'storm, tempest or flood' section of his policy where, following a period of heavy rainfall, water built up on the roof and entered the insured's house over the flashings, causing an ingress of water three to four inches deep. The Court of Appeal stated that while the events giving rise to the flood had to be abnormal, the trial judge was entitled to find on the evidence that the accumulation of water from rainfall was sufficiently rapid to be abnormal. The abnormal accumulation of water could therefore be distinguished from the seepage which formed the substance of the claim in *Young v Sun Alliance*.

Business-like interpretation

2.12 Another accepted principle of construction is that a commercial document such as an insurance policy should be construed in accordance with sound commercial principles and good business sense, so that its provisions receive a fair and sensible application. A literal interpretation of the words will therefore not be allowed where this would produce a result which is unrealistic and unanticipated. In *Fraser v B N Furman (Productions) Ltd* [1967] 1 WLR 898, the court held that in a policy where the main purpose was to insure against damage arising from negligent acts of the insured, a condition that 'the insured shall take reasonable precautions' could not be construed so that every negligent act by the insured was in breach of that clause. The reason for this was that the insured had taken out the insurance policy specifically to cover his own acts of negligence, and the policy would be worthless to him if this construction of the words were permitted.

Nevertheless, following *Arnold v Britton* [2015] UKSC 30, judicial interpretation should not disregard the literal meaning of drafting, even where the effect may result in unreasonable outcomes.

Resolution of ambiguity

2.13 Where there is true ambiguity in a contract of insurance or reinsurance, the court is entitled to rely on a rule of interpretation known as the *contra proferentem* rule. This rule states that where contractual language is capable of two alternative interpretations, it will be construed against the party which drafted the contract of insurance or reinsurance and in favour of the party which accepts the wording. The reasoning behind this rule is that the party drafting the policy will have chosen the language used and thus should not be able to rely on any ambiguity contained therein. This principle was established in *Simmonds v Cockell* [1920] 1 KB 843. In the direct insurance context, this rule protects insureds against some of the more onerous consequences of standard form policies imposed on them by insurers. However, in the case of reinsurance contracts and some commercial insurance contracts, and in cases where the policy has been drafted by the broker (the insured or reinsured's agent), the principle can operate in favour of the insurer or reinsurer (see *Abrahams v Mediterranean Insurance and Reinsurance Co Ltd* [1991] 1 Lloyd's Rep 216). Where the wording of the contract of insurance has been penned by both the insured and the insurer, this rule is unlikely to apply.

Implied term

2.14 Where there is a gap in the meaning of the contract, the court will imply a term to fill that lacuna; but there is no principle going wider than that (see the *New Hampshire* case at **2.8** above). The language of the policy may be unclear not only because of it being susceptible of more than one interpretation, but also due to the technical nature of the language used or its silence on a particular issue. The court may, in limited circumstances, imply certain terms into the contract to clarify the meaning of the words of the contract. The party seeking to imply a term must show that it is necessary to give efficacy to the contract; it is consistent with the express terms of the contract; and it would have been agreed by both parties or is a term that is considered to have widely established market usage which the contracting parties, if asked, would agree formed part of their contract. The courts are generally reluctant to imply terms into insurance contracts in this way. However, courts are generally more willing to imply a term that the insurance market would expect the parties to have included in the contract, or a term that a party has sanctioned the use of in the course of previous dealings.

Extrinsic evidence

2.15 Sometimes, the express language of the contract of insurance can be supplemented by the introduction of evidence other than the terms of the written contract itself relevant to the interpretation of the contract. This 'extrinsic evidence' will often not be permitted by the court because of the parol evidence rule. This rule states that when a contract has been committed to writing, oral or other extrinsic evidence may not be relied on for the purpose of adding to, varying or contradicting the written document. The purpose of this rule is to uphold the finality of the agreement intended by the parties when they put the contract in written form. As a consequence of this rule, the court may not consider either oral evidence or draft versions of the agreement as aids to the interpretation of the parties' intention. In *Youell v Bland Welch & Co Ltd* [1992] 2 Lloyd's Rep 127, the judgment of the Court of Appeal gives contradictory authority as to whether this type of extrinsic evidence is relevant or admissible as a construction aid. *Prenn v Simmonds* [1971] 1 WLR 1381 establishes that evidence of negotiations is not admissible as a construction aid. However, where a contract wording has superseded a previous version – for instance, where an agreed wording has followed a slip policy – the courts will look to the slip as an aid to construction (see *HIH Casualty and General Insurance Ltd v New Hampshire Insurance Co* [2001] Lloyd's Rep IR 224).

However, the courts have held that contracts are not made in a vacuum, and that the courts should know the commercial purpose of the contract and the background and the market in which the parties are operating (see *Reardon Smith Line* at **2.9**).

The courts have for many years tended to view the starting point for construction as the principles of interpretation laid down by Lord Hoffmann in *Investors Compensation Scheme Ltd v West Bromwich Building Society* [1998] 1 WLR 896. These principles are as follows:

(a) Interpretation is the ascertainment of the meaning which a document would convey to a reasonable man having all the background knowledge which would be reasonably available to the parties.

(b) The background includes everything which would have affected the way in which the language would have been understood by a reasonable man.

(c) The law excludes from the admissible background the previous negotiations between the parties.

(d) The meaning of the document is different from the meaning of the word – the meaning of the document is what the parties using those words against the relevant background would reasonably have understood them to mean.

(e) The rule that words should be given their natural and ordinary meaning reflects the common-sense proposition that courts do not usually accept that parties to a contract have made linguistic mistakes.

The commercial approach taken by the courts to the interpretation of contracts was emphasised by Lord Steyn in *Sirius International Insurance Co (Publ) v FAI General Insurance Ltd* [2005] Lloyd's Rep IR 294:

> 'The aim of the inquiry is not to probe the real intention of the parties but to ascertain the contextual meaning of the relevant contractual language. The inquiry is objective: the question is what a reasonable person, circumstanced as the actual parties were, would have understood the parties to have meant by the use of specific language. The answer to that question is to be gathered from the text under consideration and the relevant contextual scene.'

However, in recent years the higher courts have made clear that the literal wording of the contract should not be ignored in pursuit of commercial common sense. In *Arnold v Britton* [2015] UKSC 36, Lord Neuberger said (at paragraph 17): 'the reliance placed in some cases on commercial common sense and surrounding circumstances … should not be invoked to undervalue the importance of the language of the provision … the clearer the natural meaning the more difficult it is to justify departing from it.'

It therefore seems that, absent ambiguity, the courts are more likely to take a more literal approach to the words used than may have been the case in the recent past.

Chapter 3

Duration of insurance contracts

- Duration of cover
- Termination of cover

DURATION OF COVER

When does cover commence?

3.01 There is a distinction between the date of the contract and the date of the risk attaching (ie, the insurance cover starting). In principle, cover commences as soon as the contract is made.

In practice, however, policy terms may vary this possibility and may specify that cover is stated to commence:

(a) on a given date and time;

(b) on the occurrence of a given event (as in the case of a marine voyage policy where cover commences at the start of the voyage – see **Chapter 35**); or

(c) on the payment of premium by the insured to the insurer.

It is the first of these contract terms which provides the most difficulties. If cover runs 'from' a specified date, the legal presumption is that this date is excluded (*Isaacs v Royal Insurance Co* (1869-70) LR 5 Ex 296). Clear wording is needed to oust this presumption – for example, that the risk runs from a stated day inclusive or, as in *Cornfoot v Royal Exchange Assurance Corp* [1904] 1 KB 40, that cover is for a period 'beginning with' a stated day. For consumer contracts, the day on which cover starts should be made clear.

TERMINATION OF COVER

Expiry of cover

3.02 The duration of cover will depend upon the policy wording. If the cover is for a particular event, such as a marine voyage, the policy will come to an end when the voyage is completed, although it is the practice for policies to continue for a specified number of days following the safe arrival of the vessel in port. In *Cornfoot v Royal Exchange* (see **3.01** above), in which marine cover was to run for 30 days from the arrival of the vessel in port, it was held that the additional days were to be counted in consecutive periods of 24 hours, commencing from the precise time at which the vessel arrived at port; so that in this case, the vessel completed its voyage at 11.30am and was covered for a further 30 days, such that a loss occurring at 5.30pm on the 30th day was not covered.

Some policies are stated to run from one day to another. As stated at **3.01** above, in *Isaacs v Royal Insurance*, it was held that the first-mentioned day was excluded. In this case it was also held that the last-mentioned date was included. Thus, if the insurer offers cover from 1 May 1993 to 1 May 1994, the effect of the *Isaacs* case is to allow the insured to recover for a loss on 1 May 1994, while at the same time, by excluding 1 May 1993, ensuring that the insurer is liable for a calendar year and not a year plus a day.

Ambiguities in the termination date of policies are generally to be construed in favour of the insured. In *Henrich Hirdes GmbH v Edmund* [1991] 2 Lloyd's Rep 546, a marine policy commenced on 16 June 1981 was stated to run for '12 months at June 16 1981' and was renewed 'for a period of one month… until 16 July 1982'. It was held that the policy was in force on 16 June 1982, even though this meant assuming that either the original policy or the subsequent renewal lasted for one day longer than the stated fixed period. As such, the principle in *Isaacs* still applies despite the stated duration of the total policy.

Renewal of cover

3.03 Life insurance policies are generally considered to be written in the form of continuing commitments on the parties and are therefore regarded as perpetual, subject to the insured tendering the premium when it falls due. Thus, even where the premium is paid annually (although it is more common these days for payment to be made by instalments), the cover does not come to an end at the end of the year, and the insured has the right to maintain the policy by making payment by the stated date and within any days of grace allowed by the policy – see *Stuart v Freeman* [1903] 1 KB 47; although, as this case emphasises, it is important to consider the terms of the actual policy. There is academic disagreement about whether, as a result of this case and *Pritchard v Merchants' Life Assurance Society* (1858) 3 CB (NS) 622, an annual life insurance contract has an implied right to renew or whether it is a contract for life which terminates if the premium is not paid annually. Although, as stated, much depends on the terms of the policy, the policy should be regarded as continuous and not a renewal which creates a new contract (unless it lapses and has to be reinstated – *Mundi v Lincoln Assurance Ltd* [2005] EWHC 2678 (Ch)).

Indemnity policies, by contrast, are periodic, which means that at the end of the policy period, a fresh contract will be needed. The policy will come to an end at the time stated in it or on the occurrence of a stated event. The main significance of this is that the insured owes a duty to take reasonable care not to make a misrepresentation each time the policy is renewed, and must ensure that the duty is complied with when there are changes in circumstances. The insurer may, however, waive the right of disclosure by providing in the policy that the insured is entitled to an extension either on request (which is a feature of 'held covered' clauses in marine insurance and may also be found in construction insurance where the duration of the risk is uncertain), or automatically, unless the insurer has taken the positive step of giving notice of cancellation within a specified period if there is a reservation of a right to cancel in the policy (*Commercial Union Assurance Co plc v Sun Alliance Insurance Group plc* [1992] 1 Lloyd's Rep 475).

Early termination

3.04 A policy may be terminated early, either because of a breach of duty under the policy or alternatively where the insured has been given the right to terminate the policy by notice. The date from which a notice to terminate takes effect will depend upon the wording of the policy and the words used in the notice of cancellation. Ordinarily, cover will expire at the time specified or, if no time is specified, at the last moment on the date of expiry (*Isaacs v Royal Insurance Co* [1870] 6 WLUK 43) or arguably by analogy cancellation. In a Canadian case, it has been held that a notice of termination takes effect at the end of the day on which it is received by the insurer, so that an accident on that day after the notice had arrived was held by the Ontario Court of Appeal to still be insured (*Larizza v Commercial Union Assurance Co* [1990] 68 DLR (4th) 460). Some types of policies, and consumer policies, should allow a proportionate return of premium on early cancellation. In the absence of such an express right, the insured has no entitlement to a rebate.

The insurer may also reserve the right to give a notice of early termination. Some such conditions may require the insurer that seeks to cancel to show cause, but this is not essential. An old decision of the Privy Council holds that the insurer may rely upon a policy provision which gives it the right to cancel at any time and for any reason whatsoever (*Sun Fire Office v Hart* (1889) LR 14 App Cas 98). These clauses are, however, relatively unusual in England other than in the marine context, where policies are cancellable on 30 days' notice. For consumer contracts, a right to terminate without a valid reason which is set out in the contract may not be enforceable under the Consumer Rights Act 2015. Consideration should also be given to the need to treat customers fairly under the Financial Conduct Authority's (FCA) Principles and rules.

The effect of termination on claims

3.05 The expiry of the policy will prevent recovery for any losses arising after that date, subject to two modifications:

(a) In liability insurance, the policy may provide an indemnity on a 'claims made' basis or on an 'occurrence of event' basis. In the former case, the insurer is liable only for those claims made by or against the insured during the currency of the policy. In the case of 'occurrence of event' liability policy, the insurer is liable for events (eg, negligent acts by the insured) in the policy period, even though the award of damages against the insured does not occur until some years after the policy has run off.

(b) In property insurance, the general principle is that the insurer's liability under a property policy is based on the time of the occurrence of the peril and not on the time at which damage becomes apparent. Thus, in a claim for heave, the policy covering the year in which the heave occurred is responsible for the loss, and not the policy covering the subsequent year in which damage to the property first began to appear (*Kelly v Norwich Union Fire Insurance Ltd* [1989] 2 All ER 888). This rule is logical, but may cause real practical difficulties where there has been a change of insurer and the precise date at which the heave occurred cannot easily be ascertained.

The right of withdrawal under the Financial Conduct Authority Rules

3.06 Subject to certain specified exceptions, the FCA's rules (Insurance: Conduct of Business Sourcebook 7 and Conduct of Business Sourcebook 15) give consumers a right to withdraw from most consumer insurance contracts within 14 days for general insurance contracts and distance contracts (other than payment protection contracts), and 30 days for life insurance contracts and payment protection contracts. The right normally starts when the contract is concluded (or the customer is notified of it) or, if later, once the consumer has received all of the required contractual and pre-contractual information.

Chapter 4

Insurable interest

- Introduction
- Definition
- The requirement of an insurable interest
- Non-indemnity insurance: life and non-life insurance
- Indemnity insurance: marine insurance and non-marine insurance
- The indemnity principle

INTRODUCTION

4.01 The essence of an insurance contract is that the insurer pays a sum of money to the insured upon the happening of a contingency. Payment of a sum of money on the happening of a contingency is also the essence of a wager. Prior to the passing of the Gambling Act 2005 (which came into force on 1 September 2007 and which applies to contracts created on or after that date), wagers were unenforceable. What distinguished a wager from an insurance contract and so made the latter enforceable was the existence of an insurable interest. Since the Gambling Act 2005, the position has become less clear cut.

Since the legal position may be different in relation to a particular contract of insurance depending on when it was created (ie, before or after 1 September 2007), and indeed on what type of insurance it is, there are a number of stages to the analysis. First, it is necessary to consider the concept of insurable interest, since this must be present in any contract of (re)insurance created before 1 September 2007. Second, it is necessary to consider the different types of insurance, since the point in time at which the insurable interest must exist varies; and further, as regards contracts created after 1 September 2007, the Gambling Act does not dispense with the need to show an insurable interest in respect of all contracts of insurance (eg, those where such an interest is required by statute, such as for life insurance contracts). Third, and in any event, it is necessary to consider the 'indemnity principle', which is an overriding principle of insurance law. This principle has the effect of rendering the effect of the Gambling Act 2005 on the requirement of insurable interest largely academic, at least in relation to indemnity insurance.

DEFINITION

4.02 'Insurable interest' requires that the policyholder have an interest in the subject matter of the policy. This can be either in its preservation or if it would suffer some loss in the event of a diminution of its value. The classic legal definition of 'insurable interest' was given by Lawrence J in *Lucena v Craufurd* (1806) 2 B&P (NR) 269, at p 302:

> 'where a man is so circumstanced with respect to matters exposed to certain risks or dangers as to have a moral certainty of advantage or benefit but for those risks or dangers, he may be said to be interested in the safety of the thing. To be interested in the preservation of a thing is to be so circumstanced with respect to it as to have benefit from its existence, prejudice from its destruction.'

The modern definition was provided by Waller LJ in *Feasey v Sun Life Assurance Co of Canada* [2003] Lloyd's Rep IR 637 at para 95:

> '(5) It is not a requirement of property insurance that the insured must have a "legal or equitable" interest in the property as those terms might normally be understood. It is sufficient for a sub-contractor to have a contract that relates to the property and a potential liability for damage to the property to have an insurable interest in the property. It is sufficient under section 5 of the Marine Insurance Act for a person interested in a marine adventure to stand in a "legal or equitable relation to the adventure." That is intended to be a broad concept.
>
> (6) In a policy on life or lives the court should be searching for the same broad concept. It may be that on an insurance of a specific identified life, it will be difficult to establish a "legal or equitable" relation without a pecuniary liability recognised by law arising on the death of that particular person.'

THE REQUIREMENT OF AN INSURABLE INTEREST

4.03 The requirement to show an insurable interest is a rule that is governed by different statutes, depending on the type of insurance.

A crucial element in the development of the principle of insurable interest was the Gaming Act 1845. This act provided that wagers were not enforceable in English law. This led to the position that insurable interest was a necessity to escape the provisions of the Gaming Act; it prevented contracts of insurance being void. However, the Gaming Act has been repealed by the Gambling Act 2005. This has, in effect, created two regimes. Any contract effected before 1 September 2007 will be subject to the Gaming Act 1845; while any contract effected on 1 September 2007 and onwards will be subject to the Gambling Act 2005 (insofar as it applies at all).

The distinction between indemnity and non-indemnity insurance

4.04 The insurable interest that must be shown will depend on whether the policy is one of indemnity or one of non-indemnity. In its paper on insurable interest, the Law Commission provided a definition of 'indemnity insurance' and 'non-indemnity insurance' (Law Commission, Insurance Contract Law, Issues Paper 4, Insurable Interest, 2008, p3):

> **'Type 1 – Indemnity insurance**
>
> 1.16 Indemnity contracts are governed by the indemnity principle. The indemnity principle simply means that insureds can only recover what they have lost. To make a successful claim, policyholders have to show that they incurred loss. They are compensated for the amount of that loss and no more. It follows that in order to suffer a loss, the insured must have had some kind of an interest in the subject matter. This interest is not the same as the strict insurable interest required by statute.
>
> **Type 2 – Non-indemnity insurance**
>
> 1.17 Non-indemnity insurance pays a set amount on the occurrence of a specified event. Most life insurance policies are non-indemnity contracts as they pay a fixed sum on the death of the person insured. Likewise, policies that pay a specified sum on the occurrence of a defined event, such as personal accident policies or valued policies, are also non-indemnity policies.'

Non-indemnity insurance and insurable interest

4.05 As regards non-indemnity insurance, the rules concerning the demonstration of an insurable interest are governed by the Life Assurance Act 1774, which – despite its name – also applies to contracts made on human life which are not long-term insurance (eg, accidental death policies) and contracts, other than those on shops, goods or merchandise, which are not indemnity policies.

Section 1 of the 1774 Act prohibits the *making* of such insurance when there is no insurable interest. It is not necessary to have such an interest at the time of any claim. Without the required interest, a policy will be rendered null and void. This provision exists independently of the Gaming Act 1845. The position has therefore not been changed by the Gambling Act 2005.

Insurable interest in the life of another rests, with limited exceptions, upon financial interest. Insurance on the lives of family members is, therefore, not always permissible.

The basic rules are as follows:

(a) A person is conclusively presumed to have an unlimited insurable interest in his own life (*Wainwright v Bland* (1835) 1 Moo & Rob 481). If a spouse and children are the nominated payees of the policy, s 11 of the Married Women's Property Act 1882 creates a statutory trust of the proceeds in their favour.

(b) Spouses and civil partners are conclusively presumed to have unlimited insurable interests in each other's lives (*Reed v Royal Exchange Assurance Co* (1795) Peake, Add Cas 70) (policy on husband); *Griffiths v Fleming* [1909] 1 KB 805 (policy on wife); and s 253 of the Civil Partnership Act 2004.

(c) In the absence of proof of financial interest, a parent cannot insure a child (*Halford v Kymer* (1830) 10 B&C 724); although under a policy issued by a friendly society, such insurance may be taken out up to a limit of £800 (Friendly Societies Act 1992, s 99). Equally, a child cannot insure his parent without proof of financial interest (*Shilling v Accidental Death Insurance Co* (1857) 2 H&N 42).

(d) Siblings cannot insure each other's lives without proof of financial interest (*Howard v Refuge Friendly Society* (1886) 54 LT (NS) 644), and the same obviously applies to more distant family relationships.

Business relationships involving financial interest may give rise to insurable interest based on financial loss. Thus, although the amounts will be limited to financial losses (eg, under contracts of employment or partnership deeds), an employer may insure the life of a key employee and the members of a partnership may insure each other's lives. Creditors may also insure the lives of their debtors (*Hebdon v West* (1863) 3 B&S 579). *Feasey v Sun Life Assurance Co of Canada* [2003] Lloyd's Rep IR 637 reiterated the principle of insurance on the life of another based on financial loss and effectively allowed a fixed sum as an estimate of the relevant loss to be used to establish insurable interest at the outset of the policy. In that case, the insurer's (or reinsured's) insurable interest was expressed to be in the lives of employees and other persons injured who might make claims against the underlying insured (as their employer). The Court of Appeal held that there was no objection to the insurer's (or reinsured's) insurable interest being classified as a contingent one on the lives of the underlying insured's employees based on loss calculated at the outset (rather than as a simple liability cover). Such insurable interest was capable of a pecuniary evaluation and the policy itself was capable of being construed as covering that interest.

Following consideration by the Law Commission, a draft bill was introduced in 2016 in relation to insurable interest and the 1774 Act (which would have been repealed). Unfortunately, it did not progress to the statute book and it is unclear whether it will be reconsidered in the future. This bill (the Insurance Bill 2016) proposed limited changes in relation to life-related insurance. In the main, it would have extended the concept of insurable interest to cover most of the circumstances in which it is likely to be required (eg, by providing an interest in relation to co-habitees, children and grandchildren). It would also have extended the strict financial loss requirements to situations where there was a 'reasonable prospect' that the insured would suffer economic loss if the insured event occurred.

Indemnity insurance and insurable interest

4.06 The rules that govern indemnity insurance are more complicated. They are governed by a patchwork of statutes, with some dating from 1745. The important distinction for the purposes of the effect of the Gambling Act 2005 is between marine and non-marine insurance. This distinction is discussed separately below.

It follows from the definition of 'insurable interest' in *Lucena v Craufurd* (1806) 2 B&P (NR) 269 that the crucial time for the existence of an insurable interest from the insured's point of view is the time at which he makes a claim on his insurer. If the insured has no insurable interest at that point, there will be no valid claim under the insurance contract, even if the insured had an insurable interest at the time the insurance contract was entered into.

On the other hand, it is not necessary that the insured's insurable interest should have existed on the date the insurance contract was made, provided only that the insured does not enter into the insurance contract without any *bona fide* expectation of acquiring an insurable interest at some point in the future.

Marine insurance

4.07 Marine insurance is still governed by the Marine Insurance Act 1906 and the Marine Insurance (Gambling Policies) Act 1909. The effect of these statutes is that, prior to 1 September 2007, there is a legal requirement for an insurable interest for a valid contract to exist. Furthermore, the 1909 Act makes it a criminal offence to make a marine policy without any insurable interest.

The effect of the Gambling Act 2005 may be that there is no longer a need for an insurable interest in order to create a valid policy. However, the criminal prohibition on effecting such a policy remains. This means that even though the contract might be enforceable, the parties will be prevented from gaining a benefit from the enterprise.

Non-marine insurance

4.08 The law before 1 September 2007 is governed by the Gaming Act 1845. It provides that non-marine indemnity policies cannot be wagers or will be void. As such, there is a need to show insurable interest.

However, the Gambling Act 2005 has removed the prohibition on enforcing wagers. It is therefore arguable that the requirement for insurable interest throughout the contract, and in particular at outset, no longer applies to contracts that are made from 1 September 2007 onwards. However, the overriding indemnity principle remains, which means that the insured must suffer an actual loss in respect of the subject matter of the policy (and so have some relationship to the subject matter) in order to be able to recover under the policy. This is discussed further below.

Marine insurance: the time when the insurable interest must exist

4.09 As previously mentioned, the insured must possess an actual insurable interest at the date of loss; otherwise he can make no claim (Marine Insurance Act 1906, s 6(1)). The only exception to this principle is where the policy is made 'lost or not lost'. The type of policy caters for the possibility of a purchase of a vessel or cargo during the course of a voyage, at a time when it is assumed, but not certain, that no casualty has occurred. By insuring 'lost or not lost', the insured will be covered even though a loss has occurred prior to completion of the sale, but only if the insured was unaware of that loss (Marine Insurance Act 1906, s 6(1)). It is not possible for a person to insure once he has become aware that a loss has occurred.

4.10 *Insurable interest*

If an insured does not possess insurable interest at the outset of the policy, but genuinely expects to obtain insurable interest (eg, the case of a prospective purchaser of a vessel or cargo), the policy is not void by way of gaming or wagering. His ability to recover under the policy will depend upon his obtaining an insurable interest before the casualty occurs. As previously mentioned, if he has not obtained an insurable interest by that date, he will be unable to recover under the policy (Marine Insurance Act 1906, s 26(2)), although he will have a claim for his premiums (Marine Insurance Act 1906, s 84(3)(c)).

Marine insurance: illustrations of insurable interest

4.10 A variety of interests may be insured under a marine policy:

(a) the hull and machinery of the vessel;

(b) the cargo carried on board the vessel – if the cargo is in the form of an undivided bulk, consisting of goods to be allocated to individual purchaser when the vessel unloads, each has an insurable interest in a proportionate part of the bulk (Marine Insurance Act 1906, s 8);

(c) the freight – that is, the hire paid to the owner of the vessel either for space on the vessel for the carriage of cargo or for the use of the entire vessel under a chartering agreement;

(d) liability which is faced by the owner of the vessel either to the owners of other vessels or to cargo owners;

(e) the mortgagor and the mortgagee of the vessel (Marine Insurance Act 1906, s 14); and

(f) the master and crew, in respect of their wages (Marine Insurance Act 1906, s 11).

Non-marine indemnity insurance: illustrations of insurable interest

Owner of property

4.11 The owner of property has an insurable interest in it for the full value of the property, even though he has entered into a binding contract for its sale (*Rayner v Preston* (1881) LR 18 Ch D 1), and despite the fact that the property would have been subject to seizure by the customs authorities for evasion of excise duty (*Geismar v Sun Alliance and London Insurance Ltd* [1978] QB 383).

Vendor and purchase of buildings

4.12 On exchange of contracts for the sale of a building or land, a binding contract of sale comes into existence. At that stage, the vendor remains the owner, but the risk will pass to the purchaser unless the contract otherwise provides. If this is the case, the purchaser must pay the full purchase price on completion, whether or not the building has suffered loss between exchange and completion. The result is that the vendor can insure the building by reason of his ownership, and the purchaser can insure by reason of being on risk (*Collingridge v Royal*

Exchange Assurance Corpn (1877) 3 QBD 173). If the building is damaged between exchange and completion, each party can recover the value from its respective insurer; although the vendor's insurer will be able to reclaim payment from the vendor by way of subrogation when the purchaser pays the price on completion, as the vendor would otherwise receive a double indemnity.

Possessor of property

4.13 A person in possession of goods or land, even though not the owner, may have an insurable interest in the property in question. This will be the case when his possession is coupled with a right to use or enjoy the property; a thief, or a person who is in possession of goods because they have been deposited on his land, has no insurable interest (*Macaura v Northern Assurance Co Ltd* [1925] AC 619), whereas a person who has been given a right to use and enjoy property does possess an insurable interest (*Anthony John Sharp and Roarer Investments Ltd v Sphere Drake Insurance Plc Minster, Insurance Co Ltd and E C Parker & Co Ltd (The 'Moonacre')* [1992] 1 Lloyd's Rep 501).There are two forms of insurable interest which may be claimed by a person in possession of property:

(a) his personal interest; or

(b) the full value of the property.

The position may be illustrated by reference to a warehouseman storing property belonging to third parties. The warehouseman's personal interest consists of any liability which he may face to the owners of the property should it be damaged (because he has not taken proper care of it), and of the amount of any charges which he may be able to levy upon the owner as payment for his storage services. Alternatively, the warehouseman has the right to insure the subject matter for its full value; and if it is lost, he is able to claim the full value from the insurer (*Waters v Monarch Fire and Life Assurance Co* (1856) 5 E & B 870). The warehouseman may, however, retain only those sums representing his personal interest; the surplus insurance moneys are held for the true owner by the warehouseman as the owner's debtor. However, the warehouseman will hold the surplus on trust if the contract between the parties obliged the warehouseman to insure the property (*Re E Dibbens & Sons (In Liquidation)* [1990] BCLC 577). Whether the surplus is held as debtor or trustee will be significant if the warehouseman becomes insolvent, for in the latter case the owner has a secured claim on the surplus.

Given that insurance can be either personal or for full value, it becomes necessary to determine exactly which interest is being covered. The rule here is that the policy will be presumed to be one on the full value of the property unless there is clear wording to the contrary. This recognises those situations where the insured will insure the full value of loss even where this exceeds his personal interest – as where a head contractor and subcontractor each has an insurable interest in the entire contract works, despite lack of ownership or even possession. The subcontractor may only be responsible for a small part of the works, but has a sufficient connection with the entire works to justify insurable interest (*National Oilwell (UK) Ltd v Davy Offshore Ltd* [1993] 2 Lloyd's Rep 582).

THE INDEMNITY PRINCIPLE

4.14 Regardless of the question of insurable interest, indemnity insurance contracts (marine and non-marine) are governed by the indemnity principle. This requires the insured to suffer a loss in order to recover under the insurance contract. This will be implied into a policy if it is not expressly provided for in the contract. This means that the insured must have an interest in the subject matter of the insurance or exposure to legal liability for the loss of another in order to have a valid claim under the insurance. The law on the indemnity principle has not been affected by the Gambling Act 2005. Accordingly, the essential practical effect of the indemnity principle is to keep alive the requirement to demonstrate an insurable interest in the case of indemnity insurance contracts.

Chapter 5

Premiums

- Definition
- Amount of premium
- Payment of premium
- Renewal of premium
- The role of brokers
- Return of premium

DEFINITION

5.01 'Premium' can be defined as the consideration paid by the insured, in return for which the insurer undertakes to insure the risks in the policy of insurance. The premium will normally take the form of a monetary payment, although it can take other forms. Once paid, the premium applies to the whole duration of the policy and the insured cannot be required to pay a supplement should the insurer find itself faced with an undue number of claims, unless the policy contains a provision requiring payment of additional premium in these circumstances. This position can be contrasted with mutual insurance. Members of the mutual insurance organisation will generally pay a sum at the beginning of the policy year. This amount may then be increased by a 'call' from the insurer during the year, or after the year in question until it is 'closed', in order to maintain the adequacy of the insurance fund for claims.

AMOUNT OF PREMIUM

5.02 In most types of insurance, the insurer will determine the amount of the premium at the outset. This again contrasts with the position in respect of mutual insurance, which may not be ascertained until the cover period has ended. In those rare cases where there is no express agreement to set the premium at the time of the contract, there is a risk that the contract may be held to be void for uncertainty. One way to avoid this is if the court construes the contract as meaning that the insured shall pay a reasonable sum to be determined by market forces. In the case of marine insurance, there is a specific statutory provision for the fixing of a reasonable market premium in the absence of agreement (Marine Insurance Act 1906, s 31(1)). Some policies do contemplate that the insurer may be called upon to accept additional risk during the currency of the agreement. This is particularly common in marine insurance, where the insurer is obliged under 'held covered' provisions to offer cover where the insured has deviated from the agreed route, broken a warranty or entered into a war zone. Here the insured will be required to pay an additional premium to be determined on market principles (Marine Insurance Act 1906, s 31(2)); although if a premium cannot be agreed and there is no market rate, the insurer's obligation to offer additional cover is discharged (*Liberian Insurance Agency Inc v Mosse* [1977] 2 Lloyd's Rep 560).

PAYMENT OF PREMIUM

5.03 In principle, at least, premiums are payable in cash to the insurer at its principal place of business. It is for the insured to seek out the insurer and effect this payment, which should be in the form stipulated in the contract. It is more usual now for payment to be made by electronic payment or direct debit.

What is the effect of non-payment where the policy does not provide that it is a condition precedent to liability or allow for cancellation or forfeiture? Where the insured has not paid the premium on the due date, the insurer may have a number of remedies. These include bringing proceedings to compel payment of the premium. Alternatively, non-payment may be regarded as a repudiatory breach giving the insurer the right to terminate the contract.

In the absence of a non-forfeiture provision in a policy, and where the insurer has a contractual right to treat the policy as having been forfeited due to late payment of premium, the courts appear to be reluctant to exercise their equitable discretion to grant relief from forfeiture. In commercial cases, where premiums are handled by brokers acting for the parties, non-payment may be little more than an accounting error. It was held in *Fenton Insurance Co Ltd v Gothaer Versicherungsbank VVag* [1991] 1 Lloyd's Rep 172, a reinsurance case, that non-payment for a period of some eight years was not sufficient to amount to a repudiatory breach. A similar approach was taken in *Figre Ltd v Mander* [1999] Lloyd's Rep IR 193.

What then is the position if the policy takes effect even though the premium has not been paid? One has to look to the contract of insurance to determine whether the insurer is entitled to reject a claim until the premium is tendered. The insurer will normally have the right to deduct outstanding premiums from the sum due to the insured under the policy.

The payment of the premium is, in marine insurance law, a condition concurrent with the obligation of the insured to issue the policy (Marine Insurance Act 1906, s 52). The effect of this is, subject to a contrary provision in the contract, that the risk may commence from the agreed date of event, but that the insured will not be entitled to a policy (and therefore cannot enforce the contract (Marine Insurance Act 1906, s 22) until the premium has been tendered.

RENEWAL OF PREMIUM

5.04 It is now common for insurers to accept payment by instalments or by monthly direct debit. Irrespective of whether premiums are paid monthly or in a single lump sum at inception, the insured will be asked at the end of the policy period either to pay the renewal premium or to complete a further bank mandate to ensure the continuation of the direct debiting arrangement. What is the position, then, if the insured is late in complying with the insurer's instructions? A large number of insurance contracts provide that, until the premium is paid, there shall be no insurance cover. In the absence of an express contractual provision, it is unlikely that such a term would be implied. The policy, therefore, commences at its inception date and continues until lateness of payment becomes fundamental. Once time becomes of the essence, however, non-payment constitutes default whatever the reasons for, or circumstances surrounding, the non-payment. The position may be further complicated by the insurer's grant of 'days of grace' for the payments of premium. The position also varies as between life policies and other types of policy.

Life insurance

5.05 Given the nature of life contracts, it is unsurprising that punctual payment of the premium is regarded as a condition precedent to the liability of the company. The insurance is effectively regarded by the law not as periodic, but as continuing, subject to *renewal* by the insured. Failure to pay the premium by the due date will cause the policy to lapse; and if cover is to be reinstated, the insured will have to make a fresh application. The consequences of this can be extremely harsh. In order to avoid this, the insurer may give the insured a period of 'days of grace' for payment of the *renewal* premium. The effect of this is to allow the insured an extension of time for the payment of such premiums. If a loss should occur in that period, the insurer will be liable to meet the loss. This was the ruling of the Court of Appeal in *Stuart v Freeman* [1903] 1 KB 47. Certain life investment policies may provide for the policy to be paid up rather than to lapse or be forfeited. This involves the existing policy value being used to pay charges (including premiums for insurance cover provided under the policy) until the policy value is exhausted.

Indemnity insurance

5.06 An indemnity policy, unlike a life policy, is periodic and comes to an end at the end of a stated period. Renewal by the insured creates a totally new contract. The grant of days of grace by the insurer for payment of the renewal premium does not, therefore, amount to an extension of the old policy, but is an offer to the insured of fresh cover should the premium be paid in the days of grace. It follows that the insurer is not automatically liable for a loss during the days of grace; this will depend upon whether the insurer has indicated to the insured that it is prepared to accept liability in that period, and also upon whether the insured has, by conduct or otherwise, accepted the insurer's offer of temporary cover. It was held in *Taylor v Allon* [1966] 1 QB 304 that the driver of a motor vehicle was not insured during the days of grace because he had not accepted the insurer's offer and had no intention to do so. Merely driving his vehicle on the strength of the insurer's offer was held to be insufficient acceptance of it.

THE ROLE OF BROKERS

5.07 The rules applicable to the payment of premiums through brokers vary considerably as between, on the one hand, insurance placed at Lloyd's and marine policies and, on the other hand, all other policies. Lloyd's and marine insurances are governed by exceptional rules which are long established by custom. Ordinary principles are considered first in what follows.

General principles

5.08 As a general rule, the insurance broker is the agent of the insured for most purposes (see **Chapter 9**). Payment of the premium to the broker will not, therefore, satisfy the requirement to pay the premium to the insurer. Unless the broker is acting as agent for the insurer, payment is not, in fact, effective until the amount has actually been received by the insurer. One consequence of this is that, in practice, the risk of the broker's insolvency or misconduct is borne by the insured. There is, then, no legal relationship between the broker and the insurer. The law is illustrated by the unusual facts of *Wilson v Avec Audio-Visual Equipment Limited* [1974] 1 Lloyd's Rep 81, in which the defendant insured had placed insurances with the insurer through the claimant broker, but no premiums had been paid. The insurer became insolvent and premiums were demanded from the broker, which duly paid the premiums and sought reimbursement from the insured. The Court of Appeal held that the broker had no obligation to the insurer to pay the premium and, as this payment had not been authorised by the insured, the broker had no right to be reimbursed by the insured.

Where the broker is UK authorised under the Financial Services and Markets Act 2000, it will be subject to the rules set out in the Financial Conduct Authority's Client Assets Sourcebook (CASS) relating to client money. This will generally mean that monies held in connection with its UK regulated insurance distribution business must be held on trust for the client or in an approved bank until they are paid to the insurer.

Where the broker issuing a policy acts as agent of the insurer under a delegated authority, it must instead collect and hold premiums under a risk transfer arrangement with the insurer. This will mean that the insurer is liable for the money held by the broker (ie, it is deemed to be the insurer's money and premium will deemed to have been paid). Risk transfer arrangements may also be agreed between an insurer and a broker in other scenarios, and may include monies paid by the insurer in relation to claims. CASS 5.2 sets out requirements in relation to such a risk transfer arrangement, which may be summarised as follows:

(a) The broker should not receive money as agent of an insurer, unless:

   (i) it has entered into a written agreement with the insurer which expressly provides that it is to act as the insurer's agent in receiving premiums and/or holding other monies to be paid to the client (eg, refunds and claims monies) on behalf of the insurer; and

   (ii) it retains a copy of the agreement for at least six years from the date on which it is terminated;

(b) The broker must ensure that it informs those of its clients which are not insurance undertakings and whose transactions may be affected by the arrangement (whether in its terms of business, client agreements or otherwise), in writing, that it will hold their money as agent of the insurance undertaking and, if necessary, the extent of such agency (ie, whether it includes all items of client money or is restricted – for example, to the receipt of premiums); and

(c) The broker must be satisfied on reasonable grounds that the terms of the policies issued by the insurance undertaking to its clients are likely to be compatible with the risk transfer arrangement.

CASS 5.1.5A also provides that if the terms of a risk transfer arrangement permit the distributor to co-mingle risk transfer monies with client monies, the monies will effectively become client monies and the insurer's interests need to be expressly subordinated to the interests of the clients. Care is therefore needed to ensure that risk transfer arrangements do not, unless intending to apply the client money rules, permit co-mingling, as otherwise the money would become subject to the client money rules.

Lloyd's policies and contracts of marine insurance

5.09 Section 53(1) of the Marine Insurance Act 1906 codifies a market usage of the marine market at Lloyd's dating back at least to the beginning of the nineteenth century, which states that the broker is directly responsible to the insurer for the premiums. It is doubtful whether this usage applies to non-marine business at Lloyd's. In the event of non-payment, the insurer must look to the broker and not to the insured for payment, although this will be of little use to the insurer where the reason for the broker's non-payment is insolvency, as the broker is a mere debtor of the insurer and does not hold any premium paid to him by the insured on trust for the insurer. The real effect of this rule is to transfer the risk of the broker's insolvency to the insurer, as the insured cannot be made to pay the insurer once he has made payment to the broker (*Universo Insurance Co of Milan v Merchants Marine Insurance Co Ltd* [1897] 2 QB 93).

The strict legal position as set out above was avoided for a period of time by an agreement made in October 1997 between the Lloyd's Insurance Brokers' Committee, Lloyd's and the Institute of London Underwriters (now called the London International Insurance and Reinsurance Market Association) that insurers would not, notwithstanding s 53(1) of the Marine Insurance Act 1906, hold brokers responsible for payment of premiums in the event of a default by the insured. This principle applied to all business incepting after 31 August 1996; in relation to the Institute of London Underwriters, the agreement took effect in respect of all business closed on Institute policies incepting after 31 August 1997. The agreement, however, lapsed and no business going forward from 31 August 2001 is subject to it. As a result, where the relevant policy is governed by English law, the underwriters may have the option to invoke s 53(1) of the Marine Insurance Act 1906 in respect of that policy and claim unpaid premium from the broker.

In 2010 the Law Commission published Issues Paper No 8, which considered the operation of s 53(1) of the Marine Insurance Act 1906. The

Law Commission concluded that the application of s 53(1) was 'unclear' and 'anomalous', and that the 'common law fiction, which was effected to give effect to the custom before it was codified by section 53(1), has produced unprincipled and conflicting case law'.

Following a period of consultation in 2011, the Law Commission published proposals to reform s 53(1) which included amending the law so that the liability to pay premium to the insurer fell on the insured and not the broker. The Law Commission's proposals were not implemented.

RETURN OF PREMIUM

Indivisibility of premium and total failure of consideration

5.10 Notwithstanding the payment of any premium, it will be recoverable if there has been a total failure of consideration.

The common law recognises two propositions as stated by Lord Mansfield in *Tyrie v Fletcher* (1777) 2 Cowp 666:

(a) If the risk never attaches, the insurer has not earned any part of the premium and the insured is entitled to recover the full premium on the ground of total failure of consideration; and

(b) If the risk has attached, even for a day, there is no total failure of consideration and the insured is not entitled to a return of any part of his premium. In such case, the insured's right to recover any part of his premium will rest upon the policy itself.

It is worth noting that these principles may be reflected in, or modified by, the express terms of the contract.

Application of the law

5.11 The return of premium depends upon whether the risk is attached. The following situations may arise.

Lack of an insurable interest

5.12 Where the insured has no insurable interest in the subject matter but is required to have one, the risk can never attach and the premium is returnable (Marine Insurance Act 1906, s 84(3)(c)). However, there is no right to a return of premium if the insured under a life policy does not have an insurable interest, as the policy is illegal (Life Assurance Act 1774, s 1, as applied by *Harse v Pearl Life Assurance Co* [1904] 1 KB 558); although if the policy was induced by the fraud of the insurer's agent, the premium will be returnable (*Hughes v Liverpool Victoria Legal Friendly Society* [1916] 2 KB 482).

Loss of an insurable interest during the currency of the policy – for example, by sale of the subject matter – will not justify a return of premium, as the risk has been run, albeit temporarily (Marine Insurance Act 1906, s 84(3)(d)).

Risk not attaching

5.13 If the risk under the policy never attaches – for example, because the goods insured have never been transported – the premium is returnable (Marine Insurance Act 1906, s 84(3)(b)).

Mistake

5.14 If the contract is void for mistake, the consideration will fail and the premiums paid are returnable.

Avoidance for misrepresentation or non-disclosure

5.15 Where an insurer avoids a policy for breach of the insured's duty to take reasonable care not to make a misrepresentation (in the case of consumers) and the duty of fair presentation (in the case of non-consumers), whether the insurer is required to return some or all of the premiums depends on the nature of the misrepresentation or non-disclosure.

In the case of consumers, the Consumer Insurance (Disclosure and Representations) Act 2012 provides that if there has been a deliberate or reckless misrepresentation, the policy will be treated as if it never existed and the insurer is permitted to retain any premium (unless it would be unfair not to return the premium). If instead the misrepresentation was careless, the insurer can apply a proportionate remedy which reflects what the insurer would have done had it known the true facts. In some circumstances, this may result in a return of premium to reflect a reduction in the cover offered or a request for additional premium to be paid. In other circumstances, this may result in a proportionate reduction of any claims payments to reflect shortfalls in the premium that should have been paid.

In non-consumer cases, the Insurance Act 2015 provides that an insurer can avoid the contract and keep all premium where there has been a deliberate or reckless misrepresentation. In the case of a careless misrepresentation, a proportionate remedy will also be applied to reflect what the insurer would have done had it known the true facts.

Please see **Chapter 6** for further details.

Divisibility of risk

5.16 If the risk attaches to some part of the policy but not to the remainder, the insured cannot recover the premium. The position differs, however, if the contract can be shown on its true construction to be severable. The insured will be entitled to a partial return of premium to reflect those risks which have not attached at the time of loss.

Over-insurance

5.17 If the insured has insured under one or more policies for a sum greater than his insurable interest, he may not be able to reclaim the excess premium; although the position is different in marine insurance (see Marine Insurance Act 1906, s 84(3)(e) and (f)). For non-marine cases, there may be circumstances where an insured can claim a failure of consideration in relation to an innocent over insurance. Much will depend on the circumstances, including any representations made by the insured and the terms of the policy.

Chapter 6

Policyholder duties

- Law reform
- CIDRA
- Insurance Act
- Position prior to CIDRA and the Insurance Act
- Minimising loss and alteration in the risk

LAW REFORM

6.01 The law relating to the duties that policyholders owe to insurers was subject to substantial change as a result of the Consumer Insurance (Disclosure and Representations) Act 2012 ('CIDRA'), which applies to consumer insurance contracts; and the Insurance Act 2015 ('Insurance Act'), which applies to non-consumer insurance contracts. CIDRA and the Insurance Act were the result of recommendations made by the Law Commission which assessed the application of the duty of utmost good faith to insurance contracts and considered how the law could be modernised.

CIDRA came into force in respect of consumer insurance contracts on 6 April 2013 and the Insurance Act came into force in respect of non-consumer insurance contracts on 12 August 2016. They each apply to all relevant insurance contracts entered into or varied after that date.

This chapter first considers the new law as it applies to consumer insurance contracts under CIDRA. It then considers the new law as it applies to non-consumer insurance contracts under the Insurance Act. Finally, this chapter (see **6.28–6.58**) considers the law which applied prior to CIDRA and the Insurance Act coming into force, the position in relation to fraud and minimising loss.

CIDRA

6.02 CIDRA applies to insurance contracts entered into by 'consumers' or varied after 6 April 2013. For these purposes, a 'consumer' is 'an individual who enters into the contract wholly or mainly outside of their trade or business or profession'.

Duty to take reasonable care not to make a misrepresentation

6.03 CIDRA abolishes the onerous duty of disclosure which applied to consumers under the common law and replaces it with a new duty to take reasonable care not to make a misrepresentation to an insurer. This places the onus on the insurer to ask the consumer questions to establish the nature of the risk. The consumer's duty is to answer those questions accurately and fully. The consumer is no longer required to disclose material facts which are not asked about by an insurer.

The insurer will have a remedy only where a consumer has made a misrepresentation when answering those questions or in providing information voluntarily. The nature of the insurer's remedy will depend on whether the misrepresentation was 'careless' or 'deliberate or reckless'.

6.04 Whether a consumer has taken reasonable care not to make a misrepresentation is to be determined in light of all the relevant circumstances under s 3(1) of CIDRA. Examples, but not an exhaustive list, of circumstances which may be relevant to this question are provided in s 3(2) and include:

(a) the type of consumer insurance contract in question and its target market;

(b) any relevant explanatory material or publicity produced or authorised by an insurer;

(c) how clear and specific the insurer's questions were; and

(d) whether an agent was acting for the consumer.

The standard of care is by default that of a 'reasonable consumer'; but this is qualified by any particular characteristics or circumstances of the actual consumer of which the insurer was aware or ought to have been aware.

Section 3(5) provides that any misrepresentation which is made dishonestly will be automatically deemed to have shown a lack of reasonable care.

6.05 In order to have a remedy under CIDRA, s 4(1) requires the insurer to show that:

(a) the consumer has breached the duty to take reasonable care by making a misrepresentation; and

(b) had the misrepresentation not been made, the insurer would either have:

  (i) not entered into the contract; or

  (ii) done so on different terms.

In practice, this requires the insurer to provide evidence of what it would have done if the correct information had been disclosed to it.

Where the consumer fails to comply with the duty not make a misrepresentation and the insurer can show that without the misrepresentation, it would not have entered into the contract (or agreed to the variation) at all, or would have done so only on different terms, the misrepresentation is a 'qualifying misrepresentation' for the purposes of CIDRA.

Types of misrepresentation and remedies

6.06 The remedies available to the insurer will depend on whether the qualifying misrepresentation was 'deliberate or reckless' or 'careless'.

A misrepresentation can only be either 'deliberate or reckless' or 'careless' for the purposes of CIDRA, and the burden of proof is on the insurer to show that a misrepresentation was 'deliberate or reckless' or 'careless'.

Under s 5(2) of CIDRA, a qualifying misrepresentation is 'deliberate or reckless' if the consumer:

(a) knew it was untrue or misleading, or did not care if it was untrue or misleading; and

(b) knew that the matter to which the misrepresentation related was relevant to the insurer or did not care whether it was relevant to the insurer.

A consumer is presumed to know that a clear and specific question was relevant to the insurer.

All qualifying misrepresentations which are not 'deliberate or reckless' are 'careless'.

6.07 If a consumer has made a deliberate or reckless misrepresentation, the insurer is entitled to avoid the policy and to refuse all claims under it.

The insurer is not required to return any premium paid, except to the extent that it would be unfair to the consumer to retain the premium.

6.08 If a consumer's misrepresentation was careless, then the insurer can apply a proportionate remedy based on what it would have done if the consumer had complied with his duty to take reasonable care in answering the insurer's questions. These are as follows:

(a) If the insurer can show it would not have entered into the contract on any terms, it may avoid the contract and refuse all claims, but it must return the premium;

(b) If the insurer would have entered into the contract, but on different terms (excluding terms relating to the premium), the contract is to be treated as if it had been entered into on those terms at the option of the insurer; and

(c) If the insurer would have entered into the contract, but would have charged a higher premium, it may proportionately reduce the amount of any claim to be paid.

If the insurer can show that it would have entered into the contract on different terms and would have charged a different premium, the remedies set out at (b) and (c) above can both apply.

If the insurer becomes aware of a careless misrepresentation at any time before a claim arises, it can notify the insured of proposed revised terms and any additional premium. Where the contract is wholly or mainly one of life insurance, however, the insurer cannot give the consumer notice to terminate the contract. The consumer receiving notice of revised terms may terminate the contract by giving reasonable notice to the insurer. On termination, the consumer will be entitled to a refund of premiums for the balance of the contract term.

The law on careless non-disclosure and misrepresentation in relation to insurance contracts can now be seen to be similar to the practice of the

Financial Ombudsman Service (FOS) prior to CIDRA coming into force on 6 April 2013. However, it should always be remembered that the FOS is not obliged to decide cases based on the law and, for example, may impose additional requirements to the remedies provided under CIDRA.

Group policies

6.09 CIDRA includes specific provisions which apply to group insurance policies – for example, insurance policies taken out by employers for the benefit of their employees, which would otherwise be non-consumer insurance contracts and subject to the Insurance Act.

Section 7 of CIDRA has the effect that group policies (which fall within the requirements of s 7(1)) are subject to the requirements of CIDRA, and that representations made by the individuals whom the group policy covers are relevant to the duty to take reasonable care.

Section 7 of CIDRA also provides that misrepresentations made by one covered individual will not affect the cover provided to another covered individual under the same group policy. In the example of a policy taken out by an employer to cover employees, this means that one employee's misrepresentation will not affect the cover provided to another employee under the same policy.

Basis of contract clauses

6.10 CIDRA (see **1.08**) abolished 'basis of contract' clauses in consumer insurance contracts by stating that any representation made by a consumer is not capable of being converted into a warranty by means of a provision in the contract.

Agents

6.11 In circumstances where an agent is acting on behalf of the insured, information provided by the insured to the agent (but not to the insurer) is not deemed to have been provided to the insurer.

However, where the agent is acting on behalf of the insurer, information provided to the agent is deemed to have been provided to the insurer.

Schedule 2 of CIDRA sets out rules for determining whether the agent is acting on behalf of the insurer as follows:

(a) where the agent does something in his capacity as an appointed representative of the insurer;

(b) where the insurer had given express authority to the agent to collect the consumer's information; or

(c) where the agent enters into the insurance contract as the insurer's agent, with the insurer's express authority to do so.

Paragraph 3 of Schedule 2 provides some further examples of circumstances which are potentially relevant to whether an agent is acting for the insurer, including whether he is providing impartial advice to the consumer and whether the consumer pays him a fee.

If the agent does not satisfy these requirements, he is considered to be acting for the consumer for the purposes of CIDRA.

Continuation of duty of utmost good faith in consumer insurance contracts

6.12 The duty of utmost good faith still applies to consumers in relation to insurance contracts in principle. The effect of CIDRA was not to abolish the duty of utmost good faith. Section 2(5)(a) of CIDRA instead provides that the duty of utmost good faith is 'modified to the extent required by the provisions of this Act'.

INSURANCE ACT

6.13 The Insurance Act applies to insurance contracts which are not 'consumer insurance contracts' that were entered into or varied on or after 12 August 2016. In effect, this means that the Insurance Act applies to all insurance contracts which are not covered by CIDRA.

Duty of fair presentation

6.14 The changes implemented by the Insurance Act to the law of non-consumer insurance contracts are broadly similar to the changes made by CIDRA to the law of consumer insurance contracts. However, there are also a number of key differences between each piece of legislation.

6.15 One of the significant differences is that the Insurance Act applies a duty of fair presentation to non-consumer insurance contracts, rather than the duty to take reasonable care not to make a misrepresentation in CIDRA.

The duty of fair presentation requires the insured to:

(a) make a clear and accessible disclosure of every material circumstance of which it knows or ought to know; or

(b) make a disclosure which gives the insurer sufficient information to put a prudent insurer on notice that it needs to make further enquiries for the purpose of revealing those material circumstances.

The duty of fair presentation does not require the insured to disclose a circumstance if:

(a) it diminishes the risk;

(b) the insurer already knows it, ought to know it or is presumed to know it; or

(c) the insurer waives its right to receive information about those circumstances.

The requirement for the disclosure to be 'accessible' means that an insured cannot simply disclose large amounts of data or documents and expect the insurer to search through them for risks. It is hoped that in practice, insurers and insureds will agree on the scope of information that is required to be disclosed for each risk.

Knowledge of the insured and the insurer

6.16 For the purposes of the duty of fair presentation, s 4 of the Insurance Act also sets out what the insured knows or ought to know for the purposes of making the required disclosure.

Where the insured is an individual, he is only presumed to know what he personally knows as an individual and what is known to any other individuals who are responsible for his insurance.

Where the insured is not an individual, it is presumed to know only what its senior management knows and what any other individuals who are responsible for its insurance know. 'Senior management' refers to the people who have a significant role in making decisions about the management of the insured.

6.17 Section 5 of the Insurance Act also sets out what knowledge the insurer is presumed to have. An insurer is presumed to have knowledge of a circumstance only where it is known to one or more of the individuals who act for the insurer in the decision of whether to take the risk. This means that an insurer will not have knowledge for the purposes of the Insurance Act of circumstances which are known by another part of its business which is not involved in the underwriting process of the risk.

The insurer is also presumed to know things which are common knowledge and things which an insurer offering insurance of the class in question would reasonably be expected to know.

Types of misrepresentation and remedies

6.18 Similar to CIDRA, the Insurance Act provides a remedy to the insurer only for 'qualifying' breaches of the duty of fair presentation. To be a qualifying breach, the insurer must show that it would not have entered into the contract at all or would have entered into the contract on different terms if the breach had not occurred.

6.19 A qualifying breach can be either 'deliberate or reckless' or 'careless'. A qualifying breach will be 'deliberate or reckless' if the insured:

(a) knew that it was in breach of the duty of fair presentation; or

(b) did not care whether it was in breach of the duty of fair presentation.

A 'careless' breach is any breach which is not 'deliberate or reckless'.

6.20 If a deliberate or reckless breach has occurred, the insurer may avoid the contract and refuse all claims. The insurer is also not required to return any of the premiums.

6.21 If the breach is careless, one of the following proportionate remedies applies:

(a) If the insurer would not have entered into the contract on any terms in the absence of the breach, the insurer may avoid the contract and refuse all claims, but must return the premiums paid;

(b) If the insurer would have entered into the contract, but on different terms (other than terms relating to premium), the contract is to be treated as if it had been entered into on those terms; and

(c) If the insurer would have entered into the contract, but would have charged a higher premium, the insurer may proportionately reduce the amount to be paid on a claim.

The remedies specified in (a) and (b) above can both apply to the same policy if the terms and premium offered would have been different had no breach occurred.

Warranties

6.22 The Insurance Act, like CIDRA, abolished basis of contract clauses in non-consumer insurance contracts.

6.23 The Insurance Act also changed the consequences of breaching a warranty in an insurance contract. It is now possible for an insured to claim under a policy where he is in breach of a warranty, provided that the breach has been remedied when the claim is made or is not relevant to the claim. The effect of the Insurance Act is that cover is effectively suspended during the period of a breach of a warranty and comes back into force when the breach of the warranty is remedied. For example, where a home insurance policy requires a working fire alarm to be in place, cover will be suspended only for the period of time in which a working fire alarm is not in place. The breach of warranty must also be relevant to the claim for an insurer to be able to rely on its breach. For example, again in the context of home insurance, if a house is damaged during a burglary, an insurer will be unlikely to be able to rely on the breach of a warranty requiring a fire alarm to be installed to refuse the claim.

Fraudulent claims

6.24 The Insurance Act also includes provisions covering the consequences for an insured of making a fraudulent claim. Where an insured makes a fraudulent claim, the insurer is permitted:

(a) not to pay the claim;

(b) to recover any sums paid by it to the insured in respect of the claim; and

(c) to provide notice to the insured that the contract is terminated from the date of the fraudulent act.

If the insurer decides not to terminate the contract, it is entitled to refuse all liability to the insured in respect of the relevant event (eg, a loss or whatever gives rise to the insurer's liability under the contract) occurring after the time of the fraudulent act and not to return any premiums.

Contracting out

6.25 Unlike CIDRA, the Insurance Act permits insurers and insureds to agree to disapply or modify some of its requirements which would put the insured in a worse position than if the Insurance Act applied, provided that the 'transparency requirements' set out in s 17 of the Insurance Act are complied with.

Section 17 requires that:

(a) the insurer take sufficient steps to draw the attention of the insured to the relevant provision before the contract or variation is entered into; and

(b) the relevant term be clear and unambiguous as to its effect.

It is not possible for the insurer and insured to agree to contract out of the abolition of basis of contract clauses. It is also not possible to contract out of requirements relating to interest for late payment of claims in relation to consumer contracts or where the delay is deliberate or reckless.

Group policies

6.26 Like CIDRA, the Insurance Act includes provisions dealing with group policies. These have effect so that a fraudulent claim by one insured does not affect the insurance of another insured.

Interest for late payment

6.27 The Enterprise Act 2016 made subsequent changes to the Insurance Act to introduce new provisions at ss 13A and 16A covering the late payment of claims by insurers. These changes apply to all contracts entered into or varied from 4 May 2017.

Section 13A applies to consumer and non-consumer insurance contracts, and requires an insurer to pay interest on insurance claims which are not paid within a reasonable period of time.

Section 16A means that it is not possible to contract out of this requirement for consumer insurance contracts. It is also not possible to contract out of this requirement in relation to non-consumer contracts where the delay in payment of the claim is deliberate or reckless.

Continuing duty of utmost good faith

6.28 The duty of utmost good faith continues to apply to non-consumer insurance contracts in principle. The Insurance Act did not abolish the duty of utmost good faith for insurance contracts. Section 14(2) of the Insurance Act instead provides that the duty of utmost good faith is 'modified to the extent required by the provisions of this Act'.

POSITION PRIOR TO CIDRA AND THE INSURANCE ACT

6.29 The following sections set out the law which applies to contracts which were entered into, and have not been varied since CIDRA and the Insurance Act came into force on 6 April 2013 and 12 August 2016 respectively. Claims made under the previous regime are still being disputed, and therefore knowledge of the application of the Marine Insurance Act remains relevant and useful. Concepts such as material circumstances and inducement are also still relevant to the law under the Insurance Act.

6.30 Contracts of insurance are based upon the principle of utmost good faith, or *uberrima fides*. This principle can be traced back to the eighteenth century (*Carter v Boehm* (1766) 3 Burr 1905), and was adopted by the courts in recognition of the fact that it is often difficult for an insurer to ask questions about the wide range of facts which might be material to the underwriting assessment, but which are known only to the insured. Good faith is a concept which is more common in civil law jurisdictions and is a notable departure from the more normal approach of *caveat emptor*, or 'let the buyer beware', which applies to contracts in English law.

The duty of good faith was codified in s 17 of the Marine Insurance Act 1906, which provides that: 'A contract of marine insurance is a contract based upon the utmost good faith and if the utmost good faith be not observed by either party the contract may be avoided by the other party.'

Prior to amendment by CIDRA and the Insurance Act, the principle of utmost good faith imposed two essential obligations on the insured: the duty to disclose (Marine Insurance Act 1906, ss 18, 19) and the duty to make true representations (Marine Insurance Act 1906, s 20). The House of Lords in *Pan Atlantic Insurance Co Ltd v Pine Top Insurance Co* [1994] 2 Lloyd's Rep 427 affirmed that the provisions of the Marine Insurance Act 1906 dealing with utmost good faith, disclosure and misrepresentation were intended to codify the common law relating to all forms of insurance, including non-marine insurance and reinsurance, and were not confined to marine insurance. Sections 18 and 19 of the Marine Insurance Act 1906 were repealed by the Insurance Act.

Continuing duty of utmost good faith

6.31 The duties of utmost good faith, disclosure and representation were all applicable during the negotiations and placement of the insurance contract. Section 17 of the Marine Insurance Act 1906 is silent on whether the duty of utmost good faith continues during the operation of the contract. In *Manifest Shipping Co Ltd v Uni-Polaris Insurance Co Ltd (The 'Star Sea')* [2001] Lloyd's Rep IR 247, the insured had failed to disclose, after litigation had commenced, a number of documents relevant to the claim. The insurer argued that this non-disclosure was fraudulent and thus in breach of s 17 of the Marine Insurance Act 1906. The House of Lords appeared to treat this as a case of fraud, and so distinct in law from any ongoing duty of good faith, so that no issue arose of a breach of the duty of utmost good faith.

Nevertheless, while it was accepted that there was a continuing and reciprocal duty of good faith, the House of Lords was clear that the duty after a contract is concluded is different and more limited than the duty prior to the formation of the contract. The House of Lords also found that the continuing duty of good faith comes to an end once the insurer has rejected a claim and litigation in respect of that claim has commenced.

Another decision which limited the scope of the continuing duty of good faith was *K/s Merc-Scandia XXXXII v Certain Lloyd's Underwriters Subscribing to Lloyd's Policy No 25t 105487 and Ocean Marine Insurance Co Ltd and Others (The 'Mercandian Continent')* [2001] 2 Lloyd's Rep 563, in which the Court of Appeal dealt with the question of when the continuing duty of good faith applied and what the appropriate remedy was in the event of breach. The Court of Appeal held that a post-contractual duty of good faith arises where the insured has a contractual duty to provide the insurer with information, and in circumstances where a liability insurer takes control of the defence of an insured in litigation.

The Court of Appeal also held that the only remedy available for breach of the continuing duty of good faith is avoidance *ab initio*. Before the insurer can avoid the contract, it must satisfy a two-stage test as follows:

(a) There has been a breach of the continuing duty of good faith; and

(b) The breach of the continuing duty of good faith is so severe that the insurer would be justified in treating the contract as repudiated and at an end.

NON-DISCLOSURE

6.32 In the general law of contract, a contract will be voidable if a party is induced to enter into it by a false statement or misrepresentation. Under the previous law (and now under CIDRA and the Insurance Act), the duty to provide information during pre-contractual negotiations is more onerous. Under the Marine Insurance Act, not only did the usual principle of misrepresentation operate, but the insured was under an additional obligation to volunteer to the insurer all facts which are material to the risk, regardless of whether the insurer had asked any express questions. This obligation characterised the contract of insurance as one of utmost good faith, or *uberrima fides*.

Even for contracts entered into prior to CIDRA, the duty of disclosure was of diminished importance in the consumer insurance field. The Statement of General Insurance Practice, which sought to mitigate some of the harshness of the strict legal position, was replaced in a modified form by the Insurance Conduct of Business Rules with effect from 14 January 2005. Those rules were also subsequently replaced by the Insurance: Conduct of Business Sourcebook. The regulatory requirements imposed specific requirements on insurers in the context of consumer insurance contracts, which tempered insurers' ability to apply the more draconian common law remedies. Since its inception in 2001, the FOS had developed a practice which is similar to the position which now applies under CIDRA.

The nature of the obligation to disclose

Definition of 'disclosure'

6.33 Section 18(1) of the Marine Insurance Act 1906 required the insured to disclose to the insurer 'every material circumstance' known to the insured.

Section 20 of the Marine Insurance Act 1906 in turn required 'every material representation' to be truthful. All facts material to the risk therefore had to be disclosed to comply with these requirements.

Section 18(2) of the Marine Insurance Act 1906 defined as 'material' 'every circumstance which would have influenced the judgement of a prudent underwriter in fixing the premium or determining whether he would write the risk' (see **6.36** below).

The House of Lords in *Pan Atlantic* (see **6.30** above) held that for a fact to be material, it was not necessary to show that full and accurate disclosure would have led a prudent insurer either to reject the risk or at least to have accepted it only on more onerous terms. It will suffice to show that the relevant fact would have affected the judgement of the insurer, in the sense that it would have been taken into account as part of the evaluative process. It was therefore generally enough for the insured to alert the insurer that the risk has particular characteristics; the onus was then on the insurer to make further enquiries. If the insurer failed do so, it could be taken to have waived the right to the additional information (see **6.41** below). Equally, if the insured prepared detailed documentation for the insurer containing all material facts and the insurer chose not to read the documents, but relied upon summary (but not misleading) statements made by the insured, the insured was likely to have complied with his duty of disclosure (see *Pan Atlantic* at **6.30** above).

The duty of disclosure under the previous law was tempered by the concept of a 'fair presentation' of the risk. This principle, as summarised by Kerr LJ in *Container Transport International Inc and Reliance Group Inc v Oceanus Mutual Underwriting Association Ltd* [1984] 1 Lloyd's Rep 476, recognised that there is often a limit on the amount of information that the insured can disclose. The insured was required to make a judgement as to what information would be material for a prudent underwriter in order to ensure that a 'fair presentation' was made. All such information then had to be supplied. As we have already seen, this concept has been adopted and developed in the Insurance Act.

Innocent non-disclosure

6.34 The insured's duty was to disclose facts of which he was aware and facts of which he ought to have been aware (eg, in the ordinary course of business). The insured could therefore have been guilty of non-disclosure for a failure to disclose a fact which it should have known but did not. Cases – in particular, *Pan Atlantic* (see **6.30** above) – assumed that the insured constructively knew facts which he ought to have known for the purposes of disclosure. However, in *ERC Frankona Reinsurance v American National Insurance Company* [2006] Lloyd's Rep IR 157, Andrew Smith

J noted that 'the courts do not readily impute to an insured information that he did not know on the basis that he ought to have known it'. It was irrelevant that the insured did not know he was under a duty to disclose material facts; innocence of this nature did not prevent non-disclosure from being actionable.

It was not just the insured's own knowledge which was relevant, but also that of his agents. If a broker was aware of facts material to the risk, or ought to be aware of such facts (Marine Insurance Act 1906, s 19(1)), then the broker's knowledge was deemed to be that of the insured (*Blackburn, Low & Co v Thomas Vigors* (1887) LR 12 App Cas 531) and had to be disclosed. Equally, the insurer could not avoid the policy on the basis of facts which the insured or his brokers or agents had no way of knowing. In this sense, innocent non-disclosure has no legal consequences.

This should be contrasted with the position where the insured was aware of a particular fact, but chose not to disclose it in the genuine belief that it was not material. The previous law here was clear: materiality was a matter to be assessed by the standard of the prudent insurer, not by the prudent or honest insured; and the insured's belief as to materiality, whether or not reasonably held, was irrelevant (*Joel v Law Union and Crown Insurance Co* [1908] 2 KB 863 (life insurance); *Lambert v Co-Operative Insurance Society Ltd* [1975] 2 Lloyd's Rep 485 (burglary insurance); *Pan Atlantic* (see **6.01** above)).

The use of agents

6.35 Under the previous law, if the insured completed a proposal form or discussed matters to be disclosed in the presence of an agent which was acting for the insurer or which was authorised by that insurer to obtain the completed proposal, disclosure to the insurer's agent would generally be treated as disclosure to the insurer itself. All would depend, however, on the authority that would have been given to the agent by its principal, the insurer.

A different situation arose where the negotiations with the insurer were conducted by a broker (which was always then the case at Lloyd's), as the broker was deemed to be the agent of the insured. This rule had the consequence that disclosure by the insured to the broker, or the broker's knowledge of the true position, was not sufficient to satisfy the insured's duty of disclosure to the insurer (*Kenneth Roberts v Patrick Selwyn Plaisted* (1989) 2 Lloyd's Rep 341). The insured, or his agent, was required to make sure that material information was communicated to the insurer. The existence of a separate obligation on the broker to disclose material facts was confirmed by the House of Lords in *HIH Casualty and General Insurance Ltd v Chase Manhattan Bank* [2003] 2 Lloyd's Rep 61. It was therefore important under the previous law for the insured to keep the broker informed of any change in the insured's circumstances, so that relevant information could be passed to the insurer. However, if the insured became aware of a material fact too late to communicate this to the broker before the contract was concluded, the insured's non-disclosure would be excused (Marine Insurance Act 1906, s 19).

Materiality and inducement

6.36 For an insurer to be able to avoid a policy for non-disclosure, the non-disclosure had to be material and to have induced the insurer to enter into the policy.

Under the previous law, a fact was material, and had to be disclosed to the insurer, if it would 'influence the judgement of a prudent insurer in fixing the premium or in determining whether he would take the risk' (Marine Insurance Act 1906, s 18(2)). 'Every material circumstance' known to the insured was required to be disclosed to the insurer (Marine Insurance Act 1906, s18(1)).

The test of materiality was objective and was normally established by way of expert underwriting evidence. In order for a fact or circumstance to be material, it did not need to be shown that the prudent underwriter would have charged a different premium or refused the risk had it known the truth; the question was whether a prudent insurer would have been influenced by the facts withheld in the sense that it would have wanted to have known about them.

Prior to *Pan Atlantic*, the test of materiality was held, in *Container Transport International v Oceanus* (see **6.33** above), to be whether the fact or circumstance was one which a prudent insurer would have wished to take into account when deciding whether to write the risk. In *Pan Atlantic* (see **6.30** above), the House of Lords conducted a complete review of the law applicable to disclosure of material facts. Their Lordships held that:

(a) for a fact to be material, it was sufficient to show that the relevant fact would have affected the judgement of a prudent insurer, in the sense that the insurer would have taken that fact into account as part of the evaluative process, even if it was not ultimately decisive; but

(b) a material non-disclosure would entitle an insurer to avoid a contract only if that non-disclosure actually induced the underwriter to subscribe to the contract on the relevant terms (the actual inducement test).

Although the first part of the test (ie, materiality) was objective, the House of Lords introduced an important subjective element in that the insurer that wrote the risk could not avoid the contract for non-disclosure if the underwriter was not in fact influenced by the non-disclosure in question, despite the fact that a hypothetical prudent insurer may have been affected. This subjective element was confirmed in numerous cases, including by the Court of Appeal in *Assicurazioni Generali SpA v Arab Insurance Group* [2003] 1 WLR 577.

A presumption of inducement

6.37 The test established by *Pan Atlantic* (see **6.30** above) under the previous law raised the possibility that the insured or his broker could have attempted to pass poor-quality risks to the insurer, relying on the fact that the underwriter may not, in actuality, be influenced by full disclosure. Lord Mustill in *Pan Atlantic*, anticipating this problem, commented specifically that once the facts are shown to be material (in other words, the first limb of the *Pan Atlantic* test has been satisfied), a presumption arises that the non-disclosure of that fact did induce the underwriter to enter into the contract on the relevant terms. This comment was subsequently considered by the courts and in *Marc Rich & Co AG v Portman* [1996] 1 Lloyd's Rep 430, the court was asked to consider whether there was evidence to rebut a presumption of inducement. The court held that a presumption would arise only where the actual underwriter was not available to give evidence and there was no reason to suppose he acted other than prudently in writing the risk. If the actual underwriter did give evidence, but that evidence was inconclusive on the question of inducement, the presumption would not operate and the burden of proving inducement would remain on the insurer.

The position under the previous law was clarified by the Court of Appeal in *Assicurazioni Generali v Arab Insurance Group* (see **6.36** above), in which Clarke LJ summarised the position as follows:

> 'An insurer or reinsurer must prove on the balance of probabilities that he was induced to enter into the contract by a material non-disclosure or a material misrepresentation.
>
> There is no presumption of law that an insurer or reinsurer is induced to enter in the contract by a material non-disclosure or misrepresentation. The facts may, however, be such that it is to be inferred that the particular insurer or reinsurer was so induced in the absence of evidence from him.'

It should be noted that under the Insurance Act, evidence of the effect on the underwriter will be important to establish the remedies available.

Illustrations of material facts

6.38 There are many reported cases, relating to all classes of insurance, in which the courts have been required to consider whether a particular fact was or was not material in the circumstances. General guidance only may be given here. The basic principle was that a fact could be material because it contributed either to the physical hazard or to the moral hazard of the risk underwritten.

While these cases were decided under the Marine Insurance Act, the court's decisions are likely to be instructive to the position under the Insurance Act, where the duty of fair presentation still requires disclosure of material circumstances that the insured knows or ought to know.

Physical hazard

6.39 Physical hazard is constituted by those facts which increase the immediate risk to the insured subject matter. To give some obvious examples: material facts for a fire or burglary policy could include the location of the property, the uses to which the premises are put and the adequacy of security arrangements. Material facts for a life or accident policy are likely to include the insured's medical record, his occupation and his spare-time activities. Material facts for a liability policy will include the nature of the insured's activities and his knowledge of the likelihood of any claim against him arising from earlier events. Material facts for a marine, aviation or motor policy will include the qualifications of the person in control of the transport, the purposes for which the transport is required and its physical condition.

Moral hazard

6.40 Moral hazard is concerned not with the physical condition of the subject matter itself, but rather with the character of the insured and the risk that the insured in question is more likely to suffer losses or make a claim. The most important forms of moral hazard are the following:

(a) Previous losses and insurance claims – what is important for this purpose is not necessarily the amount of a loss, but the mere fact that a loss has taken place (*Anthony John Sharp and Roarer Investments Ltd v Sphere Drake Insurance plc Minster, Insurance Co Ltd and E C Parker & Co Ltd (The 'Moonacre')* [1992] 2 Lloyd's Rep 501). To be safe, an insured should disclose previous claims even if they relate to other classes of insurance (*Becker v Marshall* [1922] LI L Rep 413).

(b) Previous refusals by other insurers to issue a policy, and previous refusals to insure without additional conditions or the charging of a higher premium, are potential material facts. This may be so even if the refusal related to a different class of insurance, as in *Locker & Woolf Ltd v Western Australian Insurance Co Ltd* [1935] 153 LI L Rep 325, where a fire policy was held to be voidable in the light of the insured's failure to disclose a previous motor car insurance refusal.

(c) Double insurance or over-insurance of the insured subject matter may be material, but only if the degree of over-insurance suggests that a fraudulent claim is a possibility (*Ionides v Pender (1873-74)* LR 9 QB 531).

(d) Previous criminality on the part of the insured is likely to be a material fact. Previous criminal convictions may be material if they are directly linked to the subject matter concerned (*Jester-Barnes v Licences & General Insurance Co Ltd* [1934] 49 LI L Rep 231 – drunken driving offences not disclosed for the purposes of a motor policy), or if they indicate general dishonesty of a nature likely to pose a threat to the insurer (*Woolcott v Sun Alliance and London Insurance Ltd* [1978] 1 All ER 1253). Criminal convictions are deemed to be immaterial once they are 'spent' under the Rehabilitation of Offenders Act 1974 (legislation which wipes clean the record of a convicted person after a period of time, the relevant period being determined by a sliding scale based upon the seriousness of the offence). It is irrelevant that dishonest behaviour on the part of the insured has not come to the attention of the authorities; such dishonest behaviour is still potentially material. This includes an acquittal of a material criminal offence, which must be disclosed if the insured in fact committed the offence. An acquittal is a material fact even where the proposer maintains his innocence because it might lead the prudent underwriter to make further enquiries (*Strive Shipping Corpn v Hellenic Mutual War Risks Association (The 'Grecia Express')* [2002] 2 Lloyd's Rep 88).

> Criminal charges (and similar specific allegations of dishonesty or misconduct) outstanding against the insured at the time the insurance contract is made are material facts, even when the insured knows that he is innocent (*Brotherton v Aseguradora Colseguros SA (No 2)* [2003] Lloyd's Rep IR 746), although the insured can include within his disclosure evidence of his innocence. Colman J followed the Court of Appeal's reasoning in *Brotherton* in *North Star Shipping Ltd v Sphere Drake Insurance plc* [2005] Lloyd's Rep IR 404. In this case, it was held that the policy was voidable as the insured had failed to disclose, among other matters, four separate pending criminal proceedings against it in the Greek courts and a civil action in Panama, all of which alleged fraud. These proceedings were held to be material facts even though the insured may have genuinely believed that the allegations were groundless and three of the Greek cases had been either withdrawn or dismissed by the time of the loss. Colman J held that allegations of fraud in proceedings are material facts going to moral hazard, in the sense that they would be taken into account by an underwriter in forming a view as to the acceptability of the risk. The materiality of the information is not diminished by exculpatory evidence. If exculpatory evidence is available, it should be given to the underwriter so that it has the opportunity to consider all the evidence in forming its opinion. Colman J's decision was upheld by the Court of Appeal ([2006] 2 Lloyd's Rep 183).

However, it is not always necessary for every allegation known to the insured to be disclosed. In *Norwich Union Insurance Ltd v Meisels* [2007] Lloyd's Rep IR 69, the insurer asserted that the insured had failed to disclose irregularities in the filing of accounts and returns of companies of which he was a director, which has led to penalties being imposed and, in some cases, dissolution of the relevant companies. The insured had further failed to disclose that four of his companies had been liquidated. The facts of the case did not indicate any dishonesty. The court held, in considering generally how 'moral hazard' should be dealt with, that allegations of misconduct are not always material. There is room for a test of proportionality based on the nature of the risk. The court held that exculpatory material relating to the allegations is relevant in determining whether acts are material, or whether the insurer would have accepted the insured's explanation and disregarded the allegations.

Limitations on the duty of disclosure

6.41 The former s 18(3) of the Marine Insurance Act 1906 set out four types of facts which did not need to be disclosed to the insurer and which were immaterial unless an express question was asked.

Facts diminishing the risk

6.42 Under s 18(3)(a) of the Marine Insurance Act 1906, the insured did not need to disclose any circumstance which diminished the risk. An illustration of this situation is *Inversiones Manria SA v Sphere Drake Insurance Co plc, Malvern Insurance Co Ltd and Niagara Fire Insurance Co Inc (The 'Dora')* [1989] 1 Lloyd's Rep 69, in which the insured was held not to be in breach of the duty of disclosure for failing to disclose that the yacht to be insured was not ready to sail and was still being worked upon some time after the inception of the risk.

Facts within the knowledge of the insurer

6.43 Section 18(3)(b) of the Marine Insurance Act 1906 stipulated that the insured did not need to disclose 'any circumstance which was known or was presumed to be known to the insurer'. The insurer was presumed to know matters of common notoriety or knowledge and matters which an insurer in the ordinary course of business ought to know. There were three types of facts which fell within this provision:

(a) Facts which were actually known to the insurer: In *Cape plc v Iron Trades Employers Association Ltd* [2004] Lloyd's Rep IR 75, it was held that the assured could not, on renewal of a liability policy, be required to disclose to the insurer the fact that there had been a huge rise in the incidence of claims for mesothelioma, as the insurer was aware of such claims and had in fact paid them.

(b) Facts or circumstances which the insurer ought to have known in the ordinary course of its business, or facts of notoriety which the insurer ought generally to have known: Facts which have been held to fall into this category include the existence of war in a particular region and the dangerous properties of particular substances used in the insured's business.

(c) Facts which were specific to the form of business carried on by the insurer and which ought to have been known by an insurer involved in that form of business: An insurer of fishing boats would be assumed to know that boats of that class had been subject to an exceptionally large number of claims in recent years (*North British Fishing Boat Insurance Co Ltd v Starr* [1922] 13 LI L Rep 206). Despite this expected knowledge, an insurer will not be expected to know specific circumstances affecting limited groups within the overall market in which it works or to retain information in which it has no interest.

Waiver of the duty to disclose

Express waiver

6.44 The insured did not need to disclose 'any circumstances as to which information was waived by the insurer' under s 18(3)(c) of the Marine Insurance Act 1906. The simplest form of waiver was an express clause in the proposal form which stated that the insured's duty of utmost good faith was satisfied by answering the questions put to him on the proposal. Less obvious wording may have had the same effect. In *Hair v The Prudential Assurance Co Ltd* [1983] 2 Lloyd's Rep 667, the proposal form concluded with a warranty by the insured that 'all the information entered above is true and complete and that nothing materially affecting the risks has been concealed'. This was held by Woolf J to mean that the insured was warranting that the answers given to express questions were true and complete, and that the disclosure of anything further had been waived.

The House of Lords in *HIH Casualty and General Insurance v Chase Manhattan Bank* (see **6.35** above) accepted that it was possible for an insured to contract out of both a duty of disclosure or the duty to ensure that any representation made was correct and the consequences of non-disclosure or misrepresentation by the insured (although, as a matter of public policy, the insured could not contract out of the consequences of his own fraudulent conduct).

Implied waiver

6.45 An insurer could be held by its conduct to have waived disclosure. Waiver could arise in the following circumstances:

(*a*) The insurer had been alerted by the insured to the possible existence of special circumstances, but had failed to make further inquiry. If, for example, the insurer had been told that the insured vessel was to be carrying cargo, but neglected to seek further information as to the nature of the cargo, the insurer could not complain if the cargo proved to be inflammable (*Mann Macneal and Steeves Ltd v Capital and Counties Insurance Co Ltd* [1921] 2 KB 300).

(b) The insurer had chosen to ask a specific question on a particular matter, but had by the question restricted the amount of information required (*O'Kane v Jones (The 'Martin P')* [2004] 1 Lloyd's Rep 389). Proposals for life policies, for example, normally ask the insured about previous medical treatment, but limit the question to the previous five years. In *Roberts v Plaisted* (see **6.35** above), the Court of Appeal commented that the duty of disclosure must be considered in the light of the wording of the proposal form presented to the insured.

(c) Section 18(3)(d) of the Marine Insurance Act 1906 stated that the insured need not disclose 'any circumstance which is superfluous to disclose by reason of any express or implied warranty'. If the policy contained an express warranty, the insurer was automatically discharged from liability in the event the warranty was broken and so was not reliant upon disclosure.

(d) The failure by an insurer to ask any questions at all on a particular matter could not generally be regarded as waiver of disclosure of facts concerning that matter, as a finding of that sort would run counter to the very doctrine of disclosure. However, it was held in *Société Anonyme d'Intermédiaries Luxembourgeois v Farex GIE* [1995] LRLR 116 that if the reinsurer makes no enquiry about the cedant's retention, it must be taken to have waived disclosure of such information.

Waiver or affirmation

6.46 The insurer could waive a breach of the duty of utmost good faith (or affirm the insurance contract notwithstanding the breach); but in order to be found to have done so, the insurer must be shown to have been fully aware of the insured's breach of duty and to have chosen to regard the contract as continuing regardless of that breach (*Liberian Insurance Agency Inc v Mosse* [1977] 2 Lloyd's Rep 560; *Container Transport International v Oceanus* (see **6.33** above); *Pan Atlantic* (see **6.30** above)).

Duration of duty of disclosure

6.47 The duty of disclosure under the previous law was intended primarily to assist the insurer in its assessment of the risk. Section 18(1) of the Marine Insurance Act 1906 stated that the insured's duty of disclosure arises 'before the contract is concluded'. After the contract has been agreed, the duty of disclosure was more limited, but would revive if the insurer needs further information to make a relevant underwriting decision (*Manifest Shipping Co Ltd v Uni-Polaris Insurance Co Ltd (The 'Star Sea'), K/s Merc-Scandia XXXXII v Certain Lloyd's Underwriters (The 'Mercandian Continent')*, both at **6.31** above). It will be noted that the relevant date was the conclusion of the contract and not the date at which the insurer came on risk.

The duty of disclosure also revived when a fresh contract of insurance was made. This would have occurred in three situations:

(a) The first was on renewal, as renewal operates as the making of a fresh contract.

(b) In the case of risks written on a subscription basis, separate disclosure is required to each of the subscribing underwriters. This is so because a subscription policy is in effect a composite contract between the insured and each individual underwriter.

(c) In the case of a framework contract for insurance, such as an open cover, the insured is entitled to cover for all risks of the agreed description up to fixed or aggregate monetary limits, subject only to making appropriate declarations to the insurer. If the open cover is non-obligatory as far as the insurer is concerned – that is, the insurer can reject individual declarations – the duty of disclosure applies to each declaration (*Berger and Light Diffusers Pt Ltd v Pollock* [1973] 2 Lloyd's Rep 442). By contrast, if the cover is obligatory, no duty of disclosure arises with each declaration, but the duty of disclosure attaches to the cover itself (*Glasgow Assurance Corporation Ltd v William Symondson* [1911] 2104 LT 254).

Superfluity

6.48 The insured did not need to disclose 'any circumstance which it was superfluous to disclose by reason of an express or implied warranty' (Marine Insurance Act 1906, s 18(3)(d)). If the policy contained a warranty (or, in the case of marine insurance, an implied warranty), the insurer was automatically discharged from liability in the event that the warranty was broken. Consequently, there was little point in the insured having to disclose facts or circumstances which meant that the insurer was, in any event, off risk as a result of a breach of warranty.

The insurer's remedies for breach of duty to disclose

6.49 Under the law prior to CIDRA and the Insurance Act, only one remedy was available to the insurer where the insured had failed to disclose a material fact: the policy was rendered voidable *ab initio*, so that the insurer had the right to treat the contract as if it had never existed. The insurer had no right to maintain the contract in force and to reject the insured's claim. On avoidance of the contract, the insured was entitled to a full return of premium on the basis of total failure of consideration. The insured's premium could be forfeited if the insured was guilty of fraud or if the policy stated that the insurer was entitled to keep the premium in the event that the policy was avoided (see **6.55** below).

Damages were not available for breach of the duty of disclosure. This was because the duty did not operate as an implied contractual term (breach of which would give rise to damages for breach of contract), but rather as a rule of law.

The judicial discretion contained in s 2(2) of the Misrepresentation Act 1967 under which, following misrepresentation, the court would, instead of ordering rescission, declare that the contract was subsisting and award damages to the innocent party had no application where there had been non-disclosure in relation to a contract of insurance.

MISREPRESENTATION

6.50 As stated above, contracts of insurance are contracts of utmost good faith. This means that the insured, when applying for a policy under the previous law, not only had a duty to disclose all material facts to the insurer (see **6.32** above), but also had a duty to avoid making false statements to the insurer. If the insured failed in this latter duty, the insurer had the right to avoid the contract. The principles applicable to misrepresentation under the previous law are largely the same as those relating to non-disclosure, and therefore this section considers solely those aspects of utmost good faith which were pertinent only to the law of misrepresentation.

A misrepresentation had to be one of fact to be actionable. Statements of opinion, intention, law or expectation were not normally capable of amounting to a misrepresentation. However, such statements could have amounted to an implied representation of fact as to the maker's state of mind and so had to be made honestly (see *Edgington v Fitzmaurice* (1885) LR 29 Ch D 459 and *Economides v Commercial Union Assurance Co plc* [1998] Lloyd's Rep IR 9).

Under the previous law a 'misrepresentation' was any false statement made to the insurer by the insured or his agent prior to the making of the contract. A statement would not be regarded as false if it was substantially true (Marine Insurance Act 1906, s 20(4)). Section 20 of the Marine Insurance Act 1906 was repealed by the Insurance Act.

A misrepresentation could take one of three forms:

(a) a false statement made by the insured in response to a question put to him by the insurer, normally by means of a proposal form;

(b) a false statement made by the insured in volunteering information to the insurer – without a question having been asked by that insurer; or

(c) failure by the insured to answer a question put to him by the insurer – if the insured left a blank space in response to a question on the proposal form, his answer could be assumed to be in the negative (*Roberts v Avon Insurance Ltd* [1956] 2 Lloyd's Rep 240). Thus, in some circumstances silence could amount to misrepresentation as opposed to a breach of the duty to disclose (*HIH Casualty and General Insurance v Chase Manhattan Bank (2003)* at **6.35** above).

Materiality and inducement

6.51 Under the previous law, a misrepresentation would give the insurer the right to avoid only if it was material and the underwriter could show that he had been induced to subscribe to the contract on the relevant terms by the misrepresentation (see *Pan Atlantic* at **6.30** above). A 'material statement' was defined as a statement which would influence the judgement of a prudent insurer in accepting the risk or in determining the amount of premium (Marine Insurance Act 1906, s 20 (2)). As with non-disclosure, the misrepresentation had to be shown to have been something that would have affected the judgement of the prudent insurer, in the sense that he would have taken into account as part of the evaluative process that misrepresented fact or circumstance, even if that was not ultimately decisive (*Pan Atlantic*). It also had to be shown that the misrepresentation induced the actual underwriter as a matter of fact. The innocence or otherwise, of the insured had no bearing on the matter, since a false statement represented a misrepresentation whether the insured acted fraudulently or innocently.

Under the previous law, it was the practice in some forms of insurance for the insurer to stipulate on the proposal form that the insured's answers were deemed to be the 'basis of the contract' of insurance. Such wording converted all statements made in the proposal form into warranties, with the result that, in the event of falsity, the insurer could be discharged from liability from the date of the breach. Where a statement had been converted into a warranty, the materiality or otherwise of the falsity was irrelevant to the insurer's liability. Nevertheless, even in the absence of a basis clause, there was a general presumption that the questions on the proposal form relate to material matters. Basis of contract clauses are no longer effective in policies governed by CIDRA and the Insurance Act.

The construction of statements made by the insured

6.52 As most misrepresentations were made in response to specific questions, the issue of whether there had been a misrepresentation often depended on what question the insured had been asked. A question which asked the insured to proffer his opinion or expectation would not be construed as one which demanded a statement of absolute fact; in such a case, there could be a false statement only when the insured put forward an opinion which he did not genuinely hold or an expectation which he did not genuinely believe to be met (Marine Insurance Act 1906, s 20(3)(5)).

A question which was very broad in its ambit would be construed as being subject to a reasonableness limitation; for example, a question asking about the insured's past health record would not require him to disclose every illness, however slight, or every personal injury (*The Connecticut Mutual Life Insurance Co of Hertford v Kate Douglas Moore* (1880-81) LR 6 App Cas 644).

An ambiguous question was not falsely answered if the interpretation put upon it by the insured was reasonable in the circumstances. This principle is a specific application of the general doctrine of *contra proferentem*, whereby ambiguities are to be construed against the party drafting the wording.

A modern illustration is *Roberts v Plaisted* (see **6.35** above), where the insured completed a proposal form for insurance on his motel and, having given answers to specific questions concerning his use of the motel, left blank the general question 'Any other uses?', without stating that there was a discotheque on the premises. The Court of Appeal held that the negative answer to the general question did not amount to misrepresentation, as that question could be construed either as requiring an answer only if the specific questions which had been asked were not applicable to the risk or as requiring disclosure of an activity which was carried on in the premises as a whole and not merely a specific part of the premises.

The insurer's remedies for misrepresentation

6.53 Under the previous law, a policy which had been initiated following a material misrepresentation by the insured was voidable at the option of the insurer. The policy was set aside *ab initio* and was therefore treated as if it had never existed. This meant that the premium paid by the insured was recoverable by him; although the insurer could have been permitted to retain the premium where the insured was guilty of fraudulent misrepresentation or where the policy expressly provided that the premium was to be forfeited to the insurer in the event that the policy was set aside.

The court also had a discretionary power, contained in s 2(2) of the Misrepresentation Act 1967, to refuse to allow a contract to be avoided, on the ground of misrepresentation, and instead to award damages to the innocent party. The purpose of this provision was to mitigate the harshness of avoidance where the party making the misstatement had not been guilty of fraud and otherwise merits generous judicial treatment. The courts have held that it was not appropriate to exercise this discretion in reinsurance cases, and in other cases of commercial insurance, on the basis that the obligation to avoid false statements and the consequences of failing to comply with this obligation are well known to the parties (*Highlands Insurance Co v Continental Insurance Co* [1987] 1 Lloyd's Rep 109, *HIH Casualty and General Insurance v Chase Manhattan Bank* [2001] Lloyd's Rep IR 702 per Rix LJ in the Court of Appeal).

Although there is no possibility of damages at common law for breach of the duty of utmost good faith, the effect of s 2(1) of the Misrepresentation Act 1967 was that, if a false statement was made by one contracting party which induced the other to enter into the contract, then the other was entitled to recover damages, measured on the basis of the tort of deceit, unless the person making the statement could demonstrate that he was not negligent in making the statement. Although the question of whether s 2(1) applied to insurance contracts had not been discussed in detail by the courts, this was assumed without argument by the House of Lords in *HIH Casualty and General Insurance Ltd v Chase Manhattan Bank* (see **6.35** above).

FRAUD

6.54 Questions of fraud may arise in relation to all contracts, including contracts of insurance. Fraud arises in insurance contracts most obviously in the case of fraudulent misrepresentation. However, it should also be remembered that it is not only during the negotiations before the insurer chooses to accept the risk that fraud is an issue. Fraud often arises in the presentation of claims. The Insurance Act has clarified the position going forward in relation to fraudulent claims (see **6.24** above).

The definition of 'fraud'

6.55 In order to establish a fraudulent misrepresentation under the previous law, an insurer had to show that a statement made by the insured:

(a) was false;

(b) was made dishonestly or without belief in the truth of it or being reckless as to whether it is true; and

(c) induced the underwriter into making the insurance contract in question.

William Derry, J C Wakefield, M M Moore, J Pethick, and S J Wilde v Sir Henry William Peek, Baronet (1889) LR 14 App Cas 337 put dishonesty, as defined above, at the heart of the definition of 'fraud', and it remains of central importance today. There is clearly a line which must be carefully trodden between fraud and carelessness, even where that carelessness seems unacceptably extreme. Fraud must be interpreted strictly along the lines set out in *Derry v Peek*. It is, therefore, fraud if an insured makes a statement knowing that he is entirely ignorant as to its truth; but it is not fraud if a false statement is made simply as a result of failing to investigate the relevant facts.

The effect of fraudulent statements

6.56 Under the previous law, an insured's fraudulent statement gave the insurer the option of avoiding the contract. It could, as in the general law of contract, rescind the insurance contract and recover back any monies paid out under that contract.

Where the insurer decided to rescind the policy on the ground of fraud under the previous law, there was authority that it could cancel that policy without offering to return the premiums, as would be the case if the contract were avoided for any other form of misrepresentation or non-disclosure. Under s 84(1) of the Marine Insurance Act 1906, in marine insurance there can be no return of premium where the insurer has avoided the policy because of fraud by the insured. The reason for this rule is public policy – *viz* to discourage fraud. For policies entered into under the Insurance Act, only the fraudulent claim is tainted by the fraud. This means that the insurer will not be liable to pay the claim to which the fraud relates (regardless of honest elements), but cannot recover sums paid under the policy for previous legitimate claims.

Materiality and inducement

6.57 Under the previous law, a fraudulent statement, unlike a non-disclosure or misrepresentation, did not need to be a material fact (ie, satisfy the first 'objective' part of the usual test) in order to be actionable. This law was well established in the nineteenth century and was reaffirmed in *Pan Atlantic* (see **6.30** above). However, it still had to be shown that the fraudulent statement induced the insurer to underwrite the contract if it was to be actionable. Nevertheless, if the fraudulent statement was not material (in the objective sense), it would probably have been difficult in practice to prove that it induced the insurer to write the contract of insurance.

Fraudulent claims

6.58 In relation to fraud in the making of claims by the insured, if the insured made a fraudulent claim (ie, where he knew or did not care that the claim was inflated), the insurer could treat the policy as terminated for breach or refuse to pay the particular claims tainted by fraud. However, if there was innocent or negligent conduct by the insured in connection with the making of a claim, this would not have given rise to any remedy. It was open to insurers to include provisions in the policy for the forfeiture of benefits in such circumstances.

In *Axa General Insurance Ltd v Gottlieb* [2005] Lloyd's Rep IR 369, the court made it clear that the remedy available to insurers in relation to a fraudulent claim was forfeiture of the relevant claim, rather than avoidance of the entire contract. It was held that Axa could not recover the sums paid by it in respect of the separate valid claims prior to the fraud, as pre-existing genuine claims were unaffected by the fraud.

The Supreme Court in *Versloot Dredging v HDI Gerling Industrie* [2-16] UKSC 45 considered a circumstance where the underlying claim was valued, but was supported by 'collateral lies' calculated to speed up the payment of the claim. The court decided that the insurer had a defence to the claim if the insured's dishonesty was aimed at obtaining more than it was entitled to; but where a 'collateral lie' was not calculated to obtain more than it was entitled to, the fraudulent claim rule should not apply.

Agents of the insured

6.59 It is a general principle of contract and insurance contract law that the principal whose agent has made a misrepresentation must take responsibility for the representations of that agent. The basis for this rule is the agency principle of imputation of the knowledge of an agent to its principal and the doctrine of vicarious liability.

Section 18(1) of the Marine Insurance Act 1906 formerly provided that the insured was deemed to know every circumstance which in the ordinary course of business ought to be known by him. This included the knowledge of agents conducting the insured's business, which was imputed to the insured. However, the knowledge of an agent was not imputed to the insured in circumstances where the agent had committed a fraud upon, or other breach of duty towards, the insured; and therefore the dishonesty of an agent was not one of the matters which an insured, in the ordinary course of business, ought to know for the purpose of s 18(1) of the Marine Insurance Act 1906 (*PCW Syndicates v PCW Reinsurers* [1996] 1 Lloyd's Rep 241; *Kingscroft Insurance Co Ltd v The Nissan Fire & Marine Insurance Co* Ltd [1999] Lloyd's Rep IR 371).

Criminal liability for fraudulent statements

6.60 Part 7 of the Financial Services Act 2012 makes it a criminal offence for any person to make a statement, promise or forecast which he knows to be misleading, false or deceptive in a material particular, or which is made recklessly (dishonestly or otherwise), if its effect is to induce the making of an insurance contract.

Under s 2 of the Fraud Act 2006, a person will be guilty of fraud if he dishonestly makes a false representation and intends, by making that representation, either to make a gain for himself or another, or to cause a loss to another or expose another to a risk or loss.

Under s 3 of the Fraud Act 2006, a person will be guilty of fraud if he dishonestly fails to disclose to another person information which he is under a legal duty to disclose and he intends, by that failure to disclose information, either to make a gain for himself or another or to cause a loss to another or expose another to a risk of loss.

MINIMISING LOSS AND ALTERATION IN THE RISK

6.61 There is no common law duty in the law of insurance requiring the insured to minimise the risk of the loss insured (as opposed to the duty to mitigate a loss which has occurred). The courts assume that the insurer has taken account of the possibility that the level of risk may increase throughout the duration of the contract (*Baxendale v Harvey* (1859) 4 H&N 445). In what circumstances, then, may an increase in risk give an insurer the right to refuse to pay claims or avoid the contract? The courts at common law have stipulated that an increase in risk will allow the insurer to be protected only where the nature of the risk itself is changed. In other words, an increase in risk is generally not actionable if not disclosed, as long as the subject matter of the contract and the nature of the contract have not changed.

Clearly, where the insured intended before the making of the contract to increase the risk during the duration of the policy, there may be a non-disclosure which is actionable (eg, a breach of the duty of fair presentation).

Linked to this, if the insured is the perpetrator of a fraud and, as a result of that fraud, there is an increase in risk and/or the increase in risk is not disclosed to the insurer, then equally this will be actionable.

However, there is no clear rule as to when an increase in risk amounts to a change in subject matter. It is a matter of degree. Insurers have generally been dissatisfied with the lack of protection at common law and have therefore instituted specific policy provisions in an attempt to protect themselves. They have done this via a number of standard clauses as follows.

Increase in hazard clauses

6.62 These clauses vary in their wording; but the courts have shown themselves to be extremely wary of clauses which, instead of relating to a specific concern of the insurer, attempt to cover a possible increase in all possible dangers. In dealing with these clauses, the courts do not alter the common law position; see *Exchange Theatre Ltd v Iron Trades Mutual Insurance Co Ltd* [1984] 1 Lloyd's Rep 149, in which a bingo hall was destroyed by fire following the introduction to the premises of petrol and a petrol generator. The condition provided: 'This policy shall be avoided with respect to any item thereof in regard to which there be any alteration after the commencement of this insurance whereby the risk of destruction is increased.'

The court held in this case that there had been an alteration to the contents, but no alteration to the building. Had the building itself been turned into a petrol store, the case would probably have been decided differently (see also *Farnham v Royal Insurance Co Ltd* [1976] 2 Lloyd's Rep 437).

Reasonable care clauses

6.63 A typical clause of this nature will state that: 'although I take the risk of insuring against certain unexpected events, I expect you to take reasonable care of the insured property during the currency of the policy.'

The courts have – unsurprisingly – been reluctant to enforce these clauses if they conflict with the very underlying purpose of the insurance, which is to protect the insured from loss resulting from his own negligence (see *Fraser v B N Furman (Productions) Ltd* [1967] 2 Lloyd's Rep 1). Although the insurer may be able to rely on a clause of this nature where the insured has recognised the risk, but failed to act upon it, it is more difficult where the insured has failed to recognise the risk at all, even though a reasonable person would have done so. In those cases, the court will allow the insurer to rely upon the clause only when the insured can be shown to have acted recklessly. Leaving jewellery in the glove compartment of a car, while taking travellers cheques and money with you and locking the car, has been held not to be reckless (*Sofi v Prudential Assurance Co Ltd* [1993] 2 Lloyd's Rep 559). A householder failing to lock his backdoor or activate his alarm system upon noticing that he was being followed home, on the other hand, was found to be reckless (*Gunns v Par Insurance Brokers* [1997] 1 Lloyd's Rep 173).

It is worth noting that in property insurance, there is a simple option for insurers, which is to include a clause in the policy requiring the insured to maintain his property in a sound condition. This can be measured more objectively.

Fire protection clauses

6.64 Property insurers will often give a discount on the premium if the insured promises to keep fire extinguishing protection at the premises and to keep this in good working order. Usually, the insured is also required to warrant that the maintenance of the fire protection system will be carried out by an approved specialist contractor. In this way, insurers have successfully contracted to reduce the risk throughout the period of the contract.

Duty on the insurer

6.65 It should be noted that the insurer also has a duty to observe utmost good faith in its dealing with policyholders and prospective policyholders (*La Banque Financière de la Cité SA (Formerly Banque Keyser Ullmann en Suisse SA) v Skandia Insurance Co Ltd Westgate Insurance Co Ltd and Others (Formerly Hodge General & Merchantile Insurance Co Ltd)* [1990] 2 All ER 947).

It was recognised by the Court of Appeal in *Drake Insurance plc v Provident Insurance plc* [2004] 1 Lloyd's Rep 268 that if an insurer avoids a contract in bad faith, that avoidance may be nullified.

Chapter 7

Policyholder protection

INTRODUCTION

7.01 Provisions relating to the establishment of the Financial Services Compensation Scheme (FSCS) are to be found in ss 212–224 of the Financial Services and Markets Act 2000 (FSMA 2000). The effect of the legislation contained in the FSMA 2000 and the associated rules of the Prudential Regulation Authority (PRA) and Financial Conduct Authority (FCA) is to enable those policyholders who qualify for protection to recover 90 per cent of their claim (or 100 per cent in the case of compulsory insurances, certain other specified general insurance covers and long-term insurance). The FSCS then claims against the insurer in respect of the amount paid to the claimant and will take an assignment of the policyholder's claim against the insurer for this purpose (which could be valuable, as policyholders have priority over unsecured creditors on the winding up of an insurer).

The FSCS came into being on 1 December 2001. This chapter does not deal with the rules applicable to contracts of insurance issued prior to 1 December 2001, or with the FSCS's responsibility to compensate depositors or the holders of certain investment products which are not applicable to insurance companies. As a result of Brexit, the FSCS also now distinguishes between policies issued before and after 31 December 2020 (the end of the Brexit transitional period). This broadly retains cover for policies that were covered prior to that date, potentially for a minimum of 15 years.

When originally introduced, the scheme rules were set out in the FCA's Compensation Sourcebook (COMP). The PRA made changes to the FSCS as it applies to insurers (and Lloyd's policies) with effect from 3 July 2015. As a result of the Policyholder Protection Part of the PRA Rules, the compensation scheme available in respect of Solvency II insurers is now referred to in the PRA Rules as the 'policyholder compensation scheme'. This changed the limits applicable to policies covered by the scheme to 100 per cent of long-term insurance liabilities and compulsory insurance (and other specified general insurance obligations such as professional indemnity insurance). It also covers 90 per cent of other relevant general insurance obligations. The policyholder compensation scheme is still administered by FSCS Limited as the manager of the scheme and certain references to FSCS in this chapter are therefore to FSCS Limited.

The compensation available in relation to insurance intermediaries is provided under the FCA's COMP rules and is described separately in this chapter.

THE COMPENSATION SCHEME

Overview

7.02 Where an insurer is in 'financial difficulties' or in 'default', the FSCS may take appropriate action, including trying to transfer liabilities to another insurer. The FSCS will determine whether an insurer is in default based on whether it is unable or unlikely to be able to satisfy a protected claim. This can include situations where the insurer is in default because, in the opinion of FSCS Limited or the PRA, it is unable to satisfy a protected claim or is likely to be unable to pay its debts (eg, where there is no formal insolvency). A similar provision applies (eg, where a claim has transferred to a new insurer under a Part VII transfer) in relation to successors being in default. For long-term insurers, the FSCS must – unless it decides that it is not reasonably practicable or appropriate to do so – seek to transfer the policies to another insurer.

The scheme may pay compensation to an 'eligible claimant' in respect of claims under a 'protected contract of insurance'. This will not include contracts of reinsurance or insurance covering aircraft, ships, goods in transit, aircraft liability, liability of ships or credit. An 'eligible claimant' is a person entitled to bring a claim under r 7 of the Policyholder Protection Part of the PRA Rules. For compulsory insurance (see **7.08**), all policyholders will be covered. In addition, all long-term policyholders will be protected (even if they are large companies) unless they are connected with the insurance company (eg, directors) or brought about the relevant failure by the insurer. For other relevant general insurance policyholders, r 7 sets out the criteria to be applied and will generally cover consumers and unregulated small businesses.

In relation to Lloyd's policies, the FSCS must act, so far as is reasonably practicable, to ensure that equivalent compensation is provided to eligible claimants under those policies. This is subject to the requirements that the Central Fund must be unlikely to be able to meet the relevant claims, and that claims under the scheme against members which arise from the same loss under the same Lloyd's policy must be treated as a single claim. If the scheme pays out in relation to Lloyd's policies, the FSCS is entitled to exercise any subrogation or assignment of rights in priority to any interest that the Society of Lloyd's may have.

Qualifying conditions

7.03 The qualifying conditions for payment of compensation under the scheme are set in in r 3 and are as follows:

(a) An eligible claimant has made an application for compensation (or the FSCS has treated him as if he had done so);

(b) The claim is in respect of a protected claim against a relevant person (or, where applicable, a successor) which is in default;

(c) Where the FSCS:

(i) so requires, the claimant has assigned the whole or any part of his rights under the protected contract of insurance against the relevant person (or where applicable, a successor) or against any third party to the FSCS, on such terms as the FSCS thinks fit; and/or

(ii) so determines, the claimant has immediately and automatically subrogated all or any part (as determined by the FSCS) of its rights and claims against the relevant person (or where relevant, a successor) under the protected contract of insurance or against any third party to the FSCS, on such conditions as the FSCS thinks fit; and

(d) It:

(i) is not reasonably practicable or appropriate to make, or continue to make, arrangements to secure continuity of insurance in relation to long-term policies; and/or

(ii) would not be appropriate to take, or continue to take, measures to safeguard policyholders of a relevant person in financial difficulties.

Eligible claimant

7.04 The definition of 'eligible claimant' is a claimant who is not listed in r 7.2 – unless an exception in r 8 applies. The list of those who are not covered includes FSMA 2000 authorised persons other than specified exceptions (eg, sole traders, trustees of personal pension schemes and small businesses where the claim does not arise out of an activity for which they have permission). Bodies corporate in the same group as the insurer (or their successors) are also excluded, as are claims arising under the Third Parties (Rights against Insurers) Act 1930 or 2010.

Rule 8 effectively widens those able to claim in relation to compulsory insurance and life insurance. For compulsory insurance, all of the restrictions on eligible claimants are removed. For life insurance, claimants should be covered unless they are bodies corporate in the same group as the insurer (subject to exceptions – for example, for certain pension scheme trustees); or the FSCS considers that they have caused or contributed to the insurer's default; or they have been convicted of money laundering offences in connection with the insured transaction. The restriction on those claiming under the Third Party Rights against Insurers Acts (eg, someone claiming against the insurer in default because the insured is insolvent) are that claimants will be eligible where:

(a) the person insured would have been an eligible claimant when the rights under the Act were triggered;

(b) the claim has been agreed by the insurer or a court judgment or arbitral award had been obtained before the insurer was determined to be in default; or

(c) the liability was a liability under a contract of employer's liability insurance which would have been a liability subject to compulsory insurance had the contract been entered into after 1 January 1972.

Specific rules are also made in relation to mesothelioma claims. For relevant general insurance contracts, eligible claimants include consumers and unregulated small businesses.

The FSCS may also treat a person who is a director or responsible for the insurer's default as eligible to claim compensation where this would enable an effective transfer of liabilities to another insurer or where it considers it would be beneficial to the generality of eligible claimants to do so.

Protected contract of insurance

7.05 The claim must be in respect of a 'protected contract of insurance', which will exclude claims under reinsurance contracts or insurance covering aircraft, ships, goods in transit, aircraft liability, liability of ships or credit. The FSCS may treat a person as insured under a contract which is not evidenced by a policy if it is satisfied that he would have been covered had the policy been issued.

There are three potential categories of protected insurance contract: those issued before 1 December 2001; those issued pre Brexit – that is, before the end of the Brexit transitional period (ie, 11.00pm on 31 December 2020); and those issued post Brexit – that is, after the end of the Brexit transitional period. This chapter deals only with the latter two categories. The rules for Brexit implementation policies seek to preserve cover for policies issued by European Economic Area (EEA) insurers under the EU passporting regime. The rules for post-Brexit policies broadly remove cover for EEA policyholders and recognise the ongoing arrangements between the UK and Gibraltar which allow Gibraltar policyholders of UK insurers to be covered.

For a policy to be a protected contract of insurance, the establishment of the *relevant person* from which the policy is issued and the location of the risk or commitment (initially or, where relevant, on renewal) must meet the following criteria.

Pre Brexit

Establishment of insurer	Location of risk/commitment
UK (UK insurer or UK branch of EEA insurer)	UK, Gibraltar, EEA, CI or IoM
EEA establishment of a UK insurer	UK, Gibraltar, EEA
EEA establishment of EEA insurer	UK
CI or IoM	UK, CI or IoM
Gibraltar	UK

Post Brexit

Establishment	Location of risk/commitment
(A) UK	UK, Gibraltar, CI or IoM
(B) An EEA State TPR, SRO or CRO FOS insurer;	UK
(C) CI or IoM	UK, CI or IoM
(D) Gibraltar – UK firm	UK or Gibraltar
(E) Gibraltar – non UK firm	UK

Note: if it is a contract of insurance entered into by a member of Lloyd's, it must have been entered into on or after 1 January 2004.

Key

CI = Channel Islands IoM= Isle of Man	
TPR = Temporary Permissions Regime	CRO = Contractual run-off
SRO = Supervised run-off	FOS = Freedom of services basis

The situation of a risk or commitment is determined as follows:

(a) For a contract of insurance relating to a building or a building and its contents (insofar as the contents are covered by the same contract), the risk or commitment is situated where the building is situated.

(b) For a contract of insurance relating to vehicles of any type, the risk or commitment is situated where the vehicle is registered.

(c) For a contract of insurance lasting four months or less covering travel or holiday risks (whatever the class concerned), the risk or commitment is situated where the policyholder took out the contract.

(d) In cases not covered by any of the above, where the policyholder is an individual (including an individual trustee), the risk or commitment is situated where he had his habitual residence at the date when the contract commenced; and where the policyholder is not an individual, the risk or commitment is situated where the establishment to which the risk or commitment relates was situated at the date when the contract commenced.

Where there is more than one policyholder, only one policyholder needs to satisfy any requirement of habitual residence.

Relevant person

7.06 A claim must be made in relation to the acts or omissions of a relevant person. A 'relevant person' is someone that, at the time of the act or omission giving rise to the protected claim against it takes place, is a participant firm. A 'participant firm' is an FSMA 2000 authorised person which is an insurer, a Lloyd's member (except in rs 21, 22.6–22.8 and Annex 2 in respect of a Lloyd's member) or a CRO insurer (which – unlike firms in the TPR or SRO – would not be a FSMA 2000 authorised person (see **42.11**)).

Insurer (or successor) in default

7.07 A relevant person (or a successor) is in default if the FSCS has determined it to be in default under rs 10.3 and/or 10.4. A 'successor' is a person that has assumed responsibility for liabilities arising from acts or omissions of a relevant person (eg, under a Part VII scheme (see **Chapter 44**). This means that either:

(a) the FSCS has determined (based on its own view or that of the PRA) that the relevant person is unable (or likely to be unable) to satisfy protected claims made against it; or

(b) the FSCS has determined that a protected claim exists and the relevant person is the subject of one or more of the following proceedings in the UK (or of equivalent or similar proceedings in another jurisdiction):

   (i) the passing of a resolution for a creditors' voluntary winding up;

   (ii) a determination by the relevant person's regulator or competent authority that the relevant person appears unable to meet claims against it and has no early prospect of being able to do so;

   (iii) the appointment of a liquidator or administrator, or a provisional liquidator or interim manager;

   (iv) the making of an order by a court of competent jurisdiction for the winding up of a company, the dissolution of a partnership, the administration of a company or partnership, or the bankruptcy of an individual; or

   (v) the approval of a company voluntary arrangement, a partnership voluntary arrangement or an individual voluntary arrangement.

The FSCS may not declare a member of Lloyd's to be in default unless it is satisfied that the amounts which the Society of Lloyd's may provide from the Central Fund are or are likely to be insufficient to meet the amount of cover that would be provided under the scheme.

Compulsory insurances

7.08 For the purposes of the scheme, the following are treated as compulsory general insurance, to the extent that the policy covers a liability required under any of these enactments to be covered by insurance:

(a) s 1(4A)(d) of the Riding Establishments Act 1964;

(b) s 1 of the Employers' Liability (Compulsory Insurance) Act 1969;

(c) Part VI of the Road Traffic Act 1988 (third-party liability); and

(d) a contract of insurance effected for the purposes of s 19 of the Nuclear Installations Act 1965.

This compensation is payable in relation to all policies regardless of the identity of the policyholder (ie, large businesses are covered too).

Other categories of insurance (eg, professional indemnity insurance; policies covering liability for death or incapacity of the policyholder due to injury, sickness or infirmity; and building guarantee insurance) also benefit from 100 per cent coverage of claims (see **7.12**).

AMOUNTS PAYABLE UNDER THE SCHEME

Claims

7.09 A 'claim' is a valid claim made in respect of a civil liability owed by the relevant person or which a successor has assumed and must be calculated by the FSCS as soon as possible after the qualifying conditions (see **7.03**) have been met. The scheme specifies how the amount of a claim is to be valued, which is broadly on the basis of the amount due in respect of claims made and premium for the unexpired period of the contract for general insurance, and in accordance with the Insurers (Winding Up) Rules 2001 (SI 2001/3635) for long-term contracts – in both cases, in line with the provisions of the policy.

To clarify the position in relation to certain liabilities of an insurer, r 9.8 provides that the FSCS must treat liabilities of a relevant person (or, where applicable, a successor) which is in default, in respect of the following items, as giving rise to *claims* under a protected contract of insurance:

(a) (if the contract is not a reinsurance contract and has not commenced) premiums paid to a relevant person;

(b) proceeds of a contract of long-term insurance that is not a reinsurance contract and that has matured or been surrendered which have not yet been passed to the claimant;

(c) the unexpired portion of any premium in relation to relevant general insurance contracts which are not reinsurance contracts; and

(d) claims by persons entitled to the benefit of a judgment under s 151 of the Road Traffic Act 1988 or art 98 of the Road Traffic (Northern Ireland) Order 1981.

Subject to applicable limits (eg, under r 17), r 19 provides that the amount of compensation payable to the claimant in respect of a protected claim, and therefore a claim for the purposes of the rules, is the amount of the overall net claim against the relevant person (or, where applicable, the successor) at the quantification date. In relation to claims under a policy, the quantification date is a date determined and specified by the FSCS; whereas for amounts due in respect of unexpired premiums (treated as claims in accordance with r 9.8(3)), it is the date on which the policy was terminated or cancelled. Net claims are the amount due to the claimant net of applicable set-off. In calculating the claims amount, the FSCS may rely, to the extent that it is relevant, on any determination by a court of competent jurisdiction, the relevant insolvency practitioner or, as applicable, the certification of any net sum due which is made in default proceedings of any exchange or clearing house. Limitations in the constitution of the company (eg, in aggregate to the amount of its assets) will also be reflected. For Lloyd's policies, the amount expected to be received from the Central Fund should be taken into account and payments may include payment made from the Central Fund.

In relation to a long-term contract, unless the FSCS is making arrangements to secure continuity of insurance cover, it must calculate the liability of the relevant person (or, where applicable, its successor) to the claimant in accordance with the terms of the contract as it would be valued in a liquidation of the relevant person (or, where applicable, the successor), or (in the absence of such relevant terms in the contract) in accordance with such reasonable valuation techniques as the FSCS considers appropriate. Subject to the FSCS not exercising its right to reduce or disregard a benefit under r 20.7, where benefits have or would have fallen due, they should be paid as soon as reasonably practicable after the due date. Where the long-term contract is a with-profits contract or otherwise includes bonuses, the amount of the bonus should not be included in the amount of the claimant's claim, except to the extent that a value has been attributed to it by a court in accordance with the Insurers (Winding Up) Rules 2001 (or any equivalent rules or legislative provision in force from time to time), or the FSCS considers that a court would be likely to attribute a value to the bonus if it were to apply the method set out in those rules.

Excessive benefits and Rule 20.7

7.10 The FSCS has power under r 20.7, in connection with either securing continuity of cover or calculating the liability owed to an eligible claimant under a long-term contract, to reduce or disregard benefits if it considers that the benefits provided are or may be excessive. For this purpose, a benefit is 'excessive' only if, at the time the relevant person decided to confer or to offer to confer that benefit, no reasonable and prudent insurer in the position of the relevant person would have so decided given the premiums payable and other contractual terms. Before it does so, the FSCS must refer the contract to an actuary who is independent of the eligible claimant and of the relevant person (or, where applicable, the successor).

If, following the actuary's written recommendation, the FSCS is satisfied that any of the benefits provided for under the contract are or may be excessive, it may treat the liability of the relevant person (or, where applicable, the successor) under the contract as reduced or (as the case may be) disregarded for the purpose of any payment made after the date of that decision. The FSCS may also rely on the value attributed to the contract by the actuary when calculating the compensation payable to the claimant or when securing continuity of cover.

Other factors affecting claims value

7.11 If an application for compensation contains any material inaccuracy or omission, the FSCS may reject the application unless this is considered by the FSCS to be wholly unintentional. The FSCS must reject an application for compensation if:

(a) the FSCS considers that a civil claim in respect of the liability would have been defeated by a defence of limitation at the earlier of:

   (i) the date on which the relevant person (or, where applicable, the successor) is determined to be in default; or

(ii) the date on which the claimant first indicates in writing that he may have a claim against the relevant person (or where applicable, the successor); or

(b) the liability of the relevant person (or, where applicable, the successor) to the claimant has been extinguished by the operation of law.

The FSCS has some discretion in relation to how payments of compensation are to be paid (eg, it can make an initial payment followed by a final payment). If compensation is offered, the claimant may be required to transfer his rights to claim against other parties to FSCS Limited. The reasoning behind this is to maximise recoveries by FSCS Limited and prevent the affected consumer from taking action against the party(ies) in default. The value of such rights may be reflected in the compensation offered. Offers may be withdrawn if disputed or not accepted within 90 days. Offers may be reissued or varied. Payments are to be made directly to the claimant or on his instructions. Interest may also be payable on compensation payments at the discretion of the FSCS.

Limit on compulsory insurance policies – Rule 17.2

7.12 The percentage of the claim amount that can be recovered in respect of compulsory insurance policies is 100 per cent without upper limit. The same applies in relation to:

(a) a liability subject to professional indemnity insurance;

(b) a liability in respect of and arising from the death or incapacity of the policyholder due to injury, sickness or infirmity; or

(c) a liability subject to building guarantee insurance.

Limit on other relevant general insurance policies

7.13 The percentage of the claim amount that can be recovered in respect of protected general insurance policies, other than those specified in **7.12**, is 90 per cent.

Limit on long-term policies

7.14 If the FSCS secures continuity of insurance for eligible claimants, they will not necessarily receive any compensation, but will continue to be insured (though possibly with lower benefits than before).

However, where the FSCS does pay compensation, the percentage of the claim amount that can be recovered in respect of a protected long-term insurance contract is 100 per cent. This is subject to the power in r 20.7 for the FSCS to reduce or disregard benefits in determining the amount of the insurer's liability.

Securing continuity of long-term cover

7.15 The FSCS must make arrangements to secure continuity of insurance for an eligible claimant under a protected contract of insurance which is a contract of long-term insurance with a relevant person if:

(a) the relevant person is the subject of any of the proceedings listed in r 10.4;

(b) it is reasonably practicable to do so;

(c) in the opinion of the FSCS at the time it proposes to make the arrangements, it would be beneficial to the generality of eligible claimants covered by the proposed arrangements and, in situations where the cost of securing continuity of insurance might exceed the cost of paying compensation, any additional cost is likely to be justified by the benefits; and

(d) where the relevant person is a member of Lloyd's, the FSCS is satisfied that the amounts which the Society of Lloyd's is able to provide from the Central Fund are or are likely to be insufficient to ensure that claims against the member will provide the level of cover applicable under the scheme.

The proceedings listed in r 10.4 are one or more of the following proceedings in the UK (or of equivalent or similar proceedings in another jurisdiction):

(a) the passing of a resolution for a creditors' voluntary winding up;

(b) a determination by the relevant person's regulator or competent authority that the relevant person appears unable to meet claims against it and has no early prospect of being able to do so;

(c) the appointment of a liquidator or administrator, or a provisional liquidator or interim manager;

(d) the making of an order by a court of competent jurisdiction for the winding up of a company, the dissolution of a partnership, the administration of a company or partnership, or the bankruptcy of an individual; or

(e) the approval of a company voluntary arrangement, a partnership voluntary arrangement or an individual voluntary arrangement.

In order to secure continuity of insurance, the FSCS may take such measures as it considers appropriate to facilitate either the transfer of the policies or the issue by another firm to eligible claimants of policies in substitution for their existing policies.

If the FSCS is seeking to secure continuity of insurance, and even if it would cost more than providing compensation, the FSCS must ensure that 100 per cent of any existing benefit (due or which would have fallen due) under a contract of long-term insurance is paid to the eligible claimant. This should be paid by the FSCS or the relevant insolvency practitioner as soon as reasonably practicable after the time when the benefit in question fell due or would have fallen due under the contract. For this purpose, 'benefit' does not include any bonus provided for under the contract, unless it was declared and the policyholder was contractually entitled to it before the relevant person became the subject of the relevant insolvency proceedings. Where the FSCS has exercised the power under r 20.7 (see **7.10**), it is also subject to any reduction which the FSCS has applied (including where it has decided to disregard a benefit). Subject to any power of reduction exercised by the FSCS, the arrangements for continuity of cover should provide for 100 per cent of future benefits.

In making arrangements to secure continuity of insurance, the FSCS must use its reasonable endeavours to seek the most cost-effective arrangements available; but unless it has applied a reduction to benefits, it should not take into account that the benefits *may* be excessive in deciding whether to seek to provide continuity of cover for long-term policies.

INSURERS IN FINANCIAL DIFFICULTIES

7.16 Subject to the limits on the level of cover available under the scheme, the FSCS may take such measures as it considers appropriate for the purpose of safeguarding the rights of eligible claimants under protected contracts of insurance. For long-term contracts, this will apply where the FSCS is not securing continuity of cover. The right will apply where the relevant person is in financial difficulties – namely, where:

(a) a liquidator, administrator, provisional liquidator, administrative receiver or interim manager is appointed to the relevant person; or a receiver is appointed by the court to manage the relevant person's affairs;

(b) there is a finding by a court of competent jurisdiction that the relevant person is unable to pay its debts;

(c) a resolution is passed for winding up of the relevant person, unless a declaration of solvency has been made in accordance with s 89 of the Insolvency Act 1986;

(d) the PRA determines that the relevant person is likely to be unable to satisfy protected claims against it;

(e) approval is given to any company voluntary arrangement made by the relevant person;

(f) the relevant person makes a composition or arrangement with any one or more of its creditors providing for the reduction of, or deferral of payment of, the liabilities or benefits provided for under any of the relevant person's policies;

(g) the relevant person is dissolved or struck off the Register of Companies;

(h) a receiver is appointed over particular property of the relevant person;

(i) any of (a) to (h) or anything equivalent occurs in respect of the relevant person in a jurisdiction outside England and Wales; or

(j) in the case of a relevant person which is a member of Lloyd's, the FSCS is satisfied that any of (a) to (i) applies to the member, and the amounts which the Society of Lloyd's is able to provide from the Central Fund are or are likely to be insufficient to cover the full amount of the amount that would be available under the scheme.

The FSCS will take such steps where it determines that it would be beneficial to the generality of eligible claimants covered by the proposed measures. In situations where the cost of taking those measures might exceed the cost of paying compensation, the FSCS needs to consider that it is likely to be justified by the benefits. Under r 5.1(2), measures may be taken on such terms (including terms reducing or deferring payment of any liabilities or benefits provided under any protected contracts of insurance) as the FSCS considers appropriate. They could include arranging a transfer to (or the issuing of new policy by) another insurer or providing support to the existing insurer. The PRA may assist the FSCS in coming to a view on appropriate measures or impose constraints on the FSCS's powers. It may also require the FSCS to provide it with information about any measures which it is proposing to take.

FUNDING OF THE SCHEME'S OBLIGATIONS

7.17 The FSCS imposes levies on authorised persons in order to meet its expenses. These expenses include, in particular, expenses incurred, or expected to be incurred, in paying compensation, securing continuity of insurance or providing assistance for insurers in financial difficulties.

The FSCS may impose two types of levy on insurance companies: a management expenses levy and a compensation costs levy. The FSCS has discretion as to the timing of the levies imposed. In calculating a compensation costs levy, the FSCS may include anticipated compensation costs for defaults expected to be determined in the 12-month period following the date of the levy.

The amount of the levy is calculated by reference to the relevant class of insurance business and normally, insurers are liable for costs (including compensation amounts) incurred in relation to such classes. The calculation is based on the previous year's business covered by the scheme (ie, that could give rise to protected claims), and contributions are split pro rata among insurers with such potential liabilities in that class. The details are set out in r 21 and Annexes 1 and 2 of the Policyholder Protection Part. A tariff base for the levy is specified for the relevant classes based on a net premium income and eligible liabilities (split 75/25).

INSOLVENT INSURANCE INTERMEDIARIES

7.18 Insurance intermediaries became subject to the scheme with effect from 14 January 2005, via the FCA's COMP. This was in relation to protected non-life investment insurance mediation activities, which became FSMA 2000 regulated activities from that date. For the COMP rules to apply, the contract must be a general insurance contract, a pure protection life contract (other than a long-term care contract) or a reinsurance contract. In addition, the insurance distribution activities must have been conducted from an establishment of the insurance intermediary in the UK. However, the FSCS will not cover any claims made against an intermediary where the claimant was introduced to the intermediary via another intermediary which does not fall within the eligibility criteria above. Also, the FSCS will not cover any claims made in respect of intermediaries which are not 'relevant persons' – for example, a retailer that sells extended warranties – although it should cover a situation where a retailer has introduced a client to an authorised intermediary.

The compensation payable where an intermediary (or its successor) is at fault broadly covers the same category of claimant as the policyholder protection part of the FSCS (eg, eligible claimants in respect of protected contracts of insurance and relevant persons). However, following the introduction by the PRA of the new rules for insurers in 2015, the FCA also amended the compensation payable under the FSCS in relation to failures by intermediaries. The amount of compensation available depends upon the nature of the failure (eg, to reflect that an insured may have missed out on a policy being in place because of a relevant intermediary failure). The maximum level of compensation will be 100 per cent, as for insurer defaults – where, for example, the activities of the intermediary resulted in a compulsory insurance or pure protection contract not going on risk. In other cases, the level of compensation available will be a maximum of 90 per cent of the claim against the intermediary. Amounts paid to the intermediary as agent of the insurer or the client should also be covered up to 100 per cent.

The COMP rules on protected claims are set out in COMP 5. COMP 5.7 deals with non-investment insurance distribution of relevant general insurance and pure protection contracts (other than long-term care insurance contracts). COMP 10.2.3 sets out the limits of liability for intermediaries as follows.

Protected non-investment insurance distribution	(1) Where the claim is in respect of a liability subject to compulsory insurance: 100% of claim	**Unlimited**
	(2) Where the claim is in respect of: (a) a relevant omission; and (b) a professional indemnity insurance contract, or would be in respect of a professional indemnity insurance contract if the insurance contract had been effected: 100% of claim	**Unlimited**
	(3) Where the claim is: (a) in respect of a relevant omission; (b) in respect of a relevant general insurance contract or would be in respect of a relevant general insurance contract if the insurance contract had been effected; and (c) arises from the death or incapacity of the policyholder owing to injury, sickness or infirmity: 100% of claim	**Unlimited**
	(4) Where the claim is in respect of: (a) a relevant omission; and (b) a pure protection contract or would be in respect of a pure protection contract if the insurance contract had been effected: 100% of claim	**Unlimited**
	(5) In all other cases: 90% of claim	**Unlimited**

Note: A 'relevant omission' for this purpose is where the insurance intermediary has failed to:

(a) pay monies to an insurer;

(b) pay monies that it has received from an insurer; or

(c) take steps to cause a contract of insurance to be effected by an insurer.

Chapter 8

Global insurance programmes

- Introduction
- Obstacles to group insurance
- Retaining risk
- Fronting insurers
- Other issues with global programmes

INTRODUCTION

8.01 In most industry sectors, multinational groups may seek insurance cover on a group basis. Central purchasing of such cover also has the advantage of enabling the buyer to use its size to keep down premium rates. There are, however, a number of potential issues for insurers in seeking to provide cover to members of a group located in different countries. Such arrangements may therefore involve a number of different insurers and often what looks like a single insurance policy can be made up of a number of different contracts.

OBSTACLES TO GROUP INSURANCE

8.02 There exist at least three major obstacles to insurers covering risk of a multinational group:

(a) Regulation: There are two main issues with regulation. The first is the need for a local insurance licence and the second is conduct of business and other regulatory requirements in the country in which an insured risk is located. As regards the first point, while there may be more scope for reinsurers to cover risk located in countries in which they are not established/authorised (eg, on a non-admitted basis), direct insurers will often need to be authorised in order to cover risk located in other countries. This can mean that what looks like one policy can in fact be a series of different policies from insurers authorised in the relevant jurisdictions. As regards the second point, conduct of business rules can vary significantly from country to country and can be triggered by the use of local parties (insurers or brokers). Regulation can therefore provide a formidable barrier (for both insurers and brokers), and may lead to a local 'fronting' insurer being used to write a risk which is then reinsured to the insurer dealing with the client.

(b) Lack of global reach of insurance companies: In addition to regulatory issues, there can be capacity and expertise issues for insurers that do not normally operate in certain markets.

(c) Conflicts of law: Even if it is possible to issue a single policy covering risk across many jurisdictions, there will be potential issues in relation to the law to govern the contract, jurisdiction clauses, enforcement of judgments in other countries, local mandatory requirements (eg, insurable interest/indemnity principle) and the use/interpretation of standard wordings. Tax may also need to be apportioned across different jurisdictions. Such issues are likely to increase the greater the number of different parties involved in the arrangements. They have also, from a UK perspective, increased as a result of Brexit, as UK insurers are now required to be locally authorised to cover European Economic Area (EEA) risks. Further, choice of law, jurisdiction and enforcement of judgment issues may no longer benefit from the harmonisation applicable in EEA countries.

RETAINING RISK

8.03 Another issue with this type of insurance is that, for commercial reasons, the multinational may wish to retain part of the risk. This can be done by setting up a wholly owned subsidiary (commonly described as a 'captive insurer') which acts as an insurer or reinsurer of the group risk. The captive will then normally insure or, if it needs to do so for regulatory reasons (eg, because it is not authorised in the relevant jurisdiction), reinsure the risk that the group wishes to retain. To maximise tax advantages, captives are frequently located offshore.

The use of a captive insurer has the added advantage of enabling the group to have direct access to the reinsurance market. A disadvantage is that the captive must comply with regulations which exist in each territory. Depending on the jurisdiction in which it is based, a captive will be required to hold reserves and capital in a similar way to other insurers. However, intragroup insurance may benefit from some relaxation of regulatory requirements (eg, in relation to insurance distribution).

FRONTING INSURERS

8.04 As stated above, where an insurer is not permitted to insure a local risk, it may be able to use a locally authorised insurer to provide the cover and reinsure the risk. Different countries have different rules on how such reinsurance can work (eg, what proportion can be reinsured). Where a captive insurer has been set up by the client, it may also need to make use of fronting insurers in jurisdictions in which the captive is not authorised.

OTHER ISSUES WITH GLOBAL PROGRAMMES

Difference in conditions cover

8.05 Where fronting companies are involved, local regulatory locations may make it difficult to provide coverage which is consistent with the rest of the programme. Therefore, the insurance policy issued at a local level may only provide the basic cover needed to comply with the local regulations. The insurers or reinsurers on the main programme may issue what is commonly known as a master policy, providing 'difference in conditions' cover, which will be issued to the multinational's head office. Care will be needed with such cover so as not to breach the requirement to be authorised in the fronting insurer's jurisdiction. Sometimes additional cover can be provided in the form of insurance of a parent company's financial interest in a local subsidiary. However, this may lead to issues in establishing that the appropriate loss has been suffered. Some jurisdictions also do not permit this type of indirect insurance arrangement.

Jurisdiction and choice of law

8.06 It is not uncommon to see different parts of the programme incorporating different choice of law and jurisdiction clauses. More frequently, however, it is common to find them omitted altogether, thus relying upon local conflict of law rules. This can create inconsistency within the programme, in respect of both underlying liabilities and contractual enforcement. One solution may be to incorporate a comprehensive arbitration clause throughout the programme, but there may still be issues in applying local law and regulation.

Group and master policies

8.07 Often global insurance programmes will be covered under a group policy or a composite series of policies on the same terms (eg, between each insured and each insurer). However, there can be issues with group policies and with the way in which they are structured. There is no single structure for group policies and different jurisdictions treat group policies differently, with some completely looking through them. In the UK, issues such as insurable interest, the indemnity principle and agency law can affect the way the contract is structured. The regulatory position in the UK in relation to group policies has tightened significantly in recent years and group policies cannot be used to avoid regulatory issues (or, in a Lloyd's context, underwriting controls on cover holders).

Care should also be used with relevant terminology. For example, the term 'master policy' has a number of different meanings in different insurance markets. It can be a contract governing a relationship with the insured(s) under which cover is provided to the policyholder, who holds it for the benefit of other insureds (eg, a group policy); or it can be an overarching contract which incorporates the same terms into a series of contracts; or it can simply be a set of agreed standard terms (eg, a policy evidencing the agreed terms).

Contractual inconsistency

8.08 Where a global programme has terms which apply to the programme as a whole, care is needed to ensure that they are reflected in local policies issued. It is also necessary to consider the interaction between any aggregate level limits and limits under a local policy and any provisions for cross-default or set-off. On occasion, inconsistencies also arise in the coverage provided by the various vertical layers of risk transfer in relation to a global programme. A programme which is not carefully drafted may result, for example, in a claim being paid by a captive or fronting insurer but excluded by a reinsurer to which risk is ceded.

Controlling claims

8.09 One of the central difficulties in global programmes is that the real risk taker – for example, reinsurers above the captive – may be several contractual steps away from the person which will be paying the claims. Care is therefore required in relation to the terms on which claims are to be paid/claims handling is authorised by the reinsurer.

Risk transfer

8.10 It is unusual for captives to be rated for solvency in the same way as other insurers. Thus, an insurer or reinsurer dealing with a captive may be taking a risk as to the ongoing solvency of the captive. If the parties utilise credit mitigation or parental guarantees from the parent company of the captive, considerable care must be taken in drafting the arrangements to ensure that each contracting party retains an insurable interest (ie, is subject to the risk of the underlying loss); that the separate contracts of insurance and reinsurance are not regarded as sham transactions; and that any guarantee arrangements will not simply be overturned by the laws governing insolvency in the relevant jurisdictions.

Part 2

The Parties

Chapter 9

Brokers

- Brokers and agency law
- The regulation of brokers
- The rights of brokers
- The duties of brokers
- The liabilities of brokers

BROKERS AND AGENCY LAW

The broker as the insured's agent

9.01 In the UK, a 'broker' is an independent insurance intermediary (or in regulatory terms, an insurance distributor), appointed by the insured to perform various duties for him relating to the setting up and operation of insurance contracts, (eg, assisting the insured in the event of a claim). The broker is, therefore, the agent of the insured and not the agent of the insurer. The broker should not act for the insurer – or rather, it should not act in any manner inconsistent with its duties to the insured, without the express consent of the insured. The most important consequences of the broker being regarded as the insured's agent are that:

(a) any information which is communicated to the broker by the insured is generally not deemed to have been received by the insurer – this may be relevant in relation to pre-contractual disclosures by the insured and the giving by the insured of notice of loss; and

(b) payment of the premium by the insured to his broker is not generally treated as payment to the insurer and payment of losses by the insurer to the broker is treated as receipt by the insured – the insured, therefore, bears the risk of fraud or insolvency on the part of his broker. This risk is mitigated by regulatory requirements (see **9.21** below).

Practical difficulties

9.02 The simple legal concept that the broker is the insured's agent is blurred in practice, as brokers do not operate quite in this way. A number of areas of difficulty may be found:

(a) Brokers receive their commission not from the insured, but from the insurer (see **9.16**).

(b) Under s 19 of the Marine Insurance Act 1906, where an insurance is effected for the insured by a broker, the broker must disclose to the insurer every material circumstance which is known to himself and to the insured. In *HIH Casualty and General Insurance Ltd v Chase Manhattan Bank* [2003] UKHL 6, the House of Lords held that the effect of s 19 is to impose a duty of utmost good faith on the broker independent of that imposed on the insured by s 18 of the Marine Insurance Act 1906.

(c) In the London market, there is a long tradition – which has been criticised by the courts – of brokers acting for both the insured and the underwriters in the event of a loss. The nature of the London market means that there is necessarily a close relationship between brokers and underwriters; yet the position in law is that the broker is the agent for the person who has instructed him (and whom the broker may have never previously met), rather than the agent of underwriters with which the broker is in daily contact.

(d) A broker may be given a binding authority by an insurer, which authorises the broker to accept risks on behalf of the insurer. The fact that the broker is a coverholder acting on behalf of an insurer may not always be obvious to an insured who seeks independent advice on insurance.

(e) The large international broking firms play an active role in promoting various forms of new insurance where a market gap is perceived. This may involve a broker preparing wordings for use by insurers for insurances which are obtained by the broker for its insured clients.

(f) A broker instructed to obtain insurance may, particularly in the London market, first seek reinsurance, which enables the broker to offer to insurers a risk which is substantially covered by reinsurance and thus makes the task of finding insurance somewhat easier (see **Chapter 40**).

In the light of these practical considerations, it is by no means clear that the broker should always be the insured's agent as a matter of law. In *Roberts v Plaisted* [1989] 2 Lloyd's Rep 341, a Lloyd's broker failed to inform the underwriter that the insured's motel included a discotheque and the underwriter sought to avoid the policy for material non-disclosure and misrepresentation. The Court of Appeal was able to find on the facts that there had been no breach of duty, but went on to suggest that the law on the agency of brokers should be reconsidered (which it has been, at least in part, in relation to consumer contracts). However, in *Sphere Drake Insurance Ltd v Euro International Underwriting Ltd* [2003] EWHC 2376, it was held that a broker is free to present whatever business it thinks fit to the insurer, even if this is loss-making: the broker does not owe any duty of care to the underwriter as to the quality of business presented. The obligation of the broker is to make a fair presentation, and as long as this is done the insurer cannot expect the broker to make underwriting decisions on its behalf.

There are also cases in which it has been held that information received by a broker from the insured is deemed to be received by the insurer without further communication (*Stockton v Mason* [1978] 2 Lloyd's Rep 430, where a broker was authorised by the insurer to issue cover notes); *Woolcott v Excess Insurance Co Ltd and Miles Smith Anderson and Game Ltd (No 2)* [1979]

2 Lloyd's Rep 210), although the actual status of the intermediary in these cases is unclear.

The law has been clarified somewhat in relation to disclosures for consumer contracts by the Consumer Insurance (Disclosure and Representations) Act 2012 (CIDRA) (see **Chapter 6**). This introduced a statutory determination of when the intermediary will be considered to be acting for the insurer rather than the insured for this purpose. Schedule 2 of CIDRA states that an intermediary will be acting for the insurer in the following circumstances:

(a) The intermediary is the appointed representative of the insurer;

(b) The insurer has given the intermediary express authority to collect the information as its agent; or

(c) The insurer has given the intermediary express authority to enter into the contract on the insurer's behalf (eg, a delegated underwriting authority).

In other cases, the intermediary is presumed to act for the consumer unless, in light of relevant circumstances, it appears that it acts for the insurer. Schedule 2 sets out factors which will tend to show whether the agent is acting for either the insurer or the insured. An intermediary will be presumed to be acting for the insured where it provides impartial or whole of market advice, or is paid a fee (rather than commission). It will be presumed to be acting for the insurer where it acts for only one insurer in a particular market; it acts on a restricted advice basis for a number of insurers; or the insurer provides insurance of the type in question through only a small proportion of the intermediaries that deal in that type of insurance. Other circumstances in which the intermediary will be presumed to be acting for the insurer include where the insurer allows the intermediary to use the insurer's name in providing its services; or conversely, where the insurance products are marketed under the intermediary's name. Unsurprisingly, the intermediary will also be taken to be acting for the insurer where the insurer asks the intermediary to solicit the customer's custom.

Authority

9.03 The extent to which a broker can bind an insured depends upon its authority, which may be express, usual or apparent. The insured may also, by ratification, adopt the unauthorised acts of his broker. If, therefore, a broker has entered into a contract of insurance on the insured's behalf without the insured's authority, the insured may simply adopt the contract for his own benefit. Ratification is possible even after a loss has occurred (*National Oilwell (UK) Ltd v Davy Offshore Ltd* [1993] 2 Lloyd's Rep 582), but the insurer must have been aware that the broker was not acting on its own account and was a mere agent.

THE REGULATION OF BROKERS

9.04 Any insurance broker wishing to carry out any activities regulated by the Financial Conduct Authority (FCA) now needs to apply for authorisation by the FCA or become an appointed representative of an appropriate FCA or Prudential Regulation Authority authorised firm.

Insurance Distribution Directive

9.05 The Directive on insurance distribution ((EU) 2016/97) (Insurance Distribution Directive (IDD)) came into force in the UK on 1 October 2018 (see **Chapter 43**). The IDD amended and replaced the Insurance Mediation Directive (2002/92/EC) (IMD). The IDD applies to distributors of insurance products including by brokers.

The IDD includes provisions relating to the following:

(a) registration requirements for intermediaries;

(b) professional and organisational requirements including minimum continuing professional development (CPD) requirements;

(c) status and other (eg, remuneration) disclosure requirements;

(d) rules relating to the conduct of business, importantly including the 'customer's best interest rule' (see **9.06**);

(e) determination of the demands and needs of a customer, so that products are appropriate;

(f) product disclosure information requirements;

(g) additional requirements relating to insurance-based investment products;

(h) rules on product governance; and

(i) rules on cross-selling products.

The IDD, like the IMD before it, was mainly implemented into English Law by amendments to the FCA's conduct of business rules (the Conduct of Business Sourcebook (COBS) and the Insurance: Conduct of Business Sourcebook (ICOBS)). However, there is now a separate sourcebook – PROD – implementing its product governance requirements. UK firms are also subject to the Fundamental Rules of the Prudential Regulation Authority (insurers and managing agents) and the FCA's Principles for Business.

COBS contains the rules and guidance applicable to investment insurance contracts and is not discussed any further in this chapter. ICOBS contains the main conduct of business requirements for non-investment insurance contracts.

ICOBS

9.06 ICOBS does not apply in relation to reinsurance contracts. It also does not apply in relation to contracts of 'large risk' where the risk is situated outside the UK. Where a large risk is situated in the UK (eg, a UK registered vessel or, for financial loss, where the insured is resident in the UK), ICOBS applies in a very limited way (see below). Contracts of 'large risk' are insurance contracts covering risks in the following categories:

(a) railway rolling stock, aircraft, ships (and liability of ships), goods in transit, aircraft liability, credit;

(b) suretyship of business and professional services firms; or

(c) land vehicles, fire and natural forces, other damage to property, motor vehicle liability, general liability, and miscellaneous financial loss, insofar as the policyholder exceeds the limits of at least two of the following criteria:

  (1) balance sheet total of €6.2 million;

  (2) net turnover of €12.8 million; and

  (3) an average of 250 employees during the financial year.

Application of ICOBS (ICOBS Chapter 1)

9.07 ICOBS Chapter 1 sets out the scope of ICOBS, including to whom it applies, the activities to which it applies and its territorial scope.

In each chapter, different rules apply depending on whether the insurance broker is dealing with an individual buying insurance for himself and his family (consumer) or a business buying insurance (commercial customer). Where it is unclear whether a customer is a consumer or commercial customer, insurance brokers must comply with the rules that apply to consumers.

The following points should also be noted about the application of ICOBS rules:

(a) Although this chapter comments on its application to insurance brokers only, ICOBS applies to all insurance distributors (including insurers when selling directly and in their role as product providers);

(b) ICOBS mainly applies to the insurance broker in contact with the customer – not to insurance brokers which are in the middle of the distribution chain. However, certain rules, such as the 'customer's best interest rule' will apply to all intermediaries involved (see **9.06**);

(c) ICOBS applies in a more limited way (only the customer's best interest rule and the rules on cross-selling optional products) to transactions involving 'commercial customers' and' large risks' where the risk is located inside the UK; and

(d) ICOBS does not apply to transactions involving large risks where the risk is located outside the UK.

General matters (ICOBS Chapter 2)

9.08 ICOBS Chapter 2 outlines the general requirements of ICOBS, which relate to client categorisation, communication, inducements, record keeping and acting honestly, fairly and professionally in accordance with the best interests of the customer. In particular, ICOBS Chapter 2 states as follows:

(a) If it is not clear whether a customer is a consumer or commercial customer, an insurance broker must treat the customer as a consumer.

(b) Any communication with customers must be clear, fair and not misleading.

(c) Insurance brokers should not offer or accept an inducement if it is likely to conflict with the duty they or the recipient firms owe to customers.

(d) Insurance brokers must keep adequate records in line with high-level record-keeping requirements.

(e) Insurance brokers must act honestly, fairly and professionally in accordance with the best interests of their customers. This will include, among other things, considering the customer's information needs.

One important change made in implementing the IDD relates to the standards to be imposed on intermediaries who are not authorised because they can rely on the exemption for connection contracts (see **43.05**). Although such ancillary intermediaries (selling insurance contracts which are complementary to the goods or services they are selling) are not required to be authorised, an insurance distributor (eg, an insurer or broker selling through such an intermediary) is required under ICOBS 2.6 to impose most of the conduct of business requirements applicable to authorised insurance intermediaries (other than Continuing Professional Development requirements) on such an intermediary (eg, by appropriate contractual provisions).

Distance communications (ICOBS Chapter 3)

9.09 ICOBS Chapter 3 contains rules on distance marketing, including rules on unsolicited services (which mean that a broker cannot enforce obligations under a distance contract where the services are unsolicited).

Information about the firm, its services and remuneration (ICOBS Chapter 4)

STATUS DISCLOSURE

9.10 'Status disclosure' refers to the information that insurance brokers must provide about themselves and any fees that they charge. In summary, the information that insurance brokers need to give to customers in good time before the contract is concluded includes the following:

(a) the name and address of the insurance broker;

(b) whether it provides a personal recommendation about the insurance products offered, whether it does so on the basis of a fair and personal analysis and, if so, whether its advice is limited to certain providers (which it should name);

(c) how to complain to the insurance broker (including notification that complaints may be referred to the Financial Ombudsman Service (FOS) where relevant);

(d) a statement that it is included in the Financial Services Register (along with details of how to check);

(e) details of any holding of 10 per cent or more of voting rights or capital that the insurance broker has in an insurance undertaking;

(f) details of any holding of 10 per cent or more of voting rights or capital that an insurance undertaking (or a parent of an insurance undertaking) has in the insurance broker;

(g) the basis on which the insurance broker provides advice or information; and

(h) details of any fees, including the method of calculation.

The disclosure requirements for insurance brokers that only make introductions (eg, to other intermediaries or insurers) are significantly reduced, so that they need only disclose their name, address, statutory status and whether they are part of the same corporate group as the person to whom they are making an introduction.

ADDITIONAL REQUIREMENTS

Additional requirements apply in relation to pure protection (eg, term life insurance) and payment protection insurance. In a sale that does not involve a personal recommendation, an insurance broker must take reasonable steps to ensure the customer understands that he is responsible for deciding whether a policy meets his demands and needs. Oral communications of information relating to products must also be balanced (eg, both what is covered and main exclusions).

REMUNERATION AND DISCLOSURE

In good time before the conclusion of the initial contract of insurance and, if necessary, on its amendment or renewal, an insurance broker must provide the customer with information:

(a) on the nature of the remuneration received (eg, paid by the insurer); and

(b) on the basis of remuneration (eg, a fee, commission or other economic benefit).

Where a fee is payable, the insurance broker must inform the customer of the amount of the fee. This extends to all such fees that may be charged during the life of a policy.

MEANS OF COMMUNICATION TO CUSTOMERS

An insurance broker must communicate information to customers using either paper, a durable medium other than paper or, with the customer's consent, an appropriate website (eg, which allows the customer to access or store the information).

COMMISSION DISCLOSURE FOR COMMERCIAL CUSTOMERS

An insurance broker must, on a commercial customer's request, promptly disclose the commission that it and any associate receives in connection with a policy. Disclosure must be in cash terms and in writing or another durable medium. To the extent this is not possible, the insurance broker must give the basis for calculation.

Identifying client needs and advising (ICOBS Chapter 5)

9.11 GENERAL AND DISCLOSURE

An insurance broker should take reasonable steps to ensure that a customer only buys a policy under which he is eligible to claim benefits (eg, he satisfies the eligibility criteria or is part of the target market for the product).

An insurance broker should ensure that a customer knows what to disclose, including:

(a) explaining to a commercial customer the duty to disclose all circumstances material to a policy, what needs to be disclosed and the consequences of any failure to make such a disclosure;

(b) ensuring that the commercial customer is asked clear questions about any matter that is material to the insurance undertaking;

(c) explaining to the customer the responsibility of consumers to take reasonable care not to make a misrepresentation and the possible consequences if a consumer is careless in answering the insurer's questions or recklessly or deliberately makes a misrepresentation; and

(d) asking the customer clear and specific questions about the information relevant to the policy being arranged or varied.

DEMANDS AND NEEDS

Prior to the conclusion of a contract of insurance, an insurance broker must specify, on the basis of information obtained from the customer, the demands and the needs of that customer. The details must be modulated according to the complexity of the contract of insurance proposed and the type of customer. A statement of the demands and needs must be communicated to the customer prior to the conclusion of a contract of insurance (eg, in an application form or as a separate document). When proposing a contract of insurance, a broker must ensure that it is consistent with the customer's demands and needs.

ADVISED SALES

A firm must take reasonable care to ensure the suitability of its advice for any customer who is entitled to rely upon its judgement. If an insurance broker informs a customer that it gives advice or a personal recommendation on the basis of a fair analysis of the market, it must give such advice on the basis of an analysis of a sufficiently large number of contracts of insurance available on the market to enable him to make a recommendation; and the recommendation must be in accordance with professional criteria and adequate to meet the customer's needs.

Where an insurance broker provides a personal recommendation, the insurance broker must, in addition to the statement of demands and needs, provide the customer with a personalised explanation of why a particular contract of insurance would best meet his demands and needs.

Product information (ICOBS Chapter 6)

9.12 RESPONSIBILITIES ON INSURERS AND INSURANCE BROKERS

Insurers are generally responsible for producing information and for its content, while insurance brokers are generally responsible for providing the information to customers. There is a useful summary of responsibilities in ICOBS 6 Annex 1.

APPROPRIATE INFORMATION RULE

Insurance brokers must ensure that a customer is given appropriate information about a policy in good time and in a comprehensible form so that the customer can make an informed decision about the arrangements proposed.

LEVEL OF INFORMATION TO BE PROVIDED

An insurance broker must ensure that the level of appropriate information provided takes into account the complexity of the policy and the type of customer. The level of information required will vary according to matters such as:

(a) the knowledge, experience and ability of a typical customer for the policy;

(b) the policy terms, including its main benefits, exclusions, limitations, conditions and duration;

(c) the policy's overall complexity;

(d) whether the policy is bought in connection with other goods and services, including another policy;

(e) distance communication information requirements (eg, in some circumstances less information can be given initially during certain telephone sales, with the full information provided after the call); and

(f) whether the same information has been provided to the customer previously and, if so, when.

CONSUMERS

For consumer sales of general insurance policies, the information provided must include the insurance product information document (IPID), which is in a specified format. This must be drawn up by the manufacturer (as defined in the FCA Handbook glossary) of the product and can only contain the logo of the manufacturer. It must be provided in a durable medium; and for telephone sales that can benefit from an exemption under the distance marketing rules, it can be provided immediately after the call has ended.

COMMERCIAL CUSTOMERS

A firm dealing with a commercial customer must provide the IPID information (set out in ICOSB 6 Annex 3R), but it need not use the IPID format. It may choose to provide some or all of the appropriate information in a policy summary or a similar summary if it considers this to be a comprehensible form in which to provide that information.

OTHER INFORMATION

As well as the IPID information, other disclosures may be required for contractual or regulatory reasons. These include the Solvency II disclosures for individual customers of general insurance contracts specifying the law of the contract and complaint handling arrangements.

DISCLOSURE OF CANCELLATION RIGHT

An insurance broker must provide a consumer with information on the right to cancel a policy, how to cancel and the consequences of cancelling. The information must be provided in good time before conclusion of the contract and in writing or another durable medium.

RENEWALS

An insurance broker must provide to the consumer the following information in good time before the renewal:

(a) the premium to be paid by the consumer on renewal;

(b) in a way that is consistent with the presentation of (a) so that they can be easily compared:

 (i) except where (ii) applies, the premium for the policy which the firm proposes to renew, as set out at the inception of that policy; or

 (ii) where one or more mid-term changes were made to the policy which the firm proposes to renew, an amount calculated by annualising (or otherwise adjusting as appropriate to the duration of the proposed policy) the premium in effect following the most recent mid-term change, excluding all fees or charges associated with those mid-term changes; and

(c) a statement alongside (a) and (b) indicating that the consumer:

 (i) should check that the level of cover offered by the renewal is appropriate for his needs; and

 (ii) is able, if he so wishes, to compare the prices and levels of cover offered by alternative providers. Where the proposed renewal will be the fourth or subsequent renewal that the consumer has entered into in respect of the policy, the renewal notice must include a warning in a specified form that the customer may be able to get the insurance cover at a better price if he shops around.

The FCA intends to introduce further rules relating to renewal to enable consumers to cancel auto renewals and, for home and motor insurance, to prevent different prices being used on renewal from those used for the equivalent new business.

ADDITIONAL REQUIREMENTS

Requirements are specified in ICOBS 6A. These relate to certain types of insurance and the sale of 'add-on' products. Generally, an active election will be required before a customer can be charged for an optional additional product sold with his insurance, and the customer must be provided with information in relation to such product. Where insurance is the add-on product, it must be optional and cannot be mandatory. This does not prevent the sale of multi-risk insurance contracts.

Requirements are specified in ICOBS 6A.4 in relation to travel insurance not sold under a group policy or to a commercial customer. These relate to the provision of information relating to a medical cover firm directory to enable customers who are declined cover to seek specialist cover.

Cancellation (ICOBS Chapter 7)

9.13 THE RIGHT TO CANCEL

A consumer has a right to cancel, from the day of the conclusion of the contract, without penalty and without giving any reason, within:

(a) 30 days for a contract of insurance which is, or has elements of, a pure protection contract or payment protection contract; or

(b) 14 days for any other contract of insurance or distance contract.

There are some exceptions to this for:

(a) short-term travel and baggage or similar policies of less than one month;

(b) pure protection contracts of six months or less which are not distance contracts;

(c) sales by unauthorised intermediaries (but not appointed representatives) of general insurance (other than payment protection contracts or distance contracts); and

(d) sales under the connected contracts exemption which are not distance contracts.

A firm must, without any undue delay and no later than within 30 days, return to a consumer any sums it has received from him in accordance with the contract.

The cancellation period starts on the date the contract is concluded or, if later, the date the consumer receives the contractual terms and conditions and any other required pre-contractual information. The insurer is permitted (other than in relation to pure protection and payment protection contracts) to deduct (eg, on a pro rata basis) the cost of cover or services already received by the consumer prior to cancellation. It may also deduct the costs of concluding the contract and a proportion of fees and commissions paid to intermediaries.

Claims handling (ICOBS Chapter 8)

9.14 GENERAL

Insurers (and agents acting on their behalf) must:

(a) handle claims promptly and fairly;

(b) provide reasonable guidance to help a policyholder make a claim and appropriate information on its progress;

(c) not unreasonably reject a claim (including by terminating or avoiding a policy); and

(d) settle claims promptly once settlement terms are agreed.

Unreasonable rejection of consumer claims in relation to contracts (or variations) concluded before 5 April 2013 (for consumers) or 17 August 2017 may include rejection on the basis of non-fraudulent non-disclosure, misrepresentation or breach of a warranty unconnected to the loss.

Insurance brokers should also manage conflicts of interest in dealing with claims fairly and comply with the general law on the duties of an insurance intermediary. A firm that does not have authority to deal with a claim should forward any claim notification to the insurance undertaking promptly or inform the policyholder immediately that it cannot deal with the notification.

THE RIGHTS OF BROKERS

Commission

9.15 Except in relation to life investment insurance contracts which are sold with advice, commission may be payable to a broker that arranges or sells an insurance contract in the UK. As noted above, commission is paid to the broker by the insurer rather than by the insured, even though the broker is the insured's agent. This rule is anomalous, in that it contravenes the basic agency rule that an agent may not profit from its office other than with the express consent of its principal. However, the exception in favour of insurance brokers is well established and is subject only to the condition that the payment by the insurer conforms to usual market practice in terms of amount (*Hugh Allen & Co Ltd v A Holmes* [1969] 1 Lloyd's Rep 348 (CA)) and circumstances of payment (*NV Rotterdamse v Golding Steward Wrightson*, unreported, 1989). A broker is entitled to commission from the insurer only if the broker can demonstrate that its actions were the effective cause of the contract between the insured and insurer (*McNeil v Law Union and Rock Insurance Co Ltd* [1925] 23 LI LR 314).

ICOBS Chapter 4 requires an insurance broker to disclose the commission that it receives if it is asked to do so by a commercial customer (see **9.08** above). Disclosure may also be required to satisfy both regulatory and agency requirements where a specific request is made by a consumer.

Lien

9.16 A lien is a common law possessory security, entitling a creditor in lawful possession of the debtor's property to retain that property as security for the debt. In certain forms of insurance (eg, marine insurance), the premium is paid by the broker. If the policy is then issued to the broker by the underwriter, the broker may retain the policy as security for the payment of the premium by the insured to the broker (Marine Insurance Act 1906, s 53). The lien does not extend to a composite policy (*Eide UK Ltd v Lowndes Lambert Group* Ltd [1998] 1 Lloyd's Rep 389).

THE DUTIES OF BROKERS

Nature of the duties

9.17 Brokers, as agents, owe three classes of duty to the insured. First, the broker owes to the insured the duty to obey instructions and to use reasonable care and skill. The fact that the broker has failed to achieve what has been requested by the insured does not automatically mean that it is in breach of duty; it is sufficient if the broker exercises reasonable care. If the broker cannot obtain what is required, it must report in what respects it has failed and seek the client's alternative instructions (*Youell v Bland Welch and Co Ltd – the Superhulls Cover Case (No 2)* [1990] 2 Lloyd's Rep 431). Second, the broker owes fiduciary duties to the insured, which require the broker not to act in a manner which creates a conflict between its duty to the insured and its personal interest or duty to a third party. Third, and as noted above in relation to ICOBS, brokers owe regulatory duties under the Principles and rules of the FCA. These include similar items such as the obligation to act in the best interests of the customer, to avoid conflicts and to communicate with the customer in a way which is clear, fair and not misleading.

The Consumer Rights Act 2015 also applies to insurance brokers in relation to consumer insurance contracts. Insurance brokers providing services to consumers have a duty to perform the services with reasonable care and skill. In addition, the Act makes certain provisions in relation to unfair contract terms – unfair terms being unenforceable. Insurance brokers should note that terms such as exclusion clauses should be transparent and brought to the customer's attention; and insurance contracts should not include powers which are unreasonable or include high cancellation charges.

Finding insurance

9.18 The primary obligation of the broker is to use all reasonable care and skill to obey the instructions given to it as to the insurance required. A number of aspects of this duty have emerged from the cases:

(a) The broker must consider the market as a whole and seek to obtain the widest cover at the lowest premium. If the risk is uninsurable, the broker must inform the insured promptly (*Smith v Lascelles* (1788) 2 Term Rep 187).

(b) The broker must ensure that the security offered by the insurer or reinsurer is appropriate for the type of business being insured or reinsured (*Berriman v Rose Thomson Young (Underwriting) Ltd* [1996] LRLR 426).

(c) A broker that knows an insurer is in financial difficulties but nevertheless continues to place insurance with the insurer will be liable in negligence (*Osman v J Ralph Moss* [1970] 1 Lloyd's Rep 313).

(d) The policy must suit the insured's needs. If the broker has failed to procure insurance within the required time or of the required scope, it will be in breach of duty. There are many illustrations of this in the insurance cases. First, in *Youell v Bland Welch* (see **9.15** above), the broker had procured reinsurance for 48 months only, to cover a marine construction insurance risk of unlimited duration. Second, in *Forsikringsaktieselskapet Vesta v Butcher* (No 1) [1989] 1 All ER 402, the broker obtained reinsurance governed by English law, which gave less protection to the reinsured than the liability which it faced to its own insured under a policy governed by Norwegian law. The judges of the Queen's Bench Division, Court of Appeal and House of Lords all allowed recovery on the policy of reinsurance by a variety of different arguments, so no question of liability on the part of the broker arose. However, the House of Lords added that the broker would have faced liability if the reinsured's claim under the policy had failed. Lastly, in *McNealy v The Pennine Insurance Co Ltd* [1978] 2 Lloyd's Rep 18, the broker procured a motor policy which excluded part-time musicians, into which category the insured fell. It was held that the broker ought to have asked the insured whether the exclusion applied to him.

These obligations are now supported by the regulatory duties, including those described above in relation to the obligation to only sell products which meet the customer's demand and needs and for which the customer is part of the target market for the product – which must be identified to the broker by the insurer or manufacturer.

Completing the proposal form

9.19 In *O'Connor v BDB Kirby & Co* [1972] 1 QB 90, a proposal form completed by the broker and subsequently signed by the insured was found to contain material false statements and the insurer avoided the policy. The Court of Appeal accepted that the broker owed a duty of care to the insured to transcribe the insured's answer in an accurate fashion, but found the broker not to be liable because, first, the insured had not shown that the error was due to the broker's negligence; and second, the insured, by failing to check the form before signing it, had been the cause of his own loss.

O'Connor does not remove all possibility of action against the broker. In *Warren v Henry Sutton & Co* [1976] 2 Lloyd's Rep 276, the broker made false statements to the insurer about the driving record of a person to be a named driver under a motor policy. The broker was held to be in breach of duty for having failed to make the necessary inquiries of the insured himself. Moreover, if the completion of the proposal is entrusted to the broker due to the insured's absence, the broker is under a personal duty to check the answers. An extreme example is *Sharp v Sphere Drake Insurance Co (The Moonacre)* [1992] 2 Lloyd's Rep 501, where the broker had not only failed to inform the insured of the significance of an exclusion clause, but also forged the insured's signature on the proposal, and had thereby submitted a proposal form to the insurer containing the material false statement that the insured had personally checked the form. The broker was held to have acted negligently in these circumstances.

Payment of the premium

9.20 Where the broker is UK authorised under the FSMA 2000, it will be subject to the FCA's rules in the Client Assets Sourcebook (CASS) relating to client money. This will generally mean that monies held in connection with its UK regulated insurance distribution activities must be held on trust for the client or in an approved bank until they are paid to the insurer.

Where the broker issuing a policy acts as agent of the insurer under a delegated authority, it must instead collect and hold premiums under a risk transfer arrangement with the insurer. This will mean that the insurer is liable for the money held by the broker (ie, it is deemed to be the insurer's money and premium will deemed to have been paid). Risk transfer arrangements must comply with the provisions of CASS 5.2, which include the need for a written agreement between the broker and the insurer and for the risk transfer arrangement to have been communicated to the insured.

In marine insurance, the broker undertakes personal responsibility to the insurer to pay the premium (Marine Insurance Act 1906, s 53(1)), so that the insured is immune from an action by the insurer for the premium. The most important effect of this is that if the broker becomes insolvent having received the premium from the insured, the insured cannot be called upon to pay the premium again. This rule does not apply to other forms of insurance, so where the broker is the insured's agent, payment of the premium to the broker is not deemed to be payment to the insurer (see **Chapter 5**).

Post-formation duties

9.21 In addition to the regulatory duties referred to above, once the insurance has been arranged, the broker is under a range of further duties:

(a) If the policy is delivered to the broker, the broker must read the policy to check that it complies with the cover requested from the insurer (*King (Or Fiehl) v Chambers & Newman (Insurance Brokers)* [1963] 2 Lloyd's Rep 130).

(b) The broker must, if asked by the insured whether particular conduct is or is not permitted under the policy, act reasonably in providing advice. In the event of lack of clarity, it will not be enough for the broker to form a view of what the policy wording means (*Melik & Co v Norwich Union Fire Insurance Society and Kemp* [1980] 1 Lloyd's Rep 523), and it may be necessary for the broker to seek clarification from the insurer.

(c) When a policy is about to expire, the broker's duty may, depending upon the instructions given by the insured, be either to renew automatically or to inform the insured as to the imminent lapse of cover. If the broker's duty is to effect renewal, it must:

(i) ensure that all material facts are communicated to the insurer (*Coolee Ltd v Wing Heath & Co* (1930) 38 Ll L Rep 157; cf *Dunbar v A&B Painters Ltd* and *Economic Insurance Co Ltd and Whitehouse & Co* [1986] 2 Lloyd's Rep 38); and

(ii) inform the insured of any changes in cover imposed on renewal and obtain an acknowledgement from the insured of his willingness to accept such changes on renewal (*Great North Eastern Railway Ltd v Avon Insurance plc* [2001] 2 Lloyd's Rep 649).

(d) If the insured wishes to alter his insurance arrangements and requests that the broker make the necessary adjustments, the broker must act with reasonable care. In *Cherry Ltd v Allied Insurance Brokers Ltd* [1978] 1 Lloyd's Rep 274, the broker was instructed to cancel a policy, but informed the insured that this could not be done. The insured, acting on this advice, cancelled a substitute policy and was subsequently left uninsured when the broker did manage to cancel the original policy without informing the insured. The broker was held liable for a loss later suffered by the insured which was not covered by any policy.

(e) A broker will, depending on the type of policy, be under a duty to take reasonable steps to ensure that the client is aware of the nature and terms of the insurance, and, in particular, to draw attention to and explain (if necessary) any terms, the breach of which might result in his being uninsured (*JW Bollom & Co Ltd v Byas Mosley & Co Ltd* [2000] Lloyd's Rep IR 136).

(f) A broker must exercise all reasonable care and skill in order to be in a position to collect claims when called upon to do so. This obligation means that the broker must retain the necessary documents to enable it to collect the insured's claims. The information need only be retained so long as a reasonable broker would regard a claim as possible (*Grace v Leslie & Godwin Financial Services Ltd* [1995] LRLR 472).

Claims

Making the claim

9.22 The broker is required under its duty to the insured to seek payment of the claim from the insurer following loss. In *North & South Trust Co v Berkeley* [1970] 2 Lloyd's Rep 467, the broker acted simultaneously for the insured and the underwriter. The broker, on behalf of the underwriter, commissioned a report on the insured's loss. The insured sought possession of the report, on the basis that the broker was his agent and held the report in that capacity, rather than as agent for the underwriter. Donaldson J (at 479) rejected the insured's claim, but issued a firm warning that a broker cannot act for both parties in this fashion, and that in future cases less leniency would be shown. It is common market practice, despite this ruling, for brokers – particularly at Lloyd's – to obtain surveys and other reports for underwriters, and to appoint solicitors for underwriters on request. Such conduct is almost certainly a breach of duty towards an insured who has not been made aware of the practice.

ICOBS requirements (see **9.08-9.09** and **9.12** above) mean that an insurance broker must not put itself in a position where its own interest, or its duty to any person for whom it acts, conflicts with its duty to any customer, unless it has made proper disclosure to its customer of all information needed to enable the customer to give informed consent to the arrangement and has obtained the customer's prior informed consent.

Payment of the loss

9.23 In many cases, particularly at Lloyd's, the broker has an accounting arrangement with the underwriter whereby the broker pays losses and is subsequently indemnified by the underwriter. If the broker pays the insured in anticipation that the underwriter will accept liability, and it refuses, the sum paid by the broker to the insured may be treated as a gift. If the payment is so treated, this means that:

(a) if the underwriter is not liable, the insured retains the sums paid by the broker; or

(b) if the underwriter is liable, the insured can probably recover the full amount of his loss from the underwriter, irrespective of the fact that he has been paid by the broker, and can retain both sums. In *Merrett v Capitol Indemnity Corporation* [1991] 1 Lloyd's Rep 169, the broker paid the reinsured's claim against the reinsurer gratuitously for commercial reasons.

In the absence of any accounting arrangement, the insurer may pay the loss directly to the broker. As the broker is the insured's agent, payment to the broker (unless it is covered by a risk transfer arrangement) is deemed to be payment to the insured, so that if the broker becomes insolvent, the insured cannot require the insurer to pay again (although it should be protected by the FCA CASS rules). If the insurer, having paid the broker, discovers that the payment was made in error, the insurer can only recover the payment from the broker before the broker paid over or accounted for the money to the insured (*Holland v Russell* (1863) 4 B&S 14). The insurer must thereafter reclaim the payment from the insured itself.

THE LIABILITIES OF BROKERS

Contract and tort

9.24 There has been a move in the general law since 1986 against the co-existence of duties of care in contract and tort – the principle being that if the parties have a contract, the contract should provide an exhaustive statement of their rights and liabilities (*Tai Hing Cotton Mill v Liu Chong Hing Bank Ltd (No 2)* [1986] AC 519). This principle does not, however, apply to insurance brokers (and possibly not to other providers of professional services). The position is that a broker owes a duty to the insured to exercise reasonable care and skill in carrying out its instructions, both in contract (by means of an implied term) and in tort (by means of a duty of care). Consequently, in the event of a negligent breach, the insured may choose whether to sue in contract or in tort.

A sub-broker, which is usually the agent of the producing broker, will normally have no contractual relationship with the insured (*Pangood Ltd v Barclay Brown Co Ltd* [1999] Lloyd's Rep IR 405). A sub-broker owes no general duty of care to the insured, but such a duty may exist depending on the circumstances of the case. See, for example, *Prentis Donegan & Partners Ltd v Leeds & Leeds Co Inc* [1998] 2 Lloyd's Rep 326, where it was held that a sub-broker owes a duty of care to the insured where there was no contract between them. A sub-broker will also be subject to the client's best interest rule (see **9.06**).

Limitation of actions

9.25 Under s 5 of the Limitation Act 1980, an action for breach of contract must be brought within six years of the date of the breach. In the case of an action in tort, the action may be brought within either six years of the date of the loss or three years of the date on which a reasonable person would have the knowledge required to bring the action, whichever date is later (Limitation Act 1980, ss 2 and 14A, the latter inserted by the Latent Damage Act 1986). It is a feature of breach of duty by a broker that it may not come to light for some years after it has occurred – for example, when a policy is procured by means of false information given by the broker in year one and a loss occurs in year ten, at which date the insurer denies liability. In both contract and tort, time begins to run in year one, which is the date of the breach of contract for the purposes of s 5 of the Limitation Act 1980 and the date of damage for the purposes of s 2 of the Limitation Act 1980 (*Islander Trucking Ltd (In Liquidation) v Hogg Robinson & Gardener Mountain (Marine) Ltd* [1990] 1 All ER 826). In such a case, it is possible to sue only in tort, by relying on the three-year 'discoverability' period under s 14A of the Limitation Act 1980. There is a long-stop period of 15 years from the date of breach of duty, after which no action may be brought.

Measures of damages

9.26 It makes little difference whether the insured sues his broker in contract or tort, as the cases have established that the same measure of damages applies and the same deductions in favour of the broker are available. The basic measure of damages against a broker whose breach of duty has rendered a loss irrecoverable from the insurer is the amount of the loss itself, not the amount insured (*Charles v Altin* (1854) 15 CB 46). This is coupled with any costs incurred by the insured in unsuccessfully pursuing the insurer (*Seavision Investment SA v Evennett (The Tiburon)* [1992] 2 Lloyd's Rep 26). Damages recoverable by reinsureds from their brokers for breach of duty in obtaining cover, which underwriters are entitled to later avoid for non-disclosure of material facts, were in general limited to the value of the cover which they were instructed to obtain and reported that they had obtained. However, if the scope of the duty was wider and involved undertaking to advise on the course of action which the reinsured should pursue, the damages recoverable would be greater

(*Aneco Reinsurance Underwriting Ltd (In Liquidation) v Johnson & Higgins Ltd* [2002] Lloyd's Rep IR 91).

The amount recoverable will be reduced in two situations. First, if the broker can demonstrate that, irrespective of the broker's breach of duty, the insurer would not have paid the full amount of the loss, the broker's liability is limited to the amount which the insurer would have been likely to pay. This situation arises most commonly where the insurer has a defence against the insured which has nothing to do with the broker's breach of duty. In *Everett v Hogg, Robinson and Gardner Mountain (Insurance) Ltd* [1973] 2 Lloyd's Rep 217, both the insured and the broker had given false information to the insurer. The insurer relied upon the broker's error to deny liability. The court held that the insurer, faced with the insured's breach only, would have settled for two-thirds of the claim, and that was therefore the amount which the broker's duty had cost the insured and was the appropriate measure of damages.

The second situation is that in which the insured has in some way contributed to his own loss. In *Forsikringsaktieselskapet Vesta* (see **9.16** above), the Court of Appeal held that the Law Reform (Contributory Negligence) Act 1945 allows the apportionment of damages where it is shown that the insured is guilty of contributory negligence and where the broker's liability in contract is the same as in tort. The level of deductions has been fairly low, as the courts have taken the view that the insured, having appointed a broker, is not under a duty to monitor the manner in which the broker performs its duty. In *Youell v Bland Welch* (see **9.15** above), a reinsurance broker had sent details of cover to the reinsured, but had failed to clarify in the document the fact that reinsurance cover was to be limited to 48 months. The reinsured either did not read the document or, having read it, did not appreciate the restriction. The court felt that a deduction of 20 per cent from the damages against the broker following a loss outside the period of cover was appropriate in the circumstance. In *National Insurance and Guarantee Corporation v Imperio Reinsurance Co (UK) and Russell Tudor-Price & Co Ltd* [1999] Lloyd's Rep IR 249, damages payable by a broker to a reinsured in circumstances where the broker had produced a policy amendment which plainly did not have its intended effect, but which were nevertheless approved by the reinsured, were reduced by 30 per cent. By contrast, in *The Moonacre* (see **9.17**) – another case in which the insured had failed to read or appreciate policy wording – the court refused to make any deduction from the insured's damages against the broker. *The Moonacre* is likely to represent the position where the insured is not an expert in insurance matters. The courts are more likely to find a reinsured guilty of contributory negligence compared with an insured (but see *(1) GE Reinsurance Corporation (2) Great Lakes Reinsurance (UK) plc (3) Sphere Drake Insurance Ltd (4) Royal & Sun Alliance Insurance plc v (1) New Hampshire Insurance Company (2) Willis Ltd* [2003] EWHC 302).

Persons to whom duties are owed

9.27 The fact that the broker has a contract with the insured does not necessarily mean that the broker does not owe a tortious duty of care to third parties. The cases have established the following principles:

(a) A broker appointed to arrange insurance, which seeks reinsurance first on behalf of insurers yet to be identified and which gives a signing indication to the reinsurer, must use its best endeavours to obtain the promised level of subscription (*General Accident Fire and Life Assurance Corporation v Tanter, The 'Zephyr'* [1985] 2 Lloyd's Rep 529; see **Chapter 40**).

(b) A broker which is asked by the purchaser of a car to transfer the insured's motor policy to the third-party purchaser to accompany the sale of the car owes a duty of care to the third party to effect the insurance as required, and is in breach of that duty if it fails to inform him that the transfer has not been accepted (*Bromley LBC v A Ellis (Luff & Sons, Third Party)* [1971] 1 Lloyd's Rep 97). Similarly, if the broker is aware that the policy is to be assigned to a third party, the broker owes a duty of care to the third party to ensure that the policy is valid from its inception (*Punjab National Bank v de Boinville* [1992] 3 All ER 104). This is so because the third party in these cases has been identified and there is no danger of the broker facing liability to a large unidentifiable class of persons.

(c) A broker does not owe a duty of care to the public at large. In *MacMillan v AW Knott Becker Scott Ltd* [1990] 1 Lloyd's Rep 98, the broker made false statements to the insurer on the insured's behalf when the insured's liability policy was obtained. This rendered the policy voidable. The insured subsequently became insolvent and various third parties which had claims against the insured commenced proceedings against the insured's liability insurers in accordance with the Third Parties (Rights Against Insurers) Act 1930 (see **Chapter 20**). The claimants thus sought to sue the broker, alleging a duty of care owed to them. The court felt that it would not be appropriate to impose a duty of care upon brokers placing a liability policy towards any person who might be injured by the insured.

(d) If a broker is appointed by a company to procure insurance, its duty is – under the corporate veil principle – owed only to the company, and not to the individual shareholders. This rule may prove to be harsh in the case of a small private company where the use of corporate form was a matter of pure convenience. In *Verderame v Commercial Union Assurance Co plc* [1992] BCLC 793, the Court of Appeal held that the broker did not owe a duty of care to the two shareholders of a company to procure a valid policy for the company, and that the duty was owed to the company itself. This was significant on the facts, as the company had become insolvent so that any successful claim by the company would lead to recovery by it for the benefit of its creditors, so that the shareholders themselves received very little by way of compensation.

(e) A broker does not normally owe any duties in contract to an insurer. A broker can, however, assume specific obligations to an insurer or reinsurer (see *The Zephyr* at (a) above and *Pryke v Gibbs Hartley Cooper Ltd* [1991] 1 Lloyd's Rep 602).

If the policy wording has been prepared by the broker, as agent of the insured, the doctrine of *contra proferentem* will operate against the insured in the event of ambiguity (*Bartlett & Partners Ltd v Meller* [1961] 1 Lloyd's Rep 487). In such circumstances, the broker must exercise particular care to ensure that the wording which he has prepared meets the needs of each insured (see *Forsikringsaktieselskapet Vesta* at **9.16**).

Chapter 10

Underwriting agencies

- Nature of underwriting agencies
- Delegated underwriting agencies and Lloyd's
- Underwriting agencies and reinsurance pools

NATURE OF UNDERWRITING AGENCIES

Definition

10.01 The scope of an agent's authority depends upon the terms of its appointment. Some agents are given the right to accept business on behalf of the insurer, while others merely obtain proposals for transmission to and decision by the insurer.

An underwriting agent is a person given authority by an insurer or reinsurer to write insurance or reinsurance business on the insurer or reinsurer's behalf. Underwriting agencies or coverholders are primarily used in order to establish some form of presence in a territory or market where the insurer is itself not otherwise represented; to this extent, selling insurance through an underwriting agent is operationally an alternative to the insurer establishing a full branch in the territory in question. However, an underwriting agent with delegated authority is likely to be considered a branch of the insurer for regulatory purposes in many jurisdictions. In practice, underwriting agencies are most widely used by Lloyd's underwriters and in the placing of reinsurance risks.

Authorisation

10.02 Under the Financial Services and Markets Act 2000 (FSMA 2000), no firm or person may carry on a regulated activity by way of business in the UK unless authorised or exempt (the 'General Prohibition'). In relation to insurance, the 'insurance business' regulated activities (eg, carried on by insurers), which are specified in the Financial Services and Markets Act 2000 (Regulated Activities) Order 2001 (SI 2001/544) (RAO) are:

(a) effecting contracts of insurance as principal; or

(b) carrying out contracts of insurance as principal (art 10 of the RAO).

If either of these activities is carried on by an agent on behalf of an insurer or underwriter, the insurer or underwriter will need to be authorised under the FSMA.

There are also insurance distribution activities which may be undertaken by underwriting agents (together, 'the IDD activities'):

(a) dealing in contracts of insurance as an agent (this involves buying, selling, subscribing for, or underwriting a product as agent of the insurer or the client) (art 21 of the RAO);

(b) arranging (bringing about) deals in contracts of insurance. This involves making arrangements that would have the direct effect that a transaction takes place (art 25(1) of the RAO); or

(c) making arrangements with a view to transactions in contracts of insurance. This involves making arrangements such as introductions (other than pure introductions which are not regulated activities (art 25(2) of the RAO)). Pure introductions (art 33 B of the RAO) are introductions which:

    (i) consist of the provision of information about a potential policyholder to a relevant insurer or an insurance or reinsurance intermediary; or

    (ii) consist of the provision of information to a potential policyholder about:

        (A) a contract of insurance; or

        (B) a relevant insurer or insurance or reinsurance intermediary,

    and where the provider of the information does not take any step other than the provision of information to assist in the conclusion of a contract of insurance);

(d) advising on contracts of insurance. This involves providing advice to someone on his existing insurance or as a prospective purchaser of insurance, and must relate to/recommend a particular course of action (art 53 of the RAO);

(e) assisting in the administration and performance of contracts of insurance. This includes dealing with claims (eg, for policyholders) but not claims management and loss adjusting on behalf of an authorised insurers (art 39A of the RAO); and

(f) agreeing to carry on any of the above (art 64 of the RAO).

In relation to Lloyd's, the additional regulated activities are:

(a) advising a person to become or continue or cease to be a member of a particular Lloyd's syndicate (art 56 of the RAO);

(b) managing the underwriting capacity of a Lloyd's syndicate (art 57 of the RAO); or

(c) arranging, by the Society of Lloyd's, in the name of Lloyd's, deals in contracts of insurance written at Lloyd's (art 58 of the RAO).

Underwriting agents or coverholders need to be authorised (ie, apply and be approved for a Part 4A permission to act as an agent) by the Financial Conduct Authority (FCA).

Lloyd's managing agents must be authorised by both the FCA and the Prudential Regulation Authority (PRA), in addition to being subject to regulation by Lloyd's. Pursuant to s 55B and Sch 6 of the FSMA 2000, managing agents must satisfy the statutory conditions and must be 'fit and proper' to conduct regulated activities; and management must have adequate skills and experience, and have acted and may be expected to act with probity. They are also subject to the Senior Managers and Certifications Regime, so persons performing certain specified senior management functions in the managing agency must seek approval to do so from the relevant regulator (see **42.06**).

Where insurance contracts are made or arranged by an entity that does not have appropriate authorisation or is not otherwise exempt from authorisation, ss 26–28 of the FSMA 2000 provide that such contracts remain enforceable against the insurer by the original insured if he so elects, but are not enforceable by the insurer (eg, the insurer would be unable to enforce the provisions enabling it to receive premiums). However, this is subject to the discretion of the court to decide that the contract is enforceable on the grounds that it is just and equitable to enforce it. This decision will largely revolve around whether the entities concerned reasonably believed they were not contravening the General Prohibition. Sections 26–28 of the FSMA 2000 also provide that the insured is entitled to recover any money or property paid by him under the contract if it is not enforced, and compensation for any loss sustained by him as a result of having parted with that money or property.

Special note should be taken of ss 23–24 of the FSMA 2000, which provide that a person who contravenes the General Prohibition or who describes himself as authorised or exempt (eg, as an appointed representative), or who behaves or otherwise acts in a manner which indicates that he is an authorised or exempt person when he is not, is guilty of a criminal offence and is liable in the most serious cases to unlimited fines and imprisonment.

DELEGATED UNDERWRITING AGENCIES AND LLOYD'S

10.03 The business of a Lloyd's syndicate is managed by managing agents, which will normally underwrite risk on behalf of the syndicate. Other underwriting agents (eg, coverholders) may also be given authority to write business on behalf of the syndicate. The agreement by which the underwriting agent is authorised to accept risks on behalf of the participating syndicates is known as a 'binding authority' or 'binder'. Under the Lloyd's regulatory structure, the holders of binding authorities must be approved by Lloyd's and the agreements with approved holders are then registered at Lloyd's. The FCA requires that binding authorities expressly provide that the underwriting agent is to act as agent of the insurer for the purpose of receiving and holding premiums (if the agent has the authority to commit the insurer to risk), claims monies (if the agent has the authority to settle claims on behalf of the insurer) and premium refunds (if the agent has the authority to make refunds of premiums on behalf of the insurer). The agreement must comply with the FCA's Client Assets Sourcebook 5 rules on risk transfer, which include the need to notify the customer of the risk transfer arrangement.

The Lloyd's Underwriting Bye-law (and the Overseas Underwriting Bye-law) set out requirements for underwriting. The Lloyd's Underwriting and Controls Minimum Standard contains guidance in relation to the nature of the framework required to manage underwriting risk and in particular delegated underwriting, which must be undertaken in accordance with the syndicate business plan. Managing agents must ensure that:

(a) there is a nominated director responsible for underwriting systems and controls;

(b) for each managed syndicate, there is a written underwriting policy and/or underwriting procedures which are reviewed annually;

(c) underwriting practice is aligned to the strategy, approved business plan and underwriting policy/procedures, and takes account of pricing levels, updated aggregate exposures and reinsurance arrangements;

(d) underwriters have the appropriate experience and capabilities to write and manage policies profitably in line with the approved business plan, and to provide a good service to customers across the lifecycle;

(e) underwriters' terms of reference/authorities are in writing, properly authorised, signed and reviewed annually, and are aligned to the syndicate business plan;

(f) risks that are outside of an underwriter's agreed level of authority are referred to an appropriate individual;

(g) there are requirements for leaders to undertake pre-bind contract reviews (including checks on contract certainty, regulatory and Lloyd's advisory rules) on all risks that they lead;

(h) there are appropriate procedures and resources for review and agreement of contract wordings;

(i) there is regular review of the expertise and quality of advice given by external experts (eg, technical engineers, surveyors) used to inform underwriting decisions; and

(j) underwriting addresses external regulatory requirements.

As regards delegated underwriting in particular, where underwriting authority is delegated to a third party (eg, coverholders, or leaders of lineslips and consortia), managing agents must ensure that business written on their behalf and/or on behalf of others is profitable and proactively managed and controlled in line with their underwriting policy and procedures. Managing agents must ensure that:

(a) they have the capabilities necessary to assess the terms of the delegated authority contract and the prospects of the business that will be underwritten on their behalf to ensure alignment with their risk appetite and approved business plan;

(b) any authority granted to a third party regarding pricing, coverage and risk selection is fully aligned with the syndicate's own underwriting philosophy regarding capabilities and experience;

(c) when leading, they maintain an open and proactive engagement with the coverholder/broker to ensure that performance issues are addressed quickly and underwriting philosophies remain aligned;

(d) risk and exposure information is sufficiently detailed, allowing for robust segmental performance monitoring, analysis and challenge; and

(e) there is complete transparency and timely disclosure of any known potential conflicts of interest between leaders and followers at the commencement of the delegated authority contract.

There is also a Lloyd's Code of Practice – Delegated Authority, which highlights the main risks associated with delegating authority and provides practical guidance to help manage such risks, covering the assessment of new coverholders; the production and provision of contracts for delegating authority; the monitoring of contracts of delegation; and the cancellation or non-renewal of such contracts.

Delegated underwriting agreements will also be subject to the Solvency II rules on critical and important outsourcing which are set out in the PRA Rules and the on-shored UK Solvency II Regulation (art 275). Chapter 13 of the FCA's Senior Management Arrangements, Systems and Controls Sourcebook also provides guidance in relation to outsourcing more generally. In addition, the FCA has undertaken a thematic review in relation to delegated underwriting agreements in the insurance market. It has provided guidance in relation to the need to exercise effective supervision and control of delegated underwriting arrangements (especially where they involve sub-delegation), including through appropriate management information and review of customer outcomes (especially relating to pricing).

UNDERWRITING AGENCIES AND REINSURANCE POOLS

10.04 Much reinsurance business is conducted through reinsurance pools, the business being negotiated on behalf of the pool participants by an underwriting agent. The role of the underwriting agent acting for the pool will vary from case to case. Sometimes the agent is only the conduit for the passing of reinsurance business to the pool participants. In the majority of cases, however, the agent is given authority by the pool participant to accept risks on its behalf or on behalf of one or more pool participants.

Since the underwriting agent is, in effect, exercising its own discretion on behalf of the pool members, the contract for the appointment by the pool members of the underwriting agent gives rise to a duty of disclosure by the underwriting agent (*John W Pryke v Gibbs Hartley Cooper Ltd* [1991] 1 Lloyd's Rep 602). An underwriting agent that enters into agreements on behalf of the pool principals without disclosing this may sue and be sued on those agreements in its own name, unless it is made clear that the underwriting agent is acting purely as an agent for the principal (*Ernest Scragg & Sons Ltd v Perseverance Banking and Trust Co Ltd* [1973] 2 Lloyd's Rep 101).

Underwriting agent's authority

10.05 The relationship between the underwriting agent and its principal is governed by the agency agreement.

The extent of the agent's actual authority will be defined by any express agreement between the parties and will be a matter of the construction of the agreement. In addition to any express authority, the underwriting agent will have implied authority to do whatever is necessary in order to comply with its duties. The scope of the agent's authority will also be judged according to any trade practice or usage of the particular market in which the agent is operating. Any implied term must not, however, conflict with the express terms of the agency agreement.

The underwriting agent may also bind its principal to the extent of any apparent or ostensible authority. Third parties are, therefore, entitled to rely on any act of an underwriting agent if it is within the scope of the agent's usual authority.

If the underwriting agent exceeds its authority, its principal can ratify the actions of the agent. If the principal does not wish to ratify any act of the agent, it should make this clear to the third party as soon as possible.

An underwriting agent cannot, in the absence of express or implied authority from its principal, delegate its authority to a third party or appoint a sub-agent to perform any act within the scope of its authority. The agent must perform its fiduciary duties to its principal.

In the event of an underwriting agent both acting as an agent for a buyer of insurance by broking an insurance policy to that customer and acting as an agent for the insurer in relation to any claim made under that policy, the ICOBS rules provide that the agent must inform the customer that it is acting on behalf of the insurer in relation to that claim. The ICOBS rules require the underwriting agent to avoid conflicts of interest of this type unless it can manage them by disclosing them to, and obtaining the informed consent of, its customer.

Underwriting agent's duties

10.06 The agency agreement will usually deal with the duties of the agent. Clear underwriting guidelines should be given to the agent, whether orally or in writing.

An underwriting agent is likely to be negligent if it does not act in accordance with the basic principles of insurance; for example, it must ensure that it has spread any risk to its principal. It must also act with the reasonable skill and care expected of an underwriting agent.

An underwriting agent also has an implied duty (if the agreement does not so provide) to prepare and maintain records of the business written, the premium income received and the claims history. It is also common practice to find a clause in the agency agreement whereby the principal has the right to inspect the books and records maintained by the agent.

The agent also has an obligation not to act in furtherance of its own interests over those of its principal. In *Julien Praet et Cie, S/A v H G Poland Ltd* [1960] 1 Lloyd's Rep 420, which involved a motor insurance binder given by a Lloyd's syndicate to a Belgian insurance broker, the broker terminated the binder and offered to the insureds new policies with another Lloyd's syndicate on the expiration of their current policies. The court held that the broker was not entitled to terminate the existing policies as this interfered with the contractual rights of the parties to the policies and was contrary to the interests of the underwriters.

Where an underwriting agent is authorised by the FCA to carry on regulated activities relating to insurance, the underwriting agent is under a duty to comply with the FCA Rules and Handbook.

Chapter 11

Lloyd's

- History and structure
- Regulation of Lloyd's
- The course of business at Lloyd's
- Payment obligations at Lloyd's

HISTORY AND STRUCTURE

11.01 Lloyd's of London began life as a coffee house owned by Edward Lloyd in the seventeenth century. It proved a popular meeting place for merchants and rapidly became the focus for the underwriting of marine insurance policies. Lloyd's developed rapidly and by 1696 had begun to publish *Lloyd's News*, which gave details of marine casualties and which may be regarded as the forerunner of *Lloyd's List*. Lloyd's is now located in Lime Street in the City of London. More recently, fundamental changes in the structure of Lloyd's have occurred, as a result of the many challenges faced by the market.

Underwriting takes place at Lloyd's through syndicates. A 'syndicate', which is not a legal entity, comprises one or more capital providers – traditionally known as 'Names' – grouped together for one year of account at a time for the purpose of underwriting. Up to the end of 1993, Lloyd's Names were solely comprised of individuals who had unlimited liability in respect of their Lloyd's underwriting liabilities. As a response to the substantial losses suffered by Names in the 1980s and early 1990s, in January 1994 Lloyd's permitted companies (and, subsequently, certain limited partnerships) to become members of Lloyd's. Individual members have not been permitted to join Lloyd's on an unlimited liability basis since 2003. Members are generally assisted through the admission process and their subsequent activities at Lloyd's by a members' agent.

Another response to the serious losses of the 1980s was the creation of a reinsurance company called Equitas. The purpose of this company was to ring fence the 1992 and prior years' liabilities of Names through reinsurance of these liabilities. This allowed Lloyd's to trade forward without the burden of dealing with these earlier years.

Lloyd's syndicates operate on a year of account basis which is 'closed' (allowing the profit or loss for that year of account to be determined) and paid to or by members of that syndicate by a reinsurance to close after three years. Ordinarily a syndicate year of account would close into the next year of account of that same syndicate. If it is not possible to evaluate a premium for the reinsurance to close, then the relevant year of account may be left 'open'. A market has developed in recent years for specialist third-party managing agents to offer reinsurance to close solutions to Lloyd's businesses, either where the underlying syndicate has ceased accepting business or where it wishes to cease to have responsibility for one or more prior years of account.

The members of the syndicate are passive investors and all decision making is delegated to the managing agent of the syndicate (appointed by the members). Each managing agent must employ an 'active underwriter' which has responsibility for the syndicate's underwriting activities. Managing agents must be approved by the Council of Lloyd's, as well as the Prudential Regulation Authority (PRA). A managing agent may run more than one syndicate, but will need to satisfy conflict of interest requirements. The interests of members are protected by members' agents, whose function is to ensure that the investment in Lloyd's made by a member is spread appropriately among suitable syndicates, and that the funds provided by members are to be used for genuine underwriting purposes (*Boobyer v David Holman & Co Ltd (No 2)* [1993] 1 Lloyd's Rep 96; *Brown v KMR Services Ltd, Sword-Daniels v Michael Pitel* [1995] 2 Lloyd's Rep 513). Some members (which, with Lloyd's permission, have not engaged a members' agent) contract directly with managing agents, while those with a members' agent deal with managing agents through such members' agent. It was held by the House of Lords in *Arbuthnott v Feltrim* [1995] CLC 437 that a managing agent (whether or not it has a direct contract with the member) owes a duty of care to each member of the syndicate which it manages in respect of the underwriting activities of those syndicates.

The Society of Lloyd's itself is immune from suit by members unless bad faith can be established (s 14 of the Lloyd's Act 1982, as applied in *Ashmore v Corp of Lloyd's (No 2)* [1992] 2 Lloyd's Rep 620). The Society and Corporation of Lloyd's is a body of individual underwriters incorporated by statute and authorised by its constitution to exercise supervisory, regulatory and disciplinary powers over (among others) its members. It has been held that the Society of Lloyd's does not exercise public functions and thus is not susceptible to judicial review proceedings brought by members (*R v Lloyd's of London, ex p Briggs* [1993] 1 Lloyd's Rep 176), which was approved in *R (on the application of West) v Lloyd's of London* [2004] Lloyd's Rep IR 755 (but see **11.5** for the contrasting position of the Disciplinary Committee).

Lloyd's underwriters do not deal directly with the general public and all negotiations for insurance are conducted only with appropriately authorised intermediaries.

The Council of Lloyd's is the governing body of the Society. The Council and the Franchise Board were merged in June 2020 to form a single governing Council as a result of the Future at Lloyd's work. The Council is made up of 15 members, six nominated members, six members elected by the market and three executives.

As a result of Brexit, Lloyd's has established an authorised subsidiary, Lloyd's Insurance Company S.A., located in Brussels, Belgium in order to continue to write risks and pay claims within the European Economic Area (EEA). As an EU entity, the Brussels company benefits from the EU passport and so can write and service risk across the EEA. Any risks underwritten by Lloyd's Insurance Company S.A. are wholly reinsured into the applicable Lloyd's syndicate which, through an EEA intermediary or an underwriter seconded to Lloyd's Insurance Company S.A. for such purpose, originated the risk.

REGULATION OF LLOYD'S

11.02 The Lloyd's regulatory framework is governed partly by the Lloyd's Act 1982 and the Financial Services and Markets Act 2000 (FSMA 2000). The Lloyd's Act 1982 established the Council of Lloyd's, which performs a statutory role in relation to the legal and disciplinary functions of Lloyd's. There are a large number of byelaws, market bulletins, regulations, guidelines and codes of practice governing the entire conduct of business at Lloyd's. The Council also, critically, sets Minimum Standards (as to which see below). The Minimum Standards are expected to be replaced with Lloyd's new 'Project Rio' principles (see **11.3**).

The regulation of Lloyd's was reviewed during the consultation that led to the introduction of the FSMA 2000. Although under the FSMA 2000, much of the previous self-regulatory regime remains, the PRA also regulates managing agents and the Financial Conduct Authority (FCA) regulates conduct requirements. However, Lloyd's retains responsibility for Lloyd's members and has its own investigation and disciplinary powers for suspected breaches of its own byelaws and rules.

Both the PRA and the FCA have entered into cooperation agreements with the Society of Lloyd's, replacing two earlier cooperation agreements entered into between the Financial Services Authority and the Society in December 2001 and August 2007. The cooperation agreement entered into between the PRA and the Society sets out how both bodies envisage working together and covers such things as the role and responsibilities of the PRA and the Society; information sharing and confidentiality; authorisations relevant to managing agents; and disciplinary proceedings. The agreement also covers the supervision of the Society by the PRA. The cooperation agreement entered into between the FCA and the Society sets out arrangements to ensure an effective working relationship on 'matters of mutual regulatory interest' and covers principles of cooperation, confidentiality, authorisations, supervision and legal intervention.

Part XIX, ss 314–324 of the FSMA 2000 govern the regulation by the PRA and FCA of the Lloyd's market. Part XIX makes the Society of Lloyd's an 'authorised person' (see **44.01**). Members of Lloyd's, however, are not authorised persons. The Society is treated as having a Part 4A permission – but importantly, its Part 4A permission, is not permission to effect and/ or carry out insurance contracts. It is to carry on the following kinds of regulated activity:

(a) arranging deals in contracts of insurance written at Lloyd's (the 'basic market activity');

(b) arranging deals in participation in Lloyd's syndicates (the 'secondary market activity'); and

(c) activities carried on in connection with, or for the purposes of, the basic or secondary market activity.

The FSMA 2000 gives the PRA and the FCA certain powers to direct the affairs of the Society, its members and managing and members' agents. In general terms, the FSMA 2000 allows Lloyd's to self-regulate, although the regulators retain powers to ensure that Lloyd's regulatory approach is consistent with that of the broader UK regulatory environment. The regulators' general duty is to keep themselves informed about the way in which the Council of Lloyd's self-regulates the market and to keep under review the desirability of exercising their powers in relation to Lloyd's.

The regulators will intervene, having regard to the interests of existing and potential policyholders, where the Society of Lloyd's may have failed to satisfy any obligations under the byelaws and regulations governing its business.

Before a regulator intervenes with the regulation of Lloyd's, it must issue an insurance market direction to the Council, the Society or both. After publication of a draft direction, the FSMA 2000 provides for a period of consultation and thereafter for publication of the relevant regulator's response to the consultative process and the final direction. Under s 316 of the FSMA 2000, either the PRA or FCA may give insurance market directions which enable either regulator to direct that the general prohibition in s 19 of the FSMA 2000 does apply to a member of Lloyd's or members taken together, or that certain parts of the FSMA 2000 will apply to a member or members.

Managing agents

11.03 Managing agents must also comply with the requirements imposed on them by the Society, including under the Underwriting Byelaw (No. 2 of 2003). In particular, they must meet the standards set out by the Council and follow the requirements in the Lloyd's Minimum Standards, which cover the following:

(a) MS1: Business planning and portfolio management;

(b) MS2: Underwriting and controls;

(c) MS3. Price and rate monitoring;

(d) MS4: Governance;

(e) MS5: Risk management;

(f) MS6: Exposure management;

(g) MS7: Reinsurance management and control;

(h) MS8: Reserving;

(i) MS9: Customer;

(j) MS10: Regulatory;

(k) MS11: Cyber resilience and data management;

(l) MS12: Scope, change and use;

(m) MS13: Modelling, design and implementation;

(n) MS14: Validation; and

(o) MS15: Investment management.

As noted above, at the time of writing the Minimum Standards are expected to be replaced with Lloyd's new 'Project Rio' principles but the final timetable for this has not yet been announced.

Pursuant to s 55B of and Sch 6 to the FSMA 2000, managing agents must satisfy the statutory conditions and must be 'fit and proper' to conduct regulated activities, and management must have adequate skills and experience and have acted and may be expected to act with probity. They are also subject to the Senior Managers and Certifications Regime. This means that persons performing certain specified senior management functions in the managing agency must seek prior approval to do so from the relevant regulator (see **42.11**).

Pursuant to the PRA Rulebook, managing agents are required to ensure that the financial resources for each syndicate managed by them are adequate; that the capital resources held at syndicate level are adequate; and that they establish and maintain systems and controls for the management of prudential, credit, market, operational and insurance risks affecting each of the syndicates they manage.

Managing agents must also carry out a notional syndicate-level calculation of the applicable solvency capital requirement (SCR), which is supervised by Lloyd's and is used by Lloyd's in its member-level capital-setting process. Lloyd's is required to calculate an SCR for the entire market, but calculates this on the basis of each syndicate's notional SCR.

Lloyd's brokers

11.04 Lloyd's still registers brokers and there are a number of perceived advantages to registering, including the ability to enter into a terms of business agreement with any Lloyd's managing agent. Non-registered brokers are required to be separately assessed by each managing agent with which they intend to do business against Lloyd's Minimum Standards. Registration as a Lloyd's broker is subject to the broker successfully satisfying Lloyd's registration requirements and completing the application process.

All UK intermediaries carrying on regulated activities (see **Chapter 9**) in relation to Lloyd's policies are required to be authorised by the FCA.

Challenging the imposition of fines or suspension

11.05 Any member of Lloyd's that is accused of infringing rules of conduct is subject to disciplinary proceedings before the Disciplinary Committee, which has the power to impose fines and, ultimately, to suspend membership. There is an appeal from these proceedings to the Appeal Tribunal, except where the Disciplinary Committee has imposed a fixed penalty. Lloyd's disciplinary proceedings are subject to challenge by way of judicial review (*R v Committee of Lloyd's, ex p Moran, The Times,*

24 June 1983; *R v Committee of Lloyd's, ex p Posgate, The Times*, 12 January 1983).

THE COURSE OF BUSINESS AT LLOYD'S

The Lloyd's slip

11.06 Insurance at Lloyd's is normally initiated by the preparation of a 'slip' by the broker. Some business, however, such as personal lines, may be commenced by proposal terms. The slip sets out the details of the risk and proposes the terms upon which the risk is to be accepted. Following market reform, this should now follow the appropriate standard market format (see **1.15**). The slip is then presented by the broker to an underwriter who is known to specialise in insurance of the class sought. If the leading underwriter is prepared to accept the risk, he will execute the slip on behalf of his syndicate for a given amount and thereby bind his syndicate to accept the stated part of the risk. The broker will then present the slip to underwriters acting on behalf of other syndicates, and by this process will seek to obtain full coverage of the risk. The number of syndicates involved in a particular risk will vary. To expedite this procedure, syndicates may authorise one particular syndicate to bind them up to given financial limits in respect of risks of a particular type. This type of authority, known as a 'lineslip', means that a broker can obtain a substantial proportion of the required cover by obtaining the subscription of an underwriter administering a lineslip.

Once the slip has been fully subscribed, unless otherwise stated, it will not be replaced by a detailed policy.

Risks can also be written by way of:

(a) consortia arrangements, whereby authority is granted to a consortia leader by the followers to be able to apply a single stamp that binds all consortia members. A consortium will underwrite and bind specified classes of business produced from more than one broker – which is the main difference from a line slip; and

(b) coverholder arrangements, whereby a company or partnership is authorised by a managing agent to enter into contracts of insurance to be underwritten by the members of a syndicate managed by it and issue insurance documents as evidence that contracts of insurance have been accepted in accordance with the terms of a binding authority arrangement.

Binding nature of a slip

11.07 As soon as an underwriter executes a slip, he creates a binding contract between the member(s) of the relevant syndicate and the insured for the sum specified by the underwriter. As the slip progresses and more underwriters subscribe to it, further contracts are made. By the time the slip is fully subscribed, therefore, it will amount to a composite document evidencing a series of individual contracts with the insured. This method of contract formation gives rise to a number of issues:

(a) If a slip is not fully subscribed and the broker is unable to obtain any further subscriptions, neither the insured nor the subscribing underwriters can withdraw from the contract unless there is some mutual agreement to this effect (*General Reinsurance Corp v Forsakringsaktiebolaget Fennia Patria* [1983] 2 Lloyd's Rep 287).

(b) If the leading underwriter has executed the slip on its original terms and following underwriters insist upon new terms, the leading underwriter cannot claim the benefit of the new terms.

(c) If a loss occurs prior to full subscription and the subscribing underwriters are on risk, those underwriters who have subscribed are liable.

(d) The insured owes a duty of utmost good faith to each subscribing underwriter separately (*Bank Leumi Le Israel BM v British National Insurance Co Ltd* [1988] 1 Lloyd's Rep 71). A failure to comply with the duty to make a fair presentation of the risk by the insured to a leading underwriter may be relied upon by a following underwriter only where it is established that the following underwriters, in executing the slip, would have relied on the leader's acceptance as having been procured through a proper presentation when they agreed to subscribe to the contract themselves (*Aneco Reinsurance Underwriting Ltd (In Liquidation) v Johnson & Higgins Ltd* [2001] UKHL 51).

Oversubscription

11.08 The only situation in which the execution of a slip may be varied unilaterally is where the broker has obtained over 100 per cent subscription to the slip. Oversubscription is of little use to the insured, as he can never recover more than an indemnity. A custom has arisen at Lloyd's – which is not explained in the slip itself and which was given judicial approval in *General Accident Fire and Life Assurance Corp v Tanter, 'The Zephyr'* [1985] 2 Lloyd's Rep 529 – whereby the subscriptions of the underwriters can be signed down proportionately, giving no more than 100 per cent cover. This case further decides that a broker who indicates to the leading underwriter that he intends to seek oversubscription from the market, and thereby induces the leading underwriter to accept a greater liability than he would otherwise have done, is under a duty to use his best endeavours to obtain the level of oversubscription specified so that the leading underwriter is not left overexposed. A signing down indication given to the leading underwriter alone is not, however, deemed to have been made to the following market, so that subsequent underwriters who rely on the conduct of the leading underwriter in accepting a greater initial exposure will have no remedy against the broker.

Effect of the issue of a policy

Relationship with the slip

11.09 As the slip constitutes a binding contract between the insured and the underwriters, if a policy is issued it should not contradict what is in the slip. If there is inconsistency between the two documents, the insured is entitled to seek rectification of the policy so that it accords with the original agreement. It is unclear whether the underwriters can seek rectification, for it was held in *Eagle Star Insurance Co v Spratt* [1971] 2 Lloyd's Rep 116 that the Lloyd's Policy Signing Office was the authorised agent of the underwriters. If, therefore, the policy gives the insured a concession which was not contained in the slip, the underwriters are probably bound by the more generous terms of the policy.

While a slip may be used to rectify a policy, it cannot generally be used as evidence in any dispute as to the meaning of policy wording; although the terms of the slip may well be relevant to the factual matrix against which the policy will be construed. If the policy is unclear, generally courts seek to ascertain its meaning without reference to the slip (*Youell v Bland Welch and Co Ltd* [1992] 2 Lloyd's Rep 127). However, in certain circumstances – for example, where the slip contains a fundamental term of the insurance whereas the policy wording is silent – it may be held that the slip has not in fact superseded the policy wording, as so may be used as evidence of the contract terms (*HIH Casualty and General Insurance Ltd v New Hampshire Insurance Co Ltd* [2001] 2 Lloyd's Rep 161).

Composite nature

11.10 Like a slip, a Lloyd's policy, when issued, is a composite contract between the insured and the several syndicates subscribing to the policy. In *Touche Ross & Co v Baker (Colin)* [1992] 2 Lloyd's Rep 207, a Lloyd's liability policy issued to accountants provided that if it was not renewed, cover would nevertheless be provided in respect of events which had occurred during the currency of the policy (the 'discovery extension' clause). One underwriter of those subscribing decided not to renew and argued that he was not bound by the discovery extension clause, as that clause could operate only if there had been a collective decision not to renew. The House of Lords held that the discovery extension clause bound each underwriter individually, so that any one underwriter who refused to renew could not evade his obligations under the clause.

PAYMENT OBLIGATIONS AT LLOYD'S

Premiums

11.11 The FCA's insurance client money rules (in its Client Assets Sourcebook (CASS)) will apply to Lloyd's brokers and other intermediaries that arrange or sell Lloyd's policies. The regulatory requirements relating to brokers holding monies on behalf of insurers or as client money are set out in **Chapter 5**. However, the insurance client money rules do not apply to managing agents in acting as such (CASS 5.1.1). Premiums are held in premium trust funds established by members. Members also provide funds at Lloyd's to cover potential losses.

Losses

11.12 The Lloyd's market operates a net accounting system, under which premiums and losses are paid centrally for each accounting period.

Chapter 12

Insurance companies

- Types of insurance company
- Restrictions on insurance business
- Financial regulation and governance

TYPES OF INSURANCE COMPANY

12.01 Traditionally, in many insurance markets, including the UK, many of the original providers of insurance were mutual insurance societies owned by their policyholders rather than shareholders. In the UK, many were established by individual Acts of Parliament. Today in the UK, there are a mixture of mutual and proprietary insurance companies plus the Lloyd's market (which is a subscription market and not an insurance company). One of the interesting development in recent years has been new entrants to the market and, in particular, digital platforms looking to use mutual company structures to facilitate product innovation.

RESTRICTIONS ON INSURANCE BUSINESS

12.02 Insurance companies need to be authorised under the Financial Services and Markets Act 2000 (FSMA 2000) in order to carry on regulated activities in relation to insurance (see **Chapter 42**). Some insurance companies only write, and are only authorised to write, general insurance risk. Some only write long-term (life) insurance risk. There are also composite companies that write both. Since 1 March 1979, it has not been possible to set up new composite insurance companies. This restriction is now implemented into the rules of the Prudential Regulation Authority (PRA) for Solvency II firms in the Composites Part of its rules for Solvency II firms. It reflects the position under art 73 of the Solvency II Directive 2009/138/EU, which provides that insurance undertakings shall not be authorised to pursue life and non-life insurance activities simultaneously. There are some exceptions to this rule, in that life companies are permitted to carry on accident and sickness (class 1 and 2) general insurance business on a supplementary basis to their life business and general insurance companies can similarly carry on certain other classes of general insurance business on a supplementary basis, but not any life business (other than accidental death, which is a class of general business). However, where composite companies do carry on both general and life business, each activity must be separately managed. This requirement is reflected both in the way the businesses must be run and in the way they calculate their solvency requirements and produce regulatory reporting.

The rule against new composites does not apply to pure reinsurers, which are only authorised to write reinsurance business. The provisions do, however, apply in relation to Lloyd's business (via restrictions on managing agents (see **Chapter 11**).

12.03 Insurance and reinsurance business activities are regulated under the FSMA 2000 by reference to the activities of effecting and carrying out contract of insurance as principal. The classes of insurance business for which they are authorised are then reflected as 'investments' (due to terminology used under the FSMA 2000). It is possible to check the classes of business for which an insurer is authorised on the Financial Services Register. The classes are set out in Part I (general) and Part II (life) of Schedule 1 to the Financial Services and Markets Act 2000 (Regulated Activities) Order 2001/544 ('RAO').

Internal contagion

12.04 Insurance companies are required to restrict their commercial activities to their insurance business and activities directly arising therefrom. A similar restriction applies in relation to pure reinsurers, but the restriction is to reinsurance business and related operations. These restrictions are now to be found in the PRA Rules for Solvency II firms, Conditions Governing Business Part, r 9.1 (and r 9.2 for pure reinsurers). They implement Article 18(1) (a) of the Solvency II Directive. There is no definition of either 'directly arising' or 'related' operations. Previous Financial Conduct Authority (FCA) guidance indicated that activities directly arising from insurance business could include investing the insurer's assets and employing staff and for pure reinsurers that:

> 'related operations include, for example, activities such as provision of statistical or actuarial advice, risk analysis or research for its clients. It may also include a holding company function and activities with respect to financial sector activities within the meaning of Article 2, point 8, of the Financial Groups Directive. But it does not allow the carrying on of, for example, unrelated banking and financial activities.'

There is, however, a judgment of the European Court of Justice in relation to the underlying directive requirements in the context of the 'commercial business' point. *Association Basco-Béarnaise des Opticien Independants v Préfet des Pyrenees-Atlantique* (ECJC 109/99) related to whether a not-for-profit joint venture of two insurers providing the services of an optician constituted the carrying on of 'commercial activities'. The court held that the nature of the activities, rather than whether they were carried on for profit, determined whether they constituted a commercial business. The judgment makes the point that the 'mischief' of the rule limiting an insurer's activities is to ensure that the insurer's assets are available to pay its insurance liabilities, and that other activities do not expose it to the risk of having to use those assets for other purposes.

Any non-insurance business which is permitted within this restriction (ie, which 'directly arises' from its insurance business) should be limited, controlled and managed so that it does not lead to any significant risk that the firm might be unable to meet its liabilities as they fall due. In quantifying this risk, a firm should consider how likely it is that financial risk from this type of business could diverge from expectations.

FINANCIAL REGULATION AND GOVERNANCE

12.05 UK insurers are subject to regulation by the PRA and the FCA. The PRA regulates prudential issues (eg, financial condition and governance), and the FCA regulates conduct (eg, sales and fair treatment of customers).

Most UK insurers, other than those whose premiums or assets do not meet a minimum threshold, are regulated for prudential purposes under the Solvency II Directive as implemented in the UK via the PRA Rules for Solvency II firms and the on-shored UK Solvency II Regulation. Solvency II firms will be insurers other than those that fulfil all of the following conditions:

(a) The firm's annual gross written premium income does not exceed €5 million;

(b) The total of the firm's technical provisions, gross of the amounts recoverable from reinsurance contracts and UK insurance special purpose vehicles (ISPVs), does not exceed €25 million;

(c) Where the firm belongs to a group, the total of the technical provisions of the group – defined as gross of the amounts recoverable from reinsurance contracts and UK ISPVs – does not exceed €25 million;

(d) The business of the firm does not include insurance or reinsurance activities covering liability, credit and suretyship insurance risks, unless they constitute ancillary risks; and

(e) The business of the firm does not include reinsurance operations:

    (i) exceeding:

        (A) €500,000 of its gross written premium income; or

        (B) €2.5 million of its technical provisions gross of the amounts recoverable from reinsurance contracts and UK ISPVs; or

    (ii) with more than 10 per cent of its gross written premium income or more than 10 per cent of its technical provisions gross of the amounts recoverable from reinsurance contracts and UK ISPVs.

The Solvency II requirements detail how an insurance company should manage its business, invest its assets and calculate its liability position and its reserves. They also require insurers to calculate and hold a risk-based capital amount. There are also a significant reporting requirements for Solvency II firms (see **Chapter 42**).

Part 3

The Claim

Chapter 13

Causation

- Proximate cause
- Sequential causes of loss
- Concurrent causes of loss
- Mitigation
- Insured's negligence
- Alternative policy formations

PROXIMATE CAUSE

13.01 The insurer is liable only for those losses proximately caused by an insured peril (Marine Insurance Act 1906, s 55(2)(a)), and it is for the insured to prove that his loss was so caused. If the policy is all risks – meaning that the insured's burden is simply to demonstrate that he has suffered a loss – the insurer can escape liability by demonstrating that the loss was proximately caused by an uninsured peril.

SEQUENTIAL CAUSES OF LOSS

13.02 Causation is a crucial matter, but it is not possible to lay down any single test for ascertaining the proximate cause of a loss where there has been a series of contributing factors. Each case must turn on its own facts. The most difficulty is occasioned by cases in which there are two operative and interacting events occurring sequentially. The law does not accept that the last event is necessarily the proximate cause of the loss, and a court might take the view that the earlier event was the start of an unbroken chain of events leading to the loss. The cases fall into three general classes: unbroken chain of events, broken chain of events and linked events.

Unbroken chain of events

13.03 In this type of case, the first peril to occur is bound ultimately to lead to a loss, and the occurrence of the second peril is simply the inevitable or other means by which that loss occurs. The position may be illustrated by *Reischer v Borwick* [1894] 2 QB 548, in which a vessel was holed following a collision and was lost due to the ingress of water. The court held that the proximate cause of the loss was collision, and that the ingress of water was an inevitable consequence of the collision.

Broken chain of events

13.04 Perhaps the best illustrations of this situation are provided by a series of wartime marine cases in which a vessel, seeking to avoid enemy submarines, deviated from its course and was lost in bad weather – for example, *Yorkshire Dale Steamship Co Ltd, Appellants v Minister of War Transport, Respondent* [1942] AC 691. In those cases, the proximate cause of loss was clearly perils of the sea, and not war risks.

Linked events

13.05 The most complex cases are those in which the first and second perils are equally efficient in their operation, in the sense that the loss would not have taken place had just one of the perils occurred. The decided cases can be difficult to apply in practice. In *Leyland Shipping Co Ltd, Appellants v Norwich Union Fire Insurance Society, Ltd Respondents* [1918] AC 350, the insured's vessel was holed by a torpedo and put into the port of Le Havre for repairs. The port authorities refused to allow the vessel to berth, as storms were expected and the authorities feared that the vessel would sink in the port's vicinity. The vessel left port and was subsequently lost outside the vicinity of the port in a storm. The House of Lords held that the proximate cause of the loss was war risks and not perils of the sea, as the storm had not broken the chain of causation. Similar results were reached in a serious of accident policy cases, of which *Mardorf v Accident Insurance Co* [1903] 1 KB 584 is typical. In this case, the insured under an accident policy was accidentally scratched; the wound became infected and resulted in blood poisoning, from which the insured died. The cause of death was held to be the accidental scratch, and not natural causes.

These cases may be contrasted with two other accident policy claims. In *Winspear v The Accident Insurance Company, Limited* (1880-81) LR 6 QBD 42, the insured suffered a fit, which caused him to fall into a river and drown. It was held that his death was proximately caused by accidental drowning rather than by the natural cause of the fit. A similar decision was reached soon afterwards in *Lawrence v The Accidental Insurance Co (Ltd)* (1880-81) LR 7 QBD 216, where the insured's fit led to him falling onto a railway line in front of a train.

CONCURRENT CAUSES OF LOSS

13.06 A loss may be attributable to two events working chronologically alongside each other. Here, the issue is not whether the chain of causation from one event has been broken by the second event, but rather which of the two events is the greater contributor to the loss. This is again a question of fact in every case. It may not always be possible for the court to disentangle the causes, in which case it must conclude that the loss has been proximately caused by two concurrent causes.

Such a finding is of little significance for the insured where the concurrent causes consist of an insured peril and a peril which is not specifically excluded under the policy, as the rule here is that the uninsured peril is disregarded. In *JJ Lloyd Instruments Ltd v Northern Star Insurance Co Ltd*

[1987] 1 Lloyd's Rep 32, the insured's vessel, which was unseaworthy, was lost in bad weather. As the vessel was insured under a time policy, there was no warranty of seaworthiness under s 39(1) of the Marine Insurance Act 1906, and the insurer was unable to rely upon s 39(5) of that Act (which provides a defence under a time policy where a loss is attributable to seaworthiness) because he had been unaware of the unseaworthy state of his vessel (see Chapter 35). The Court of Appeal was thus faced with a situation in which there were concurrent perils operating: perils of the sea (an insured peril); and unseaworthiness (an uninsured, but not excluded peril). The insured was held to be able to recover, as he had proved that his loss had been proximately caused by an insured peril.

A finding that a loss has concurrent causes is, however, fatal to the insured's claim if the loss caused by one of those two perils is specifically excluded under the policy. In *Wayne Tank and Pump Co Ltd v Employers Liability Assurance Corporation Ltd* [1974] QB 57, the insured installed into premises belonging to a third party equipment for storing and cooling wax. The equipment malfunctioned, causing a disastrous fire, for which the insured was held to be liable to the third party on two grounds:

(a) Unsuitable material had been used in the manufacture of the equipment; and

(b) The insured had failed to carry out proper monitoring tests.

The insured's liability policy covered the second of these risks, but specifically excluded 'damage caused by the nature or condition of any goods', the first of the risks. The Court of Appeal held that the proximate cause of the loss was the condition of the equipment, so that the insured was unable to recover. However, the Court of Appeal went on to suggest that, even had it not been possible to distinguish the two causes of loss, thereby rendering them concurrent causes, the insured would also have failed to recover. The reason was that if a loss is caused proximately by the interaction of an insured risk and an excluded risk, the exclusion takes priority.

This principle was applied by the Court of Appeal in *Midland Mainline Ltd v Eagle Star Insurance Co Ltd* [2004] 2 Lloyd's Rep 604 and by the Supreme Court in *Navigators Insurance Company Limited and others v Atlasnavios-Navegacao LDA* [2018] UK SC 26.

In the first case, following a rail disaster which had been caused by a rail fracturing, restrictions were imposed by the rail network operator on other parts of the railway network where it was known that the rails were also suffering from stress fatigue. The claimant, a train operating company, had an insurance policy covering business interruption losses, but excluding liability for losses arising from wear and tear. The Court of Appeal held that there were two concurrent causes of the loss – wear and tear and the imposition of emergency speed restrictions – and applied the rule that in cases of concurrent causes, any specific exclusion prevailed over the cover. Therefore, the insurer could rely upon the exception.

In the second case, the Venezuelan authorities had found drugs attached to the hull of a vessel, placed there by an unknown third party. The vessel owner served a notice of abandonment, giving rise to a constructive total loss. The vessel owner's insurance policy contained an exclusion for loss arising from 'detainment…by reason of infringement of any customs or regulations'. The Supreme Court held that if there had been a loss caused by an insured peril, it would have been excluded, as the principle in *Wayne Tank* would nevertheless have applied.

Finally, the rules on concurrent causation received significant attention in *The FCA v Arch & Others* [2021] UKSC 1 – the Supreme Court's judgment in the FCA test case relating to Covid-19 business interruption insurance. One of the issues considered by the Supreme Court was whether business interruption insurance policies providing cover for occurrences of disease within a specified radius were triggered where the business closures were caused by multiple nationwide occurrences of Covid-19, prompting lockdown measures. The Supreme Court analysed the existing case law on concurrent causes, observing that it generally concerned two interdependent causes, where the losses would not have happened without both causes being present. It then extended the existing principles to multiple causes which acted in combination, finding that each case of Covid-19 was an individual cause of the UK government introducing lockdown restrictions.

MITIGATION

13.07 As a general principle, the insured has a duty to take steps to avoid or mitigate a loss, and within the policy of insurance this obligation generally takes the form of a reasonable care clause. As noted below, such clauses do not have the effect of preventing recovery when mere negligence by the insured has been involved.

Whether or not the insured is under a duty to take steps to avoid a loss, the fact that it has done so may give rise to causation issues. The general principle is that as long as the insured has acted reasonably, steps taken by him to avert loss by a peril insured against will not prevent recovery, even if the steps taken by the insured resulted in loss from an uninsured peril. This point was made by Kelly CB in *Stanley v The Western Insurance Co* (1867-68) LR 3 Ex 71:

> 'I agree that any loss resulting from an apparently necessary and *bona fide* effort to put out a fire, whether it be by spoiling the goods by water or throwing the article of furniture out of a window, or even the destroying of a neighbouring house by an explosion for the purpose of checking the progress of flames, in a word, every loss that clearly and proximately results, whether directly or indirectly, from the fire, is within the policy.'

This principle was applied by the Court of Appeal in *Symington & Co v Union Insurance Society of Canton, Ltd* (1928) 32 Ll L Rep 287. In this case, a fire broke out at a quay. A quantity of cork was stored on the quay, some of which was doused with water and some of which was thrown into the sea in order to prevent loss by fire. The Court of Appeal held that the water damage to the cork had been proximately caused by fire.

All depends, however, upon the insured having acted reasonably. If the insured, anticipating the occurrence of an insured peril, takes avoidance measures which result in loss by an uninsured peril, the insurer will not be liable if it can be demonstrated that the likelihood of loss from an insured peril was remote in the extreme (see *Kacianoff v China Traders Insurance Co, Ltd* [1914] 3 KB 1121).

INSURED'S NEGLIGENCE

13.08 Negligence by the insured has a neutral effect on his ability to recover. This is stated specifically by s 55(2)(a) of the Marine Insurance Act 1906: '[the insurer] is liable for any loss proximately caused by a peril insured against, even though the loss would not have happened but for the misconduct or negligence of the master or crew.'

The effect of this provision is that negligence is not regarded as a peril in its own right, but merely as the method by which a peril can be brought into existence. The only question, therefore, is whether the peril occasioned by the insured's negligence is an insured or excluded peril. The point is illustrated by *Harris v Poland* [1941] 1 KB 462, in which the insured, for safety reasons, hid her jewellery in a fire grate. She subsequently forgot what she had done and lit a fire, as a result of which the jewellery was lost. The judge, allowing recovery under the insured's householder policy, held that the loss had been caused by the insured peril of fire, and the fact that the loss by fire had resulted from the insured's negligence did not defeat the claim. The position is not affected by a clause requiring the insured to take reasonable care of property, as such a clause has been held to mean no more than that there can be no recovery where the insured has deliberately or recklessly caused the loss.

As a review of cases in this areas demonstrates, there is an implied duty on every insured at common law to take reasonable care of his property and to act as though he was uninsured. Whether an insured has deliberately or recklessly caused the loss will depend upon the factual circumstances of each case. The following cases demonstrate the different factual circumstances that the court will need to consider.

In *Sinnott v Municipal General Insurance* [1989] CLY 2051, the claimant was moving property with a total value of £3,000 from her flat to a house some miles away. She stopped in a city area that she knew had a high incidence of car theft and left her car unattended for 30 minutes while she visited a library. The car was stolen (with the contents) and was never recovered. The insurer argued that the claimant had failed to take 'reasonable precautions'. It was held that the claimant was entitled to recover her insured loss. It would have been otherwise had she left the goods on view in the car (they were in the boot) or had there been an express clause that such goods were not to be left an unattended motor car.

In *Devco Holder Ltd and Burrows & Paine Ltd v Legal & General Assurance Society Ltd* [1993] 2 Lloyd's Rep 567 the claimant company purchased a Ferrari and insured it with the defendant against theft. One of the claimant's employees left the car temporarily unattended in a station car park, with the keys in the ignition, while he went to his office on the first floor of the building opposite the station. The car was stolen and damaged. It was a term of the policy that the claimant take all reasonable steps to protect the car against loss or damage. The question was whether reasonable steps had been taken. The judge found that the employee had not taken reasonable steps by leaving the car unlocked in a public place with the key in the ignition deliberately, rather than inadvertently. The defendant appealed.

It was held, in dismissing the appeal, that:

(a) by deliberately leaving the key in the ignition of a car attractive to thieves, the employee deliberately courted a danger in the breach of the condition;

(b) there was a breach even though the employee underestimated or did not contemplate the risk of theft or thought the absence from the car park would be short; and

(c) (*obiter*) the position might have been different if the keys had been left inadvertently.

In *Sofi v Prudential Assurance Co Ltd* [1993] 2 Lloyd's Rep 559 the insured had a household policy covering theft and a travel policy. Both obliged him to take 'all reasonable steps to safeguard … property'. The claimant decided to take jewellery valued at £42,000 away on holiday, as he had been burgled at home. After a discussion with members of his party, the claimant decided to leave the jewellery locked in the glove compartment of a car for 15 minutes while visiting Dover Castle, the car being in view for most of that time. The car was ransacked and the jewellery and all of the claimant's suitcases were stolen. The insurer argued that the claimant had failed to take reasonable steps and should have taken the jewellery with him or left someone in the car. The judge found in favour of the claimant and the insurer appealed.

It was held, in dismissing the appeal, that:

(a) the burden was on the insurer to prove a breach of the condition;

(b) the correct test was to consider the recklessness on the part of the claimant and there was no distinction between property and liability insurance; and

(c) in applying the test, it was relevant to take into account the value of the goods at risk; but the claimant was not reckless, as he had considered the security position and was not away from the car for a long period.

ALTERNATIVE POLICY FORMATIONS

13.09 The principles of causation outlined in this chapter represent the default position and can be ousted by contrary wording. The policy may, for example, state that the insurer is liable for loss by a particular peril only if that peril is the 'direct and sole' or an 'independent' cause of the loss. This means that the operation of any other peril, even in a minor role, will deprive the insured of an indemnity. The same will follow if the insurer is stated to be discharged from liability where an excluded peril has indirectly caused the loss. Both possibilities are illustrated by *Jason v Batten (1930), Ltd* [1969] 1 Lloyd's Rep 281, in which the insured, who suffered from heart disease, was involved in a motor accident. Six days later, he suffered a heart attack, which disabled him for a year. The insured claimed under his accident policy, which stated that he could recover for disablement sustained in any accident, and independently from all other causes, but that the insurer was not liable for disablement directly or indirectly caused by pre-existing physical defect. Fisher J held for the insurer: while it was the case that the insured's heart attack would not have occurred without the accident, the insured's disablement was not caused independently by the accident; and in any event, the insured's latent medical problem had been an indirect cause of his disablement within the meaning of the exclusion. The advantages to the insurer of a widely phased exclusion are also demonstrated by *Coxe v Employers' Liability Assurance Corporation, Ltd* [1916] 2 KB 629, where the insured's death resulted from being hit by a train during a blackout enforced under wartime regulations. The insurer was held not to be liable under the policy, which excluded death caused directly or indirectly by war risks. Similar wording was also considered in *The FCA v Arch & Others* [2021] UKSC 1; but in that case, the words 'solely and directly' in the relevant clause were found to link the losses with the interruption, and not to link the losses with the causes of the interruption. As a result, the clause did not oust the normal rules on concurrent causation.

Chapter 14

Claims

- Notification of claims
- Proof of loss
- Fraudulent claims
- Limitation

NOTIFICATION OF CLAIMS

14.01 The simple existence of a policy of insurance to cover a particular type of loss does not mean that payment under the policy automatically follows upon the event of the loss occurring. Having issued the policy, the insurer is likely to be oblivious to the subject matter of the policy, and remain so unless and until the insured notifies the insurer that he has suffered a loss in respect of which he believes he has cover under the policy.

If the insured fails to give proper notice of loss to the insurer, then the insurer may be prejudiced by being unable to respond under the policy to the loss. Can the insurer confirm that the policy covered the loss? Can the insurer investigate the circumstances in which the loss is alleged to have occurred? Can the loss be properly quantified? Can the insurer be satisfied that the insured is complying with his duty to act in good faith? Is it a fraudulent claim?

Most policies stipulate the manner and time within which a loss is to be notified to the insurer. If the notice clause is a condition precedent to the insurer's liability, breach of its terms will entitle the insurer to refuse to pay the claim, even if there is no actual prejudice to the insurer. This remains the case under the Insurance Act 2015. If the clause is a bare condition, then, depending on the wording of the clause itself, the insurer may still be liable to pay the claim even though there has been a breach by the insured. However, in both scenarios the insurer will need to act in a way which is consistent with its regulatory obligations (eg, to treat customers fairly and to comply with ICOBS 8 in relation to the payment of claims). For consumer contracts, terms relating to notification of claims will also need to comply with the requirements relating to unfair contract terms in the Consumer Rights Act 2015 (see **Chapter 43**).

Unless expressly stated in the policy as a requirement, notification of a claim to the insurer may be given verbally and by someone other than the insured. While notice may be given to an agent of the insurer duly authorised to receive it, notice to the insured's broker does not amount to notice to the insurer, as the broker is the agent of the insured.

Losses occurring versus claims made policies

14.02 In first party insurance policies, such as property damage insurance, the insured is normally indemnified for losses occurring and reported in the policy period. Some types of first-party insurance may operate on a slightly different basis (eg, crime insurance, which operates on a 'losses discovered' basis, also requiring notification within or shortly after the policy period). However, the general approach is similar, in that the policy covers losses occurring (or discovered) during (or shortly after) the policy period, with the insured obliged to notify the insurer within a similar period of time.

By contrast, third-party insurance or 'claims made' policies, such as professional indemnity insurance, respond to claims made against the insured during the policy period or to subsequent claims arising from circumstances that are notified during the policy period. In the latter case, the policy should contain a 'deeming provision' that provides for the subsequent claim to be treated as if it were made in the policy period when the circumstances were notified. Notifications of circumstances can give rise to disputes about whether the subsequent claim is attributable to, or within the scope of, the circumstances that were notified at an earlier stage. These disputes are fact specific, and the principal authorities are *HLB Kidsons (A Firm) v Lloyds Underwriters subscribing to Lloyds Policy No 621/PK1D00101 & Ors* [2007] EWHC 1951 (Comm); *Kajima UK Engineering Ltd v The Underwriter Insurance Company Limited* [2008] EWHC 83 (TCC); and *Euro Pools Plc v Royal & Sun Alliance Insurance Plc* [2019] EWCA Civ 80.

Time for giving notice

14.03 Notice of loss provisions tend to fall into three categories:

(a) Provisions under which the insured is required to give immediate notice of loss. If the provision is a condition precedent to liability, an insured who delays in any way in giving notice under this type of claim will lose his right to claim. The cases are clear that the insured's obligation is absolute and is not excused by events beyond his control. In *Re Williams and Thomas and Lancashire & Yorkshire Insurance Co* [1902] 19 TLR 82, the insured's obligation was to give notice of any accident causing injury to a third party. An accident occurred, but the injury to the third party did not become manifest for some seven weeks, at which point notice of loss was given. It was held that the insured had failed to comply with his notice obligation. While conditions precedent such as this are extremely rare, they do still arise. In *Aspen Insurance UK Limited and others v Pectel Limited* [2008] EWHC 2804 (Comm), the notification clause required 'immediate written notice' of an occurrence that may give rise to a covered loss. The term 'immediate' was agreed to mean 'with all reasonable speed in the circumstances'. The notification clause was found to be a condition precedent by virtue of a so-called 'sweep up' clause that purported to make the insurer's liability contingent on the terms and conditions of policy being met. As a result, the insured was found to be in breach of a condition precedent and the insurer was entitled to decline cover.

(b) Provisions under which the insured is required to give notice of loss or of an event likely to lead to a loss within a specified period – generally within seven or 14 days of the loss occurring. Once again, if the provision is a condition precedent, the insured cannot successfully plead any excuse for failing to notify. In *Cassel v Lancashire & Yorkshire Insurance Co* (1885) 1 TLR 495, the insured under a policy against accidents was required to give notice to the insurer within 14 days of the occurrence of an event giving rise to a claim against the insured. An accident to the third party occurred, but it did not become clear for some nine months that the third party had suffered injury. The insured was held to be too late to seek an indemnity despite the surrounding circumstances.

(c) Provisions under which the insured is required to give notice of loss as soon as is reasonably practicable. This type of clause is much more generous and, even if it is a condition precedent to liability, permits the insured some leeway if, for good reason, the claim could not be presented immediately. Such a case was *Verelst's Administratrix v Motor Union Insurance Co Ltd* [1925] 2 KB 137, in which a claim on an accident policy was allowed even though it was not made for a year after the insured's death, as the existence of the policy had not been known to the insured's representatives until that time.

In consumer cases, the combined effect of obligations on the insurer to treat customers fairly and to handle claims fairly/not unreasonably reject a claim, together with the need to comply with the unfair contract terms provisions in the Consumer Rights Act 2015, will mean that notification requirements need to be reasonable in all the circumstances. In addition, the significantly increased jurisdiction of the Financial Ombudsman Service in terms of small businesses and the maximum award may result in a different approach in those cases too (see Chapter 43).

PROOF OF LOSS

14.04 In the same way that the insurer needs to know of a loss occurring, it also needs to know the nature and extent of the loss that has to be met. Accordingly, the policy will normally stipulate in what manner and what particulars of loss are to be notified to the insurer, usually requiring the completion of a claim form. The policy will require the insured to provide particulars of the loss in such detail as is reasonably practicable, and to do so within the time specified in the policy. Certain policies (eg, crime insurance) may include an express requirement to file a 'proof of loss' without prescribing what that document should contain. A general rule of thumb is that the proof of loss should set out the key details of the loss that has occurred, including how it happened and its quantum.

While the insurer is entitled to seek more detailed information about the circumstances of the loss or the quantification of the claim in order to decide whether it is obliged to indemnify under the policy, the insurer cannot make unreasonable demands. The insurer must limit the enquiry to information that appears to be relevant to the claim, in which event the insured must comply with the request, even though the information supplied may subsequently be found irrelevant.

In certain situations – for example, where the insured has lost documentary evidence that would substantiate his claim – the insurer may require the insured to complete a sworn statement detailing his loss and entitlement to claim. However, such a sworn statement does not override the insured's duty to prove his loss in any subsequent trial should the insurer continue to refuse to meet the claim. In the alternative, the insurer can also request an indemnity from the insured or claimant.

In relation to life insurance, the rules in respect of proof of title are the same as for other forms of policy. However, in situations where there is uncertainty as to survivorship, all the evidence of the circumstances that is available should be submitted to either a registrar or district registrar at the earliest opportunity. The registrar or district registrar can then decide whether a grant of representation may be issued on that evidence or whether further enquiries should be made (see *Practice Direction (PDAD: Commorientes Grants)* [1964] 1 WLR 1027). Therefore, for example, the insurer may, within a reasonable time, require a post-mortem examination of the deceased (*Ballantine v Employers Insurance Co of Great Britain* [1893] 21 R 305).

Waiver of breach of condition precedent

14.05 An insurer may lose the right to rely upon a breach of condition precedent if its conduct has been such as to lead the insured to believe that the claim will be paid and the insured has in some way relied upon the insurer's conduct. In all cases, there can be a waiver only if the insurer is aware of the insured's breach. An insurer that proceeds with arrangements to deal with the insured's claim may potentially be treated as having waived the breach, whereas an insurer that does nothing while considering its position will not be taken to have waived the breach (*Allen v Robles* [1969] 3 All ER 154). It is normal practice for insurers to reserve their rights to avoid inadvertently waiving a potential coverage defence.

Burden of proof

14.06 When a claim is made by an insured against an insurer, a number of issues may be in dispute between them. These may relate to the circumstances of the loss, the amount of the loss or the possibility that the insured has broken a term of the contract. The law has developed a series of rules for determining which party bears the burden of proving these respective issues. The general principle is that the party who alleges must prove, so that the insured must prove his loss and the insurer must prove any exception or fraud by the insured; but there are various special cases where the burden is reversed.

The standard of proof required is the usual civil standard of the balance of probabilities. However, if the insurer is alleging fraud on the insured's part, this will have, in practice, to be demonstrated to a higher standard approaching the criminal 'beyond reasonable doubt' standard.

Proof of loss by an insured peril

General rule

14.07 The insured bears the burden of proving that he has suffered a loss and that the loss was attributable to a peril insured against under the policy. Unless this can be done, there is no possible claim. If, therefore, the insured has suffered a loss but cannot demonstrate how it has occurred, the claim will fail. This possibility is most likely in the context of marine insurance, where a vessel is lost without explanation. The House of Lords faced this situation in *Rhesa Shipping Co SA v Edmunds (The Popi M)* [1985] 2 All ER 712, and ruled that the insured could not recover without proving that an insured peril had occurred. The House further determined that in such cases, the court is not required to adjudicate between possible explanations in order to determine which is the least implausible and for this to be taken as the likely cause of the loss. In *The Popi M*, the insured relied upon evidence that submarines had been seen in the area, and that the most likely explanation for the loss was accidental collision. The insurer asserted by way of defence that the vessel was probably unseaworthy. As there was no evidence for either argument, the claim was dismissed. The position is that unless the insured can produce an explanation which, on the balance of probabilities, is correct, he must lose. The House of Lords did concede that it is possible that the insured might be able to demonstrate that an insured peril has caused the loss by showing that all other possible causes could not have operated; but the prospects of success by elimination are not great, simply because no evidence is available (*Lamb Head Shipping Co Ltd v Jennings (The Marel)* [1994] 1 Lloyd's Rep 624). The principle was subsequently confirmed in *Nulty v Milton Keynes Borough Council* [2013] EWCA Civ 15, where the Court of Appeal reiterated that a claimant must demonstrate that the particular version of events on which it relies is more likely to have happened than not.

At this stage in the process, the insured need not prove that the loss was accidental and unforeseen, as it is enough for the insured to show that a loss has taken place. If the insurer wishes to allege that the insured was in some way implicated in the loss by fraud, and the insurer's response to the claim is that the entire loss was a figment of the insured's imagination, then the insured is required to prove that the loss actually occurred.

All risks insurance

14.08 Under an all risks policy, the insured need only prove that he has suffered a loss, without having to point to the precise event which has caused that loss (see **Chapter 24**).

FRAUDULENT CLAIMS

14.09 If the insured submits a fraudulent claim to the insurer, the insurer has the right at common law to reject the claim while maintaining the policy in force, or may simply treat the contract as terminated for breach of contract by the insured. Most policies contain provisions governing fraudulent claims, conferring one or both of these rights upon the insurer independently of the insurer's common law rights. The Insurance Act 2015 provides that the insurer is under no obligation to pay the claim; may recover any payments made in respect of any fraudulent claims; may elect to terminate the insurance cover as from the date of the fraudulent act; and may retain the premium.

Fraudulent claims can take many forms, of which the following are the most common:

(a) Deliberate destruction of the subject matter by the insured.

(b) An exaggerated claim by the insured: This is the most frequent problem faced by insurers, but one where the courts have historically failed to give clear guidance. Overvaluation of a loss is not evidence of fraudulent conduct on the part of the insured; whereas if the overvaluation is particularly gross or excessive, having regard to all circumstances of the case, then that may constitute fraud. Fraud relating to just part of a claim will vitiate the entire claim, as is now codified in the Insurance Act 2015. In *Lek v Mathews* [1927-28] 29 LI L Rep 141, the insured claimed for the loss of his stamp collection, including for the loss of some stamps which he did not own. The court held that the entire claim was fraudulent, even though the insured's apparent purpose was to ensure that he did not suffer a financial loss on the stamps which were actually lost.

    The difficulty for the insurer in establishing that a claim is fraudulent rather than merely inadvertently exaggerated by the insured was recognised by the Court of Appeal in *Orakpo v Barclays Insurance Services Co Ltd* [1995] LRLR 443. The court recognised that where an insured places an inflated value on the claim, and provided that nothing is misrepresented or concealed, his actions may be regarded as no more than a legitimate starting point for negotiations with the insurer or the insurer's appointed loss adjuster.

    However, there is also an important distinction between dishonestly exaggerated claims and 'collateral lies' which ultimately have no relevance to the insured's claim. This distinction was considered by the Supreme Court in *Versloot Dredging BV and Anor v HDI Gerling Industrie Versicherung AG and others* [2016] UKSC 45. The claim concerned damage caused when the engine room of a vessel was flooded. During the claim, a director of the vessel's owner made a false statement, aimed at fortifying the claim. This statement was found to be a 'collateral lie' which did not forfeit the claim because it did not affect the claim's validity.

(c) Fraudulent description of the circumstances of the loss: This will prevent proper investigation by the insurer. In *Cox v Orion Insurance Co Ltd* [1982] RTR 1, the insured claimed that his vehicle had been stolen and damaged, when in fact the damage had been caused by the insured himself while intoxicated. The insured's claim was held to be fraudulent even though, had the truth as to the circumstances of the loss been disclosed to the insurer, it would have been liable.

A claim which is not fraudulent, but which involves false statements, cannot be rejected. A merely innocent misrepresentation does not give the insurer the right to reject the claim or to terminate the contract (*Bucks Printing Press Ltd v Prudential Assurance Co* [2000] CLY 880).

Proof of fraud

14.10 Any defence of fraud must, other than in the exceptional case of perils of the sea, be made out on the basis of evidence produced by the insurer. As an allegation of fraud is also an allegation of potential criminal offence by the insured (seeking to obtain money by deception or, possibly, criminal damage), the insurer must demonstrate fraud according to the criminal burden of proof (*Broughton Park Textiles (Salford) Ltd v Commercial Union Assurance Co Ltd* [1987] 1 Lloyd's Rep 194). There may nevertheless be a number of indications that the loss was brought about by the insured's connivance. These will include:

(a) over-insurance;

(b) inability of the insured to produce proof of loss (in the case of a business, this will often mean evidence of stock in trade);

(c) the insured's insolvency or urgent need for funds;

(d) loss occurring in unexplained circumstances;

(e) failure by the insured to make any inquiries into the circumstances of the loss; and

(f) refusal by the insured of assistance (eg, in the case of a stranded vessel, failing to take advantage of the offer of salvage).

LIMITATION

The Limitation Act 1980

14.11 The Limitation Act 1980 provides that an action for breach of contract is to be brought, by the issue of a writ, within six years of the date of breach. An action on an insurance contract is treated by the law as one for breach of contract and the breach of contract is deemed to be the loss itself.

Consequently, in the case of a life, marine or property policy, the insured has six years from the date of his loss to bring an action against the insurer. It is important to stress that time begins to run at this early date, and not at any later dated at which the insurer refuses to pay (*Bank Of America National Trust & Savings Association v Christmas (The Kyriaki)* [1993] 1 Lloyd's Rep 137). The insured must, therefore, disregard events taking place after the loss should it be necessary for proceedings to be commenced.

As far as liability is concerned, the insured's loss occurs when he has been found to be liable to a third party. The six-year limitation period will thus commence when there is a judgment or award against the insured, or when a settlement is reached with the third party (*London Steamship Owners Mutual Insurance Association Ltd v Bombay Trading Co Ltd (The Felicie)* [1990] 2 Lloyd's Rep 21). There may have been prior negotiations between the insurer and the insured in the course of which the insurer has indicated that it does not intend to indemnify the insured in the event that the insured is found to be liable to the third party. The position here is that the insurer's mere denial of liability does not start the limitation period running; although if the insured informed the insurer that he regards the insurer as in breach of contract, the limitation period will begin to run there and then. If, therefore, the insured under a liability policy wishes to preserve his six-year limitation period running from the date at which he is found liable, he must refrain from acknowledging any earlier breach of contract by the insurer (*Lefevre v White* [1990] 1 Lloyd's Rep 569).

Contractual limitation periods

14.12 Some types of policy may substitute a lesser contractual limitation period for the statutory six years. This is a regular feature of credit insurance policies, in particular. In *Walker v Pennine Insurance Co* [1980] 2 Lloyd's Rep 156, a motor policy provided that the insured had to commence an action against the insurer within 12 months of the date on which the insurer denied the insured's claim. The clause was enforced against the insured; and it was held to be irrelevant that at the date of the insurer's denial of liability, the injured third party had not obtained judgment against the insured. The insured was, therefore, in the unfortunate position of having time running against him, and potentially expiring, before he could know whether there was a successful claim against him.

The insurer's obligation to pay

14.13 Section 13A of the Insurance Act 2015 imposes a duty on insurers to pay claims promptly, within 'a reasonable time'. If the insurer breaches that duty, the insured may claim damages in addition to interest. However, the insured must prove on the balance of probabilities that the loss for which it claims damages was caused by the insurer's breach. Any action for such damages must be brought within one year of the date on which the insurer makes a final payment to the insured.

The insurer's obligation to make payment arises as soon as the insured's loss occurs, as that is the date on which the insurer is deemed to be in breach of contract. Any delay by the insurer in making payment is not, therefore, a further breach of contract in respect of which additional damage can arise (*Ventouris v Mountain (The Italia Express) (No 3)* [1992] 2 Lloyd's Rep 281). Instead, the insured will be entitled to interest for late payment, which will generally be calculated to run from the date at which the insurer, acting reasonably, would have made payment. In exceptional cases, the insured may also be entitled to damages to compensate him for the distress caused to him in consequence of the insurer's delay.

Payments in respect of assigned policies

14.14 As a result of the Policies of Assurance Act 1867 and s 136 of the Law of Property Act 1925, it is possible for the benefit of an insurance policy to be assigned at law. If an assignment (eg, of the whole policy) fails as a legal assignment, it may still operate as a valid equitable assignment.

A legal assignment gives the assignee the right to sue for the debt at law and therefore the ability to give the company good legal discharge, without having to join the assignor. Furthermore, the whole or part of any proceeds of an insurance policy are also assignable in equity. An equitable assignment gives the equitable assignee either, with the consent of the insured, the right to sue the insurer in the name of the insured; or, without such consent, the right to join the insured as a joint defendant in an action against the insurer.

Chapter 15

Valuation of loss

- Loss
- Indemnity
- Valued policies
- Unvalued policies
- Insurance on a 'reinstatement' basis
- Late payment by the insurer
- Restrictions on recovery
- The insurer's right of salvage
- Reinstatement

LOSS

General meaning of 'loss'

15.01 Most contracts of insurance are contracts of indemnity, which means that the insured must prove that he has suffered a loss in order to substantiate a claim (for the burden of proving loss, see **Chapter 14**; and for assessing the value of a loss, see **15.5** et seq below). A loss may be either total or partial; and in the case of property, may take the form of either damage to or deprivation of possession of the property. Marine insurance law, by way of contrast to all other forms of property insurance, recognises an intermediate form of loss, known as 'constructive total loss' (see **Chapter 35**). A constructive total loss is something less than a total loss of the property, but which permits the insured to recover the full insurable value of the subject matter on a total loss basis either where the property is damaged beyond economic repair or where the property has been seized by a third party and is unlikely to be returned within a reasonable time.

Loss of possession of property

15.02 In marine insurance, an insured who has been deprived of use or possession of his property by the act of a third party – often in the form of seizure of property or arrest of a vessel – can frequently claim for constructive total loss of the property. In non-marine insurance this possibility does not exist, and the insured must demonstrate a total loss in full. A number of different situations might arise:

(a) The insured's property has disappeared without explanation and cannot be found on reasonable search. Here there is clearly a loss. For example, in *Holmes v Payne* [1930] 2 KB 301, the insured's necklace went missing and she was paid by the insurer for its loss. Interestingly, the necklace was subsequently found in the lining of her cloak, but it was held by the court that the insurer was entitled only to claim the necklace and not to reclaim its payment. This was because if the insured item is missing and a reasonable time had elapsed to allow for a diligent search and that search has failed to recover the item, then it may properly be said to be lost, as recovery of the item appears uncertain.

(b) The insured's property has been stolen by persons unknown. Even though there is the theoretical prospect of recovery, because a thief cannot obtain or pass on good title to the property, goods which have been stolen are likely to be treated as lost if their whereabouts cannot be ascertained after reasonable efforts, subject to the insurer's right of salvage if the goods are ultimately returned. Also see *Webster v General Accident Fire and Life Assurance Corporation Limited* [1953] 1 QB 520, in which it was held that a car passed to an auctioneer for sale on the purchaser's behalf, but which the auctioneer purported to sell on his own behalf, had been 'lost' because the insured had taken all reasonable steps to recover it and, having taken all reasonable steps, recovery had not been achieved and was uncertain.

(c) The insured's property has been seized by a third party who has refused to return it. In *London and Provincial Leather Processors v Hudson* [1939] 2 KB 724, the insured sent skins to a firm in Germany to be processed. The German firm entrusted some of these skins to a subcontractor. The German firm became insolvent and the skins were retained by the subcontractor as security for sums owed to it by the German firm. This was held to be a loss of the skins, even though their whereabouts was known.

(d) The insured's property is in safe hands but the insured cannot obtain possession of it. This was the situation in *Moore v Evans* [1918] AC 185, where pearls sent from England to potential customers in Europe were insured under a goods in transit policy, but on the outbreak of war were deposited for safekeeping with a bank in Brussels to protect them from seizure by the German authorities. The House of Lords held that the pearls were not lost, even though the insured was deprived of the use of them for four years. Equivalent facts in marine insurance would plainly have amounted to a constructive total loss.

(e) In certain cases it may not be immediately apparent that the possibility of recovery of an insured item is subject to a 'mere chance'. Whether or not there is an uncertainty as to recovery may require a 'wait and see' period, which is discussed in *Scott v The Copenhagen Reinsurance (UK) Ltd* [2003] EWCA Civ 688, where a British Airways aircraft was stranded in Iraq when war broke out in 1991 and was subsequently destroyed by bombing. The court said that 'wait and see' cases in their real sense refer to the situation where property cannot immediately be said to have been lost, but the insured has been deprived of it in circumstances which are subject to a process of development and change. The process of development and change may indicate that the prospects of recovery are uncertain. As in that case, where the aircraft was subsequently blown up, the development of circumstances determined what originally was not immediately apparent as a loss.

The 'wait and see' test might also refer to the emergence of evidence which impacts upon the assessment of the probabilities of recovery. Thus, where a car is taken without the owner's consent, if it is discovered that the car was taken by a joy rider instead of a thief, the probability may be that it will soon be found and recovered.

The defrauded insured

15.03 An insured may be tricked by fraud into giving possession of his property to a third party, who absconds with the property. The insured is *prima facie* entitled to recover even if he was negligent in his conduct, but a further question may arise as to whether there has been a 'loss' in such circumstances.

The situation must be considered where the insured has been induced to sell his property to a third party in return for what proves to be a stolen or otherwise worthless cheque. In *Eisinger v General Accident Fire and Life Corporation Limited* [1955] 2 All ER 897, the court ruled that an insured who had exchanged his car for a cheque which was subsequently dishonoured had lost not the car, but rather the proceeds of the sale, the latter not being insured under the policy. This decision is inconsistent with a later decision of the Court of Appeal, *Dobson v General Accident Fire and Life Corporation plc* [1989] 3 All ER 927, where the insured sold jewellery to a third party who paid by means of a stolen cheque. The policy covered 'loss by theft' and the Court of Appeal ruled that, as what had occurred had amounted to 'theft' (see Chapter 26), the insured was entitled to recover. It was not suggested to the Court of Appeal that there had been no 'loss'. If, in the case of fraud, the insured's policy covers theft, the *Eisinger* decision would appear to have been superseded by that of *Dobson*.

INDEMNITY

15.04 Contracts of insurance confer upon the insured the right to receive a sum of money on the happening of an uncertain event or fortuity. This is subject to the common law principle of indemnity, under which the insured is entitled to recover at most a sum equivalent to the amount which he has lost by reason of the happening of the uncertain event (see **Chapter 4**). Not all insurance contracts are indemnity contracts. Life and accident policies fall into this excluded category, on the basis that it is not possible to calculate the value of a life or a limb. The amount recoverable under a life or accident policy is, therefore, the amount agreed between the parties.

Property and other indemnity policies may be written on a valued or unvalued basis. If the policy is valued, the parties agree the insurable value of the subject matter, so that in the event of loss the insurer is liable for the agreed value or the relevant part of the agreed value. If the policy is unvalued, it will be necessary for a calculation of the amount actually lost to be made. The use of valued policies for the most part eliminates post-loss disputes as to the measure of indemnity, and such policies are common on items which have no readily ascertainable market value. Policies on unique items such as works of art and jewellery are often valued, as are the vast majority of marine policies.

VALUED POLICIES

Valuation

15.05 The value of the subject matter agreed between the parties for the purposes of the policy is deemed to be conclusive (Marine Insurance Act 1906, s 27(3) and, *inter alia, Irving v Manning and Anderson* [1847] 1 HLC 287). It is rarely appropriate for the insurer to contest the agreed valuation once a loss has occurred, as the premium has been paid on the basis of that valuation. There are nevertheless exceptional situations in which an excessive valuation may be relevant.

It has been said that if the insured has warranted that the subject matter is of a certain value, and this proves to be false, the insurer may apparently rely upon the breach of warranty as discharging it from liability irrespective of the small amount of any discrepancy. However, note the Court of Appeal's decision in *Economides v Commercial Assurance Co plc* [1998] 1 QB 587, in which it was held that a representation of belief or opinion as to the value of property to be insured need only be made honestly – there is no requirement of reasonable grounds for the belief or opinion. That said, however, there must be some basis for the representation before it can be said to have been made honestly. This decision has subsequently been applied in a commercial context in *Eagle Star Insurance Co Ltd v Games Video Co (GVC) SA, 'The Game Boy'* [2004] 1 Lloyd's Rep 238 and *Rendall v Combined Insurance Co of America* [2005] Lloyd's Rep IR 732.

If the agreed valuation proves to be wildly excessive, to the extent that there is good reason to consider that there may have been fraud, the insurer may be able to plead that there has been a breach of the duty of fair presentation, entitling it to set the policy aside or claim another remedy available under the Insurance Act 2015. The leading authority is *Ionides v Pender* [1874] LR 9 QB 531, where a cargo which had cost £8,000 was insured for £16,500. The insured's stated purpose was to insure against loss of profits on resale. There was evidence, though, that while profits as high as 30 per cent were conceivable, anything higher than that would render the risk speculative and this should have been disclosed. The excessive estimation of profits had not been disclosed and the policy was therefore voidable for non-disclosure.

See also *Eagle Star Insurance Co Ltd v Games Video Co (GVC) SA, 'The Game Boy'* [2004] 1 Lloyd's Rep 238, in which the vessel was insured for $1.8 million but, due to its condition, only had a value of $100,000. This overvaluation was found to be material. The underwriting expert for the insured gave evidence that an overvaluation was only material if it was extreme. However, Simon J accepted that an overvaluation 'in multiples' was also material and the insurer was entitled to avoid for misrepresentation as to the value of the vessel.

An insured who insures property for the price paid for it by him cannot be guilty of misrepresentation if he insures for that amount, even though the price was excessive (*Inversiones Manria SA v Sphere Drake Insurance Co plc, The 'Dora'* [1989] 1 Lloyd's Rep 69).

Total loss under a valued policy

15.06 Total loss under a valued policy is determined strictly in accordance with the agreed valuation. If the property has been insured for its full value, the insured is entitled to the full value. If the property has been insured for a sum less than the full value, the insurer is liable only for the agreed amount.

Partial loss under a valued policy

15.07 Where there has been a partial loss, the amount recoverable is again calculated in accordance with the agreed value. This will depend, however, upon whether the insured has insured for the full agreed value or a lesser sum and whether the policy is or is not subject to average (see **15.8–15.9** below).

Valued policy not subject to average

15.08 Under a valued policy not subject to average, the insured recovers that proportion of the agreed value of the subject matter which the amount lost bears to the true value. In *Elcock v Thomson* [1949] 2 KB 755, a building with an agreed value of £106,850 and insured for that amount was damaged to the extent of 30 per cent. The insured was held to be entitled to recover 30 per cent of the agreed value and so recovered £32,055. This was so despite the court's conclusion that the true value of the building had been only £18,000 before the fire, so that the insured's actual loss was a mere £5,400.

If the insured is insured for the full agreed value, the position is governed by the *Elcock v Thomson* principle. By contrast, the insured may have deliberately insured the property for a sum less than the agreed value. If the policy is not subject to average, the fact of its underinsurance makes no difference to the *Elcock v Thomson* principle, except that the insured value operates as a ceiling on recovery. Thus:

(a) if property with an agreed value of £200,000 is insured for £100,000 and suffers a 50 per cent loss, the insured is entitled, in accordance with *Elcock v Thomson*, to recover £100,000 whatever the actual cost of reinstatement or repairs might be; and

(b) if property with an agreed value of £200,000 is insured for £100,000 and suffers a 75 per cent loss, the insured can recover only £100,000, as that is the maximum sum insured under the policy.

Valued policy subject to average

15.09 If a valued policy is subject to average, the insured is deemed to be his own insurer for the uninsured proportion of the loss. The parties are deemed to have jointly insured the subject matter. For example, suppose that property with an agreed value of £100,000 is insured for £100,000 and suffers 25 per cent damage. In these circumstances, the insured recovers £25,000, as the insurer has accepted 100 per cent of the risk. Average does not apply.

By contrast, suppose that property with an agreed value of £100,000 is insured for £80,000 and suffers 25 per cent damage. The loss is £25,000 but this must be divided between the insurer and the insured in accordance with their respective proportions as joint insurers, so that the insurer pays £20,000 (80 per cent) and the insured bears a loss of £5,000 (20 per cent).

UNVALUED POLICIES

Valuation

15.10 The insured under an unvalued policy may be required to state a valuation of the property to the insurer even though the valuation is irrelevant to the sum recoverable, as this is determined by the value at the date of the loss. The value will, however, normally be relevant in fixing the insurer's maximum liability under the policy and forms the basis for the calculation of the premium. It will rarely be a material fact, for duty of fair presentation purposes, for the insured to overstate the value of the subject matter, as the insured will not be able to recover any more than his actual loss and the main consequence is that the insured has paid a superfluous premium. An overvaluation which is material for the purposes of a valued policy may, therefore, not be material for the purposes of an unvalued policy. However, if the sum stated is grossly excessive and points towards potential fraud on the insured's part, the policy may be regarded as voidable. In *Parker & Heard v Generali Assicurazioni SpA*, unreported, 1988, goods worth £38,000 were insured for £200,000 (5.5 times the real value), but this was held not to be excessive. The case of *Williams v Atlantic Assurance Co Ltd* [1933] 1 KB 81 is an exceptional case: a valuation of £8,000 in respect of goods worth £250 (32 times the real value) was held to be sufficient to allow the insurer to avoid the contract.

Total loss under an unvalued policy

Valuing the insured's loss: buildings

15.11 Under an unvalued policy, the sum insured under the policy is normally the maximum amount which may be recovered in respect of a loss. The sum which is recoverable will, subject to that maximum amount, depend upon the actual amount of the insured's loss. This is determined by the value of the insured property immediately prior to the loss. The method of determining the value may vary according to the intentions of the insured and so the basis of the calculation may vary from case to case. A good example is a restaurant being operated in ornate Victorian premises in a busy city centre. If the building is totally destroyed, the insured's loss may be calculated on one of three assumptions:

(a) The value of the building to the insured was its uniquely ornate construction and décor. Here, the insured will be entitled to recover the cost of reinstating the building in more or less its original form (reinstatement cost).

(b) The value of the building to the insured was its city centre location and its actual appearance was of marginal significance. In such a case, the insured's indemnity is to be calculated on the provision of a modern equivalent cost building.

(c) The insured had, prior to the loss, evidenced an intention to sell the building. Here, the value of the building to the insured is its investment worth and not its physical appearance or location. The insured's loss will, therefore, be determined in accordance with market value. This is likely to be a sum less than both reinstatement cost and modern equivalent cost.

'Reinstatement cost' is the appropriate measure where a building's particular features are the reason for the insured's occupation of the building. In the case of a domestic dwelling of unique characteristics, this is almost certain to be the case. In the case of commercial premises, all will depend upon the evidence. In *Reynolds and Anderson v Phoenix Assurance Co Ltd* [1978] 2 Lloyd's Rep 440, the insured purchased for £18,000 an old maltings, which he used for the storage of grain. The building was insured for £628,000 and was destroyed by fire. The cost of reinstating the maltings in their original condition was £250,000, while the cost of erecting a modern equivalent building was £50,000. The trial judge was persuaded that the insured used the maltings in the light of their aesthetic features and awarded £250,000. An insured who is paid on a reinstatement basis is not generally obliged, as far as the insurer is concerned, to use the money to reinstate the premises; although the insured may be under a contractual duty to a third party to reinstate (as in the case of a landlord insuring a building for the benefit of tenants – see **15.30** et seq below). A person interested in the property may, however, under s 83 of the Fires Prevention (Metropolis) Act 1774, require the insurer to use the insurance monies to reinstate the property rather than pay the proceeds of the policy over to the insured (see **15.34** below).

'Modern equivalent cost' is appropriate for business premises which are used without regard to their particular aesthetic qualities. In *Exchange Theatre Ltd v Iron Trades Mutual Insurance Co Ltd* [1983] 1 Lloyd's Rep 674, the building in question was a Victorian public hall, which was used by the insured to operate a bingo hall and discotheque. The Court of Appeal ruled that the insured was entitled to a modern equivalent reinstatement, although a retrial was subsequently ordered on the basis of an allegation of fraud.

'Market value' is appropriate where the insured's intention, at the time of the loss, was to dispose of the property. This was the position in *Leppard v Excess Insurance Co Ltd* [1979] 2 All ER 668, in which the insured's house was destroyed by fire. Before the fire, the market value of the property had been £4,500. After the fire, its market value was £1,500. The reinstatement cost would have been £8,694 and the sum insured covered the cost of reinstatement, but the insured was held to be entitled only to the lower figure of £3,000 (ie, the difference between the market value before the fire (£4,500) and the market value after the fire (£1,500)), in the light of his intention at the time of the loss to sell the property.

Valuing the insured's loss: goods

15.12 In the event of a total loss, the general principle remains that the insured can recover the value of the goods immediately prior to the loss.

In the case of mass-produced goods, this figure will nearly always be the cost of replacing the goods in their actual condition immediately prior to the loss. However, if the policy is written on a 'new for old' basis, the insured will be entitled to a sum sufficient to enable him to purchase new goods without any reduction for wear and tear.

Where the market value test is applicable, the fact that the insured originally acquired the goods cheaply is immaterial, as this does not bear upon the market value of the goods at the date of their loss (*Dominion Mosaics and Tile Co Ltd v Trafalgar Trucking Co Ltd* [1990] 2 All ER 246). In *Quorum v Schramm* [2002] 1 Lloyd's Rep 249, where there were two markets (the auction market and the private dealers' market) for determining the value of a damaged pastel by Degas, the court in determining the value decided that it should have regard to the market where it was likely that the higher price would be obtained. In any event, on the facts this was the market where the picture was likely to be sold. Therefore, it more accurately reflected the loss. The market value of goods is to be assessed on an objective basis and disregards the vagaries of particular potential buyers. This is understood to be consistent with the practice of the Financial Ombudsman Service (FOS).

It should also be noted that when dealing with complaints about motor valuations, the FOS is likely to treat the 'market value' as the 'likely cost to the customer of buying a car as near as possibly identical to the one which has been stolen or damaged beyond economic repair', and not the value which could have been obtained upon sale.

In determining the value of goods, other forms of loss are to be disregarded. The loss of a treasured heirloom or article of sentimental value does not entitle the insured to any sum in excess of market value (*Re Earl of Egmont's Trusts, Lefroy v Earl of Egmont* [1908] 1 Ch 821), and for this reason items of that sort are commonly insured under valued policies. Equally, the loss of an article used in a process of manufacture does not, unless the policy expressly provides, justify a claim by the insured for loss of profits pending the replacement of the item. The exclusion of less tangible forms of loss is illustrated by *Richard Aubrey Film Productions Ltd v Graham* [1960] 2 Lloyd's Rep 101, in which a film nearing completion was lost. The court allowed the difference between the market value of the completed film and the costs of completion and excluded any claim based upon emotional and aesthetic loss.

Partial loss under an unvalued policy

The general measure of loss

15.13 If a building or goods are damaged but not totally destroyed, the insured will normally be entitled to the reasonable cost of effecting repairs. This may be subject to the principle of average (see **Chapter 19**): if the insured is under-insured and the policy is subject to average, the insured and the insurer are treated as co-insurers for their respective proportions of the market value of the loss, so that an insured who is 30 per cent under-insured will have to bear 30 per cent of the cost of repairs (see **15.09** for the application of average to partial loss under a valued policy, where precisely the same principles apply).

The fact that the cost of reinstating a building or repairing goods is greater than their pre-loss market value does not give the insurer any common law right to pay only the market value. Many policies do nevertheless provide that in such a case the insurer may treat the property as totally destroyed and pay only the property's market value to the insured.

Damage to a distinct part of a property

15.14 A perennial problem for insurers is the situation in which the insured suffers loss of or damage to property which forms part of a wider article, the loss diminishing the value of the wider article despite lack of physical harm to it – for example, damage to the fabric covering an armchair forming part of a three-piece suite, where the fabric is no longer available. The insured can clearly claim the cost of re-covering the armchair, but he is left with a non-matching three-piece suite. The question here, which has yet to reach the English courts, is whether the insured can claim the cost of re-covering the entire three-piece suite. In the absence of a clear legal principle, the FOS has a general rule of thumb the practice of awarding to the insured one-half of the cost of re-covering the remaining items.

Consequential loss

15.15 As with total losses, consequential losses – loss of profits, compensation for sentimental value – are not recoverable where goods have been partially damaged. One exception to this principle would appear to be depreciation. If an item (eg, a car) is damaged and repaired, it will probably be less saleable whatever the quality of the repair; and the FOS would be expected to recognise a reduction in the value of goods due to repair as a part of an insured's loss under the policy.

INSURANCE ON A 'REINSTATEMENT' BASIS

15.16 Policies on buildings are commonly written on a 'reinstatement' basis. This does not mean that the insured is entitled to have his building reinstated, but merely that the cost of reinstatement is recoverable under the policy (always assuming that the insured intends to reinstate, as discussed below). In most cases, the reinstatement value will represent the actual value of the premises to the insured. In particular, where the insured is under a contractual duty to reinstate the premises, the amount recoverable is based upon the reinstatement cost (*Lonsdale & Thompson Ltd v Black Arrow Group plc* [1993] 3 All ER 648). Such costs are to be assessed as at the date of loss: *Tonkin v UK Insurance Ltd* [2006] 2 All ER (Comm) 550.

An issue may arise where the insured wishes to undertake some improvements to the building as part of the reinstatement. *Tonkin* provides useful guidance on what information an insured should provide to insurers in order to calculate the value of a claim. Where minor improvements are to be undertaken, the insured needs to make it plain to the insurer at the outset that the scheme will include some elements of improvement and identify those improvements. In the case of major changes to improve what was there before, it may be better to draw up a notional reinstatement scheme that is accurately priced and this can be used to calculate the insurer's contribution towards reinstatement. HHJ Peter Coulson QC made it clear that an insured should never try to put forward a reinstatement scheme without identifying any improvements:

> 'It is never acceptable to be less than direct and open with insurers. At the worst end of the scale, such conduct can easily amount to fraud … [at the very least it] will inevitably cause delay suspicion and antagonism. It is a clear failure on the part of the insured to comply with these obligations under the policy.'

Conversely, if the evidence demonstrates that the value of the property to the insured immediately prior to the loss was some lesser amount, the insured is entitled to recover only that amount. In *McLean Enterprises Ltd v Ecclesiastical Insurance Office plc* [1986] 2 Lloyd's Rep 416, premises with a market value of £250,000 were insured on a reinstatement basis for £375,000, the latter sum being the estimated cost of reinstatement. Prior to the loss, the insured had been involved in negotiations to sell the premises, although there was no binding contract. The premises were the subject of a partial loss and the court ruled that the insured was entitled to recover only the difference between £250,000 and the post-loss market value of the premises.

The principles for measuring the indemnity for property damage losses, and the relevance and timing of the intention to reinstate, were also reviewed in *Endurance Corporate Capital Ltd v Sartex Quilts & Textiles Limited* [2020] EWCA Civ 308. In 2011, the insured property suffered fire damage. In 2013, the insurer paid the insured a sum equivalent to the diminution in market value. It was not until 2018 that the insured started reinstatement works, at that point seeking additional sums from the insurer. The Court of Appeal decided in favour of the insured. The basis for its decision was that, as the insured intended to use the site for manufacturing when the fire occurred, the appropriate measure was the cost of reinstatement and any subsequent change of intention was irrelevant. In reaching that conclusion, the Court of Appeal distinguished an earlier decision in *Great Lakes Insurance UK v Western Trading Ltd* [2016] EWCA Civ 1003, where a 'fixed and settled intention' to reinstate was considered necessary.

The reinstatement basis of coverage also received particular attention following the earthquake and aftershocks in Christchurch, New Zealand in 2011. In *Turvey Trustee Ltd v Southern Response Earthquake Services Ltd* [2012] NZHC 3344, it was found on the applicable wording that the insurer did not have to pay for the cost of building a new property using identical materials to the original building. In *TJK (NZ) Ltd v Mitsui Sumitomo Insurance Co Ltd* [2013] Lloyd's Rep IR Plus 32, the court found that, having elected to reinstate, the insured was entitled to receive an interim payment that would be topped up to the full reinstatement value if it did in fact reinstate.

LATE PAYMENT BY THE INSURER

Damages for breach of contract

15.17 Insurance contracts are treated as contracts to hold the insured harmless against the liability or loss insured against. Therefore, a claim under a contract of insurance is properly viewed as a claim for breach of contract. In the case of a life or property policy, the date of the insurer's breach of contract will be the date of the event causing loss; and in the case of a liability policy, the date of the insurer's breach of contract is the date on which the insured's liability to a third party is established. The insurer has no implied right to postpone payment for a reasonable time while investigating the claim, for example. The fact that the insurer is liable in damages from the outset necessarily means that, if payment of such damages is not made or delayed, the insurer cannot be liable for any further breach of contract.

In *Ventouris v Mountain, The Italia Express (No 2)* [1992] 2 Lloyd's Rep 281, the underwriter under a marine policy delayed in making payment and was sued for additional damages, representing distress. The judge ruled that the underwriter could not be liable for damages for distress, as to award damages would be tantamount to regarding the underwriter as being in further breach of its original breach of contract. In addition, the judge held that the Marine Insurance Act 1906 did not contemplate any claim against the insurer other than for an indemnity calculated in accordance with that Act and, on the facts, there had been no distress as the insured was a company. This decision was approved and applied in *Sprung v Royal Insurance (UK) Ltd* [1997] CLC 70. In that case, the insured argued that he had been unable to continue to run his business and as a consequence had lost the opportunity to sell it as a result of the insurer delaying payment of a material damage claim for three and a half years. The Court of Appeal approved and applied *The Italia Express* and held that there could be no recovery of damage in respect of a failure to pay or a delay in payment of the original damages, and that the insured would only be compensated by payment of interest. See also *Normhurst Ltd v Durnoch Ltd* [2004] EWHC 567; *Mandrake Holdings Ltd v Countrywide Assured Group plc* [2005] EWCA Civ 840; and *Tonkin v UK Insurance Ltd* [2007] Lloyd's Rep IR 283. It is perfectly possible, however, that in appropriate circumstances in the future, a court might rule that an insured can recover damages for delay if the insurance policy contains a term (express or implied) that payment of a claim will be made without delay. This possibility was hinted at by the Court of Appeal in *Sprung v Royal Insurance (UK) Ltd*. However, to date, such arguments have not succeeded. In *Tonkin*, the insured sought to claim damages for breach of contract, relying on a provision that the insurer would 'always try to be fair and reasonable whenever you have need of the protection of this Policy. We would also act quickly to provide that protection'. The court concluded that there was no separate breach of contract arising out of the general obligations set out in the care clause, on the basis that this obligation was too general. It would appear, therefore, that to have any chance of succeeding in such a claim, the separate provision would need to be more specific.

Prior to the Enterprise Act 2016, it was established law following *Sprung v Royal Insurance (UK) Ltd* that damages could not be recovered for losses incurred by an insured due to the insurer's failure to pay the claim promptly. However, this position was changed by the Enterprise Act 2016, which introduced a new s 13A to the Insurance Act 2015 whereby, pursuant to an implied term in every contract of insurance, damages can now be recovered where:

(a) the insurer fails to pay the claim within 'a reasonable time'; and

(b) the insured has incurred a loss as a result of the insurer's duty to make such payment.

Section 13A does not provide guidance on what constitutes 'a reasonable time' and it is therefore considered a fact and policy specific matter. Note, however, that the insured must establish its claim to loss; and there is a one-year limitation period for bringing such claims, running from the date on which the insurer eventually made payment. It is also worth noting that the Consumer Rights Act 2015 requires that services performed for a consumer be provided within a reasonable time. The interaction between the Consumer Rights Act and the Enterprise Act is as yet untested in the courts.

Interest

15.18 The proper remedy against a dilatory insurer is ability to claim damages under Section 13A of the Insurance Act 2015. This remedy is separate and additional to the existing remedy of an award of interest from the date on which the indemnity should have been paid. The High Court has a general discretion under s 35A of the Supreme Senior Courts Act 1981 to award interest on a claim for damages. As a matter of logic, it would follow from the nature of a claim under an insurance contract (see **15.17** above) that interest should be awarded from the date of the event insured against. The court's usual practice, however, has been to award interest from the date when the claim ought to have been paid in the ordinary course of events. Therefore, insurers will be allowed some time to consider the claim. The time will vary according to the nature of the loss, the way the claim is presented and the circumstances which require investigation. That interest may be reduced in circumstances in which the court feels that there has been unreasonable delay on the part of the insured in bringing proceedings: see *Quorum AS v Schramm (No 2)* [2002] 2 Lloyd's Rep 72. The power to award interest is not confined to sums unpaid by the date of the judgment; the court can order interest on sums paid at an earlier date, such as payments into court or payments on account (*Edmunds v Lloyd Italico e L'Ancora Cia di Assicurazioni e Riassicurazioni SpA and Another* [1986] 2 All ER 249).

RESTRICTIONS ON RECOVERY

Betterment

15.19 An insured whose property is destroyed or damaged and is subsequently reinstated or repaired at the expense of the insurer may be obtaining something better than what was actually lost. Where the insured does stand to make a profit, the insurer is generally accepted to be entitled to deduct from the amount payable a sum representing the notional profit to be gained by the insured as a result of receiving something better. The concept of a deduction for betterment has been objected to, however, as 'the equivalent of forcing the [insured] to invest money in the modernising of their plant which might be highly inconvenient for them' (per Widgery LJ in *Harbutt's*

'Plasticine' Ltd v Wayne Tank & Pump Co Ltd [1970] 1 QB 447). On the other hand, it is always open to an insured specifically to insure his property on a 'new for old' basis, if he is prepared to pay the additional premium.

The calculation of betterment may be a somewhat arbitrary exercise. In practice, it is frequently excluded in the case of household goods under 'new for old' policies. The FOS may also allow some betterment where it considers it to be fair.

Contractual limitations

Excess clauses

15.20 The insured is often required, and sometimes has the option, to carry an excess (or similarly a retention or deductible) in respect of every claim. Unless the claim reaches the excess figure, the insurer is not liable at all; and if the claim is greater than the excess figure, the insurer is entitled to deduct the amount of the excess from its payment. The use of excesses recognises that most claims are relatively small. If the insurer were liable for small claims, the administrative and liability costs to the insurer would be greatly increased; and for this reason the premium for a policy without an excess is disproportionately high. In addition, the presence of an excess means that the insured shares in the risk of loss and, therefore, is intended to encourage the insured to guard against losses.

It is particularly important to define the risk insured against, as this will determine whether the insured bears one single excess as a result of a particular incident or a number of excesses in respect of each individual claim flowing from the incident. This raises the distinction between 'events', 'occurrences', 'accidents' and 'claims', and the aggregation language that insurers use in their policies to determine how many losses occurred and therefore how many excesses apply.

Franchise clauses

15.21 A franchise clause, like an excess, lays down a sum which must be exceeded before the insured can make a claim. The difference between the two types of clause is that where the loss exceeds the amount stated in a franchise clause, the insurer bears the entire loss and not merely the amount by which the loss is greater than the franchise figure.

A series of losses

Unconnected loss

15.22 The insured may suffer a series of losses, such as burglaries, within the period covered by the policy. There will generally be a maximum sum insured under the policy. The application of the maximum liability figure will depend upon the proper construction of the policy's wording. The policy might provide that the maximum sum insured relates to single losses so that the insurer is liable for more than one loss even though their aggregate cost is greatly in excess of the maximum sum insured.

Conversely, the policy may lay down a maximum figure, not just per claim, but per year. If the policy is silent, the former construction appears to be the correct one – a principle which has been codified in s 77 of the Marine Insurance Act 1906.

Successive claims for the same subject matter

15.23 If the insured's property is damaged by fire, repaired and then damaged again, the insured can, in accordance with the principles set out in **15.22** above, recover for the successive losses. The position is different, however, if the original damage has not been repaired. Three different situations might arise:

(a) The insured's car is damaged in a road accident and is left in his garage pending repair. The garage catches fire and renders the vehicle a total loss. Here, the obvious solution is that the partial loss is merged into the total loss, so that the insured can recover only for the total loss (*British and Foreign Marine Insurance Co Ltd v Wilson Shipping Co Ltd* [1921] 1 AC 188).

(b) The insured's car is damaged in a road accident and is deposited with a repairer (the car being uninsured while in the possession of a person other than the insured), where it is destroyed by fire. Here, the merger principle again operates, depriving the insured of the right to recover anything at all, even for the insured partial loss. In practice, this is an unlikely event today.

(c) The insured's car is damaged in a road accident and is left in his garage pending repair. The policy then expires and the insured does not renew. The car is subsequently destroyed by a fire in the insured's garage. The rule, laid down in the marine case of *Lidgett v Secretan* (1871) LR 6 CP 616, is that the insured's position has to be viewed at the date of the expiry of the policy. As at that date the insured had an outstanding partial loss, he is entitled to recover for that loss.

The issue of successive losses arose in *Ridgecrest New Zealand Ltd v IAG New Zealand Ltd [2014] NZSC 129*, where the insured owned a building that was damaged by multiple earthquakes during the period of insurance. By the time the building was destroyed, some repairs had been undertaken. The New Zealand Supreme Court held that, on the specific wording, the insured could recover up to the sum insured for each earthquake, but that the total claim could not exceed the replacement value of the building on account of the indemnity principle.

Losses with a common cause

15.24 Rather different considerations arise where the insured suffers a series of different losses flowing from the same event. This is particularly significant in liability insurance, where one negligent act by the insured can give rise to a range of liabilities. Assuming that the policy contains a maximum liability figure faced by the insurer, it will be necessary to determine whether that figure relates to individual claims by (or in the case of liability insurance, against) the insured, or whether it relates to an aggregation of claims flowing from some single unifying factor – an event, for example. The result may vary, depending upon whether the maximum liability figure relates to 'accidents', 'occurrences', 'events' or 'claims'.

Settlements between insurer and insured

Binding nature

15.25 The payment of a loss by the insurer is frequently made conditional upon the insured entering into a contract with the insurer under which the insurer's payment is to be accepted in full and final settlement of the loss. Should additional loss subsequently come to light, the insured will have no right to claim against the insurer for that loss. In the absence of a full and final settlement agreement, the insured can look to the insurer for an indemnity for loss which comes to light at a later date. These principles are illustrated by *Kitchen Design & Advice Ltd v Lea Valley Water Co* [1989] 2 Lloyd's Rep 221, in which the claimant insured's premises were damaged by flooding caused by the defendant. The insurer paid the insured for the flood damage and recovered its payment from the defendant on a 'full and final settlement' basis. Subsequently, the insured put in a claim against its insurer for consequential loss, which the insurer had to pay as it had not settled the original claim as a full and final settlement. The insurer was, however, precluded from reopening the agreement with the defendant and was thus unable to seek indemnification from it.

Settlements made under a mistake

15.26 In English law, where the parties involved in negotiating a contract are under a common misapprehension as to a fundamental matter which affects the very basis of their negotiations, their subsequent contract is void. If the mistake is of lesser significance, the contract is not to be treated as void, but voidable, and either party may ask the court to exercise its discretion to set the contract aside. A settlement contract based on an error is, therefore, potentially void or voidable, and the insurer can either reclaim its payment or, if it has not paid, refuse to make payment.

The decided cases provide specific illustrations of these rules:

(a) Where the insurer makes payment under a lapsed policy, the payment may be recovered (*Kelly v Solari* (1841) 9 N&W 54);

(b) Where the insurer makes payment in the erroneous belief that the insured had an insurable interest, the payment may be recovered (*Piper v Royal Exchange Assurance* [1932] 44 Lloyd's Rep 103);

(c) Where the insurer makes payment in ignorance of the fact that the loss has not been caused by an insured peril, the payment may be recovered (*Norwich Union Fire Insurance Society v Price* [1934] AC 455); and

(d) Where the insurer makes payment unaware of the existence of grounds which would have entitled it to set aside the insurance contract for breach of duty by the insured, the payment may be recovered (*Magee v Pennine Insurance Co* [1969] 2 QB 507 – misrepresentation by the insured when applying for the policy). Presumably the same

> principle would apply if the insurer was unaware of a breach of condition or warranty by the insured. The mere fact that the insurer has paid does not amount to waiver of the defence, as there can be waiver only where the insurer was aware of the facts giving rise to a defence and nevertheless made payment.

In *Kyle Bay Ltd (T/A Astons Nightclub) v Underwriters* [2007] EWCA Civ 57 both the insured and the insurer agreed settlement on the basis that the policy was written on a 'gross profits basis' subject to the application of average, whereas it was in law a declaration linked policy to which average did not apply. As a consequence, the insured recovered £108,319.46 less than it ought to have. The Court of Appeal upheld the first instance decision that the settlement contract was not void for mistake. A claim settled on a mistaken legal basis will not be void for mistake unless the mistake either renders the agreement to settle impossible to perform or renders the subject matter of the agreement radically different from the subject matter that the parties believed to exist. The fact that the settlement agreement is to one party's disadvantage does not render it void.

Settlements induced by misrepresentation

15.27 If the insured's claim is fraudulent, the insurer may refuse to pay it and generally has the additional right under the Insurance Act 2015 to terminate the policy (see Chapter 13). If the insured's claim is not fraudulent or reckless but contains innocent misstatements, there is no breach by the insured of his continuing duty of utmost good faith and (subject to any other relevant policy conditions) the claim must be paid.

The insured can set aside a settlement contract if it has been induced by a false statement made on behalf of the insurer. In *Saunders v Ford Motor Co Ltd* [1970] 1 Lloyd's Rep 379, the plaintiff signed a document presented to him by his employer in respect of an injury at work, for a full and final settlement at £100. The plaintiff had been led to believe that this was an interim payment only and the court held that the document signed by the plaintiff could not stand.

However, in *Kyle Bay Ltd v Underwriters* the insured sought to argue that it was entitled to rescind the settlement agreement for misrepresentation on the basis that the insurer had represented that the policy was not declaration linked and average applied. Jonathan Hirst QC concluded that the insurer's letter was not to be read as a representation as to the contents of the policy, but rather as a statement of the underwriter's opinion of the overall effect of the policy. It was, therefore, a representation as to belief or opinion, and was an accurate representation of the insurer's opinion and therefore made in good faith. There had been no misrepresentation.

Unfair settlements

15.28 In general, other than in relation to consumer contracts, the courts will not overturn a contract on the basis that its terms are unfair to one of the parties, as it is not regarded as the function of law to rewrite bargains. This principle is modified where a contracting party can be shown to have been pressurised into making the contract. Pressure may be physical or economic (duress) or psychological (undue influence). A possible example of economic pressure might arise where an insured trader whose business premises are destroyed by fire in what appear to be suspicious circumstances feels obliged to accept a low settlement offer in order to minimise disruption to the business and loss of goodwill. An example of undue influence is provided by *Horry v Tate & Lyle Refineries Ltd* [1982] 2 Lloyd's Rep 416, in which a claimant injured at work was pressurised into accepting a settlement of £1,000 by statements to the effect that he was, due to his own lack of care, probably not entitled to any payment at all. The judge held that the settlement signed by the claimant should be set aside.

THE INSURER'S RIGHT OF SALVAGE

15.29 Once the insured and insurer have agreed upon a settlement, the insured is entitled to the policy monies. If there has been a total loss of the subject matter insured, the insurer has a common law right of salvage – that is, to take possession of whatever is left of the insured subject matter and deal with it as the insurer thinks fit. Thus, an insured whose car is treated as a total loss by the insurer must hand the wreckage to the insurer and the insurer is entitled to sell the wreckage (for scrap or repair) for its own benefit.

The principle of salvage also operates where insured subject matter, which has been lost and paid for as a total loss, once again comes into the insured's possession. This was the situation in *Holmes v Payne* (see **15.02** above), where the insured rediscovered her lost jewellery in her cape after the insurer had indemnified her for the loss. The insurer claimed repayment of the policy monies, but the trial judge held that, following settlement, the insurer was entitled only to the insured subject matter by way of salvage and could not overturn the settlement for mistake. The position is presumably the same when the insured wishes to retain the property and repay the policy monies (as will be the case where the property has a sentimental value or is underinsured); the insurer again has the right to demand the property by way of salvage but will need to act in a way which is consistent with its regulatory obligations to the customer.

The insurer's right of salvage is different in many ways from its rights of subrogation. One example is as follows. If an insurer takes possession of property by way of salvage and then sells it (or what remains of it) at a profit, the insurer is entitled to retain the profit. If, on the other hand, an insurer exercising its rights of subrogation recovers from a third party a sum in excess of its outlay under the policy, the insurer holds the balance on trust for the insured. For a fuller discussion of subrogation, see **Chapter 16**.

REINSTATEMENT

Definition

15.30 'Reinstatement' in this context is not the cost of reinstatement, as described at **15.11** above, but rather the actual repair or rebuilding of damaged property by or on behalf of the insurer. Reinstatement is only available if there is an express provision in the contract of insurance or under statute as between the insurer and a third party who, while not a party to the insurance, has some interest in the property.

The insured may himself be under an obligation to a third party to use the policy monies to reinstate the damaged property. Examples of this situation are:

(a) a policy procured by a landlord on a block of flats, with each lease requiring the landlord to use the policy monies to effect reinstatement;

(b) a hire purchase agreement on a motor vehicle under which the hirer is required to insure the vehicle and to use the insurance monies to repair it in the event of damage; and

(c) express provisions in a mortgage deed requiring the lender to reinstate.

Whether or not the insured is under an obligation depends upon the nature of his relationship with the third party. The general rule is that, unless there is an express obligation on the insured to reinstate, the third party has no right to require the insured to use the policy monies to do so (*Leeds v Cheetham* [1827] 1 Sim 146). However, where the insured is under a contractual duty to reinstate, he is under a corresponding implied duty to pursue the claim against the insurer and to reinstate the premises in the same condition as they were previously. In *Vural v Security Archives* [1990] 60 P&CR 258 it was held that the landlord of premises was required to reinstate the building using a floor covering which was suitable for the tenant's business. Furthermore, a person interested in the property may, under s 83 of the Fires Prevention (Metropolis) Act 1774, require the insurer to use the insurance monies to reinstate the property rather than pay the proceeds of the policy over to the insured. In addition, the Contracts (Rights of Third Parties) Act 1999 provides that third parties other than the insured who are identified in the policy by name, class or other description (and upon whom the policy purports to confer a benefit) may enforce the policy direct against the insurer. Thus, for example, a tenant or a lender whose interest is noted in the policy may be able to make a claim direct against the insurer even if he is not the insured under the policy (so long as the policy does not provide that the third party is not entitled to enforce his rights directly).

Reinstatement under the policy

The availability of reinstatement

15.31 Most policies on property confer upon the insurer the alternative rights, following damage to the property, either to indemnify the insured by means of the payment of money or to have the insured's property reinstated. The option is there for two reasons: reinstatement may be cheaper than a cash indemnity; and the insurer may suspect some form of malpractice on the part of the insured and may wish to ensure that the insured cannot gain in any way as a result of the loss. The option to reinstate is normally for the benefit of the insurer only; the insured has no right at common law to insist upon reinstatement as opposed to payment

(*Leppard v Excess Insurance Co Ltd* [1979] 2 All ER 668) and policies rarely confer that right.

The obligation to reinstate

15.32 Once a loss has occurred, an insurer that has a contractual right either to pay or to reinstate must exercise the option within the time limits set down by the policy or, if no limits are specified, within a reasonable time. As soon as the insurer has unequivocally stated its intention to reinstate or to pay, that decision is binding on the insurer: *Scarf v Jardine* (1882) 7 App Cas 345.

If the insurer has chosen to reinstate, a fresh contract for repair or rebuilding between the insurer and the insured comes into being. As is the case with all contracts for the supply of work and materials, the insurer is under an implied obligation to reinstate the property to an appropriate standard and must perform this obligation within a reasonable time. An illustration of the point is a Scottish decision, *Davidson v Guardian Royal Exchange Assurance* [1979] 1 Lloyd's Rep 406, where the insured was entitled to claim damages against the insurer for the failure of its agent (a garage) to repair the insured's car within a reasonable time.

Even if the insured nominates a repairer or builder to reinstate, the contractual position would appear to remain unchanged, in that the insurer remains liable to the insured for failure to reinstate or for defective reinstatement and there is no contract between the insured and the repairer. If, therefore, the repairer is negligent, the insured's claim remains one against the insurer. Conversely, the repairer has no claim against the insured for the cost of effecting the repairs and the repairer's rights can be enforced only against the insurer (*Godfrey Davis v Culling and Hecht* [1962] 2 Lloyd's Rep 349).

Unforeseen complications

15.33 An insurer that has elected to reinstate is under a contractual obligation to do so. If it proves to be the case that the cost of reinstatement is greater than originally anticipated (and even if the cost exceeds the monetary amount which would have been payable under the policy), the insurer is not excused from the obligation to reinstate in full.

A greater problem, however, arises in the situation in which the insurer, having opted to reinstate, finds that reinstatement is not merely more expensive than was originally contemplated, but impossible as a matter of law (eg, by reason of the intervention of planning authorities). The position here is as follows.

If the insurer has not commenced reinstatement when impossibility intervenes, the insurer's exercise of the option to reinstate is frustrated and the insurer's obligation reverts to the provision of a financial indemnity under the policy (*Anderson v Commercial Union Assurance Co* [1885] 55 LJQB 146).

If the insurer has commenced reinstatement when impossibility intervenes, the same position would appear to apply. The difficulty is that the insurer will have incurred expense, but it would seem that there is no legal basis upon which the insurer can seek to deduct any expenditure already incurred from the full sum owing to the insured.

In either case, if the insured has agreed with a third party that the policy monies are to be used to reinstate the property, and reinstatement is impossible, the general principle is that the policy monies must be divided between the insured and the third party in accordance with their respective interests in the property (*Beacon Carpets Ltd v Kirby* [1984] 2 All ER 726).

Statutory reinstatement

15.34 In the eighteenth century a particular form of insurance fraud gave rise to great difficulty. A tenant would procure a short-term (possibly weekly) lease on a building and would then start a fire, having insured the building for its full value. Insurers are not, of course, liable to the insured in such circumstances (see **Chapter 14**) but deterrence rested upon the chances of detection. Parliament ultimately rendered the practice unprofitable in an ingenious fashion by passing s 83 of the Fires Prevention (Metropolis) Act 1774 – a provision which has been copied throughout the common law world. Section 83, which is lengthy and complex, provides that an insurer of a house or building damaged or destroyed by fire is required, on the request of any person interested in the property, to cause the insurance monies to be laid out for the purpose of reinstatement. This ensures that any person setting fire to a building for the insurance money will not actually receive the money as long as a third party interested in the property intervenes and requests reinstatement.

The operation of s 83 is subject to a number of conditions, which are as follows:

(a) The section extends to England and Wales but not Scotland, and operates only in respect of buildings rather than their contents (*Re Barker, ex parte Gorely* [1864] 4 De G J&Sm 477). Moreover, the damage must be caused by fire.

(b) The section applies to insurance companies, but not to Lloyd's underwriters.

(c) Application by a person interested must be made to the insurer before the insurance money has been paid to the insured. Once the insured has received the insurance monies, notice to the insurer is ineffective.

(d) Persons interested in property in addition to the insured have been held to include the parties to a lease (*Wimbledon Park Golf Club Ltd v Imperial Insurance Co Ltd* [1902] 18 TLR 815), the parties to a mortgage (*Sinnott v Bowden* [1912] 2 Ch 414) and the parties to a contract of sale (see *Lonsdale & Thomson Ltd* at **15.16** above). A party to the policy cannot, however, give notice. In *Reynolds and Anderson* (see **15.11** above) a mortgagor was held not to be able to require the insurer to reinstate his house under a policy procured by the mortgagee to which the mortgagor was a named party.

(e) The insurer is liable to reinstate the premises, but only to the extent of the sum payable under the policy. This should be compared and contrasted with reinstatement under contract with the insured, where the insurer is liable to reinstate whatever the cost.

(f) The insurer's liability under s 83 arises only where the insurer would otherwise be liable to the insured under the policy. If, therefore, the insurer has a defence against the insured, s 83 cannot be relied upon. This point is particularly important where the property is damaged by fire after the insured has entered into a binding contract to sell the property. While the purchaser is an interested person, he will be unable to give notice to the insurer once he has made payment to the insured as at that stage the insured has suffered no loss. If, however, the insured vendor has agreed with a third party, such as a tenant, that he will reinstate the property in the event of loss, the insured is not indemnified by the payment by the purchaser and retains the right to claim under the policy: this will permit the purchaser to give notice to the insurer despite having made payment to the insured (see *Lonsdale & Thomson* at (d) above).

(g) The insurer, having received a valid notice, either must apply the insurance monies to reinstate the building or may pay them directly to the insured on receipt of some security for the insured's promise to reinstate.

(h) An insurer that refuses to reinstate may be restrained by an injunction in favour of the third party from making payment to the insured (see *Wimbledon Park Golf Club* at (d) above).

Chapter 16

Subrogation and assignment

- Nature of subrogation
- Scope of the right of subrogation
- Indemnification of the insured
- Actions against the emergency services
- Procedural aspects of subrogation actions
- Sums recovered by way of subrogation
- Assignment
- Assignment of the policy
- Assignment of the proceeds of the policy

NATURE OF SUBROGATION

Role of subrogation

16.01 The insurer's right of subrogation has been recognised in England since at least the middle of the eighteenth century. The principle is that an insurer, having indemnified the insured for his loss, is entitled to 'step into the shoes' of the insured and may commence proceedings in the insured's name against the third party who has caused the insured's loss. The sum recovered may then be retained by the insurer. The insurer's right of subrogation is codified in s 79 of the Marine Insurance Act 1906, which states that an insurer which has indemnified the insured for a total or partial loss is entitled to exercise all the rights and remedies of the insured arising as from the date of the loss, in relation to the insured subject matter. Subrogation does not give the insurer the right to take the insured subject matter itself; although in the case of a total loss, the parallel doctrine of abandonment confers upon the insurer the right to take possession of what is left of the insured subject matter.

Subrogation has two functions. Firstly, it ensures that the person who is actually responsible for the loss will pay for it, despite the fact that the victim of the loss has private insurance. In practice, however, the wrongdoer is himself likely to be insured, so that many subrogation actions are in effect attempts to seek to move the loss from one insurer to another. Secondly, the doctrine of subrogation furthers the indemnity function of insurance, by ensuring that the insured does not recover both from his insurer and from the wrongdoer to compensate him for a single loss.

Although the conceptual origins of an insurer's right of subrogation are not entirely clear, it is suggested that, following the House of Lords decision in *The Right Honourable Francis Nigel Baron Napier and Ettrick and Richards Butler v R F Kershaw Ltd* [1993] 1 Lloyd's Rep 197, subrogation is in fact fundamentally a legal doctrine which arises from the very nature of the contract of indemnity, albeit that it is customarily enforced by equitable remedies. The authorities are unclear as to whether the right to subrogate arises by virtue of an implied term of the contract (*Yorkshire Insurance Co Ltd v Nisbet Shipping Co Ltd* [1962] QB 330) or arises automatically on payment of the indemnity but independently of, or at best parasitically on, the express or implied terms of the insurance contract. (Note that the concept of a common law right distinct from the express or implied terms of the insurance contract is now the favoured analytical basis for the insurer's right to decline a fraudulent insurance claim and recover payments already made to the insured in respect of that claim (*Agapitos v Agnew* [2002] 3 WLR 616).) Irrespective of how it arises, however, the operation of subrogation in insurance cases can be modified by express contractual provisions and also by various terms implied into insurance policies by the courts. Subrogation is, therefore, a combination of equitable principles and express and implied policy terms.

An excellent summary of the historical genesis of subrogation is set out in *England v Guardian Insurance Ltd* [1999] 2 All ER (Comm) 481.

Practical operation of subrogation

16.02 In *Castellain v Preston* (1882-83) LR 11 QBD 380, Brett LJ stated the principles applicable to subrogation rights in the following words:

> '… as between the underwriter and the insured, the underwriter is entitled to the advantage of every right of the insured, whether such right consists in contract, fulfilled or unfulfilled, or in remedy for tort capable of being insisted on, or in any other right, whether by condition or otherwise, legal or equitable, which can be or has accrued, and whether such right could or could not be enforced by the insurer in the name of the insured by the exercise or acquiring of which right or condition the loss against which the insured is insured, can be, or has been diminished.'

In the actual case, the insured building was destroyed by fire between contract and completion, and the vendor had received both the insurance monies and the purchase price at the time of the action. The insurer was held to be entitled to recover the sum paid by the purchaser to the vendor by way of subrogation. The insurer is entitled to make a claim of this type only in respect of sums which have been paid to the insured by the third party to diminish his loss. This may give rise to fine distinctions. For example, in *Arthur Charles Burnand v Rodocanachi Sons & Co* (1881–82) LR 7 App Cas 333, compensation paid to the insured by the US government in the aftermath of the American Civil War was held, on the proper construction of the authorising legislation, to be by way of personal compensation and not in diminution of loss. Consequently, the insurer had no claim to the sum. By contrast, in *Steams v Village Main Reef Gold Mining Co* [1905] 21 TLR 236, compensation paid to the insured by the South African government following requisition of the insured's property was held to be intended to diminish loss and was thus subject to a subrogation recovery.

Subrogation is not in any event confined to insurers, but extends to any person giving an indemnity. An insurance-related question was discussed by the House of Lords in *Giles v Thompson* [1994] 1 AC 142. This case considered the validity of an agreement between a driver whose car had been damaged in a motor accident and a car-hire firm. The firm agreed to provide a hire car free to the insured pending the repair of his own vehicle (such loss being generally outside the cover provided by a motor policy) in return for the transfer to the firm of the insured's right to sue the wrongdoer for damages representing these costs. The House of Lords held that the agreement was valid, and in particular did not amount to champerty (interference with a cause of action).

Assignment as an alternative to subrogation

16.03 The insurer's right of subrogation arises automatically on the indemnification of the insured by the insurer, so that, in principle, an insurer can rely upon subrogation to recover from the third party a sum equivalent to that paid to the insured without having to take any further steps in relation to the insured. However, in some situations, insurers prefer to take an assignment of the insured's cause of action against the third party. Assignment has two main advantages:

(a) The insurer need not pay the insured before exercising assigned rights against the third party; and

(b) Under an assignment, the insurer is able to retain the entire sum recovered from the third party, whereas under subrogation the insurer retains only the nominal amount actually paid to the insured.

Assignment has two potential drawbacks. Firstly, the insurer has to call upon the insured to assign his rights after the loss. However, there is no objection to a policy term which effects such an assignment. Secondly, if the insurer has taken a legal assignment of rights, the action must be brought in its own name; many insurers prefer anonymity in the process of pursuing third parties.

SCOPE OF THE RIGHT OF SUBROGATION

Indemnity contract

16.04 The doctrine of subrogation applies only to insurance contracts which are contracts of indemnity, given that one of the primary purposes of subrogation is to prevent the insured from recovering more than an indemnity. All forms of property insurance are indemnity contracts; whereas the same is not true of all forms of life policies, so the holder of a life policy may be able to recover both the policy monies and damages from the person causing the insured's death. Personal accident policies are, for subrogation purposes, classified as non-indemnity contracts, so that an insured who suffers personal injuries can claim both from the insurer and from the wrongdoer in each case without discount for the other's payment (*Theobald v Railway Passengers Assn* (1854) 10 Ex 45). As new insurance products develop, the courts may be called upon to decide whether these new policies are indemnity policies for subrogation purposes.

Insured must have a cause of action

16.05 An insurer exercising subrogation rights can obtain no better rights against the wrongdoer than the insured himself possessed at the date of the loss. If, for some reason, the insured has no cause of action against the third party, the insurer itself cannot sue the third party; although in some circumstances the insurer may have a right to proceed against the insured for failing to protect the insurer's subrogation rights. The insurer's rights will depend upon why the insured has no cause of action against the third party. A variety of situations might be found.

Wrongdoer is a party to the policy

16.06 Subrogation rights cannot be exercised against a person who is party to the contract of insurance. In *Simpson and Co v Thomson, Burrell* (1877–78) LR 3 App Cas 279 the insured's two vessels were involved in a collision. The House of Lords held that the insurer could not deny liability for the damage to one of the vessels by arguing that the damage was caused by the negligence of the insured's own agents, and that the liability was cancelled out by the right to claim the loss from the insured by way of subrogation.

The same principle applies where the wrongdoer is a co-insured (ie, where the parties are co-owners or where the parties have different interests under the policy (see Chapter 17)). The difficulty here is in determining whether there is co-insurance. In *Petrofina (UK) Ltd v Magnaload Ltd* [1983] 3 All ER 35, a policy taken out by a head contractor for itself and all subcontractors was held to be intended to make subcontractors co-insureds. Thus, when a subcontractor negligently damaged property on the site, the insurer, having paid for the loss, was unable to exercise subrogation rights against the subcontractor. If, by contrast, the policy does not specifically state that subcontractors are to be co-insureds, and the arrangements between the contractor and the subcontractor do not contemplate that the contractor will insure on the subcontractor's behalf, the subcontractor cannot claim to be party to the insurance and will face a subrogation claim (*Stone Vickers Ltd v Appledore Ferguson Shipbuilders Ltd* [1992] 2 Lloyd's Rep 578). A policy which does cover subcontractors will extend to a subcontractor that has not authorised the contractor to procure a policy, provided that it ratifies the contractor's act of insuring for it, ratification being possible even after the loss has occurred (*National Oilwell (UK) Ltd v Davy Offshore Ltd* [1993] 2 Lloyd's Rep 582). Consideration must also be given to the type of losses covered by the co-insurance: in *Kruger Tissue (Industrial) Ltd v Franks Gallier Ltd* 57 Con LR 1 the policy provided co-insurance in respect of existing structures and their contents, but not in respect of loss of profits or increased costs of working resulting from damage to the existing structures and their contents. Thus, the insurer was able to subrogate against the contractor in respect of consequential losses, although not in respect of the loss to the existing structures and contents themselves.

Wrongdoer contemplated as a beneficiary of the policy

16.07 In some situations, two parties holding different interests in the same subject matter may agree that only one of them is to be a named insured under the policy, although the intention is that the policy should cover their respective interests. This arrangement is commonly found between a landlord and a tenant: the landlord (although it may be the tenant) insures, but the premium is paid by the tenant and it is intended that the policy monies are to be used in reinstating the premises in the event of a loss. Insurers generally require the interest of the tenant to be 'noted' on the policy, although noting does not have the effect of creating a co-insurance.

An arrangement of this type is intended to obtain insurance for the benefit of both landlord and tenant even though only the landlord is a party to the insurance. In *Mark Rowlands Ltd v Berni Inns Ltd and Others* [1985] 3 All ER 473, the policy was taken out by the landlord with the premiums paid by the tenant, and the building was damaged by fire due to the apparent negligence of the tenant. The insurer paid the landlord and sought to exercise subrogation rights against the tenant. The Court of Appeal held that a term was to be implied into the lease to the effect that, in the event of any loss to the premises caused by the tenant, the landlord had no right to proceed against the tenant but must instead recover from the insurer. Given that the landlord had no right to sue the tenant, the insurer had no subrogation rights against the tenant and must bear the loss.

Wrongdoer exempted from liability by contract with insured

16.08 If the insured has agreed to exempt the third party from liability, the insurer is bound by the insured's agreement. In *Tate & Sons v Hyslop* (1884-85) LR 15 QBD 368, a cargo owner entered into an agreement with the carrier under which the carrier was to be liable only for negligence. The cargo owner subsequently insured the cargo, but did not disclose to the insurer the restriction on his rights. Following loss caused by the carrier without negligence on its part, it became clear that no subrogation rights could exist against the carrier. However, the insurer was held to be able to avoid the policy for the insured's failure to disclose to the insurer that subrogation rights had been prejudiced in this way.

The opposite can arise where a contractual indemnity gives rise to rights of the insured which it might otherwise not have. These indemnities are common in complex construction projects. One issue for the courts is whether the right of an insurer where such indemnities exist is one of contribution, as if the contractual indemnity were itself an insurance policy (see **Chapter 18**), or one of subrogation. In a Scottish case arising out of the Piper Alpha oil rig disaster, *Caledonian North Sea v London Bridge Engineering* [2002] 1 Lloyd's Rep 553, the court decided that such contractual indemnities allocated primary responsibilities and that the insurance was in case of non-recovery under the indemnity. As such, subrogation rights against the giver of the indemnity could arise.

Loss of cause of action by the insured

16.09 There is an implied term in every contract of insurance that the insured will not, after the loss, throw away his cause of action against the wrongdoer and thereby prejudice the insurer's subrogation rights (see *Lord Napier and Ettrick* at **16.01** above). If the insured does enter into arrangements with the wrongdoer under which the wrongdoer is excused liability, the insurer is bound by those arrangements, although the insurer will have an action against the insured for the loss caused by his conduct. The question of whether the insured faces liability to the insurer for a post-loss settlement of rights depends upon whether the settlement was or was not *bona fide*. If the settlement is based upon the fact that the insured has received, or is to receive, an equivalent sum from the insurer, the settlement is plainly prejudicial to the insurer's rights and the insured must make up the amount lost (*West of England Fire Insurance Co v Isaacs* [1897] 1 QB 226). By contrast, if the settlement is based upon genuine negotiations, the insurer is bound by it and has no cause of action against the insured.

These principles were applied in *Horwood v Land of Leather (in administration) & Zurich Insurance plc* [2010] EWHC 546 (Comm), also known as 'the toxic sofas litigation'. In that case, the claimants brought personal injury claims against a retailer of sofas that they had purchased. The retailer, which was insured, had entered into settlement agreements with its suppliers without consulting its insurer. The judge found that the insurer was not liable because a claims control clause operated as a condition precedent to the insurer's liability. The judge also found that there was an implied term in each insurance policy that an insured must act reasonably and in good faith with due regard to the insurer's interests and subrogation rights.

Waiver of subrogation rights by the insurer

16.10 An insurer may stipulate in the policy that subrogation rights are not to be exercised against named persons or classes of persons. This form of provision is common in construction contracts where co-insurance arrangements are not used, the object being to eliminate the cost of allocating any losses on site between the contractor and the various subcontractors by requiring the contractor's insurer to bear the loss. The subrogation waiver clause is not, however, effective in law with respect to parties who are not co-insureds. In *National Oilwell* (see **16.06** above) the High Court ruled that a subcontractor who was not party to the contract of insurance could not rely upon a subrogation waiver purported to be in his favour. If he was a party to the policy, he was a co-insured protected from subrogation; and if he was not a party to the policy, then the doctrine of privity of contract prevented reliance on the subrogation waiver clause.

INDEMNIFICATION OF THE INSURED

Actual payment by the insurer

16.11 Before the insurer can be subrogated to the rights of the insured against the wrongdoer, the insurer must have provided an indemnity to the insured. If the insurer has failed to pay the entire sum due under the policy, subrogation rights cannot arise. This is illustrated by *Page v Scottish Insurance Corporation, Ltd* (1929) 33 Ll L Rep 134, where the insurer refused to admit liability to the insured in respect of his possible liability following a motor vehicle accident. The insurer was held not to be able to claim from a third party the costs of repairing the insured's car.

The insurer's liability to indemnify the insured

16.12 As long as the insurer has paid the insured, the insurer will obtain subrogation rights. This is so even if the payment is made by way of settlement, without the insurer's liability having been fully established as a matter of law. This was held to be the case in *King v Victoria Insurance Co, Ltd* [1896] AC 250; and in *Lord Napier and Ettrick* (see **16.01** above) the Court of Appeal and House of Lords simply assumed that an insurer which settles is permitted to claim from the third party.

An insurer which pays in the clear knowledge that it is not liable under the policy will not, however, obtain subrogation rights, as subrogation is not available with respect to pure *ex gratia* payments. This rule can be sidestepped by means of express agreement between the insurer and the insured. In *Naumann v Ford* [1985] 2 EGL R 70, the insured tenant agreed with the insurer that the insurer would pay the loss *ex gratia* (the policy having lapsed), and that the insured would bring an action against the wrongdoer and would hold the proceeds on trust for the insurer. The High Court ruled that the insured's action against the wrongdoer was permissible and was not defeated by the fact that the insured had been indemnified by the insurer.

Rights of the insurer prior to payment

16.13 The insurer has no subrogation rights against the third party prior to making payment to the insured. At this stage, the action against the third party belongs entirely to the insured; although if the insured prejudices the insurer's rights by entering into a settlement with the wrongdoer which cannot be justified on objective grounds, the insurer will have an action against the insured for breach of contract (*Faircharm Investments Ltd v Citibank International plc* [1998] Lloyd's Rep Bank 127; and see also *Horwood v Land of Leather (in administration) & Zurich Insurance plc*, discussed above). Most of the authorities, however, consider positive acts by the insured not acts of omission.

A further question is whether the insured is, in this pre-indemnification period, under a positive duty to preserve the insurer's rights. This creates a potential difficulty where the insurer anticipates that, unless speedy action is taken against the third party, any right of recovery against him may prove to be unenforceable. This might arise, for example, where the third party has taken steps to transfer his assets outside the UK, or where the insured is faced with a limitation period (the latter being particularly important in marine cargo claims, where the contractual limitation period may be no more than one year). In such cases, the insured is perfectly free to seek a Mareva injunction against the third party freezing his assets or to issue a 'protective' writ preserving the cause of action against the operation of a limitation period; but an insured who is fully covered by insurance has no particular incentive to incur the expense of doing so. It is undecided whether the insurer can require the insured to take a pre-emptive step of this type.

Some policies may impose the necessary obligation upon the insured, but in the absence of an express obligation it is far from clear that the insurer could insist upon this. In *AB Svensk Exportkredit v New Hampshire Insurance Co*, unreported, 1998, the Court of Appeal held that a reasonable care clause in an insurance policy (obliging the insured to take reasonable care to avoid incurring a loss) did not have the effect of allowing the insurer to control the insured's conduct prior to having been paid by the insurer. In *Noble Resources Ltd and Unirise Development Ltd v George Albert Greenwood ('The Vasso')* [1993] 2 Lloyd's Rep 309, it was held that a sue and labour clause in a marine policy did not operate to require the insured to seek a Mareva injunction, and it was not suggested by the insurer that subrogation might have had any different effect. Thus, insurers generally include a wide-ranging clause allowing them to exercise the rights of the insured and commence proceedings prior to payment of the indemnity.

Loss exceeding the sum insured

The insured's right to proceed

16.14 It is commonly the case that the amount lost by the insured exceeds the sum payable by the insurer under the policy. This may arise either because the insured bears an excess (also known as a retention or deductible) which requires him to meet the first part of his own loss, or because the insured is underinsured. The two forms have very different consequences.

Turning first to the case in which the insured bears an excess under the policy, it was held by the House of Lords in *Lord Napier and Ettrick* (see **16.01** above) that the amount of the excess is deemed not to be a loss within the terms of the policy as the insured has agreed to bear the amount of the excess. Consequently, full payment by the insurer after deducting the excess means that, as far as the insurer is concerned, the insured has received a full indemnity. In such a case, the control of the action passes to the insurer under the doctrine of subrogation, which means that the insured will recoup his excess only if the insurer is able to recover the full amount of the claim from the third party, as the insurer can retain only the amount of its own payment and must hand over the surplus to the insured.

By contrast, if the insured is underinsured because the policy limits do not extend to the full amount of the loss, the insurer obtains subrogation rights by virtue of its payment, but the insured retains the right to control the action against the third party (*Commercial Union Assurance Co v Lister* (1873-74) LR 9 Ch App 483). The insurer is, therefore, bound by any settlement reached between the third party and the insured (although the insurer will have an action against the insured for breach of an implied term in the insurance policy prohibiting the insured from prejudicing the insurer's subrogation rights – see above). Equally, the insurer is bound by the insured's conduct of the action. In *Terence Trevor Hayler v D G Chapman*

[1989] 1 Lloyd's Rep 490, a motor case, the insured obtained judgment against the wrongdoer only for the uninsured sum, as the rest of the insured's loss had been recovered from his own insurer. The insured's insurer sought to have the judgment set aside on the ground that the insured had sought an inadequate amount. The Court of Appeal ruled that a judgment could not be set aside unless fraud on the part of the defendant (or the defendant's insurer) could be shown (eg, by not contesting the insured's claim in the knowledge that an inadequate sum had been claimed). As there was no fraud, the judgment had to stand: the insured's insurer in such a case would, therefore, be required to proceed against the insured for prejudicing his subrogation rights. In *Buckland v Palmer* [1984] 3 All ER 554, another motor case, the insured commenced an action against the third party for the uninsured sum. The insurer here stepped in at an earlier stage, and before the case had been heard the insurer issued its own proceedings against the defendant for the sum which had been paid to the insured under the policy. The Court of Appeal held that two sets of proceedings could not be commenced in relation to the same cause of action, and held that the proper approach was for the insurer to apply for the insured's action to be set aside and fresh proceedings for the entire loss to be commenced.

Stopping an action by the insured

16.15 An insurer which has subrogation rights is likely to wish to use them. However, there may be cases in which the insurer does not want proceedings against the third party to be pursued. The most likely explanation for this is the existence of a 'knock-for-knock' or equivalent agreement between the insured's motor insurer and the wrongdoer's liability insurer, under which each insurer has agreed to bear first-party losses and not to pursue liability claims. This situation arose in *Hobbs v Marlowe* [1978] AC 16, although the House of Lords did not go as far as ruling that an insurer has a right under the doctrine of subrogation to halt an action by the insured; in this case, such a right was to be found in the express subrogation clause in the policy. If an insured has initiated proceedings on his own initiative, then generally he cannot be restrained by the insurer.

An insured who did successfully proceed against the third party contrary to his own insurer's wishes would not, of course, be able to retain both the insurance monies and the damages recoverable from the third party; a sum equivalent to the insurer's payment to the insured would have to be returned to the insurer.

ACTIONS AGAINST THE EMERGENCY SERVICES

16.16 The courts have been reluctant to impose a positive duty of care upon emergency services to protect property owners. They have distinguished between the statutory duty which might be owed by the emergency services, making them liable under any particular legislation, and the establishment of a common law duty of care which, if proven, may lead to the payment of substantial damages. It is rare for substantial damages to be awarded against an emergency service In *Digital Equipment Co Ltd v Hampshire County Council and Capital & Counties plc v Same* [1997] 2 Lloyd's Rep 161, it was established that a fire brigade did not owe a duty of care to individual owners of premises other than in special circumstances. Those circumstances would normally involve the emergency service intervening and aggravating the damage by way of a positive act of negligence. Thus, for example, if the fire brigade failed to respond in time or respond with sufficient engines, the property owner would be unable to establish the requisite duty of care. On the other hand, in this particular case, the fire brigade intervened and turned off the sprinkler protection system, thus substantially aggravating the problem. In those circumstances, the brigade had created a fresh danger or substantially increased the risk of damage. The ongoing reluctance of the courts, however, to impose such duties is demonstrated by the decision of *OLL v Secretary of State for Transport* [1997] 3 All ER 897, in which the court purported to follow the above case, but decided that the failures of the coastguard when positively misdirecting the rescue attempts of others did not create a duty and breach so as to establish a claim for damages. It is difficult to distinguish between the two cases.

PROCEDURAL ASPECTS OF SUBROGATION ACTIONS

16.17 Subrogation proceedings must be brought by the insurer in the name of the insured. If the insured's name, for some reason, cannot be used – for example, because the insured is a company which has been dissolved and has thus ceased to exist (*M H Smith (Plant Hire) Ltd v D L Mainwaring (T/A Inshore)* [1986] 2 Lloyd's Rep 244) – subrogation rights will be lost. In other cases, the insurer can compel an unwilling insured to lend his its name to the action, and can also compel the insured to permit the insurer to control the conduct of the action. It was indeed suggested by the House of Lords in *Lord Napier and Ettrick* (see **16.01** above) that the insurer possesses an equitable charge over the insured's action, although their Lordships were not prepared to go any further than ruling that there is an implied term in the contract of insurance under which the insured is under a duty to allow the use of his name.

The fact that the insurer is not suing in its own name should not be overlooked. In *Russell v Wilson*, Independent, 2 June 1989, the plaintiff's insurer brought a subrogation action against the defendant motorist, represented by his liability insurer. Since the claim was for a small amount, the matter was heard under the small claims procedure in the county court, under which procedure each party bears its own costs. The court ruled that the successful insurer had to bear its own costs, despite the fact that these greatly exceeded the sum in dispute.

In *Kitchen Design and Advice Ltd v Lea Valley Water Co* [1989] 2 Lloyd's Rep 221, the plaintiff was insured against property damage and consequential loss. The defendant's conduct resulted in water damage to the plaintiff's property, for which payment was made by the plaintiff's insurer. The insurer, exercising subrogation rights, then reached a full and final settlement with the defendant's insurer for a slightly smaller sum. Subsequently, the plaintiff made a further claim against its insurer for consequential loss. This claim was met, but the insurer found itself unable, by reason of its settlement with the defendant's insurer, to seek indemnification from it. The plaintiff's insurer commenced proceedings against the defendant in the insured's name, arguing that the settlement which had been reached bound only the two insurers, and that it did not affect the plaintiff and defendant themselves. This argument had become possible only because the insurers, in settling, had done so in their own names and not in the names of the parties. The High Court nevertheless dismissed the action, holding that the plaintiff's policy was to be construed as authorising the insurer to enter into settlements on the plaintiff's behalf, so that the insurer had settled the plaintiff's rights by its agreement with the defendant's insurer.

SUMS RECOVERED BY WAY OF SUBROGATION

Ownership

16.18 Sums in respect of which the insurer may have a subrogation claim may be received in one of two ways:

(a) By virtue of the fact that the third party has made payment to the insured: In such a case, the insured must account to the insurer for some or all of that payment. The capacity in which the sum is held by the insured is of importance in the event that the insured becomes insolvent before payment has been made to the insurer; if the insured is merely a debtor of the insurer, the insurer is purely an unsecured creditor and will have no prioritised claim in the event of insolvency. If, by contrast, the insured holds the money in a fiduciary capacity, the insurer has a priority in any bankruptcy or liquidation proceedings. The question was resolved in the insurer's favour by the House of Lords in *Lord Napier and Ettrick* (see **16.01** above). Their Lordships ruled that the insurer had an equitable charge or lien over the money, so that it was impressed with a security interest in favour of the insurer. This conclusion was the direct result of the equitable nature of subrogation.

(b) By means of an action against the third party brought by the insurer in the insured's name: Here, the money will go directly to the insurer. If the insurer has recovered a sum greater than its own payment to the insured, that must be paid to the insured; and pending payment is, it might be assumed in the light of *Lord Napier and Ettrick,* to be held subject to an equitable charge or lien in the insured's favour.

Allocation

16.19 When a sum of money has been obtained from the third party by either the insurer or the insured, the question arises of how it is to be allocated between them. There are two general principles here.

The first is that the insurer can never recover by way of subrogation a nominal sum greater than had been paid to the insured. In *Yorkshire Insurance Co Ltd v Nisbet Shipping Co Ltd* [1962] 2 QB 330, the insured suffered a loss of £72,000, which was paid by the insurer. The insured then recovered £126,000 from the wrongdoer (the Canadian government). The discrepancy arose because of alterations in the exchange rate; and the reality of the situation was that the amount recovered, although nominally greater than the loss, was in practical terms equal to it. The court nevertheless held that subrogation operated on nominal payments, and held that the insurer could claim only £72,000 of the recovery, leaving the insured with a windfall of £54,000. In this type of situation, the insurer would be better advised to seek an assignment of the insured's rights, as assignment allows the insurer to retain the full amount of any recovery.

The second general principle is that the insured is entitled to receive an indemnity, so that any monies recovered from the third party must first be allocated to the insured to make up any shortfall between his loss and the sum recovered from the insurer. In determining the total amount of the insured's loss for this purpose, any excess borne by the insured is to be disregarded. The principle is well illustrated by *Lord Napier and Ettrick* (see **16.01** above). Here, the insureds (Lloyd's Names) were insured against underwriting losses, and also had causes of action against those responsible for the losses. The House of Lords worked on assumed figures of:

Recovery from wrongdoer	£150,000
Total loss	£160,000
Sum insured	£100,000
Uninsured excess	£25,000

The insureds were paid the sum insured of £100,000, but this still left the insureds with a loss of £60,000, consisting of £25,000 excess and £35,000 above the policy limits. The House of Lords held that the uninsured excess was to be disregarded in determining the insureds' loss, as that sum had been agreed to be borne by the insured. This left a 'recover down' principle, under which the £150,000 recovered was to be applied in the following order:

(a) The first £35,000 went to the insureds, to provide them with an indemnity;

(b) The next £100,000 went to the insurer, by way of subrogation; and

(c) The balance of £15,000 went to the insureds, on the principle that the insurer can never retain more than the nominal amount which it had paid.

The 'recover down' principle is equally applicable to a commercial insurance which is arranged in layers: any subrogation recovery goes to the top layer insurer first, on the basis that the layering arrangement is intended to ensure that it is the last insurer to bear any loss.

Costs

16.20 Insurance policies commonly contain clauses which, notwithstanding all of the above, specify in detail how recoveries are to be allocated between the insurer and the insured. Such clauses often reflect the 'top-down' approach recognised in *Lord Napier and Ettrick*, although different approaches are also possible (eg, the insurer may recoup either a proportion of or its entire loss at an earlier point than would be the case under the 'top-down' approach). Such clauses also typically provide for the costs of the recovery action to be reimbursed first.

The costs of a subrogated action will normally be paid by the insurer if the insured has been fully indemnified. Where the action includes claims for insured and uninsured losses, the insurer and the insured are free to agree how the action is to be funded, in whatever proportions they consider to be appropriate.

ASSIGNMENT

16.21 English law provides different mechanisms for the assignment, or transfer, of 'choses in action', such as contractual and other rights. Insurance policies and rights of payment under insurance policies are choses in action, and are therefore, in principle, transferable from the insured to a third party. The assignment of insurance rights concerns two very different matters:

(a) the assignment of the policy itself; and

(b) the assignment of the right to recover the debt owed by the insurer under the policy.

The differences flow from the fact that where the policy itself is assigned, there is a change of insured; whereas where there is an assignment of the right to recover, the insured stays the same. It is important to note that an assignee of the policy of insurance can only recover losses sustained by him to his interest, whereas an assignee of a right of recovery can only recover for losses sustained by the insured (who stays the same).

Assignment, for the purposes of this book, is concerned only with voluntary assignment of policies and their proceeds. Transfer may also occur by operation of law on the death or insolvency of the insured.

ASSIGNMENT OF THE POLICY

General prohibition

16.22 The general rule is that a contract of insurance is a personal contract between the insurer and the insured, in that the insurer only undertakes the risk having considered with care the character of the insured and the potential for loss under the policy. The law does not, therefore, permit the insured to transfer his policy to a third party and thereby to change the nature of the risk originally accepted by the insurer.

The general rule disallowing assignment is nevertheless subject to three exceptions. A policy may be assignable if:

(a) the insurer consents to the transfer;

(b) the policy is a marine policy; or

(c) the policy is a life policy.

Consent of the insurer

16.23 The insurer may consent to the transfer of the policy either by including a right to transfer in the policy itself or by consenting to an express request for a transfer. An illustration of the former possibility is the clause sometimes found in policies on buildings which states that the purchaser of the property is to be entitled to the benefit of the seller's insurance for the period between exchange of contracts and conveyance to the purchaser. Similar clauses also appear in credit insurance policies, when it is envisaged that the underlying loan may be assigned to other lenders.

The effect of failure to obtain the insurer's consent to assignment is demonstrated by *Peters v General Accident Fire & Life Assurance Corporation* (1938) 60 Ll L Rep 311, which held that where the insured sold his motor vehicle and assigned his motor policy covering the motor vehicle contemporaneously to a third party, the assignment of the policy without consent had the effect of terminating the policy automatically.

Where the insurer has consented to the assignment of the policy, it is important for reasons of insurable interest that there is a simultaneous assignment to the third party of the subject matter insured by the policy and the policy itself.

If the insured purports to assign the property before he assigns the policy, his insurable interest in the policy will lapse and the policy will become ineffective. This was so held in *Rogerson v Scottish Automobile & General Insurance Co Ltd* [1931] 41 Ll L Rep 1, in which the insured's motor policy was held to have lapsed on his selling the car which was insured under it. The policy can survive in this situation only if the insured has retained some insurable interest – for example, in the case of a motor policy where the policy covers the insured while driving other vehicles (*Dodson v Peter H Dodson Insurance Services* [2001] 1 WLR 1012, disapproving of *Boss v Kingston* [1962] 2 Lloyd's Rep 431), or in the case of a property policy where the insured retains legal ownership until the purchase price on the sale of a property has been paid (*Rayner v Preston* (1881) 18 Ch D 1).

If, by contrast, the insured purports to assign the policy before he assigns the property, the assignee of the policy does not at that stage have any insurable interest in the property. It was held in *Lloyd v Fleming* (1872) LR 7 QB 299 that a third-party assignee cannot recover as at the date of the assignment of the policy, as he did not possess an insurable interest, and the insured cannot recover as he has assigned the policy. This disregards the insurable interest rule that a policy on property is lawful as long as the insured has a reasonable expectation of obtaining an insurable interest (see Chapter 4). The correct rule seems to be that the insured assignee cannot recover if a loss occurs before the property is transferred to him, but he can recover if the loss occurs after the policy and the property have both fallen into his ownership.

Formalities

16.24 A contract of insurance, as a chose in action, can be assigned either at law or in equity. There is a need for an express assignment in all cases, as the mere fact that the subject matter of a contract of insurance is transferred to a purchaser does not have the effect of carrying with it any policy on that subject matter (Marine Insurance Act 1906, s 15). A legal assignment must comply with s 136 of the Law of Property Act 1925, the requirements of which are as follows:

(a) The assignment must be in writing and signed by the assignor;

(b) The assignment must be intended to transfer the entirety of the assignor's interest (and not merely a part of the interest – eg, where the policy is mortgaged); and

(c) Written notice of the assignment must be given to the insurer.

An assignment which fails to meet one or more of these requirements will nevertheless take effect as an equitable assignment, as long as an intention to assign can be demonstrated.

A legal assignment is preferable from the assignee's point of view, for two reasons:

(a) A legal assignment allows the assignee to bring proceedings against the insurer in his own name. As the law does not recognise an equitable assignment, an action on the policy must be brought by the assignee and the assignor jointly. This is only a technical problem, as the court can force the assignor to lend his name to the proceedings.

(b) Taking a legal assignment protects the assignee against fraud. Priorities of competing assignments, whether legal or equitable, are determined by the dates of notice of the assignment being given to the insurer. Thus, if the insured assigns his policy to A without giving notice to the insurer, and then fraudulently assigns his policy to B, B (assuming that he was not, at the time of assignment to him, aware of what has gone before) may obtain priority over A by being first to notify the insurer of his interest.

Marine policies

16.25 It is a long-established principle in the common law, as codified in s 50(1) of the Marine Insurance Act 1906, that marine policies can be assigned unless the terms of the policy say otherwise. This recognises the basis upon which shipping business is transacted, and in particular the 'cost insurance freight' form of export contract, under which the seller of goods is obliged to arrange for the transport, as well as arranging the insurance policy, to be assigned to the buyer on payment for the goods.

The procedure for, and effect of, assigning marine policies are set out in ss 50(3) and 50(2) respectively of the Marine Insurance Act 1906, which provide that:

(a) a policy may be assigned by endorsement or in any other customary manner;

(b) assignment has the effect of allowing the assignee to proceed against the insurer in the assignee's own name; and

(c) there is no requirement for the assignee to give notice of assignment to the insurer in order to create a legal assignment.

A marine policy is assignable only if it does not contain terms expressly prohibiting assignment.

Life policies

16.26 A life policy requires the insurer to make payment to the policyholder on the death of the life insured. As long as the policyholder has an insurable interest in the insured life at the date the contract is made, the policy will be freely assignable unless the policy provides otherwise (which today is rare). Life policies may be sold or mortgaged.

A life policy may be assigned in any of the following ways:

(a) under the provisions of the Policies of Assurance Act 1867;

(b) in compliance with s 136 of the Law of Property Act 1925; or

(c) in equity.

Policies of Assurance Act 1867

16.27 Prior to the Policies of Assurance Act 1867, a life policy was not assignable at law. However, under the 1867 Act, an assignment is valid if it is of the assignor's whole interest in the policy.

A policy may be assigned under the 1867 Act, either by endorsement on the policy or by a separate document in the form set out in the schedule to the 1867 Act. Notice of the assignment must be given to the insurer.

Section 136 of the Law of Property Act 1925

16.28 A life policy is a chose in action and as such can be assigned under the provisions of the Law of Property Act 1925. An assignment of a life policy under this provision requires that the assignment of the life policy be absolute, so that the assignor must transfer the entirety of his interest.

The formalities are as follows:

(a) The assignment must be in writing and signed by the assignor; and

(b) Written notice of the assignment must be given to the insurer.

Equity

16.29 An assignment of a life policy may also be assigned in equity without formality and without notice to the insurer. Various forms of assignment will commonly overlap. Where a number of successive assignments by a fraudulent policyholder have been made, the first assignee to give notice to the insurer will take priority, as long as he was not aware of any previous assignments when he took his own assignment.

Consequences of assignment of a policy

16.30 An assignment, whether legal or equitable, of a policy has the effect of bringing into existence a new contract between the insurer and the assignee. This does not mean, however, that previous matters affecting the policy are disregarded, for the rule is that assignment is always 'subject to equities'. This means that any defence to a claim, or any right to avoid the policy which the insurer had obtained before the assignment remains in place and can be relied upon against the assignee after the assignment. The position is spelled out by s 50(2) of the Marine Insurance Act 1906, which provides that the insurer 'is entitled to make any defence arising out of the contract which he would have been entitled to make if the action had been brought in the name of the (original insured)'. A similar wording is found in s 136 of the Law of Property Act 1925 and s 2 of the Policies of Assurance Act 1867. Matters which can be pleaded against the assignee include failure by the insured to disclose a material fact when the policy was taken out and breach of warranty by the insured.

ASSIGNMENT OF THE PROCEEDS OF THE POLICY

Principles governing assignment

16.31 The proceeds of the policy constitute a debt payable by the insurer to the insured. Debts are freely assignable as choses in action. The proceeds of a policy may be assigned either:

(a) under s 136 of the terms of the Law of Property Act 1925; or

(b) in equity.

The differences between an assignment of the policy and an assignment of the proceeds are as follows:

(a) An assignment of the proceeds does not give rise to a new contract between the insurer and the assignee, which means that the insured is still the assignor, and for that reason the consent of the insurer to assignment is not needed unless the policy expressly so provides.

(b) The assignee does not need to have an insurable interest in the subject matter of the policy and as such, the subject matter does not also have to be assigned.

An assignment of the proceeds of the policy can be effected at law, by compliance with s 136 of the Law of Property Act 1925 or in equity (see **16.28** above). If the assignment is legal, the assignee can sue the insurer in his own name; if not, the assignor must be joined to the action. An assignee of the proceeds, nevertheless, is in a somewhat weaker position as regards the insurer than is an assignee of the policy itself. This is the case because there is no change of insured, so that the rights of the assignee are purely dependent upon the conduct of the insured. Not only is the assignee's right to recover limited by any wrongful conduct by the insured prior to the assignment (eg, breach of the duty of utmost good faith, breach of warranty, etc) (see **Chapter 2**), but the assignee is affected by post-assignment misconduct. The point is that the assignee can claim the proceeds only if the proceeds would have been payable to the insured.

If, therefore, the insured fails to make a claim under the policy within the time allowed by the policy, the insurer has a defence to the claim and the assignee has no rights. Similarly, if the insured, having assigned the right to recover, breaks a warranty in the policy, there are no proceeds payable and there is no available fund against which the assignee can press his claim (*Bank of Nova Scotia v Hellenic Mutual War Risks Association (Bermuda) Ltd (The 'Good Luck')* [1991] 3 All ER 1 – breach of warranty by the insured vessel's entering into a war zone). It is for this reason that an assignee would be well advised to procure his own fall-back policy which will provide an indemnity to him in the event that the insured's own policy for some reason does not provide an indemnity. An example of this would be a mortgagee's interest policy providing for indemnity in the event that the primary insurer repudiates liability.

Sale of land

16.32 The problem here is the two-stage process applicable to a contract for the sale of land. At the initial contract stage, the purchaser bears the risk while the seller remains the owner, and ownership is transferred to the purchaser only at the second stage of completion. The effect of the purchaser bearing the risk in the period between contract and completion is that the purchaser must pay the full price on completion, irrespective of any damage which may have taken place regarding the property (see *Rayner v Preston* at **16.22** above). To reverse this rule, which in effect requires both parties to maintain insurance for that period, s 47 of the Law of Property Act 1925 provides that any sum payable to the seller under its own policy shall be held for the purchaser on completion. The purchaser is therefore only liable to pay the purchase price, net of the insurance recovery, by virtue of a statutory assignment of the policy proceeds. This provision is subject to various conditions including, *inter alia*, obtaining the consent of the insurer.

The section is, however, fundamentally flawed as it disregards the fact that the seller's insurer, having paid the insured, is entitled to exercise subrogation rights against the purchaser and to claim payment under the contract of sale from the purchaser. The problem is largely resolved by the Law Society's Standard Conditions of Sale (5th edition), which provide that the seller is under no obligation to insure the property from the date of the contract, when the property becomes at the risk of the purchaser.

Chapter 17

Co-insurance

- Introduction
- Joint insurance
- Composite insurance
- Co-insured subrogation immunity
- Insurance for the benefit of another

INTRODUCTION

17.01 'Co-insurance' is a collective term for any form of arrangement under which the interests of two or more persons are insured under a single policy. It is also used in other contexts to denote sharing of risk among insurers and in the US to cover quota share reinsurance. This chapter deals with sharing of risk among insureds other than by the use of group policies.

There are two forms of co-insurance: joint insurance and composite insurance. The distinction is important, for reasons that follow.

This chapter will also consider a third possibility: that a policy has been taken out by a single insured, under contractual arrangements with another, whereby that other is directly or indirectly an intended beneficiary of the insurance.

JOINT INSURANCE

17.02 'Joint insurance' is where there is more than one insured under a policy and each has a common and indivisible interest in the insured subject matter (*General Accident Fire and Life Assurance Corp Ltd v Midland Bank Ltd* [1940] 2 KB 388). The clearest example of a common and indivisible interest sufficient to give rise to joint insurance is that of joint ownership of the insured property.

The general principle with joint insurance is that the rights of the joint insureds stand and fall together. This has the following consequences:

(a) Any application for the policy is made by both parties, as each will have completed the application. A false statement, or a failure to disclose the required information or to make misrepresentation, by one party will therefore provide the insurer with a remedy against both parties to avoid liability against both parties (*United Shoe Machinery v Brunet* [1909] AC 330, 340).

(b) The conditions in the policy must be complied with by both parties. If, for example, a burglary policy provides that the insured must take reasonable care to avoid a loss and one of the joint insureds neglects to secure the premises from which the insured property is stolen, the other (innocent) party has no claim against the insurer. The same principle applies to other breaches of duty by one of the parties, such as a breach of warranty or deliberate destruction of the property (*P Samuel & Co Ltd v Dumas* [1924] AC 431, 445).

(c) In the event of a loss, the insurer may pay the insurance monies to any one of the joint insureds.

COMPOSITE INSURANCE

Definition and significance

17.03 'Composite insurance' is where there is more than one insured and each has a diverse interest in the insured subject matter. Where the policy is composite, each insured in effect has a separate contract with the insurer, albeit embodied in a single policy document. Typical examples of composite insurance are policies taken out by a mortgagor and a mortgagee, a landlord and a tenant, an owner and a hirer of goods, and a contractor and subcontractor of building works.

The implications of composite insurance are as follows:

(a) Because the contracts are separate, if one insured has made a non-disclosure or misrepresentation at inception and the other has not, any rights available to the insurer may only be used against the 'guilty' insured (*New Hampshire Insurance Co Ltd v MGN Ltd* [1997] L RLR 24, 57-58). An illustration may be found in the context of mortgagor and mortgagee. A mortgage lender may procure a block insurance policy covering its interests as mortgagee in all properties. Each mortgagor choosing to insure with the mortgagee's insurer will then be added to the block policy as well. If the mortgagor infringes his duty of utmost good faith in applying for cover, he will be unable to recover under the policy, but the mortgagee's cover under the block policy will be unaffected (*Woolcott v Sun Alliance and London Insurance Ltd* [1978] 1 Lloyd's Rep 629). However, a point to note – other than in relation to group policies, where the Consumer Insurance (Disclosure and Representations) Act 2012 and the Insurance Act 2015 provide otherwise – is that where one proposal form is completed by all the insureds or by one as agent for the others, if this contains a non-disclosure or misrepresentation, then the insurer will have remedies available against all the insureds.

(b) Breach of duty by one party will preclude recovery by him, but will not affect the other's right to recover. To give some examples: in the case of a life policy under which A and B insure each other's lives and A murders B, A cannot claim under the policy, but the policy monies will be payable to B's estate (*Davitt v Titcumb* [1989] 3 All ER 417); under a policy taken out by the mortgagor of property covering the interests of himself and the mortgagee, deliberate destruction of the property by the mortgagor will not preclude recovery by the mortgagee (*P Samuel & Co Ltd v Dumas* [1924] AC 431).

(*c*) Losses under the policy must be paid to each composite insured in respect of his own interest (*General Accident Fire and Life Assurance Corp Ltd v Midland Bank Ltd* [1940] 2 KB 388). A co-insured with an insurable interest in the entire subject matter may, however, recover the full sum insured, although he must account to his co-insureds for any sums which are in excess of his own interest in the subject matter.

Creation of composite insurance

17.04 A composite policy may be formed by the co-insureds making simultaneous applications to the insurer. More commonly, however, an insured will insure on behalf of himself and other persons, either specifically identified or forming part of a definable class. A good example of the position is found in the context of the insurance of a construction project, the head contractor insuring himself and all subcontractors. Whether a person is co-insured under a policy depends upon whether the primary insured was or was not authorised to procure insurance for that person (eg, whether he was acting as agent).

Where the primary insured is authorised

17.05 Where X is authorised by Y or required by a contract with Y to take out a composite policy with Y (ie, a policy under which both their respective divisible interests in the subject matter of the insurance are covered), the policy will cover the interests of both where:

(a) X's authority/contractual obligation extends to procuring the policy in question: In *National Oilwell (UK) Ltd v Davy Offshore Ltd* [1993] 2 Lloyd's Rep 582, for example, the main contractor was obliged by the terms of the subcontract to procure an all risks property insurance policy for the subcontractor, covering the equipment due to be supplied under the subcontract, up to the point of delivery of the equipment. In fact, the main contractor procured a policy which covered both itself and the subcontractor against liability incurred due to defects in the subcontract equipment occurring before or after delivery. Defects arose in the equipment post-delivery, with the result that construction was delayed, causing the main contractor to incur substantial losses. These were paid by the insurer, which sought in turn to recover its payment from the subcontractor by way of subrogation. The subcontractor resisted this claim by asserting that it was a party to the contract of insurance and therefore immune from subrogation proceedings, in accordance with the general rule that subrogation rights cannot be exercised against an insured party (see **17.7** below). The court held that the subcontractor was not a co-insured *vis-à-vis* post-delivery risks, since to be a co-insured the main contractor must have been authorised to insure on the subcontractor's behalf. This had not been the case, as the subcontract obliged the main contractor to insure for the subcontractor only in respect of pre-delivery losses. The main contractor's authorisation to insure could not be any wider than its obligation. The subcontractor was, therefore, co-insured under the policy only in respect of pre-delivery risks.

(b) X intended to cover Y's interests when taking out the policy: It has been held that X's intention to include Y was an obvious inference in the circumstances – it was a replacement policy (*O'Kane v Jones (The Martin P)* [2004] 1 Lloyd's Rep 389); but that was not the case where the wording (eg, contractor) did not extend to someone providing advice in a professional capacity (*Hopewell Project Management Ltd v Ewbank Preece Ltd* [1998] 1 Lloyd's Rep 448, 456-457).

(c) The policy does not preclude the extension of coverage to Y: Usually, the policy will identify the insured persons, by either name or description. But the description must be apt to cover the purported co-insured in question. In *Talbot Underwriting v Nausch Hogan & Murray Inc ('The Jascon 5')* [2006] 2 Lloyd's Rep 195, for example, the question was whether the ship owner's repairer was a co-insured by virtue of policy phrase 'and/or Subsidiary, Affiliates, Associated and Interrelated Companies and/or Joint Ventures'. The court held that it was not, since the repairer was not in the same group of companies, and something more than a repairing contract was required to give rise to a joint venture.

If the purported co-insured (Y) is not named or otherwise described as being an insured by the policy, then the question is whether the actual proposer (X) was acting as his agent – that is, whether Y was X's undisclosed principal. In *Siu Yin Kwan v Eastern Insurance Co Ltd* [1994] 1 All ER 213, for example, a shipping agent was requested by a ship owner to obtain a policy covering the ship owner's potential liability to its employees. A policy was issued, but with the shipping agent named as the insured. An accident occurred for which the ship owner was held to be liable, and the Privy Council ruled that the ship owner was the proper insured under the policy by reason of the agency law doctrine of the undisclosed principal, given that the requirements of authorisation and intention had been met.

A potential problem which may arise when a person not identified in the policy claims to be the insured, on the basis that the actual proposer acted with his authorisation and intended to do so, is the duty on the proposer to disclose all material facts to the insurer. Is the existence of the undisclosed principle a material fact? In *Talbot Underwriting*, Cooke J stated *obiter* that in his view, in the connection of the marine policy there under consideration, this would certainly be the case.

If the purported co-insured is not named or otherwise described as being an insured by the policy and is unable to successfully argue that he was the actual proposer's undisclosed principal, he may still be able to enforce the policy, by virtue of the Contracts (Rights of Third Parties) Act 1999.

Where the primary insured is unauthorised

17.06 Where the primary insured under an insurance contract is not authorised to obtain cover for another person, that other may in some circumstances be able to ratify the unauthorised act and thereby claim to be a party to the contract. Ratification was discussed by the court in *National Oilwell* (see **17.5** above), where the following conditions for ratification by the subcontractor were laid down:

(a) The contractor had to be a person identified in the policy as a co-insured, either by name or by description. This is based on the common law rule that an undisclosed principal cannot ratify.

(b) The contractor must have intended to insure on behalf of the subcontractor. As above, this requirement was held by the court in *National Oilwell* not to have been met, as the contractor's intention to insure could not be regarded as any wider than its obligation to do so. In the result, even though the subcontractor was stated to be a co-insured, the fact that the contractor was not obliged to insure for post-delivery losses meant that it could not have intended to do so.

Where ratification is possible, it can be effected at any time, even after the person seeking to ratify has become aware that a loss has occurred. But a company which was not formed at the date that the policy incepted cannot ratify the contract, since it did not exist at the material time (*Natal Land & Colonization Co v Pauline Colliery and Development Syndicate* [1904] AC 120).

CO-INSURED SUBROGATION IMMUNITY

17.07 An insurer has no right of subrogation in the name of one co-insured against another under the same policy (*Petrofina (UK) Ltd v Magnaload* [1984] QB 127). There is debate as to the basis for this rule. On one view, it is to avoid the circuity that would arise if an insurer could recover from one of its insureds what it had paid out to another, under a policy insuring both (eg, see *The Yasin* [1979] 2 Lloyd's Rep 45). However, in *Co-operative Retail Services Ltd v Taylor Young Partnership Ltd* [2002] 1 WLR 1419, Lord Hope stated that the better view on the facts there under consideration was that such a recovery was prevented by virtue of an implied term in the contract between the co-insureds, pursuant to which the composite policy had been taken out.

The prohibition on subrogation against a co-insured only applies to those risks in respect of which the co-insured has cover under the policy. In the *National Oilwell* case (see **17.5** above), the co-insured subcontractor was insured only against losses occurring prior to its delivery of products to the contractor. The products were allegedly defective and caused the contractor loss due to delay in completing the project. The court held that the subcontractor was not immune from a subrogation action regarding post-delivery losses, as it was not a co-insured in respect of such losses. Also, if the co-insured is guilty of wilful misconduct and either deliberately or recklessly causes the loss, the insurer, having paid other co-insureds, is not precluded from proceeding against the guilty co-insured by way of subrogation (*P Samuel & Co Ltd v Dumas* [1924] AC 431, 445).

INSURANCE FOR THE BENEFIT OF ANOTHER

17.08 Where a number of interests are to be insured, an alternative to composite insurance is a policy taken out in the name of one insured but for the benefit of himself and other persons who are unidentified. The premium will often be paid, directly or indirectly (eg, in the form of rent or other charges to the named insured), by the other persons. The interests of those other persons are frequently 'noted' on the policy, although the effect of such noting is unclear (eg, it may have no legal effect or it could, in some cases, evidence an implied trust for those policy proceeds).

There are a number of situations that can be covered by this type of arrangement (eg, leasing arrangements which effectively cover the lessee for loss or damage). In those cases, the terms of the contract will leave the risk with the insured, but the indirect beneficiary of the insurance is the lessee. In other cases, the beneficiary may be the only insured in relation to part of the risk. Care is required in these cases, especially where the beneficiary is effectively paying for the cover. FCA rules (eg, on cross-selling and bundling) would apply where the insurance is an add-on . Additional considerations apply to vendor extended warranties which can only be offered at point of sale on terms which are consistent with the relevant market practice.

However, where an insurance contract which is neither joint nor composite insurance is taken out for the benefit of someone other than the policyholder, the following points should be considered:

(a) The right to sue: Although there is no privity of contract between the insurer and the potential beneficiaries, and if not excluded by the policy terms, the Contracts (Rights of Third Parties) Act 1999 can be used to enable beneficiaries under the policy to enforce their rights where they are expressly named (or identified as a class) or where the policy purports to confer a benefit on them.

(b) Payment of proceeds: All insurance proceeds are payable to the named insured and the unnamed insureds have no general right to require the insurer to apply the insurance monies in any other way. There is one statutory exception to this principle, contained in s 83 of the Fires Prevention (Metropolis) Act 1774, under which a person with an interest in a building insured under a fire policy can require the insurer to apply the insurance funds on reinstatement of the building.

(c) Unnamed insured subrogation immunity: While the unnamed insureds can derive no direct benefit from the policy, an indirect benefit may accrue in the form of immunity from a subrogation action (see **Chapter 16**).

In *Mark Rowlands v Berni Inns Ltd* [1985] 3 All ER 473, the claimant was the landlord of a building, the basement of which was leased to the defendant. The tenant covenanted to repair the basement when necessary, and to pay to the landlord an insurance rent related to the premium paid by the landlord for insurance of the whole building. The lease contained a provision that, in the event of fire, the tenant was to be relieved of the duty to repair the building and the landlord was to use the insurance money to repair it. Subsequently, the whole building was destroyed by a fire. The insurer indemnified the landlord and sought to recover from the tenant, whose negligence had allegedly caused the fire. The Court of Appeal held that, although the tenant was not a party to the insurance contract, under the lease the insurance was taken for the joint benefit of landlord and tenant; and this arrangement revealed that the parties' intentions were that the tenant was exempt from any liability to the landlord for the loss covered under the insurance policy.

Thus, an unnamed co-insured's immunity from subrogation may rest upon a term in the contract with the named insured (possibly implied), whereby the named insured agrees to look to the proceeds of the insurance policy rather than to the 'co-insured' for indemnification for loss. Arguably, in the absence of an obligation to insure and reinstate, and some contribution to the premium by the unnamed co-insured, it will rarely be possible for a term of the *Mark Rowlands* case type to be implied. In *National Oilwell* (see **17.5** above), the subcontractor claimed to be an unnamed co-insured for losses occurring after its delivery of products to the named insured contractor. Colman J ruled that it was not possible to imply into the subcontract any term giving the subcontractor the benefit of the contractor's insurance, not least because the subcontractor had not contributed any part of the premium for post-delivery losses.

The essential question which the court must look at is whether it was the parties' common intention that the insurance should inure to both parties' benefit, even in the absence of one of the parties being a named insured. Indeed, in looking for that intention, the courts have now decided that they can look outside of the precise contractual arrangements between the parties, as in the case of *Lambert v Keymood Ltd* [1997] 2 EG 131, where the court determined that it was entitled to take that intention outside of the terms of the lease by examining ancillary correspondence between the tenant and the landlord.

(d) Rights of the unnamed insureds against the insured: Any rights which the unnamed insureds possess against the insured derive from the contractual relationship between them. Two particular issues arise:

  (i) Can the unnamed insureds force the named insured to make a claim under the policy? This may be a particularly important issue in the context of policies taken out by a landlord intended to benefit tenants, for if the premises are destroyed, the tenants will be under a continuing obligation to pay rent and the landlord will have no incentive to make a claim against the insurer. In some cases the courts will be willing to imply a term into the contract between the named and unnamed insureds that the named insured will make a claim (*Vural Ltd v Security Archives Ltd* [1990] 60 P&CR 258); and in residential tenancies (including statutory tenancies), there is a statutory procedure under which the tenant is provided with information about the insurance and can prevent the insurer from denying liability for want of a claim pending proceedings to require the landlord to make a claim (Landlord and Tenant Act 1985, s 30A and, Sch 1).

(ii) Can the unnamed insureds claim any interest in the policy monies? The general rule is that, unless the contract gives any specific right to the unnamed insureds, the named insured can deal with the insurance monies exactly as he thinks fit (*Leeds v Cheetham* (1827) 1 Sim 146). However, if the amount recovered exceeds the insured's own loss, he will in certain circumstances have to account to third parties for the excess.

Chapter 18

Double insurance and contribution

- Introduction
- Double insurance
- Double insurance and contribution

INTRODUCTION

18.01 Where the insured takes out insurance for a sum greater than his potential loss, he is said to be over-insured. Over-insurance, which occurs because there are two or more policies on a single risk (or at least a substantial part of it), is known as 'double insurance'. For there to be double insurance, it is necessary that both insurances cover the same property/risk and the same interest (eg, of the insured). In the event of double insurance, the insured may be able to seek indemnity from any one of the insurers involved; in that case, the paying insurer should have the right to recoup a proportion of its payment from the other insurer. This right is referred to as the insurer's 'right of contribution'; it is an equitable remedy and is only applicable to indemnity contracts.

DOUBLE INSURANCE

The insured's rights

18.02 It is a cardinal rule of indemnity insurance law that the insured can only recover the amount of his loss, irrespective of whether he is insured for a greater sum. In the event of double insurance, the insured can still only recover an indemnity, but he is free to make up that indemnity from the insurers in such proportions as he thinks fit (a rule confirmed by s 32(2) of the Marine Insurance Act 1906; see also s 80, which provides for marine insurers to pay loss in proportion to the amount for which they are liable under their contracts and a right of contribution against the other insurers).

The surplus premium paid by the insured may be recoverable from the insurers. This is clearly the case in marine insurance (under s 84(3)(f) of the Marine Insurance Act 1906). The position is less clear in other forms of insurance; but it is arguable that an insured should be able to seek a return of premium in relation to which there is failure of consideration.

Variation by contract

18.03 Insurers are wary of over-insurance and particularly of double insurance, as this may be an indication of potential fraud by the insured.

Insurers may also be unwilling to face the entire burden of a claim when other insurances are in place. For these reasons, a number of contractual devices may be used by insurers to overcome the common law principle that the insured can claim from the insurers in such order as he thinks fit. The following are typical clauses:

(a) an unconditional prohibition on the taking out of further insurance;

(b) a prohibition on the taking out of any further insurance without the consent of the insurer;

(c) an avoidance (or limitation) of the insurer's liability in the event that any other insurance covering the risk is in existence; and

(d) a policy provision that the contract is not to come into force if any other insurance covering the risk exists at the date of inception.

It will frequently be the case, where there is double insurance, that both policies involved contain clauses of the above types. Which of the two policies bears the risk will depend upon a number of factors, including the wording of the clauses, the specific nature of the risk and which of the policies was incepted first. The most common forms of wording used in relation to double insurance can be broadly categorised into three types:

(a) Escape: This states that an insurer will not be liable if another policy is in force (effectively a 'non-contribution clause');

(b) Excess: This states that an insurer will only be liable where another policy has been exhausted; and

(c) Rateable proportion: This states that an insurer will only pay its share of the loss. This type of clause is often included with an *escape* clause.

There is some uncertainty in the case law relating to the precedence of conflicting clauses (see below) and each policy should be looked at on its specific facts to determine whether there is in fact any double insurance (eg, as a result of one of the clauses described above).

In addition, as regards contracts with consumers, it should be noted that the law in this area is subject to the rules on unfair contract terms in the Consumer Rights Act 2015; the Financial Conduct Authority's (FCA) principles and rules relating to treating customers fairly (TCF); and the 'fair and equitable' jurisdiction of the Financial Ombudsman Service (FOS). It appears that the underlying aim of the courts and the FOS will be to prevent double recovery by the insured, but not to uphold escape clauses that leave the insured without cover. The FOS may also prevent insurers from forcing the insured to claim against a number of insurers.

DOUBLE INSURANCE AND CONTRIBUTION

Escape clauses

18.04 In *Equitable Fire and Accident Office, Ltd v The Ching Wo Hong* [1907] AC 96, policy A required the insured to obtain the insurer's consent for the taking out of further cover on the same risk. The insured, without seeking the consent of the insurer, entered into an agreement for the issue of policy B, but this never came into force as the premium for it was not paid. It was held that the condition in policy A had not been broken. In *Home Insurance Co of New York v Gavel* [1928] 30 Ll L Rep 139, policy A provided that the insurer would not be liable in the event that the insured took out further insurance of which the insurer had not been notified. The insured procured policy B, which stated that it was not to come into force if an earlier policy covering the risk was in place. It was here held that the wording of policy B prevented it from coming into operation, and that the entire risk was borne by policy A.

The courts have refused to adopt a construction of contractual restrictions which leads to neither insurer being liable. If the circular position is reached whereby each policy casts the risk onto the other and a different result is reached depending upon which policy is looked at first, the courts will disregard the contractual restrictions and hold each insurer to be liable for the full loss (*Weddell v Road Transport and General Insurance Co, Ltd* [1932] 2 KB 563; *National Employers Mutual General Insurance Association Ltd v Haydon* [1980] 2 Lloyd's Rep 149).

Further, where only one contract contains an escape clause (eg, which states that the insurer is not liable if there is a right to claim on another policy), the exclusion of liability under the policy with the escape clause should take precedence over the policy which only contains a rateable proportion clause (see *NFU v HSBC Insurance* [2010] EWHC 773, in which the NFU policy included a rateable proportion clause but did not contain an escape clause).

Rateable proportion clauses

18.05 A rateable proportion clause is intended to restrict the insurer's liability to a proportion of the ultimate claim. If the policy issued by insurer A contains a rateable proportion clause and the insured procures a policy from insurer B, insurer A is liable only for the proportion of the cover which its policy represents – in this case 50 per cent.

The effect of a rateable proportion clause is that the insured is unable to claim against only one insurer. If he wishes to obtain his whole indemnity, he must claim against all of the relevant insurers (see *Structural Polymer Systems Limited v Brown* [2000] Lloyd's Rep IR 64). A key disadvantage of a rateable proportion clause for the insured is that, in the event of the insolvency of any one of the co-insurers, subject to its ability to claim under the Policyholder Protection Scheme, the insured may not be able to make a full recovery, even with multiple policies. In consumer cases, unfair contract terms rules (which are enforced by the FCA) and TCF requirements will cut across contractual provisions. In addition, in such cases the FOS decides cases on the basis of what is fair and equitable and not based on the strict legal position. It is expected that the FOS would not enforce terms that enable one insurer to force the insured to claim from multiple insurers. This argument would be strongest where cover is taken out for a particular or specified risk/purpose and the insured claims against that insurer.

Definition of 'contribution'

18.06 Contribution is an equitable doctrine, and operates where there has been double insurance and the insured has claimed from one insurer rather than another. Let it be supposed that the insured has procured a policy from insurer A and a policy from insurer B, and the claim has been made against insurer A alone. Contribution is insurer A's right to claim from insurer B a proportion of A's payment to the insured.

Contribution can operate between insurers only where, leaving aside the respective financial limits of the policies, the policies involved are more or less the same in terms of coverage. The following features must be present:

(a) The policies must cover the same subject matter. It will be a matter of construction whether this is the case. Moreover, the overlap between the policies must be substantial rather than merely coincidental (see the Irish case of *Zurich Insurance Co v Shield Insurance Co* [1988] IR 174, which concerned a motor policy and an employers' liability policy, and where the interests under and risk assumed by the insurers on each policy were not the same).

(b) The policies must cover the same insured interests in that subject matter. Different interests may exist in the same property. A quantity of goods in store may, for example, be insured by their owner for their value and by the warehouseman in respect of his own liability for them. If the goods are destroyed and the warehouseman's insurer makes payment, that insurer has no right to seek contribution from the owner's insurer (*North British and Mercantile Insurance Co v London, Liverpool and Globe Insurance Co* (1877) 5 Ch D 569). Note, however, that there will be, on the facts of some cases, the same insured interests even where there may appear to be different insureds. This was the case in *O'Kane v Jones (The 'Martin P')* [2004] 1 Lloyd's Rep 389, where the manager of a ship was held to be acting as the undisclosed principal of the owner of the ship when effecting insurance on the ship (see **Chapter 17**).

The conditions for contribution

18.07 For there to be contribution, both insurers must face legal liability to the insured. The implications of this are explained in the following paragraphs, in which it is assumed that insurer A has been called upon by the insured to make payment, and then makes a claim against insurer B for contribution.

Insurer A's legal liability

If insurer A is not obliged to make payment to the insured, but does so on an *ex gratia* basis, insurer A, in effect, makes a gift to the insured. English law does not, however, allow restitutionary claims in respect of gifts. In *Legal and General Insurance Society Ltd v Drake Insurance Co Ltd* [1992] QB 887, the insured had procured two motor policies covering the same losses. The insured incurred liability to a third party and a claim was made against insurer A, whose policy contained a rateable proportion clause. Insurer A settled the entire claim and sought contribution from insurer B. The Court of Appeal held that A's claim had to fail. A was, by the terms of its own policy, liable only for one-half of the loss, but had chosen voluntarily to pay the entire loss. There was, therefore, no legal basis upon which A could recover the excess payment from B.

Insurer B's legal liability

If insurer B has a defence against the insured, there is no concurrent liability under the two policies and insurer B has an equivalent defence against a contribution claim brought by insurer A. Based on the decision in *O'Kane* (above), which rejected the view of the Privy Council in *Eagle Star Insurance Co Ltd v Provincial Insurance plc* [1993] 3 All ER 1 and followed the view of the *Legal & General* case (above), it appears that the time at which the right of contribution of insurer B to insurer A arises is at the date of loss, not at the time of the contribution claim. *O'Kane* concerned two insurances taken out on a ship: one which the insurer had threatened to cancel but did not, and one which was taken out in anticipation of this cancellation but which, subsequent to the loss, had itself been cancelled. If the time for assessing contribution had been at the time the claim was made, then the cancellation of the second policy would mean only one policy was in force at the time. The court's decision that the relevant time was when the loss occurred meant there was double insurance and the paying insurer could claim a contribution from the other insurer.

However, a rateable proportion clause will not necessarily preclude contribution. In *Drake Insurance plc v Provident Insurance plc* [2003] EWCA Civ 1834, the Court of Appeal held that insurer A, which had the benefit of a rateable proportion clause in its policy but which was in dispute with insurer B over the validity of a concurrent policy (and therefore B's need to contribute to the settlement of the claim), was not in the position of a volunteer when it paid 100 per cent of the claim 'under reserves'. Insurer A had made it clear to insurer B that it would pay the claim and later litigate the issue of its entitlement to a contribution if it had to. The court held that insurer B should bear the risk of the facts not supporting its avoidance of the second policy.

The amount of contribution

18.08 There are two ways of calculating the amount from which the paying insurer, insurer A, can recover from the contributing insurer, insurer B. The first is the independent liability calculation (where each insurer is fully liable up to its own limits and thereafter is liable in the proportion that such limits bear to the total amount of cover), which is applicable in liability insurance. The second is the maximum liability (pro rata to each insurer's policy limits) calculation, which applies in property policies.

Chapter 19

Average

- 'Average' defined
- Policies subject to average

'AVERAGE' DEFINED

19.01 The concept of average is intertwined with that of contribution between policies There are two conditions:

(a) relating to pro rating claims where the insured is under insured; and

(b) relating to contribution between more specific and less specific insurance.

The general term 'average' may be used to describe both 'conditions' (or clauses) of average (ie, the first condition of average and the second condition of average). This section only deals with the principle in the context of the first condition.

The first condition of average (or the pro rata condition of average) concerns the situation where the insured is under-insured and a partial loss has occurred. Where a policy is subject to average (for which see **19.02** below), the insured is deemed to be his own insurer for the proportion of the value of the subject matter by which he is uninsured (in the case of marine policies this is codified in s 81 of the Marine Insurance Act 1906).

The formula for calculating how the first condition of average is applied is as follows:

Sum insured ÷ True value × loss = Amount payable under policy

Set out below are some practical examples of average:

(a) If subject matter worth or valued at £100,000 is insured for £80,000 and is totally destroyed, the insured recovers the full sum insured under the policy, £80,000. This is so whether or not the policy is subject to average.

(b) If the subject matter worth or valued at £100,000 is insured for £80,000 under a policy not subject to average and suffers 50 per cent damage, the insured will recover his full £50,000 loss.

(c) If subject matter worth or valued at £100,000 is insured for £80,000 under a policy subject to average, and suffers 50 per cent damage, the insured and the insurer are deemed to be co-insurers in the respective proportions 2/10: 8/10. The insured will therefore recover only 8/10 of his loss – namely £40,000.

POLICIES SUBJECT TO AVERAGE

19.02 All marine policies, valued and unvalued, are deemed to be the subject of average (Marine Insurance Act 1906, s 81). Fire policies on commercial property have frequently been written on an average basis by inclusion of an express clause. However, as yet, there is no clear authority as to whether, in the absence of such an express clause, average is to be implied as a matter of law. In *Carreras Ltd v Cunard Steamship Co Ltd* [1918] 1 KB 118, a case involving the insurance of goods stored in a warehouse, the court read an average clause into the contract in question without an express condition to that effect. Bailhache J's reasoning was that fire policies on goods were so often written on that basis that an average clause was to be implied. It does not appear clear, however, whether the court had heard any expert evidence to that effect, and it is at least arguable that the very existence of express clauses in the majority of fire policies is evidence that there was an intention to omit such a clause if one is not included. It is probably the better view that commercial property policies are not subject to average unless an express clause is included. In the absence of an express clause and in the case of a gross undervaluation, the only remedy available to the insurer is to allege a non-disclosure or misrepresentation (see Chapter 6). However, such allegations are made difficult by the fact that the valuation representation will probably be characterised as an opinion (see *Economides v Commercial Union* [1998] QBD 587). Therefore, to succeed, the insurer must establish that in all the circumstances, the opinion could not have been honestly held.

Purely domestic property risks are not normally written subject to average (Lloyd's policies being an exception), and clear wording would be required to produce that effect (*Sillem v Thornton* (1854) 3 E & B 868). Equally, commercial policies other than those on property (eg, fidelity policies) are not presumed to be subject to average (*Fifth Liverpool Starr-Bowkett Building Society v Travellers Accident Insurance Co Ltd* [1893] 9 TLR 221). However, there is a separate issue as to what the effect of under insurance is where, for example, there have been questions or representations as to the value of the property insured.

Chapter 20

Third Parties (Rights Against Insurers) Act 2010

- Background
- Conditions for the operation of the Third Parties (Rights Against Insurers) Act 2010
- Compliance with policy terms
- Limitation periods
- The third party's right to information
- The effect of the transfer of rights under the 2010 Act
- Policies written outside the UK

BACKGROUND

20.01 In *Re Harrington Motor Insurance Co Ltd, ex p Chaplin* [1928] Ch 105, it was held that where an insured incurs a liability to a third party but then becomes insolvent, the insurance policy proceeds must be paid into the insolvent insured's estate for distribution to the insured's creditors generally, and cannot be redirected to meet the third party's claim.

The Third Parties (Rights Against Insurers) Act 1930 (TP(RAI)A 1930) was passed specifically to resolve the problem which had emerged in *Re Harrington*. The broad effect of the Act was to transfer to the third party the rights of the insolvent insured against his liability insurers. This had the effect that policy monies would go directly to the third party, and not pass into the general insolvency.

The TP(RAI)A 1930 applied to all forms of liability insurance, compulsory or non-compulsory; but it did not apply to motor insurance, where the principle of the Act is embodied in the Road Traffic Act 1988, or to reinsurance.

A number of shortcomings were identified by the Law Commission in relation to the TP(RAI)A 1930, including that the third party had to establish the existence and amount of the insured's liability before it could bring proceedings against the insurer. The proceedings had to be brought against both the insured and the insurer, sometimes requiring a dissolved company to be restored to the register; insolvency law no longer aligned with the TP(RAI)A 1930; and it had an inadequate system for the disclosure of information to third parties.

CONDITIONS FOR THE OPERATION OF THE THIRD PARTIES RIGHTS (AGAINST INSURERS) ACT 2010

20.02 The Third Parties Rights (Against Insurers) Act 2010 (TP(RAI)A 2010) came into effect on 1 August 2016. It applies to all contracts concluded after that date. The TP(RAI)A 1930 will continue to apply to contracts that pre-date the 2010 Act. The TP(RAI)A 2010 was delayed in its coming into effect by changes required to be made under the Insurance Act 2015 and the Third Parties (Rights Against Insurers) Regulation 2016/570.

The TP(RAI)A 2010, unlike its predecessor, applies to voluntarily incurred liabilities, with the result that it will apply to legal expenses insurance. It does not apply to reinsurance policies.

Transfer of rights to third parties

20.03 The TP(RAI)A 2010 transfers the rights of a 'relevant person' to a third party in specified circumstances. Section 1(2) of the TP(RAI)A 2010 enables the rights of a relevant person against an insurer in respect of liability to be transferred to and vest in a third party to whom the liability has been incurred.

The transfer of rights to the third party will occur when either a relevant person incurs a liability (against which he is insured under a contract of insurance) or when a person who is insured becomes a relevant person (TP(RAI)A 2010, s 1(1)). The transfer therefore will take place regardless of whether the liability occurred before or after the person became insolvent.

Establishing liability

20.04 The third party may bring proceedings to enforce the rights against the insurer without having first established the insured's liability (TP(RAI)A 2010, s 1(3)). This is in contrast to the position under the TP(RAI)A 1930, where the third party first had to establish the insured's liability towards him by admission or judgment, in some cases requiring a dissolved insured to be restored to the register of companies. Under the TP(RAI)A 2010, the third party is still required to establish the insurer's liability under the contract of insurance.

Liability is established (in accordance with s 1(4)) only when its existence and amount are established by a declaration concerning the insurer's liability, a judgment or decree, an arbitral award or an enforceable agreement.

Section 2 of TP(RAI)A 2010 enables the third party to bring a claim against the insurer for a declaration as to either the insured's liability towards him or the insurer's potential liability towards him (where the liability under the policy has yet to be established). Importantly, and in contrast to the TP(RAI)A 1930, these declarations can be sought in one set of proceedings.

Where the third party is required by the policy to bring a claim against the insurer in arbitration, the third party can obtain through the arbitral proceedings a declaration as to the insured's liability and the insurer's potential liability (TP(RAI)A 2010, s 2(7)).

The third party may add the insured as a defendant to any proceedings, but is not obliged to do so (TP(RAI)A 2010, s 2(9)).

Relevant persons

20.05 The TP(RAI)A 2010 sets out which persons (whether individual or corporate) fall within the definition of 'relevant person'. Broadly, these are individuals or corporates that have become insolvent. The triggering events include bankruptcy, voluntary or compulsory winding-up, administration, receivership and court-sanctioned compromises or arrangements.

COMPLIANCE WITH POLICY TERMS

20.06 The third party cannot be placed in any better position against the insurer than the insured would have been under the policy. Thus, if the insurer has any defence against the insured, that defence can be used against the third party equally. Furthermore, if the policy imposes conditions upon the insured which have to be met before the insurer is liable, such as premium payment or claims notification, such conditions must be met before the third party can use the TP(RAI)A 2010 against the insurer.

The TP(RAI)A 2010 limits the insurer's ability to run technical defences against a third-party claimant. Accordingly, it enables the third party to fulfil some of the conditions required of the insured. Section 9(2) provides that anything done by the third party which, if done by the insured, would fulfil a condition must be treated as so fulfilled if done by the third party. Similarly, s 9(3) removes any condition that requires the insured to provide information where the insured has died or, if a company, has been dissolved. Any sums owed to the insurer by the insured (eg, premium) can be offset against sums paid towards the third party (TP(RAI)A 2010, s 10).

Section 9(5) of the TR(RAI)A 2010 states that transferred rights are not subject to prior discharge by the insured of his liability to the third party. This has the effect of making any 'pay to be paid' condition in any non-marine policy of no effect. Such clauses will still apply to marine policies (with the exception of claims for death or personal injury). In *Firma C-Trade SA v Newcastle P&I Association (The Fanti)* [1991] 2 AC 1 the insured was required to have in fact paid the amount of its liability if it was to be indemnified by the insurer. The House of Lords held that this term was a condition precedent to the liability of the insurer and did not change on the insolvency of the insured.

Any term in the insurance contract to the effect that the policy is avoided when the insured becomes a relevant person has no effect in accordance with s 17 of the TP(RAI)A 2010.

LIMITATION PERIODS

20.07 Subject to s 12 of the TP(RAI)A 2010, the insurer may rely upon a limitation defence that would have been available against the insured. Therefore, if the third party fails to bring either a claim against the insured or a claim for declaratory relief under s 2 of the TP(RAI)A 2010, the insurer may rely upon the defence that the claim is time barred. The six-year limitation period for the third party runs from when liability has been established against the insured (TP(RAI)A 2010, s 12(4)).

Section 12 of the TP(RAI)A 2010 provides that where a third party has issued proceedings against the insured, the expiry of any limitation period will not bar his claim against the insurer while that action is still in progress. This further aligns the rights of the third party with those of the insured.

THE THIRD PARTY'S RIGHT TO INFORMATION

20.08 Under the TP(RAI)A 1930, the third party had the right to obtain information from the insured as to his insurance position following a bankruptcy or insolvency event. However, it was only possible to find out about any insurance policy once liability had been established. This meant that litigation had to be conducted without the benefit of knowing whether the insured was covered by insurance. Section 11 and Schedule 1 of the TP(RAI)A 2010 set out a clear process by which a third party can discover whether the insured was covered by insurance and the extent of any coverage.

Schedule 1 to TP(RAI)A 2010 sets out the circumstances in which a third party can get information about whether someone who has incurred a liability against him has insurance cover. Under paragraph 1 of the Schedule, person (A) can request certain information in writing from a relevant person (B) where A reasonably believes that he has incurred a liability towards B. Under paragraph 2, information can also be obtained where A believes that rights under a contract of insurance held by a person (B) have been transferred to him and another person (C) has the relevant information. Information can be requested by A from either or B or C, depending on the scenario. C might include a broker, for example.

The information that can be obtained is set out in paragraph 3 of the Schedule. It covers:

(a) the name of the insurer;

(b) the terms of the contract of insurance;

(c) whether the insurer had informed the insured that he had no liability under the policy;

(d) whether there are or have been proceedings in relation to the policy and details about those proceedings (including the name of the court and case number);

(e) whether there are any limits of recovery and the amounts already paid out in claims in respect of those limits; and

(f) whether any sums which would be paid out under the policy would be subject to a fixed charge.

THE EFFECT OF THE TRANSFER OF RIGHTS UNDER THE 2010 ACT

20.09 Section 14 of the TP(RAI)A 2010 provides that a third party cannot recover against the insured what he is able to recover under the transferred rights. In other words, the third party will not be able to recover twice in respect of the same liability. The third party may, however, seek to recover sums that are not covered by the policy.

POLICIES WRITTEN OUTSIDE THE UK

20.10 The application of the TP(RAI)A 2010 applies regardless of where the liability occurred and the residence or domicile of the parties. It also applies regardless of whether the law of the policy is governed by the laws of the UK or a foreign law. Accordingly, it will apply in situations where the insurance policy was written by a foreign insurer.

Part 4

Dispute Resolution

Chapter 21

Arbitration

- The arbitration agreement and arbitration clause
- The scope of arbitration
- Procedure governing arbitrations
- Confidentiality
- Honourable engagement clause
- Right to appeal

21.01 Arbitration is an alternative method of dispute resolution to court proceedings. In practice, the use of arbitration in insurance disputes is largely limited to commercial insurance, and in particular to shipping and reinsurance disputes. English law on arbitration is governed by the Arbitration Act 1996. Arbitration is consensual and private. The parties to a contract of insurance can agree to resolve any dispute relating to that contract by reference to arbitration. The parties will agree to be bound by the decision of the arbitrators. An arbitration clause can be included in the contract of insurance or a separate agreement can be created; in whatever manner it is formulated, the arbitrators derive their powers from the agreement to arbitrate.

THE ARBITRATION AGREEMENT AND ARBITRATION CLAUSE

21.02 Section 7 of the Arbitration Act 1996 gives explicit statutory recognition to what has become known as the 'doctrine of severability'. This doctrine means that the arbitration agreement contained in the insurance contract concerned is treated as separate to the main contract, unless otherwise agreed by the parties. This prevents potential legal difficulties at a later date if one party alleges that the contract in dispute has been rescinded or avoided. Logically, this would result in the arbitration clause which forms part of that contract also being treated as avoided. However, by treating the arbitration agreement as a separate contract, this problem is circumvented. Arbitrators, therefore, can be appointed to adjudicate on whether a party's avoidance of the contract is valid.

THE SCOPE OF ARBITRATION

21.03 The matters which can be referred to arbitration will depend upon the scope of the wording of the clause or agreement in question. An arbitration clause should be drafted in the widest possible terms to try to ensure that all disputes which could arise concerning the contract in question can be referred to arbitration for resolution. However, since arbitration is a consensual and private method of resolving disputes, it is impossible to compel third parties to join the proceedings. In the context of insurance, this may be a major drawback if a party to, for example, a dispute between an insurer and an insured, or a reinsurer and a reinsured, wishes to join the broker as a party to proceedings for misrepresentation, breach of the duty of fair presentation and/or negligence.

Arbitration clauses can also state the type of person to be appointed as arbitrator and how such appointments are to be made. Such clauses in reinsurance contracts will often stipulate that the arbitrators must have requisite amounts of experience in the London insurance and reinsurance market. The advantage of this is that the panel of arbitrators will have relevant expertise to determine any dispute which arises between the parties to the contract.

Various organisations have drafted or recommended arbitration clauses, such as the London Court of International Arbitration (LCIA), the International Chamber of Commerce and – particularly in respect of insurance and reinsurance arbitrations – ARIAS and the International Association for Insurance Law Reinsurance and Insurance Arbitration Society.

PROCEDURE GOVERNING ARBITRATIONS

21.04 The arbitration agreement will normally specify which procedural rules apply. The LCIA, ARIAS and other arbitration authorities have produced comprehensive sets of rules to deal with the conduct of arbitration proceedings from commencement until termination.

In the absence of specific procedural rules set out in the arbitration agreement, the parties can decide between themselves how the arbitration should be conducted. In the absence of agreement between the parties, even with regard to how the arbitrators should be appointed, the Arbitration Act 1996 sets out rules for the commencement of arbitration proceedings and the appointment of arbitrators, as well as providing those arbitrators with powers to determine the manner in which the dispute between the parties should be resolved.

CONFIDENTIALITY

21.05 Arbitration decisions are confidential, although in certain circumstances the arbitrators' award will need to be disclosed if it becomes necessary, by way of example, to enforce the award.

The award of the arbitrators is binding only upon the parties to the arbitration. Thus, unlike the court system, there is no operation of precedent. This does not mean that arbitrators are not bound by the published decisions of the English courts – assuming, of course, that the governing law of the contract in dispute is the law of England and Wales. The contract could be governed by the laws of other countries; in such case, the arbitrators will be bound by the laws of that jurisdiction.

For this reason, the parties to arbitration proceedings will usually wish to have at least one lawyer (usually a senior Queen's Counsel with relevant experience) as part of the arbitration tribunal. He or she will usually chair the tribunal and prepare the reasons for the arbitrators' decision, as well as advising the other members of the tribunal (who will often be practising or recently retired market practitioners) of the details of law and procedure relevant to the particular hearing.

HONOURABLE ENGAGEMENT CLAUSE

21.06 Arbitration agreements, particularly in reinsurance contracts, often include a clause known as an 'honourable engagement clause'. In essence, an honourable engagement clause allows the arbitrators flexibility when making their decision; they can take notice of market practice based upon their own knowledge and resolve the dispute based upon what is fair and reasonable, as opposed to a strict legal approach. The courts have deemed such a clause to be valid as long as it does not attempt to alter or oust the substantive law. An example of an honourable engagement clause is as follows: 'The arbitrators and the umpire shall interpret this reinsurance as an honourable engagement and they shall make their award with a view to effecting the general purpose of this reinsurance in a reasonable manner, rather than in accordance with a literal interpretation of the language.'

That particular clause was the subject of a court decision in *Home & Overseas Insurance Co Ltd v Mentor Insurance Co (UK) Ltd* [1989] 1 Lloyd's Rep 473. The court gave full effect to the requirement that the arbitrators in that case, in reliance upon the honourable engagement clause, should make a decision based upon equitable grounds rather than by a strict legal interpretation of the issues in dispute.

Honourable engagement clauses appear to have been given statutory effect in the Arbitration Act 1996, potentially rendering the necessity to include such a clause in an arbitration agreement superfluous. Section 46(1)(b) of the Arbitration Act 1996 provides: 'The arbitral tribunal shall decide the dispute … if the parties so agree, in accordance with such other considerations as are agreed by them or determined by the tribunal.'

In a decision under s 46(1), the Court of Appeal held that an arbitrator could determine any issue which the parties to a dispute chose to put before him, and that it was irrelevant that the arbitration clause was silent as to the issue in dispute (*Wealands v CLC Contractors Ltd* [1999] 2 Lloyd's Rep 739). One key question which remains is whether s 46 will have the effect of reducing the grounds upon which parties can appeal arbitrators' awards on the grounds of an error of law to the courts of England and Wales.

RIGHT TO APPEAL

21.07 The right to appeal the decision of an arbitration panel to the courts of England and Wales is restricted to questions of English law. The court has first to give leave before an appeal can take place. The Arbitration

Act 1996 (in particular, s 69) clarifies the previous statute law and court practice. It is vital that an arbitral award is in writing and fully reasoned if there is to be any possibility of an appeal by either party of the tribunal's decision. There are limited grounds on which to challenge an arbitration award. Under ss 67–69 of the Arbitration Act 1996, there are three ways in which an award can be appealed in the English courts:

(a) lack of jurisdiction;

(b) serious irregularity; or

(c) on a point of law.

An appeal on a point of law is only possible where the decision is either obviously wrong or of general public importance and at least open to serious doubt. There is therefore a relatively high threshold to appeal an award. The applicable procedural rules may also place further restrictions on the right to appeal.

Chapter 22

Court proceedings

- Civil Procedure Rules
- The overriding objective
- The court's case management powers
- Pre-action protocols
- The three 'tracks' to litigation
- Part 36 offers
- Disclosure
- Expert evidence
- Summary

CIVIL PROCEDURE RULES

22.01 In 1999 the civil justice system in England and Wales underwent its most fundamental changes in many years. Since 1999, procedure in the English High Court and county courts has been governed by the Civil Procedure Rules (CPR), also referred to more colloquially by lawyers as 'the White Book'. The CPR provide a comprehensive set of rules and practice directions for the conduct of litigation in England and Wales.

THE OVERRIDING OBJECTIVE

22.02 The key principle which runs through the entirety of the CPR is the court's overriding objective, which is set out in Part 1. This overriding objective is for the court to deal with cases justly. Rule 1.1(2) sets out the following matters which, as far as practicable, must be considered by the court when dealing with a case 'justly':

'(a) ensuring that the parties are on an equal footing;

(b) saving expense;

(c) dealing with the case in ways which are proportionate:

(i) to the amount of money involved;

(ii) to the importance of the case;

(iii) to the complexity of the issues; and

(iv) to the financial position of each party;

(d) ensuring that it is dealt with expeditiously and fairly; and

(e) allotting to it an appropriate share of the court's resources, while taking into account the need to allot resources to other cases.'

The concept of proportionality as set out above is a vital element of the new rules. The courts no longer give the parties the free hand they once had to deal with their disputes in any way that they choose, without regard to the issues and the amounts involved. The court's duty is to manage cases. That duty is set out in r 1.4, which states: 'the court must further the overriding objective by actively managing cases.' The CPR also requires the court to actively manage cases.

Rule 1.4 goes on to describes what active case management includes – for example, 'encouraging the parties to co-operate with each other in the conduct of the proceedings'; 'identifying the issues at an early stage'; 'encouraging the parties to use an alternative dispute resolution procedure'; and 'helping the parties to settle the whole or part of the case'.

THE COURT'S CASE MANAGEMENT POWERS

22.03 The courts have significant powers of case management to assist them with implementing the overriding objective and fulfilling their duty to manage cases. One of Lord Woolf's key concerns was that parties had previously been allowed to let the litigation process drag on unnecessarily, which was wasteful – not only in terms of time, but also in terms of costs. Judges have, therefore, changed from being reactive to proactive and wide-ranging case management powers have been bestowed upon the courts.

Part 3 sets out the judge's case management powers. The courts have powers to fix strict direction timetables; to adjourn or bring hearings forward; to require not only a party's legal representatives, but also the party itself, to attend before the court; and to stay the whole or any part of the proceedings to encourage the parties, for example, to explore alternative dispute resolution (ADR). The courts even have powers to decide which issues are to be tried and to exclude an issue from consideration.

In order to assist the court with its greater powers of intervention, r 3.3 gives the court the power to make an order of its own initiative. The court has also been given wide powers to impose sanctions on parties that fail to comply with its orders. The sanctions available to the courts include costs penalties (r 44.3), and even the power to strike out a party's statement of case (r 3.3).

Since the Court of Appeal decision in *Mitchell v News Group Newspapers* [2013] EWCA Civ 1537, it has become clear that the courts will not be sympathetic to parties that breach orders, inadvertently or otherwise. If a party has, for example, missed a deadline, it must apply for 'relief from sanctions'.

In addition, the courts also have the power, for example, to strike out a party's case where 'it discloses no reasonable grounds for bringing or defending the claim' (r 3.4(2)(a)); or to grant summary judgment against either a claimant or a defendant in relation to the whole or part of a claim if they consider that the claim has no real prospect of being successfully made or defended, unless there is another compelling reason why a trial should take place (Part 24).

PRE-ACTION PROTOCOLS

22.04 The CPR also includes 'pre-action protocols', aimed at encouraging parties to reach an early settlement before proceedings are issued and significant legal expenses are incurred. Under the pre-action protocols, the courts are able to interfere with parties' pre-action behaviour in order to encourage them to address the issues in dispute as they arise, with a view to reaching an early settlement if possible. This is achieved by, for example, requiring the parties to disclose the nature of their case, as well as key documents, even before proceedings have commenced. The pre-action protocols are also designed to encourage ADR.

There are currently approved pre-action protocols in respect of eight types of action: construction and engineering disputes; defamation claims; personal injury claims; clinical disputes; professional negligence claims; judicial review; disease and illness claims; and housing disrepair cases. Whatever the nature of the dispute, the courts will expect the parties, in the light of the overriding objective in Part 1, to act reasonably and to exchange information relevant to the issues in dispute before proceedings commence. Pre-action conduct will be taken into account when the court considers the issues of costs at the end of the case.

In addition, pursuant to r 31.16, parties are entitled to make an application for pre-action disclosure of documents relevant to the claim if there has not been voluntary disclosure. The court will grant pre-action disclosure if it is satisfied this will aid the fair disposal of any proceedings brought subsequently or, in addition, will assist the resolution of the dispute without the need for bringing proceedings, or to save costs generally.

THE THREE 'TRACKS' TO LITIGATION

22.05 Disputes are allocated to three different tracks:

(a) Small claims track: This is an informal procedure with limited rights to recover costs, together with no disclosure or experts other than with leave of the court.

(b) Fast track: This was introduced by the CPR and is designed to deal with reasonably straightforward cases. Cases allocated to the fast track will be subject to a fixed timetable of 30 weeks from the date of allocation to trial. Once set, the timetable must be complied with and sanctions will be imposed in the event of default. The trial itself will normally be restricted to one day.

(c) Multi-track: This covers all other types of cases. On allocation to multi-track, there will usually be a case management conference to decide upon how the case is to be conducted. One important aspect is that a trial window will be fixed, which will be a period of time during which the trial will take place. The actual date of the trial will be fixed later.

Rules 26.6–26.9 set out the rules governing allocation of a dispute to one of the three tracks. Track allocation occurs once a defence has been filed. The parties at that stage complete an allocation questionnaire. It asks the parties to consider identify to which track the case should be allotted. Although other factors are relevant, allocation depends largely on the financial value of the claim; the small claims track deals with claims with a financial value of up to £10,000 (with some exceptions); the fast track deals with claims between £10,000 and £25,000; and the multi-track deals with cases over £25,000. If the court considers it so appropriate, it has the discretion to allocate a case to a different track, even if the financial value falls outside these limits.

The allocation questionnaire also asks the parties a variety of other questions relevant to case management concerns. It asks the parties to set out whether they have complied with pre-action protocols; whether there are any specific applications they wish the court to consider; details of who their witnesses of fact will be; and what expert evidence the parties require. The parties are also asked whether they wish to have a one-month stay of the proceedings in order to attempt to settle. If either side indicates positively to that question, the court has the power to stay the proceedings.

A failure to provide proper information concerning allocation will result in sanctions being imposed by the court on the defaulting party. Such sanctions can be punitive.

PART 36 OFFERS

22.06 One of the most important parts of the CPR is Part 36. This aims to encourage the parties to settle cases before trial. Both claimants and defendants are able to make Part 36 offers, either to accept or pay a certain sum, or the equivalent where a claim does not have a monetary value. Such offers are made 'without prejudice save as to costs'. This means that no admission as to liability is made and the court will not be made aware of the existence of a Part 36 offer until the issue of costs is dealt with after a trial (if the case proceeds that far). The making and acceptance of Part 36 offers by both claimants and defendants are encouraged by a variety of provisions dealing with those costs arising after a Part 36 offer is made. These costs consequences make Part 36 an important tactical consideration in any litigation.

DISCLOSURE

22.07 'Disclosure' is the process whereby the parties to the proceedings disclose the documents which are relevant to the issues in dispute. Disclosure is governed by Part 31.

The normal order will be for standard disclosure. This requires a party to disclose those documents on which it relies; those which adversely affect its case or another party's case; and those which support the other party's case. A party is only obliged to undertake a reasonable search for documents relating to the issues in dispute, and factors such as the number of documents involved will be taken into account when deciding whether such a search has been reasonable.

A party can seek disclosure of additional documents which fall outside the scope of the standard disclosure rules by making an application to court if the other party will not voluntarily disclose the documents sought. When making its decision, the court will consider the principles set out in the overriding objective at Part 1.

EXPERT EVIDENCE

22.08 Expert evidence is likely to have an important role in most many disputes relating to insurance law. In particular, expert underwriting evidence will tend to need to be adduced to assist the court to determine what a prudent underwriter would have wanted to know by way of material circumstances in the context of a breach of the duty of fair presentation dispute. Expert evidence is governed by Part 35 which, in furtherance of the overriding objective, aims to ensure that such evidence is given as objectively and efficiently as possible.

The court has case management powers to limit what expert evidence the parties can adduce, including encouraging the parties to appoint a single joint expert. If two experts are appointed, they will be expected to cooperate and the parties will be required to disclose the substance of the instructions given to their appointed expert.

SUMMARY

22.09 The key theme of the CPR is to achieve a resolution of the dispute as swiftly and economically as possible. The principles of the overriding objective will be applied to all elements of court procedure leading to trial. In order to achieve this objective, the courts have been given far-reaching powers and the parties are under a duty to assist the court in achieving the overriding objective. In many cases, litigation is now a swifter way to resolve a dispute than arbitration, where the strict rules, time limits and sanctions of the CPR do not apply.

Chapter 23

Alternative dispute resolution

- Mediation
- Executive tribunal (or 'mini trial')
- Expert determination
- Early neutral evaluation
- QC clauses

23.01 Alternative dispute resolution (ADR) has taken on a new importance since the introduction of the Civil Procedure Rules in April 1999, and of various practice directions which govern court procedure in England and Wales, for the simple reason that the courts are now under a duty to consider and encourage the parties in dispute to use ADR if it is considered appropriate. The court specifically asks the parties in the allocation questionnaire, which they complete after the defence has been filed, whether they have considered ADR and whether they think it is appropriate. The courts are under a duty to consider and encourage the parties to use ADR, and there is a general expectation that parties will take part in ADR at some stage in the litigation or arbitration process.

ADR is a concept which originates from the US. It is a generic name given to a variety of procedures which are designed to assist parties in dispute to resolve their differences. In basic terms, it is the private resolution of disputes with the use of a neutral third party. The procedures are usually without prejudice to the parties' rights to proceed to litigation or arbitration, which are mutually exclusive forums for resolving disputes. The aim of ADR is to seek a swifter resolution to the dispute than more 'traditional' processes, to save costs and, by adopting a commercial approach to resolving the dispute, to enable the parties at the end of the day to maintain their commercial relationship. These aims translate into the potential advantages of using ADR to resolve a dispute.

ADR comes in varying forms. The methods include mediation, executive tribunal (also known as 'mini trial'), expert determination, early neutral evaluation and QC determination. Of these, mediation is by far the most widely used. Each one will be looked at in turn.

MEDIATION

23.02 This is a commonly used ADR procedure. Generally, all parties to the dispute must agree for their differences to be dealt with by way of mediation, as it is essentially a voluntary process. The Court of Appeal in *Halsey v Milton Keynes General NHS Trust* [2004] EWCA Civ 576 affirmed this position by holding that the courts can merely encourage parties to mediate, rather than ordering them to do so; and that a party which is ultimately successful in proceedings, but which has refused mediation, will not be penalised for that refusal by any costs order unless the refusal to mediate is unreasonable. As the costs consequences for unreasonably refusing to mediate can be severe, a party which is offered the opportunity to mediate should not reject that offer lightly. Mediation, however, will not be suitable in all cases. The Court of Appeal envisioned a situation in which a defendant which considers itself to have a very strong defence may not wish to mediate so as to avoid having to make any 'nuisance payment' simply to dispose of an unmeritorious claim against it.

The parties to the mediation will select a neutral party to assist them in reaching an acceptable agreement. The mediator is usually an expert in the subject matter of the dispute as well as being a trained mediator. The mediator's role is to persuade the parties to focus on their underlying concerns and differences. Although the process is not binding, it tends to operate as a concentrated period of negotiation which can lead the parties towards a binding settlement agreement, which may otherwise take much longer to achieve. As a consequence, mediation can be a cost-effective way to resolve a dispute. Talks can break down; if they do, the parties can proceed to litigation or arbitration instead, although a mediation which does not provide an immediate resolution may often narrow the issues in dispute such that a settlement follows shortly after. Mediation is a consensual process carried out under privilege and the mediator's focus will be on bringing the parties together, rather than expressing a view on the merits of each party's case.

EXECUTIVE TRIBUNAL (OR 'MINI TRIAL')

23.03 This again is a voluntary procedure and is non-binding. The parties appoint a neutral expert to whom they present an abbreviated version of their case. The expert then supervises the proceedings. It is a more formal process than mediation, which involves discussion rather than presentation. At the close of a mini trial, the neutral expert gives a non-binding opinion as to his view on the case. The purpose behind this process is that, with views having been expressed as to the merits of the parties' agreements, the parties thereafter attempt to negotiate a binding settlement.

EXPERT DETERMINATION

23.04 This is a binding form of mini trial or executive tribunal, but only if the contract between the parties in dispute provides for dispute resolution by way of expert determination. It is the contract which gives this binding effect. It is closer in nature to arbitration than it is to mediation or an executive tribunal. The expert is again neutral, and is either agreed upon by the parties or appointed by a third party. The expert's role is similar to that of a judge or arbitrator.

EARLY NEUTRAL EVALUATION

23.05 This combines elements of both mediation and expert determination. The process involves the parties in dispute engaging a neutral independent person, who has expertise in the subject matter of the dispute, at an early stage in the dispute. The independent expert reviews the merits of each party's case and delivers an opinion on the likely outcome of the dispute.

QC CLAUSES

23.06 Finally, insurance policies sometimes contain 'QC clauses'. These clauses provide for certain issues to be resolved by a QC. A common example of an issue that is resolved by this route is where, in the professional indemnity insurance context, the insurer and the insured do not agree about whether a settlement offer should be accepted. QC determinations of more substantial disputes are also possible.

Part 5

Specific Types of Insurance

Chapter 24

All risks insurance

- Nature of all risks insurance
- Effect of the policy being all risks

NATURE OF ALL RISKS INSURANCE

24.01 Various forms of property insurance are written on an all risks basis. Historically, goods in transit insurance and marine cargo insurance were frequently written on this basis. This trend then spread to householders' insurance and property insurance for most large-scale commercial risks. It frequently forms the core of global property insurance programmes placed for multinational corporations (see **Chapter 8**).

The term 'all risks' is certainly misleading, as such policies do not cover all forms of loss. Most all risks policies will exclude a number of perils as well as certain types of property.

EFFECT OF THE POLICY BEING ALL RISKS

24.02 The main advantage of an all risks policy is to make it somewhat easier to substantiate a claim than under a specific risks policy. The insuring clause in an all risks policy will simply specify that the policy covers the insured property for physical loss or damage during the underwriting period.

Therefore, to fall within that cover, the insured must prove that:

(a) the claim is in respect of insured property;

(b) physical loss or damage has occurred to that property; and

(c) the cause of the loss was fortuitous (ie, as a result of an accident or casualty).

When the insured has overcome those hurdles, the burden of proof will then pass to the insurer to demonstrate that the peril which caused the loss was excluded from cover. This was established in *British and Foreign Marine Insurance Co, Ltd Appellants v Gaunt Respondent* [1921] 2 AC 41. In *Re National Benefit Insurance Co* [1933] 45 LI L Rep 147, it was alleged that goods in transit had failed to arrive at their destination, and the court decided that it was sufficient for the insured to prove the non-arrival of the goods to satisfy its burden of proof.

In contrast, in specified perils insurance, such as fire, the insuring clause will state additionally that the physical loss or damage must be caused by a particular peril (eg, fire). In those circumstances, the insured has an additional hurdle to overcome – namely, the proof that the particular physical loss and damage was proximately caused by the specified peril (see **Chapter 13**).

The insuring clause in the all risks policy does not specify that the peril causing the physical loss or damage must be accidental. This is a fundamental requirement of valid insurance policies (ie, not to bring about the insured risk) and will therefore be implied into any policy.

The legal authorities, however, are unclear as to whether fortuity is judged from the perspective of the insured or from that of the reasonable bystander. Clearly, if the test is subjective, then the only question that needs to be asked is whether the insured knew that the physical loss or damage was likely to occur. Certainly, in *Kier Construction v Royal Insurance* (UK) 30 Con LR 45, the court appeared to consider the question of inevitability from the viewpoint of the insured. In other words, if at the time of the purchase of the cover the parties did not expect the damage to occur, then even if objectively, and with the benefit of hindsight, the loss was inevitable, it was still an insured loss.

Chapter 25

Aviation insurance

- Introduction
- Aircraft operators' insurance
- Airport owners' and operators' liability insurance
- Spares cover

INTRODUCTION

25.01 The term 'aviation insurance' is generally regarded as encompassing three types of risk:

(a) aircraft operators' hull risks and third-party liability;

(b) aviation manufacturers' and suppliers' product liability; and

(c) airport owners' and operators' liability.

Given the nature of the underlying industry and the sums involved, in terms of both liability exposure and hull values, aviation insurance is an international business. Much of it is led (at either primary or reinsurance level) in the London market, where a significant number of insurers and brokers are engaged solely in, or maintain teams dedicated to, the aviation business. Many overseas insurers write the primary business but reinsure the majority – often as much as 90 per cent – through London.

This chapter addresses the principal risks insured under conventional aircraft, airport owners' and operators' policies. It describes a typical level of cover; but of course, such policies may well be bespoke to the particular airline. In some cases, key exclusions are highlighted but the chapter does not detail all of the exclusions likely to be applicable to particular type of cover.

AIRCRAFT OPERATORS' INSURANCE

25.02 The policy will insure the aircraft owner against loss or destruction of, or damage to, the aircraft named on the policy, and will indemnify the operator against liabilities to third parties arising out of the operation of the aircraft. This will include liability to passengers (whether fare paying or not) in the event of an accident and liability for damage to property and people on the ground.

Usually, an airline's aircraft fleet policy will exclude liability for death or injury to crew, which will be covered under a separate employer's liability policy. The airline may additionally effect death in service or personal accident insurance for the benefit of its crew. Comprehensive liability insurance for airlines is essential, as the exposure is often of high value. The total value of aircraft insured may be significantly greater than the liability limit. However, the risk of total loss of the entire fleet is remote and would probably only be a threat for war risks underwriters.

Aviation insurers tend to provide cover in respect of the following categories of loss or damage:

(a) loss and damage to the aircraft itself;

(b) legal liability to passengers;

(c) legal liability to third parties other than passengers; and

(d) cover in respect of loss or damage to cargo.

Loss of or damage to aircraft

25.03 Cover is normally provided in respect of loss of, or damage to, aircraft named in the schedule to the policy. Provision is made for aircraft to be added during the term of the policy. Each aircraft named in the schedule is insured up to a maximum sum, referred to as the 'amount insured'. It is not uncommon for aircraft to be insured at an agreed value which may be in excess of the market value.

Under the terms of cover, insurers normally have the option to repair or pay for the loss or damage and may arguably also have the option to replace an aircraft with an equivalent aircraft in the event of a total loss. Provision will also be made for payment by insurers of emergency expenses necessarily incurred by the insured to ensure the security of the aircraft following damage or a forced landing.

Typically, insurers will exclude liability for wear and tear, deterioration, breakdown, defect or failure in or of any 'unit' of the aircraft – for example, an engine – unless the resulting damage is attributable to a single recorded incident. However, where wear and tear, deterioration or similar in a unit results in damage being caused to some other part of the aircraft, insurers will normally accept liability for that separate damage.

The interests of parties other than the aircraft operator may be recognised and protected under the policy. Of course, few airlines own their aircraft outright nowadays, and often large numbers of banks or financial institutions have an interest in any given aircraft through syndication or security arrangements. Many such lenders will also take out credit insurance in the event that the airline is unable to pay the financing.

Liability of operators to passengers

25.04 Insurers will typically be liable to indemnify the operator for, or pay on behalf of the operator, compensatory damages (including costs awarded against the insured) in respect of the following risks:

(a) accidental bodily injury (including death) to passengers sustained on board an aircraft or sustained while embarking or disembarking an aircraft; and

(b) loss of, or damage to, baggage and personal effects of passengers arising out of an aircraft accident.

In international carriage by air, a commercial operator's liability will usually be determined by reference to an international convention system based on international conventions. The detail of this system is beyond the scope of this chapter; but in brief, it provides for a presumption of liability in favour of the passenger in particular circumstances, subject to a limit of liability (save in specified circumstances).

Liability to third parties other than passengers

25.05 Standard policy terms will make insurers liable to pay compensatory damages (including costs awarded against the insured) in respect of the following risks:

(a) accidental bodily injury (including death); and

(b) accidental damage to property caused by the aircraft or by any person or object falling from the aircraft.

General exclusions to cover

25.06 As stated above, although policies may include standard exclusions (eg, risks resulting from noise and pollution, war, hijacking and nuclear risks), the policy is likely to be bespoke and include specific exclusions. It may also include terms requiring the insured to avoid losses and ensure airworthiness.

Liability for loss of or damage to cargo

25.07 The aircraft operator will be indemnified for all monies payable up to a specified limit for loss of or damage to cargo under international conventions or the terms of the policy.

AIRPORT OWNERS' AND OPERATORS' LIABILITY INSURANCE

25.08 This form of insurance covers the liability risks faced by airport owners and airport operators and various services that they provide. Maintenance suppliers, air traffic controllers and others involved in the operation of an airport may have their own policies.

Premises liability

25.09 A standard policy will typically cover bodily injury, including death resulting from bodily injury; and loss or damage to the property of others caused by accident during the policy period.

Hangar keeper's liability

25.10 Cover may be provided in respect of liability arising from loss or damage to aircraft or aircraft equipment not owned, rented or leased by the insured while on the ground and in the care, custody or control of (or being serviced or handled or maintained by) the insured or any employee of the insured.

SPARES COVER

25.11 Subject to stated exclusions, insurance is generally available for engines, spare parts and equipment which are to be fitted to an aircraft. Such cover will apply only where the property is owned by the insured or is the property of another party for which the insured is responsible.

Chapter 26

Buildings and property insurance

- Introduction
- Types of building and property insurance
- Exclusions
- Typical conditions
- Extensions to buildings and property insurance

INTRODUCTION

26.01 This chapter is concerned with the particular features of building and property insurance, and most importantly, policies on commercial premises and dwellings and their contents. **Chapter 33** considers goods and transit policies. Other aspects of property insurance have been considered elsewhere – in particular, insurable interest (**Chapter 4**); policyholders' duties, which include utmost good faith, non-disclosure and misrepresentation (as amended by the Consumer Insurance (Disclosure and Representations) Act 2012 and the Insurance Act 2015), fraud, minimising loss and increase in risk (**Chapter 6**); and insurance contracts (**Chapter 1**).

TYPES OF BUILDING AND PROPERTY INSURANCE

26.02 There are as many types of property insurance as there are properties. The types of policies will vary from cover for a simple semi-detached house in Hounslow to global programmes of property insurance covering a multinational for damage to property throughout its offices and manufacturing centres.

Buildings insurance is not compulsory, but may be required by providers of finance for the property in order to protect their interests.

Specified perils versus all risks

26.03 Traditionally, property insurance has been provided on a specified perils basis. In other words, the insuring clause will limit cover to physical loss and damage caused by a named peril such as fire. Other specified perils might include storm or flood etc. Thus, the insured must prove the causal connection between the peril and the loss.

In contrast, all risks cover places no limitations in the insuring clause on the type of peril and, therefore, the burden of proof rests with the insurer to prove that a particular cause of loss is an excluded peril. This type of cover has become more popular, especially among larger commercial insureds.

It is possible to purchase combined lines policies which provide insureds with cover not only for property, but also employers' liability, public liability and other forms of cover. In some larger property programmes, insureds are provided with aggregate cross-class deductibles. It has become common for a wider range of property to be included in commercial property insurance. Boiler and machinery coverage used to be dealt with under separate and specific insurance, but it has now become common for this sort of coverage to be provided under a general all risks property programme.

Some policies historically included coverage for losses attributable to failures in computer systems or loss of data. With the advent of increasing cybercrime, coverage for such losses is no longer typically included in all risks policies and must be bought separately. Following concerns about ambiguity of coverage, policies must be unambiguous as to coverage in respect of malicious and non-malicious cyber risks.

Trigger of cover

26.04 Most property policies are triggered by physical loss or damage occurring during the policy period, caused by a peril occurring during the same policy period. 'Claims made' policies provide coverage for claims submitted during the relevant policy period, while 'losses occurring' policies provide coverage when an event occurs within the policy period.

Disclosure of risk

26.05 The duty of utmost good faith and disclosure on the part of the insured is crucial to any insurance, but especially where buildings and property insurance is concerned. This subject is dealt with in depth in **Chapter 6**, but some particular issues arise in respect of this class of business. The duty of utmost good faith is characterised in statute (in the Insurance Act 2015) for commercial insureds as the duty to make a fair presentation of the risk.

In respect of smaller commercial risks, proposal forms will be used by insurers and will, to some extent, set out the type of information sought by insurers. In the absence of a proposal form, what should the insured expect to disclose? He should disclose both the moral hazard and the physical hazard. The moral hazard to the insurer would include a criminal record or claims history, or any factor which casts doubt upon the honesty of the insured or the company, even when the circumstances cover the insured's relationship with third parties (see *Insurance Corp of the Channel Islands and Royal Insurance (UK) v Royal Hotel Ltd* [1998] Lloyd's Rep IR 151).

As to the physical hazard, it would of course be relevant to the underwriter to know the location and the construction of the property. For example, is the property in close proximity to an area which floods regularly? It may also be relevant to the insurer to know what steps have been taken in respect of fire prevention and security. Do the premises, for example, have the benefit of a sprinkler system or smoke detectors? Both security and fire prevention are often dealt specifically in the policy as either a warranty or a condition precedent.

If, however, it is the intention of the insurer to incorporate such clauses as warranties and/or conditions precedent, it is important that they are drafted most precisely. For example, in *Hussein v Brown* [1996] 1 Lloyd's Rep 627, the insured in the proposal form confirmed that the premises were fitted with a security alarm. In fact, the alarm was fitted; but when a fire destroyed the factory in question, the alarm did not work. The insurer argued that the warranty provided must be construed as an ongoing obligation to maintain the alarm system. The court determined, however, that in the absence of precise words, no such obligation could be imputed, and thus by simply installing an alarm the insured had complied with the warranty.

It would of course be highly relevant to the insurer to know of any peculiarities of the premises which characterise them as a high risk.

EXCLUSIONS

26.06 The number and importance of exclusions depend, to some extent, upon the type of cover. In respect of specified perils cover, some exclusions become less important because the burden of proof would be upon the insured to prove that the proximate cause of the loss is covered by the specified peril – for example, flood.

In contrast, however, properly drafted exclusion clauses are critical to the operation of an all risks insurance policy. Such exclusion clauses are numerous and can be difficult to categorise. Generally, however, the exclusions fall into two categories: either excluded property or excluded perils.

Certain property will usually be excluded from such policies, such as land, roads, pavements and bridges. It would also be unusual for vehicles, watercraft and aircraft to be covered under a typical property policy.

Perils exclusions may also be subdivided into sub-categories as set out below.

Natural peril exclusions

26.07 On occasion, flood, storm, tempest, earthquake, earth subsidence and earth movement may be excluded. It will depend to a large extent on whether the underwriter considers that that an area is particularly susceptible to such a risk.

Storm, tempest and flood are standard insured perils under a buildings policy. The term 'storm' generally means high winds accompanied by rain or snow; although it was held in one Scottish case that a heavy fall of snow, with little wind, which accumulated on the insured's roof and caused it to collapse constituted a loss by storm (*Glasgow Training Group (Motor Trade) Ltd v Lombard Continental plc* 1989 SC 30 r). 'Tempest' plainly entails high winds. The word 'flood' taken alone probably means no more than an undesired accumulation of water; but in the context of 'storm, tempest, flood', a flood requires something violent, sudden and abnormal. In *Young v Sun Alliance and London Insurance Ltd* [1976] 2 Lloyd's Rep 189, a gradual seepage of water into the insured's house to a level of about three inches was held not to be a flood, as the ingress of water did not meet this requirement (see also *Rohan Investments Ltd v Cunningham* [1999] Lloyd's Rep IR 283).

Unlike 'storm' and 'tempest,' 'flood' can overlap with non-weather related perils. For example, in *The Board of Trustees of the Tate Gallery v Duffy Construction Ltd* [2007] EWHC 361 (TCC) Jackson J held that the discharge of a large volume of water into the Tate Gallery from a burst pipe outside (but within the boundary of the insured location) fell within both 'flood' and 'bursting or overflowing of water tanks, apparatus or pipes', which was another specified peril.

Industrial perils

26.08 More usually, however, certain types of perils associated with manufacturing are excluded so as to avoid underwriters becoming guarantors for products and/or workmanship. Thus, usually, faulty design and workmanship are excluded; although resulting damage not otherwise excluded may be brought back into cover. For example, a defectively welded pipe in a manufacturing process would not itself be covered under a typical policy, but any damage caused by the escaping fluid to other machinery may well be covered under the resulting damage proviso.

Courts have distinguished between faulty design and faulty workmanship. It is generally easier to prove the former. In respect of faulty design, the courts have determined that it is not necessary to prove that the defective design was negligently drawn (see *Queensland Government Railways and Electric Power Transmission Ltd v Manufacturers Mutual Insurance Ltd* [1969] 1 Lloyd's Rep 214). In contrast, to rely upon a faulty workmanship exclusion, it is necessary to prove that the workman was negligent in some way.

Other exclusions may be boiler and mechanical breakdown, although this is now more often covered under all risks property insurance policies (see **Chapter 24**). Frequently, nipple or joint leakage, failure of welds, contamination and damage caused by the escape of water from tanks, apparatus or pipes are also excluded.

Cyber risks

26.09 Many property policies will cover physical damage to computers and IT equipment, but will not cover damage to, or loss of, the information stored in such equipment.

'Cyber risk' is exposure to loss resulting from damage to or destruction of information systems or data. Coverage for cyber risks within property insurance is increasingly being excluded as the risk of substantial losses from cyber-attacks increases. Cyber exposures have increased exponentially as individuals and organisations rely on interconnected information systems. There have been concerns in the insurance market that many policy wordings inadvertently cover greater cyber risks than underwriters had intended. This problem of 'silent cyber' coverage in property and other business insurance policies has required intervention from regulators and market representative groups.

Cyber risk is covered in greater detail in **Chapter 29**.

War and allied perils exclusions

26.10 Most property insurance will exclude war and allied perils, which would include riot. A typical example of a war exclusion might be as follows: 'Damage occasioned by war, invasion, act of foreign enemy, hostilities (whether war be declared or not), civil war, rebellion, revolution, insurrection or military or usurped power, nationalisation, confiscation, requisition, seizure or destruction by government or any public authority.'

One of the key problems in relying on such an exclusion is the difficulty that insurers find in proving the causal nexus between the excluded peril and the loss. Frequently, it is difficult to gather sufficient evidence in war-affected territories to prove that cause of particular damage (eg, a looted supermarket) was in fact caused by the war. Insurers have attempted to improve their position by removing the proximate cause test using words such as 'contributing to' or 'indirectly', thus requiring them only to prove that war was a contributing factor to the loss rather than the sole or dominant cause. However, care is needed to ensure, in designing products, that they are providing a valuable benefit to the target market for the product and meeting their needs. See also *Financial Conduct Authority v Arch Insurance (UK) Ltd and others* [2021] UKSC 1).

Indeed, in some policies insurers have even included a reverse burden of proof clause whereby if the underwriter has proved *prima facie* that the loss has taken place in a war-affected territory, and provided that some basic evidence is available as to causation, the burden of proof will transfer to the insured to satisfy the court that the loss was not caused by war or allied perils.

One of the more comprehensive accounts on the effect of causation and description of the different types of perils covered by such clauses was provided by Mustill J (later Lord Mustill) in *Spinney's (1948 Ltd) v Royal Insurance Co Ltd* [1980] 1 Lloyd's Rep 406.

Theft and fraud exclusions

26.11 The fraud of the insured or a corporation is usually dealt with under the conditions section of a property policy. Some policies, however, will exclude specifically the fraud or theft by certain persons such as employees of the company.

Where theft is an insured peril, the term is to be given a meaning which accords with the definition under the Theft Act 1968 – namely, appropriation of the property of another with the intention of permanently depriving that other of the property. This technical meaning in the Theft Act 1968 is less likely to be applied in respect of risks outside the UK. It is possible for the property to be appropriated where the owner is deprived of it by trick. In *Dobson v General Accident Fire and Life Assurance Corp* [1990] 1 QB 274, the insured sold the insured jewellery to a purchaser who paid with a stolen cheque. The Court of Appeal held that the insured had been the victim of a 'theft'. It might be added that s 18 of the Sale of Goods Act 1979 provides that ownership of goods is presumed to pass to the buyer as soon as the agreement is made even though payment is deferred to a later date. It follows that the result in *Dobson* would have been different had the insured not reserved ownership of the jewellery pending his receipt of full payment, for otherwise the property would have belonged to the purchaser and it could not have been said that the purchaser had appropriated property 'belonging to another'.

Theft policies may be restricted to theft 'committed by persons present on the premises of the insured'. This wording was considered by the High Court in *Deutsche Genossenschaftsbank v Burnhope* [1995] 1 WLR 1580, in which an innocent agent collected securities from the insured bank for his employer and the employer subsequently absconded with the securities. It was held that there was a theft, but that it had been committed not by the agent, but rather by his employer. As the employer had not been physically present on the premises when the appropriation occurred, the policy exclusion prevailed.

The need for a physical link to the premises is illustrated by the approach of the Court of Appeal to the rather dramatic events in *Canelhas Comercio Importacao e Exportacao Ltd v Wooldridge* [2004] EWCA Civ 984. The managing director of the insured jewellery company was kidnapped along with his family. A bomb belt was attached to his son and he was ordered to drive to his business premises and persuade his staff to hand over some emeralds. He told his staff of the threats to his family and they complied. The Court of Appeal held that his insurer was not entitled to rely upon a term in an all risk policy limiting its liability for 'robbery when the premises are open for business' because the reference in the clause to the premises being open for business made it clear that it only applied to theft by threats of violence made to the insured's staff at the insured's premises (whereas here the kidnappers were not on the premises).

Policies on premises which insure against burglary frequently require theft from the premises following forcible and violent entry. These words were considered by the Court of Appeal in *Nash (t/a Dino Services Ltd) v Prudential Assurance Co Ltd* [1989] 1 Lloyd's Rep 379, where the insured's car was broken into and the keys to his premises removed, and these were subsequently used to gain access to his premises. The Court of Appeal decided that the robbery had involved the use of 'force', as physical effort – albeit nominal – had been needed to use the keys. The entry had not, however, been violent, and the claim failed.

Inevitable loss

26.12 It might be thought that inevitable loss would be implicitly excluded from an insurance policy, as insurance is only intended to cover accidental loss. These types of exclusions are frequently included either to increase the effectiveness of the exclusion or to point out to the insured that such loss is not covered. Typical exclusions are latent defects, gradual deterioration, inherent vice, wear and tear, corrosion, rust, wet or dry rot, evaporation and shrinkage.

Other exclusions

26.13 This 'catch-all' section will vary widely from policy to policy, but it will certainly include consequential loss, and possibly goods in transit and lack of incoming utilities. Most policies will not indemnify the insured in respect of losses which are covered under other policies. On the other hand, some policies will cover such perils within the policy or by way of endorsement for additional premium.

TYPICAL CONDITIONS

26.14 Many conditions which are to be found in building or property policies will also be found in other forms of insurance and are dealt with elsewhere in **Chapter 14** (in particular, notification of claims, fraudulent claims and proof of loss) and policyholders' duties (**Chapter 6**).

Insurance contracts will invariably contain express conditions in relation to fraudulent claims. The insurer bears the burden of establishing that a claim is fraudulent. Where the insured has made a fraudulent claim, the insurer has no liability in respect of that claim, as the fraud taints not only the elements of the claim that are untrue, but also genuine aspects of the claim. Accordingly, any sums already paid to the insured in respect of the particular claim can be recovered. However, can claims under the policy that are not related to the fraudulent claim be recovered? A number of cases had considered whether the duty of utmost good faith would be breached by a fraudulent claim and the policy avoided *ab initio* (see *Orakpo v Barclays Insurance Services* [1995] LRLR 443). Section 12 of the Insurance Act 2015 has clarified the position with the effect that only the claim tainted by fraud is affected, and not previous honest claims. The following clause reflects the changed law:

> 'If the insured makes a fraudulent claim under this contract, the insurer:
>
> (a) shall not be liable to pay the claim;
>
> (b) may recover from the insured any sums paid by the insurer to the insured in respect of the claim; and
>
> (c) may by notice to the insured treat the contract as having been terminated with effect from the time of the fraudulent act.'

How will the law treat dishonest statements made in respect of a genuine claim? A 'collateral lie', being a lie that has no direct bearing on the insured's right to recover, will not defeat the claim (*Versloot Dredging BV v HDI Gerling Industrie Versicherung AG* [2016] UKSC 45). Insurers will be relieved of liability for any made-up claim and where the amount of loss has been exaggerated, as the insured will be using fraud to get something that he would not otherwise be entitled to under the contract.

Buildings and property insurance will also frequently include increase in hazard clauses which will attempt to prevent the insured increasing substantially the nature of the risk, and also reasonable care clauses attempting to place upon the insured an obligation to take reasonable care of the insured property. In both instances, however, the courts have proved to be remarkably creative in circumventing their effect in protecting insureds (see **Chapter 6**).

Typical conditions specific to property policies also include the following:

(a) clauses excluding inherent vice, latent defect, wear and tear or other discoverable and preventable problems with the property;

(b) the 'non-invalidation' clause. This is often found in policies designed for landlords and states that the cover provided shall not be prejudiced by any act or default of the tenant that increases the risk of loss or damage, as long as immediate notification is given by the landlord when he becomes aware of this; and

(c) the 'unoccupied premises' clause. There are several variations on this clause. Some provide that cover ceases altogether if the premises are left unoccupied for more than 30 consecutive days. Others provide that cover will continue (sometimes for restricted perils), but only on condition that the insured inspects the property weekly, shuts off all services and boards up accessible windows.

Courts are more likely to uphold conditions which are specifically drafted to deal with a type of risk, such as a sprinkler warranty which might require the insured to maintain sprinklers on a regular basis. Frequently, premium is clearly rated on the basis of such undertakings and courts are more likely to enforce such specific conditions or warranties. This would also apply to security requirements.

An example of a very commercially minded approach to the construction of an alarm warranty is found in *Anders & Kern UK Ltd (t/a Anders & Kern Presentation Systems) v CGU Insurance plc (t/a Norwich Union Insurance)* [2007] EWCA Civ 1481. The judge upheld a term requiring a key holder to remain at the premises in the event that the insured received notification from the alarm monitoring company that the line was down. The court refused to imply a term that the key holder would not be required to remain at the premises if it would put him in personal danger because the alarm warranty and its accompanying terms showed a clear allocation of risk such that the insurer was to be off risk if the premises were unattended unless the alarm was fully operational.

Average clauses are found in buildings and property insurance (see **Chapter 19**). It is also quite usual to find subrogation waiver clauses in this type of cover, but this is dealt with in **Chapter 16**.

EXTENSIONS TO BUILDINGS AND PROPERTY INSURANCE

Business interruption

26.15 As indicated at **26.13** above, consequential loss is excluded from property insurance in respect of commercial premises, but may be brought back in by way of business interruption extension.

A policy insuring property does not, in the absence of express wording, cover financial loss accruing to the insured as a direct result of damage to the property. In *Maurice v Goldsborough Mort & Co Ltd* [1939] AC 452, a firm of wool brokers insured a quantity of wool in their possession belonging to a wool grower. The wool was destroyed, and a question arose as to how the insurance monies received by the brokers were to be allocated as between themselves and the grower. The House of Lords ruled that the brokers could retain only an amount equal to the cost of services rendered and were unable to retain a sum representing loss of profits on warehouse charges and on resale, as these matters were not insured under the policy. Again, in *Re Wright & Pole* (1834) 1 Ad & El 621, an innkeeper who had insured his inn against fire was entitled to recover the value of the buildings, but could not recover the financial cost of hiring other premises and loss of trade pending repair.

Loss of profits and other consequential business interruption losses must, therefore, be insured separately. Policies or policy extensions of this type are subject to general principles of insurance law. In particular, the insured must comply with his duty to make a fair presentation of the risk, which should include the profitability or otherwise of the business.

Most business interruption policies include a clause requiring that cover can only be provided for financial loss in conjunction with material damage to the property. Sometimes business interruption cover will simply be an extension of the material damage policy or, alternatively, it might be covered under a discrete policy. Generally speaking, however, the payment under the business interruption policy in addition to its own terms of cover will be dependent upon the insured being entitled to make a claim under the material damage policy. The importance in drafting such provisos carefully was made clear in *Glengate-KG Properties Ltd v Norwich Union Fire Insurance Society Ltd* [1996] All ER 487, where the insurer certainly did not draft the material damage proviso carefully enough to produce the result they intended.

Denial or prevention of access

26.16 This is a common extension in the business interruption section of a property policy and provides cover for financial loss when access to the insured premises is prevented or hindered due to damage by an insured peril to a neighbour's property. A common example of when this might apply would be a fire in a unit in a shopping centre – businesses in neighbouring units may suffer no physical damage, but it may be many weeks before they can resume trading while the fire is investigated and the area made safe. Prevention of access clauses provide cover for business interruption losses resulting from public authorities preventing or hindering access to, or use of, the premises.

Disease

26.17 Disease extensions to business interruption cover provide an indemnity for financial loss suffered when the occurrence of a notifiable disease within a specified area prevents access to business premises. For example, a policyholder may recover financial loss as a result of premises being forcibly closed during an epidemic or pandemic (see *Financial Conduct Authority v Arch Insurance (UK) Ltd and others* [2021] UKSC 1).

Debris removal

26.18 This provides for removal of the debris off site and/or the temporary removal of property from premises for cleaning and renovation etc after loss. Debris removal coverage is usually dependent upon physical loss or damage to property covered under the main policy, and frequently it is limited financially as a proportion of the material damage loss.

In certain types of property insurance, it can be an important extension. For example, if earthworks are covered within an open pit mine, the removal of debris from site in the event of an earthworks failure could constitute a very large part of the loss.

Increased cost of construction

26.19 Cover is provided under a property policy for the cost of repairing the property or replacing it with an equivalent property in a condition equal to, but not better than, the property destroyed. If an old building is damaged beyond repair, the Building Regulations may not allow the insured to rebuild without making improvements to the specification, such as fitting double glazing, which will increase the cost and would otherwise be regarded as betterment and so be irrecoverable.

However, because the insured has no choice but to comply with these statutory requirements, most policies contain an extension allowing the insured to recover such costs, as long as the insured was not already required to make these improvements prior to the damage. This is also known as a public authorities extension because only improvements required by an authorised public body or required by law are covered.

Chapter 27

Construction risks insurance

- Risk issues
- Project insurance
- Insurance under the JCT construction contracts
- Issues arising from the operation of contractors' all risks insurance
- Latent defects insurance

RISK ISSUES

27.01 A typical construction contract exposes all the participants to risk of different kinds. Some of the risks arise under the general law of contract and tort. For example, the owner/client (referred to as the employer in many standard form contracts such as those of the Joint Contracts Tribunal (JCT)) could incur liability as an occupier of a site for injury or damage suffered by a visitor to the site under the Occupiers Liability Acts 1957 and 1984. The main contractor can also incur liability as an occupier.

However, some of the risks to participants in a construction contract are created, or at least allocated, by the contract itself. The participants will wish to insure against many of those risks, and may be required to do so as part of the contractual responsibilities. Modern construction (and engineering) contracts invariably contain sophisticated insurance provisions regulating the insurance cover that must be obtained, by whom and exceptions and extensions to the cover.

PROJECT INSURANCE

27.02 It would be possible for each party to take separate insurance for each of the risks to which it is exposed. However, there are good commercial reasons, especially on very large projects, for obtaining comprehensive project insurance. There should be significant savings in premiums over piecemeal cover by several parties, and administrative costs are typically reduced. This type of insurance is attractive in traditional projects, subject to the argument that the employer ought not to transfer a burden from the contractor to itself without good reason; but it is more problematic in a design and build contract, where truly comprehensive project insurance would need to include the professional indemnity cover of the designers and other consultants used by the contractor.

Even if project insurance is not obtained, there are 'composite' or 'combined' policies for contractors that include the employer's liability risk, public liability risk and loss or damage to the contract work (the part usually covered by an all risks policy).

To the advantages of economy and simplicity of project insurance can be added some certainty on the part of the employer as to the cover in place. For these reasons, the major standard form construction contracts often require the contractor to take out comprehensive insurance, including the misleadingly named 'contractors' all risks', but also insurance of its other potential liabilities to the employer. The contractor is also typically required to indemnify the employer against loss and to be insured in order to be able to discharge this responsibility. The indemnity provisions of a contract such as the JCT form must be read with its insurance provisions to obtain an accurate account of the position.

On large projects, it is also sometimes the case that the employer will arrange the project insurance under an owner-controlled insurance programme (OCIP). An OCIP enables the employer to control the cost, scope and limits of cover, and to select the insurers.

INSURANCE UNDER THE JCT CONSTRUCTION CONTRACTS

27.03 The JCT Standard Building Contract, 2016 Edition, provides for five types of insurance to be purchased: public liability; employers' liability; insurance against non-negligent withdrawal of support; insurance of the works and existing structures; and professional indemnity insurance. With respect to insurance of the works and existing structures, the parties have the ability to select one of three options:

(a) Option A: The contractor insures the works under an all risks policy in the joint names of the employer and contractor.

(b) Option B: This is the same as Option A, except that it is the employer which insures the works.

(c) Option C: Whereas Options A and B are suitable for new build projects, Option C is typically used where the works relate to existing structures. Under this option, the employer effects a joint names policy for the existing structure and contents, on an all risks basis.

The JCT forms of contract are considered to be the most commonly used standard construction contracts in the UK, with the Standard Building Contract designed for large or complex construction projects. It is therefore an important example of how responsibility for arranging insurance on construction projects may be allocated, particularly in relation to the critically important contract works cover.

ISSUES ARISING FROM THE OPERATION OF CONTRACTORS' ALL RISKS INSURANCE

Coverage

27.04 The basic principle is that all risks insurance covers any loss not caused by an 'excluded peril'. The benefit to the insured lies in not having to prove that the loss falls within the cover. It is enough to show that loss has occurred in order to initiate a claim under an all risks policy. To resist the claim, the insurer would have to show that the cause of the loss fell within an exclusion, the burden of proof being upon the insurer.

Risks excluded

27.05 By way of example, the JCT Standard Building Contract, 2016 Edition, authorises the exclusion of certain risks from its definition of all risks insurance, such as property defects due to 'wear and tear, obsolescence, deterioration, rust or mildew'. There are also exclusions of loss or damage arising out of war and various other types of civil and military conflict. Perhaps the most contentious exclusion is for faulty workmanship and faulty design, expressed as follows:

> 'any work executed or any site materials lost or damaged as a result of its own defect in design, plan, specification, material or workmanship or any other work executed which is lost or damaged in consequence thereof where such work relied for its support or stability on such work which was defective.'

LATENT DEFECTS INSURANCE

27.06 The essential components of latent defects insurance (LDI) are as follows: it is a non-cancellable material damage insurance against specified latent defects and damage caused by them. It gives protection for a period of ten or 12 years. It is funded by a single premium paid 'upfront' at the inception of the project or in two stages, the first at the preliminary design stage and the second at the date of practical completion. It is only after practical completion that the insurer is on risk. The premium is paid in principle by the developer (employer), although there is nothing to prevent it from negotiating with its design and construction team to share it. LDI is needed because most buildings insurance policies exclude cover for damage arising from an inherent or latent defect. While one might consider that the employer could simply claim against the contractor and consultants, which would in turn be covered by professional indemnity insurance, the 'claims-made' nature of such policies puts the employer at risk if the contractor/consultant is insolvent.

It should also be borne in mind that LDI engages from practical completion. Up to that point, the project insurance programme may provide a degree of cover for damage caused to the works arising from a defect. The London Engineering Group and Design Exclusion clauses are commonly used.

Basic cover is limited to structure and weather shield envelope (although additional optional cover for some types of consequential loss, such as loss of rent, can be purchased). The benefit of the cover is to be transferable to successive owners and to whole-building tenants (ie, tenants of part of the building or individual units receive an indemnity). Deductibles apply, but are set at levels designed to impose discipline on the conduct of developers and producers (ie, contractors and consultants).

Chapter 28

Crime insurance

- Nature of cover
- Key insuring clauses
- Exclusions
- Other notable provisions

NATURE OF COVER

28.01 Companies purchase crime insurance to protect themselves against a number of risks. Two of the key risks insured against are losses caused by employee dishonesty, and losses caused by physical loss or damage to currency and other valuable items (generally defined as 'property') while on the insured's premises.

However, crime insurance policies also provide other important coverage, including loss or damage to property while in transit; loss caused by reliance on forged or fraudulently altered payment instructions or counterfeit currency; loss caused by the erroneous transfer of funds to incorrect third parties; loss resulting from payment to extortionists; and various other losses arising from matters such as the introduction of a virus into the insured's system or the insured's reliance on fraudulently modified data. As discussed below, these policies also cover legal defence costs in certain situations.

This type of insurance is particularly important to financial institutions, although it has wider appeal as, to a greater or lesser degree, most companies are exposed to employee fidelity risks and theft or damage of valuable items from their premises. A further point to stress is that some of the risks insured under a crime insurance policy could also be insured under a kidnap and ransom, cyber or standalone specie insurance policy. If a company purchases a number of these products, it is likely that they will have been arranged carefully so that the policies interlock, with a view to recovering certain losses under specific policies and thereby avoiding the complications caused by double insurance.

KEY INSURING CLAUSES

28.02 Many crime insurance policies are structured as a series of insuring clauses, followed by a number of extensions, exclusions and conditions.

Ordinarily, the insuring clauses will start with employee fidelity, indemnifying the insured for direct financial loss resulting from a dishonest, fraudulent, criminal or malicious act by an employee. Employee fidelity insuring clauses commonly have two important features:

(a) For cover to be triggered, the employee must have acted with the intent to obtain an improper financial gain. 'Improper financial gain' is typically stated to exclude the customary benefits of employment, such as salary, commissions and bonuses. These requirements may be modified slightly with respect to losses arising from loans and trading.

(b) The term 'employee' is broadly defined, covering not only individuals under contracts of employment with the insured, but also those acting under the direct control and supervision of the insured, as well as other categories of personnel

Another prominent insuring clause provides 'premises and contents' cover in respect of the physical loss, damage or destruction of property while on the insured's premises. It is important to stress that this insuring clause only covers on-premises losses; the policy may provide a degree of off-premises cover under a subsequent 'transit' insuring clause where property is in the custody of an employee or security company; however, that is typically the limit for physical losses under crime insurance policies. 'Premises and contents' insuring clauses tend to be widely drafted, covering loss by any means but also, specifically, by theft, burglary and vandalism.

EXCLUSIONS

28.03 At first sight, traditional insurance policies may appear to have an unusually large number of exclusions. However, on closer scrutiny, it will be seen that many of the exclusions are deployed with a view to boxing in certain risks to specific insuring clauses. For example, there may be an exclusion for loss, damage or destruction of property due to fire, except under the 'premises and contents' cover. Similarly, there may be an exclusion for loss resulting from forgery, counterfeiting or alteration, except under the employee fidelity insurance policy and other insuring clauses where such matters are integral to the cover provided (eg, the 'forgery and alteration' insuring clause).

While there may be some generally applicable exclusions (eg, for indirect and consequential loss), the result is that very careful regard must be given to the exclusions by anyone reviewing a crime insurance policy to assess the scope of cover that is provided.

OTHER NOTABLE PROVISIONS

28.04 In the event of a claim, crime insurance policies normally require a proof of loss to be submitted within six months of notification or some other period. There may be a prescribed format for the proof of loss; but there quite possibly may not be, in which case the insured will have a discretion to determine which facts and documents are material. If the insurer disagrees with the approach taken, the insured can expect to receive further requests for information. In some instances, compliance with the timeframe in the proof of loss clause may be a condition precedent to liability.

Such policies also contain detailed basis of valuation clauses, setting out how losses are to be calculated. Lost or damaged currency or precious metals may be valued by reference to a particular exchange or publication on the date of discovery. The indemnity payable in respect of electronic data may be limited to the cost of replacing the storage media and the cost of labour to replace the lost or damaged data.

Finally, the policy may also cover a range of costs and expenses, such as defence costs, stolen identity costs (ie, costs, including legal costs, for dealing with the consequences of identity fraud) and rewards for information. Of these categories, defence costs are likely to be the most material for insureds, particularly in the case of financial institutions which incur liability to their customers due to employee infidelity or another insured peril.

Chapter 29

Cyber insurance

- Introduction
- What cyber insurance policies cover
- Relevant provisions

INTRODUCTION

29.01 In the past decade, cyber risk has risen to the top of the agenda for most boards of directors. This is due to the way in which business is now conducted, heavily relying on technology and data. As a result, there can be serious financial and reputational consequences for a company if its technology or the data that it holds is compromised.

Cyber risks may be deliberate or accidental. In this regard, the Prudential Regulatory Authority (PRA) has identified two types of cyber exposures:

(a) losses resulting from malicious attacks (eg, cyberattacks or the introduction of malicious code); and

(b) losses resulting from non-malicious acts (eg, inadvertent loss of data or other accidental acts).

While the first of these exposures is more prominent in the public consciousness, losses resulting from non-malicious acts may be equally damaging. For example, third parties whose data has been lost may bring claims against the company in its capacity as a data controller or processor. A company that is responsible for losing its customers' data may suffer just as serious reputational consequences as a company whose IT security system is breached.

In the UK in recent years, increased regulation and a stream of cyberattacks against well-known organisations have resulted in high demand for cyber insurance.

On the regulatory side, the General Data Protection Regulation 2016/679 (EU GDPR) came into force in the UK on 25 May 2018, alongside the Data Protection Act 2018. Article 5(1)(f) implemented the 'security principle': a requirement that personal data be processed in a manner that ensures appropriate security, including protection against unauthorised or unlawful processing, as well as against accidental loss, destruction or damage, using appropriate technical or organisational measures. Article 5(2) also implemented the 'accountability principle', requiring data controllers to be able to demonstrate compliance with the various EU GDPR principles. The EU GDPR also provided supervisory authorities (in the UK context, the Information Commissioner (ICO)) with the power to impose administrative fines on controllers and processors of up to 4 per cent of their total worldwide annual turnover or €20 million; and gave data subjects an automatic right to compensation. Following the UK transition period, the UK GDPR replaced the existing regime via the Data Protection, Privacy and Electronic Communications (Amendments etc.) (EU Exit) Regulations 2019, but materially the same regulatory framework remains in place.

As for the cyber threat environment, the number of successful cyberattacks has increased in line with cyber criminals' deployment of more advanced methods and techniques. In recent years, this has extended from malicious actors seeking financial reward to carefully planned and executed attacks on high-value data by state-sponsored actors. As technology has diversified, so the range of potential vulnerabilities has increased. The resulting consciousness of a high cyber threat level, coupled with a more stringent regulatory framework and an appreciation of the significant financial consequences that may follow, has led many companies to purchase cyber insurance policies. The relatively recent phenomenon of UK group litigation actions arising out of mass data breaches is another development that may generate further interest in the product.

In addition, there has been a concerted effort by insurers under non-cyber policies – prompted by the PRA – to reduce their unintended or 'silent cyber' exposure by making clear within their policy wordings whether there is cover for cyber risks. This has led to the widespread adoption of cyber exclusions in many classes of insurance, making it more difficult for insureds to rely on their non-cyber policies to cover cyber risks and in turn promoting cyber insurance as the solution.

WHAT CYBER INSURANCE POLICIES COVER

29.02 Cyber insurance wordings frequently change to take account of the evolving threat landscape and there are many different forms. However, the following are typically within the scope of many policies:

(a) the various costs that may be incurred following a cyber incident, such as legal expenses, the cost of retaining public relations consultants and fees charged for technical and IT forensic services. These are essentially crisis management costs, incurred in the aftermath of a cyber incident when specialists are retained to help investigate what has happened and mitigate the effects. Policies often contain a list of pre-approved providers to avoid unnecessary delay following an incident;

(b) extortion costs, including ransom payments and the costs of retaining ransom negotiators. This is a particularly important element of cover due to the relative frequency of ransomware attacks. English law does not prohibit the payment of ransoms, although care must be taken not to contravene sanctions legislation or provide funds to terrorist organisations;

(c) compensation paid to third parties in respect of actual or alleged breaches of the insured's legal and regulatory obligations, and associated defence costs. This element of cover would therefore respond in the event that an individual or group claim is brought by affected parties seeking recourse for breaches of the UK GDPR;

(d) business interruption loss, triggered by IT outages caused by cyber-attacks. Ransomware viruses, in particular, have the capacity to cause serious disruption to businesses for prolonged periods of time; and

(e) regulatory fines, to the extent that they are insurable. Under English law, the general position is understood to be that regulatory fines imposed on a party for its wrongdoing are contrary to public policy and are therefore not insurable. However, fines issued by the ICO can be significant.

Other types of cover are also possible. For example, some policies provide cover for theft of funds, reputational damage and property damage. It is also worth stressing that, at the time of writing, as a general observation, cyber insurance policies are continuing to evolve. As with other types of insurance, it is therefore not the case that there is a settled insurance framework which most policies adopt. It is highly likely that additional types of valuable cover will be identified in the coming years, and that existing policies will be adapted as risk appetites change (for both insurers and policyholders).

RELEVANT PROVISIONS

29.03 Any cyber insurance policy is very likely to contain a double insurance clause, providing for the policy to operate in excess of any other responsive insurance or not at all. As has been explained, other types of policy can provide a degree of cyber coverage, though not to the same extent as a dedicated cyber insurance policy. Of particular note in this regard are crime policies, which may indemnify the insured for financial loss resulting from unauthorised access to its IT system; public liability policies, which sometimes contain data protection extensions; property damage policies, which can provide cover for physical damage arising from cyber incidents; and professional indemnity insurance policies. While efforts have been made to clarify and confirm the extent of cyber coverage that non-cyber policies provide, overlapping cover remains a distinct possibility.

Policies typically exclude war and terrorism. The latter is particularly relevant in a cybersecurity context, on account of the scope for cyberattacks by state-sponsored threat actors. It is presently understood that insurers are prepared to cover losses arising from such attacks (and not rely on this exclusion).

Cyber insurance policies exclude loss arising from the failure of utilities and other infrastructure as standard. This reflects an understandable concern on the part of cyber insurers not to assume responsibility for widespread, catastrophic losses where an attack on essential infrastructure impacts multiple insureds.

Chapter 30

Directors' and officers' liability

- Nature and scope of directors' and officers' insurance
- Common sources of liability for directors

NATURE AND SCOPE OF DIRECTORS' AND OFFICERS' INSURANCE

Background

30.01 Section 233 of the Companies Act 2006 expressly permits a company to purchase insurance on behalf of its directors and officers in respect of liabilities which they may incur in relation to the company. A directors' and officers' (D&O) policy is designed to provide protection to a company's directors and officers in respect of many forms of civil liability and defence costs (including defence costs) in relation to their activities, or arising out of their capacity as a director or officer of a company.

A typical D&O policy will have two insuring clauses. The first, sometimes known as 'Side A', provides direct indemnification by the insurer to the director or officer. The second, sometimes known as 'Side B', provides that the insurer will reimburse the company to the extent that the company has already indemnified its directors or officers. Most standard D&O policies do not provide any 'entity cover' to the company in respect of its own exposure to civil liability or defence costs, although this type of cover may be available on payment of additional premium, sometimes known as 'Side C'.

Side A and Side B may be purchased together because the insured directors and officers may benefit from a company indemnity. Side B therefore indemnifies the company to the extent that the company indemnifies the director or officer, and Side A indemnifies the director or officer in the event that the company is unable to do so.

The trigger for cover under a D&O policy is a 'wrongful act' or a notice to attend an investigation. This is generally widely defined to include any act, error or omission committed by directors in their capacity as such.

Most policies are written on a composite basis for the benefit of each director or officer individually rather than jointly as a group.

D&O policies do not typically contain many exclusions. Perhaps most materially, loss is excluded if it arises out of the insured director or officer obtaining personal financial profit or acting dishonestly. Most policies also oblige the insurer to advance defence costs pending the determination of coverage issues. This can be an important benefit where fraud is alleged, requiring the insurer to fund the director or officer's defence; should the allegation of fraud succeed, the insured director or officer will need to repay the funded costs on account of the dishonesty exclusion, but will have had the benefit of a funded legal defence in the meantime.

Permutations of cover

30.02 Cover varies considerably from policy to policy, but some general points should be borne in mind:

(a) Virtually all D&O policies are written on a 'claims made' basis, which means that they only cover losses arising and notified during the policy period. Retired directors facing a claim in relation to their period in office may not be covered.

(b) Criminal fines and penalties are generally not insurable under English law, particularly where resulting from intentional conduct. However, costs incurred defending criminal prosecutions will generally be covered, subject to fraud and dishonesty exclusions.

(c) Many D&O policies exclude claims brought or liabilities incurred in certain jurisdictions.

(d) A director may be called upon to participate in a regulatory, disciplinary or criminal investigation.

COMMON SOURCES OF LIABILITY FOR DIRECTORS

Duties to the company

30.03 All directors owe a number of fiduciary duties to the company on whose board they sit, codified in the Companies Act 2006.

Sections 171–177 set out a number of general duties with which directors must comply. Section 170(3) states that the 'general duties are based on certain common law rules and equitable principles as they apply in relation to directors and have effect in place of those rules and principles as regards the duties owed to a company by a director'.

Section 170(4) goes on to provide that the 'general duties shall be interpreted and applied in the same way as common law rules or equitable principles, and regard shall be had to the corresponding common law rules and equitable principles in interpreting and applying the general duties'.

The general duties owed by directors include:

(a) to exercise reasonable care, skill and diligence;

(b) to exercise independent judgement;

(c) to act in the way that they consider, in good faith, would be most likely to promote the success of the company for the benefit of its members as a whole (having regard to six specified factors);

(d) to act in accordance with the company's constitution and to exercise their powers for the purposes for which they are conferred;

(e) to avoid conflicts of interest;

(f) not to accept benefits from third parties; and

(g) to declare any interest in a proposed transaction or arrangement with the company.

These duties are only enforceable by the company rather than by individual shareholders (Companies Act 2006, s 170(1)). However, a so-called 'derivative' action, to allow shareholders to bring claims in the name of the company against directors, is possible under the Companies Act 2006. The Companies Act 2006 does not require a shareholder to hold any minimum number of shares in order to have standing to bring a claim, and the claim can be brought in respect of breaches of duty alleged to have occurred before the shares were purchased (s 260(4)). A claimant bringing a derivative action must seek the court's permission to continue its claim.

Duties to third parties

30.04 Following the House of Lords decision in *Williams v Natural Life Health* Foods [1998] 2 All ER 577, the scope for third parties to bring direct claims for negligent misstatement against a company director acting in his capacity as such is limited. This case decided that in the absence of clear evidence that a director has assumed personal and direct responsibility for advice or information to an individual, the individual will not have a right of action against him.

Other statutory liabilities

30.05 Under the statutory regimes that affect directors, there are many ways in which a director can incur civil liability or liability for fines and penalties. These include:

(a) civil liability for wrongful trading under s 214 of the Insolvency Act 1986 in circumstances where a director allows a company to continue trading beyond the time at which he should reasonably have concluded that it was insolvent;

(b) disqualification under the Company Directors Disqualification Act 1986 on a variety of grounds, including a general provision enabling a director to be disqualified in circumstances where his conduct was such as to make him unfit to be concerned in the management of a company; and

(c) civil liability under s 90 of the Financial Services and Markets Act 2000 to any investors in a company who can show that they have suffered a loss as a result of reliance on untrue or misleading statements contained in listing particulars or as a result of the omission from the particulars of any matter required to be included by the Act.

In addition to these examples, there are many other statutory provisions in respect of which a director can incur civil or criminal liability. Much will depend on the scope and sphere of the operations conducted by the company on whose board he sits.

Chapter 31

Employers' liability insurance

- Introduction
- Compulsory insurance for injuries at work
- Contents of the policy
- Liabilities faced by an employer
- Who is the employee?
- Transfer of liabilities
- Enforcement

INTRODUCTION

31.01 English law imposes a variety of common law and statutory duties upon employers to secure the safety of their employees. The growth of personal injury claims in the early twentieth century led to the development of employers' liability insurance. The Employers' Liability (Compulsory Insurance) Act 1969 (EL(CI)A 1969), which entered into force on 1 January 1971, made it compulsory for employers to insure against liability to employees. Under s 3 of the EL(CI)A 1969, local authorities are exempt from the requirement to effect insurance.

COMPULSORY INSURANCE FOR INJURIES AT WORK

The obligation to insure

31.02 Every employer carrying on any business in Great Britain is required to take out and maintain insurance against liability for bodily injury or disease sustained by its employees arising out of and in the course of their employment in Great Britain (EL(CI)A 1969, s 1(1)). This includes death as a result of an injury at work and mental illness arising as a result of their work. The policy must be issued by an insurer authorised to carry on insurance business of the class in question (EL(CI)A 1969, s 1(3)(b); see **Chapter 42**). The policy must be 'approved' – that is, not narrower in scope than is required by the Act (EL(CI)A 1969, s 1(3)(a)). (For exceptions to the obligation to insure, see **31.12** below.)

Compulsory insurance requirements in relation to motor vehicle accidents involving employees are covered by either the EL(CI)A 1969 or the Road Traffic Act 1988 (RTA 1988). Generally, accidents occurring while an employee is travelling in (or getting into or out of) a motor vehicle being used by his employer should be covered by s 145 of the RTA 1988 (requirements in respect of compulsory motor insurance). This is an exception to the general rule (RTA 1988, ss145(4) and145(4)A)) that compulsory motor insurance does not need to cover liabilities which are 'in fact' covered by employers' liability insurance.

Other liabilities to employees for personal injury (or death) as a result of a motor accident in the course of their employment will need to be covered by employers' liability insurance. It is therefore important to understand the situations covered by the RTA, which are set out in reg 9 and sch 2 of the Employers' Liability (Compulsory Insurance) Regulations (SI 1998/2573) and are as follows:

(a) The employee is, in the course of his employment in Great Britain, being carried in/upon or getting into/on or alighting from a motor vehicle;

(b) The motor vehicle is being used on the road by the employer (see **Chapter 36** in relation to the meaning of the term 'used' in this context); and

(c) The bodily injury is caused by or arises out of that use.

In *AXA Insurance UK Plc v Norwich Union Insurance Ltd* [2007] EWHC 1046 (Comm), it was held that 'carried in or upon' meant travelling in and not using equipment forming part of the vehicle while stationary. This meant that the employer's liability for the accident was required to be covered by the employer's liability insurance rather than its motor insurance policy. Had the accident occurred while the employee was temporarily parked in the vehicle, the outcome may have been different.

Regulation 9 and sch 2 of SI 1998/2573 also exempt certain classes of employer from the requirements of the EL(CI)A 1969. They are principally bodies issued with certificates of exemption by government departments, foreign and Commonwealth governments and certain public bodies.

Amount of cover

31.03 The amount of cover to be procured is specified by statutory instrument made under s 1(2) of the EL(CI)A 1969. The present figure is £5 million 'in respect of claims relating to any one or more of his employees arising out of any one occurrence' (SI 1998/2573, reg 3). The level of cover required relates not to individual injuries, but rather to the occurrence which gives rise to individual injuries and is therefore an aggregate figure for each such occurrence. In practice, higher levels of cover may be maintained.

Course of employment

31.04 Compulsory insurance need not extend to injuries suffered by an employee acting outside the course of his employment. It should be noted that an employee is acting in the course of his employment even though he may be disobeying his employer's orders: the test is whether the employee is going about his employer's business at the time. An employee travelling to and from work is not acting in the course of his employment unless the job requires travelling between sites or offices (*Smith v Stages* [1989] 1 All ER 833); neither is an employee who is engaged in after-hours social activities, such as playing football for his employer's team (see *R v National Insurance Commissioner* [1977] 1 WLR 109).

CONTENTS OF THE POLICY

31.05 An employers' liability policy follows the pattern of general liability policies. However, under reg 2(1) of SI 1998/2573, four types of policy condition are prohibited from inclusion in a compulsory policy. The prohibited conditions relate to the insurer seeking to avoid liability:

(a) in the event of some specified thing being done or omitted to be done after the happening of the event giving rise to a claim under the policy (eg, notice of loss clauses or admissions of liability);

(b) unless the policyholder takes reasonable care to protect its employees against the risk of bodily injury or disease in the course of their employment (reasonable care clauses have, independently of this provision, been given limited meaning by the courts and have been confined to recklessness);

(c) unless the policyholder complies with the requirements of any enactment for the protection of employees against the risk of bodily injury or disease in the course of their employment (so that, for example, breaches of health and safety legislation by the employer cannot provide a defence to the insurer); and

(d) unless the policyholder keeps specified records or provides the insurer with or makes available to it information therefrom (a clause of this type may relate to a record of wages paid or to an accident book).

An insurer remains free to provide that the employer is to indemnify the insurer for sums required under the legislation to be paid by the insurer to an injured employee where any of the above terms have been broken by the employer (SI 1998/2573, reg 2(2)).

LIABILITIES FACED BY AN EMPLOYER

Common law liability

Direct liability

31.06 An employer owes a duty of care to its employees to take reasonable care for their safety. The leading authority is *Wilsons & Clyde Coal Co, Ltd v English* [1938] AC 57, in which the employer of a miner killed due to the operation of an unsafe system of work was sued by the miner's family. The House of Lords rejected the employer's defence that the duty to organise working systems had been delegated to an employee and held that the employer's duty could not be delegated. Lord Wright's speech contains the classic statement of the scope of an employer's duty – namely, to provide 'a competent staff of men, adequate material, and a proper system and effective supervision'.

The duty is not absolute and merely requires the employer to act reasonably. In *Latimer v AEC LD*, [1953] AC 643, for example, in which an employee was injured having fallen over on a floor made slippery by flooding, the House of Lords ruled that the employer had, in clearing up the flood, taken all reasonable care to overcome the danger, and that it was unreasonable to expect the employer to provide absolute protection by closing the factory down until the floor was completely dry. In *Dixon v London Fire and Civil Defence Authority*, *Times*, 22 February 1993, a fireman was injured due to slipping on wet quarry tiles at his place of work. The Court of Appeal held that the employer had not broken its duty of care, as it had taken reasonable care to fix the leak which had caused the wetting. The Court of Appeal further held that it would have been unreasonable for the employer to install an entirely different floor surface despite the fact that the quarry tiles were not the safest possible flooring in the circumstances.

Vicarious liability

31.07 In addition to an employer's direct liability to its employees, it may also be vicariously liable for the negligent acts of fellow employees and independent contractors working on its premises. As far as vicarious liability for employees is concerned, the employer is liable for all injuries negligently inflicted by one employee on another if the negligent employee was acting in the course of his employment. The concept of 'course of employment' is a wide one and may include the activities of an employee acting contrary to the employer's business. In *Rose v Plenty and Another* [1976] 1 WLR 141, the employer of a milkman was held to be liable for injuries to a child falling from one of its milk floats, even though the employee milkman had been specifically forbidden to carry children in this way.

Where an employer is held to be vicariously liable for the acts of an employee, the employer is entitled at common law to be indemnified by the employee by reason of an implied term to that effect in the contract of employment. The real impact of this rule is to permit the employer's liability insurer, having indemnified the employer, to exercise subrogation rights against the employee (see *Lister v Romford Ice and Cold Storage Co Ltd* [1957] AC 555 – a case in which the employer's insurer was able to recoup its payment to an injured employee from the guilty employee, who happened to be the injured employee's father). This rule remains the law, but insurers agreed with the government in the wake of this case not to exercise subrogation rights against negligent employees. In a later case, *Morris v Ford Motor Co Ltd* [1973] QB 792, the Court of Appeal refused to extend the *Lister* case to injuries caused by an employee who had been borrowed from another employer.

In the case of an independent contractor, the employer's liability is personal rather than vicarious. The employer is liable only if its own conduct has been negligent – for example, if it has failed to exercise reasonable care in selecting a competent independent contractor or adequately to supervise the independent contractor's performance of its obligations. Whether a contractor is properly to be regarded as independent or falls within the category of an employee is considered below at **31.09**.

Liability arising under statute

31.08 The Health and Safety at Work etc. Act 1974 (HSWA 1974) established a system of administrative control and penal sanctions relating to general duties requiring safety in the workplace. However, the HSWA 1974 does not confer any civil rights upon an employee injured in consequence of his employer's breach of any provision of the Act. The employee's civil rights are available either under the common law or by means of an action based upon other health and safety legislation for breach of statutory duty.

Over the decades, the range of different statutes provided for regulation within different industries – most notably the various Factories Acts, mines and quarries legislation and regulations governing offices, shops and railway premises.

This industry-by-industry approach to health and safety was eventually superseded by the implementation in the UK of the European Framework Directive on Safety and Health at Work (Directive 89/391 EEC), introducing a wide-ranging series of regulations governing workplace health and safety.

Just as the HSWA 1974 does not afford any civil remedy, the Management of Health and Safety at Work Regulations 1992 (SI 1992/2051) (revoked and superseded by the Management of Health and Safety at Work Regulations 1999 (SI 1999/3242)) similarly, when first introduced, did not attract civil liability. However, following the Management of Health and Safety at Work (Amendment) Regulations 2006 (revoked and superseded by the Health and Safety at Work etc. Act 1974 (Civil Liability) (Exceptions) Regulations 2013 (SI 2013/1667)), compensation claims can now be brought based directly on a breach of the 1992 Regulations. Claims may also be brought against employees by third parties who were affected by their work. In *Stark v The Post Office* [2000] 3 WLUK 75, the claimant was employed as a delivery postman and suffered injury during the course of his employment when the front wheel of the bicycle that he was riding locked, causing him to be thrown over the handlebars. The accident was caused by a defect in the bicycle which would not have been detected upon a thorough examination. The Court of Appeal held that reg 6(1) of the Provision and Use of Work Equipment Regulations 1992 (SI 1992/2932) imposed an absolute obligation on the employer to maintain work equipment in efficient working order and good repair. Note that the Provision and Use of Work Equipment Regulations 1998 (SI 1998/2306) revoked and re-enacted the Provision and Use of Work Equipment Regulations 1992, which broadly gave effect, as regards Great Britain, to Council Directive 89/655/EEC (OJ No L393, 30 December 1989, p 13) on the minimum health and safety requirements for the use of work equipment by workers at work.

In *Fytche v Wincanton Logistics plc* [2004] UKHL 31, the House of Lords considered whether the duty placed on an employer under the Personal Protective Equipment Regulations 1992 to keep personal protective equipment in repair extended only to the risk in relation to which the equipment was supplied or whether it extended to all possible risks.

The claimant lorry driver was provided with steel-capped safety boots when collecting milk from farms, to protect him from dropping milk churns on his feet. Water got into his boots, causing frostbite. The House held that the obligation to keep the boots in good repair extended to keeping them free from defects relating to the risks that the boots had been provided to provide protection against.

By comparison, in *Hawkes v London Borough of Southwark*, unreported, 1998 (CA) the Court of Appeal held that a test of 'reasonable practicability' is still relevant when considering the system of work giving rise to a claim pursuant to the Manual Handling Operation Regulations 1992 (SI 1992/2793). See also *Koonjul v Thameslink Healthcare Services* [2000] 3 WLUK 838. The claimant was an experienced care assistant who worked at a small residential home for children with learning disabilities. In the course of making a bed, she bent down and pulled the bed away from a wall, injuring her back. The bed was unusually low in case children with epilepsy fell out of bed (which was against the wall for the same reason). It was accepted that the force required to move the bed was very modest. The Court of Appeal held that the defendant was not liable. Lady Justice Hale stated:

> 'It is an employment involving a number of everyday tasks, any one of which could involve something which could be described as a manual handling operation – lifting bedding, moving beds around in order to make them, moving the chest of drawers, or moving the chair in order to make the bed. There are innumerable tasks around such a home, and the idea that the level of risk involved (which I have already said was very low) should be met by a precise evaluation of each of those tasks and precise warnings to each employee as to how each was to be carried out, seems to me to take the matter way beyond the realms of practicability.'

In addition to applicable European legislation (eg, EU regulations which have been onshored to the UK as a result of Brexit), the Employers' Liability (Defective Equipment) Act 1969 entitles an injured employee to sue his employer where he suffered injury as a result of using defective equipment that had been manufactured and supplied to the employer by an independent manufacturer. It is for the employer to sue the manufacturer for the liability that it has incurred towards its employee.

The word 'equipment' covers both 'plant' (tools and machinery to be used by the employee), and 'stock in trade' (articles produced by the use of plant). In *Knowles v Liverpool City Council* [1993] 1 WLR 1428, a flagstone which the employee had been employed to lay was held to be 'equipment'.

In *Wright v Romford Blinds & Shutters Ltd* [2003] EWHC 1165 (QB), the claimant was standing on top of a van, loading shuttering that was being passed up to him, when he lost his footing and fell. The fall was held to be directly associated with the work being undertaken. The defendant had not put up guard rails or raised edges on the roof surface. No risk assessment had been carried out. It was held that there was a breach of reg 13 of the Workplace (Health, Safety and Welfare) Regulations 1992, as the roof of the van was a 'workplace' and the defendant had failed to prevent the claimant from pulling a distance likely to cause injury.

As the title suggests, the Work at Height Regulations 2005, which came into force on 6 April 2005, govern all aspects of working at height and place duties upon an employer for his employee and any other person under his control.

WHO IS THE EMPLOYEE?

An 'employee'

31.09 The term 'employee' is defined as meaning 'an individual who has entered into or works under a contract of service or apprenticeship with an employer whether by way of manual labour, clerical work or otherwise, whether such contract is expressed or implied, oral or in writing' (EL(CI)A 1969, s 2(1)). The most important distinction to be drawn here is between an employee and an independent contractor.

Over the years, various tests have been developed to identify who should properly be classed as an independent contractor and therefore not an employee. The courts have gradually moved away from tests such as 'who controls and directs the work' to an assessment of the 'economic reality' of the relationship between the parties. Even where an independent contractor describes himself as such and provides his own equipment, he may well be held to be an employee when the financial reality of the relationship between the parties is considered (see *Lane v The Shire Roofing Company (Oxford) Ltd* [1995] IRLR 493; *Wharf v Bildwell Insulations Ltd* [1999] 2 WLUK 38).

Residence in Great Britain

31.10 An employee must be ordinarily resident in Great Britain to obtain the benefit of the EC(CI)A 1969 (EC(CI)A 1969, s 2(2)(b)). SI 1998/2573 extends protection to an employee who is not ordinarily resident in Great Britain, but who is injured in the course of his employment while present in Great Britain for a continuous period of not less than 14 days. An employee who is not ordinarily resident in Great Britain may, of course, be covered by employers' liability insurance on a voluntary basis; but the employer is under no common law duty of care either to take out such insurance or to warn the employee that he should take steps to procure first-party insurance against injury incurred abroad (*Reid v Rush & Tomkins Group plc* [1989] 3 All ER 228). This does not apply to work on offshore installations, which are covered separately by SI 1998/2573 (reg 5(4)).

Relatives

31.11 The EL(CI)A 1969 does not require insurance to be taken out in respect of an employee who falls into any of the following categories of relation to the employer: husband, wife, father, mother, grandfather, grandmother, stepfather, stepmother, son, daughter, grandson, granddaughter, stepson, stepdaughter, brother, sister, half-brother or half-sister (EL(CI)A 1969, s 2(2)(a)).

Specific exceptions

31.12 The compulsory insurance requirement does not apply in respect of:

(a) various categories of local authority employees (EL(CI)A 1969, s 3(1)(a)(2));

(b) employees of a statutory body under national ownership or control (EL(CI)A 1969, s 3(1)(b));

(c) employees of various bodies listed in reg 9 and sch 2 of SI 1998/2573, including transport and judicial authorities; or

(d) an employer's liability for the death of or personal injury to an employee in a motor vehicle accident (while he is being carried in/on or entering/alighting from a motor vehicle) which arises in the course of his employment in Great Britain and where the liability is caused or arises out of the use by the employer of the vehicle on the road (SI 1998/2573, reg 9, para 14 and schedule 2).

TRANSFER OF LIABILITIES

31.13 Regulation 5 of the Transfer of Undertakings (Protection of Employment) Regulations 1981 (SI 1981/1794) (TUPE 1981) provides that on the completion of a transfer of a business, all the 'old' employer's rights, powers, duties and liabilities under or in connection with any such contract shall be transferred to the 'new' employer. In addition, anything done before the transfer is completed by or in relation to the old employer in respect of that contract, or a person employed in that undertaking or part, shall be deemed to have been done by or in relation to the transfer.

These regulations have caused confusion in circumstances where a worker suffers a personal injury due to the employer's negligence, but then thereafter the business is transferred to a new employer. Which employer should the worker sue?

This issue was considered by the Court of Appeal in *Bernadone v Pall Mall Services Group* [2001] ICR 197 and *Martin v Lancashire County Council* [2000] 3 All ER 544. The Court of Appeal held that reg 5 was wide enough to allow for a liability for personal injury to arise in connection with the contract, and as such it was transferred to the new employer under the TUPE 1981. In addition, the court held that the old employer's right to recover from its insurers in respect of liability to an employee for personal injury arising under the EL(CI)A 1969 also transferred to the new employer, thereby transferring the old employer's insurance cover to the new employer.

Although the new employer will have the benefit of the old employer's insurance cover, the new employer will still be responsible for the excess or deductible under the policy.

ENFORCEMENT

Sanctions

31.14 It is a criminal offence for an employer to fail to procure the required insurance. Criminal liability, in the case of a company, may be extended to any officer of the company who was responsible for the default (EL(CI)A 1969, s 5). However, if the employer's default is not remedied and an employee is injured, the employee will simply be left uncompensated if the employer cannot afford to pay the damages.

Certificates

31.15 To guard against failure to insure, the EL(CI)A 1969 sets up an inspection regime (EL(CI)A 1969, s 4). An employer taking out insurance must, within 30 days, be issued by the insurer with a certificate in the statutory form, stating the name of the policyholder; the date of the commencement of the insurance; the date of the expiry of the insurance; and the name of the insurer (SI 1998/2573, regs 4 and 5). A copy of the certificate must be displayed at each of the employer's places of business (SI 1998/2573, reg 5), and must be produced for inspection to the Health and Safety Executive or an inspector appointed by the Department of Trade and Industry (SI 1998/2573, regs 6, 7 and 8).

Chapter 32

Environmental insurance

- Forms of environmental risks and liabilities
- Sources of environmental liability
- Insurance against environmental liability

FORMS OF ENVIRONMENTAL RISKS AND LIABILITIES

32.01 Greater awareness of the effects of environmental degradation has led to the development of environmental liability regimes in England and Wales. The enforcement of these regimes means that companies are no longer able to ignore environmental liabilities arising from their acts or omissions. Environmental risks and liabilities may take the form of:

(a) civil penalties under specific environmental regimes;

(b) payment of damages under civil actions (including liabilities to third parties for damage to their person or property);

(c) costs of carrying out works to a site or installation to comply with environmental laws or permits, including where responsibility for cleaning up the environment has been imposed by a regulator such as the Environment Agency;

(d) closure or temporary suspension of a site or operations by regulators where the site or operations do not comply with environmental laws or permits;

(e) business disruption as a result of clean-up or upgrade works;

(f) costs of compliance with an injunction;

(g) fines, imprisonment or other sanctions for criminal environmental offences; and

(h) legal costs.

One way of managing these liabilities – other than fines for criminal offences, which are not insurable as a matter of public policy – is to insure them.

SOURCES OF ENVIRONMENTAL LIABILITY

32.02 Insurance may be sought against environmental liabilities arising from the common law and from statute.

Common law

32.03 The principal common law sources of environmental liability are nuisance (public and private); negligence; the rule in *Rylands v Fletcher* (1868) LR 3 HL 330; and, to a much more limited extent, trespass. For the first three torts, there must be damage and that damage must be reasonably foreseeable. For the fourth tort, damage is not a prerequisite; the claimant need only show interference with its land.

Statute and regulation

32.04 Environmental legislation imposes criminal liability on polluters and, as noted in **32.01** above, for public policy reasons, it is not possible to insure against fines. In addition, there are statutory provisions which authorise regulatory authorities to require the remediation (clean-up) of polluted land and/or water. Examples include s 161A of the Water Resources Act 1991, which authorises the Environment Agency to serve a notice requiring a person who caused or knowingly permitted a pollutant to enter a body of water to remediate it and, if practicable, restore the aquatic environment; and s 78E of the Environmental Protection Act 1990 which, subject to certain conditions, requires a local authority which has identified land as contaminated to serve a notice requiring the person who caused or knowingly permitted the contamination – or, if that person cannot be found after a reasonable inquiry, the owner or occupier of the land – to remediate it.

Other statutory provisions also impose civil liability on a polluter. An example is s 73(6) of the Environmental Protection Act 1990, which authorises a person who has suffered property damage or personal injury caused by an unlawful deposit of waste to bring an action for damages against the person who deposited the waste, or knowingly caused or knowingly permitted it to be deposited.

The liabilities outlined above may be covered by public liability or environmental insurance policies.

The main environmental statutory regimes in the UK are as follows:

(a) The contaminated land regime is set out in Part 2A of the Environmental Protection Act 1990. Its aim is to remediate significant historic contamination. Regulators will use this regime where other regimes under which contamination could be cleaned up do not apply. The contaminated land regime does not make it an offence to contaminate land; however, non-compliance with a remediation notice is an offence. The purpose of the regime is to ensure the remediation of contaminated land, rather than to punish those responsible. Liability for the remediation of contaminated land lies with those who caused or knowingly permitted the contamination, referred to as 'Class A persons'. However, if those persons cannot be identified, liability will pass to the owners and occupiers of the land (referred to as 'Class B persons'). This is the case regardless of whether such Class B persons were aware of the contamination or not.

(b) Water pollution and water discharges are regulated by the Environmental Agency in the UK under the Water Resources Act 1991, and discharges to water require an environmental permit. Environmental permits are subject to conditions and an operator may be required by the terms of its permit to pre-treat the discharge before it can be discharged into water (eg, rivers, streams or groundwater). Failure to comply with the terms of an environmental permit is a criminal offence, as is causing or knowingly permitting a discharge to water or groundwater without an environmental permit.

(c) The environmental 'permitting' regime is primarily set out in the Environmental Permitting (England and Wales) Regulations 2016 (SI 2016/1154). Operations that fall under the Environmental Permitting Regulations must either obtain a permit (standard or bespoke) or be exempt, as operating a regulated facility without a permit or in breach of a permit's conditions is an offence; as is failing to comply with an enforcement notice or suspension notice. The operations covered by the Environmental Permitting Regulations include industrial operations; waste disposal or recovery; water discharges; radioactive substances; management of waste from mining operations; and activities on or near a watercourse.

(d) Under the asbestos regime, it is now illegal to use any form of asbestos in the construction or refurbishment of any buildings. The Control of Asbestos Regulations 2012 (SI 2012/632) impose an obligation on the 'dutyholder' – who may be an employer – in relation to non-domestic premises, to determine whether asbestos is or is likely to be present in a building and/or to manage any asbestos that is or is likely to be present. Failure to comply with the Control of Asbestos Regulations is a criminal offence.

INSURANCE AGAINST ENVIRONMENTAL LIABILITY

Public liability policies

32.05 Public liability policies generally cover the insured in respect of damages or compensation that the insured is legally liable to pay to third parties for personal injury and property damage which takes place during the policy period and which is connected with the insured's activities. Personal injury or property damage may result, among other things, from pollutants or exposure to pollutants. Claims for such injury or damage may be made many years after the policy period has ended. A typical coverage clause might cover sums which the insured becomes legally liable to pay as damages because of bodily injury or property damage occurring during the period of insurance.

Issues may arise in determining when an occurrence took place and whether liability to remediate a third party's land can be said to be damages within the terms of a general liability policy. Other issues include whether liability for remediating groundwater which is not owned by a landowner is covered by the policy.

English courts have been called upon to determine the extent to which public liability policies cover environmental liability less frequently than the courts in some other countries. A significant English case is that of *Bartoline Ltd v Royal & Sun Alliance Insurance plc* [2006] EWHC 3598 (QB). In this case, water pollution resulted from foams used to fight a fire at Bartoline's warehouse. Under powers contained in the Water Resources Act 1991, the Environment Agency took emergency measures to clean up and sent Bartoline the bill. It also ordered Bartoline to carry out further clean-up works. Bartoline claimed its and the Environment Agency's costs under its public liability insurance, but the court decided that these did not constitute 'damages' and were not therefore covered.

Over time, increases in environmental liabilities in the UK led insurers of UK risks to restrict cover for pollution under public liability policies. Since 1990, on the recommendation of the Association of British Insurers, virtually all public liability policies exclude cover for gradual pollution.

Environmental insurance policies

32.06 The exclusion of cover for gradual pollution in public liability policies and the increase in environmental liabilities encouraged the development of environmental insurance policies. Generally speaking, such policies:

(a) are written on a claims-made – and reported – basis: to trigger the cover, the insured must make a claim and report it to the insurer during the policy period or an extended reporting period;

(b) are written on a site-specific basis; and

(c) cover liability arising from gradual as well as sudden pollution without differentiating between them.

Environmental insurance policies are available to cover liabilities arising from pollution (both sudden and gradual) to third parties for bodily injury, property damage and – depending on the policy – remediation costs, nuisance claims, legal defence costs and certain specified economic losses. Other environmental insurance policies cover the cost of remediating an insured's own site; remediation costs above a specified amount; and errors and omissions of environmental consultants and laboratories.

A typical coverage clause in an environmental insurance policy designed to cover third-party claims might cover amounts that the insured is legally liable to pay as a result of a claim for property damage, bodily injury or clean-up costs arising from pollution conditions on an insured site.

Chapter 33

Goods in transit insurance

- Goods in transit insurance in context
- Goods in transit and carrier's liability distinguished
- Coverage under goods in transit policies
- Exclusions and conditions
- The Marine Institute Cargo Clauses

GOODS IN TRANSIT INSURANCE IN CONTEXT

33.01 Goods in transit insurance is the means by which a person with an interest in goods while en route from, say, a seller to a purchaser insures the goods for their full value against the risk of loss or damage during transit. Usually the carriage will be associated with the sale of the goods, but it is also employed where goods are conveyed to the custody of a hirer.

It is important to distinguish three separate contracts that may exist:

(a) a contract between vendor and purchaser for sale of the subject goods;

(b) a contract of carriage (usually) between vendor and carrier; and

(c) a contract of insurance between cargo interests or the carrier and the insurer.

Where, as may often occur, insurance is taken out by the carrier, the carrier (rather than the owner) may be the named insured on the policy. As a bailee, the carrier has an insurable interest, even though it has no ownership interest in the goods. Alternatively, the carrier may take out insurance as agent for the owner. This agency relationship will extend to the claims stage where, for instance, a freight forwarder lodges a claim on behalf an owner (*Granville Oil & Chemicals Ltd v Davis Turner & Co Ltd* [2003] 2 Lloyd's Rep 356). For the avoidance of confusion, the carrier is referred to as such in this chapter, and not as 'the insured'. If ambiguity arises as to whether the policy protects the owner's full interest in the goods or indemnifies the carrier for its legal liability, the policy will be construed as covering the value of the goods (*Hepburn Appellant v A Tomlinson (Hauliers) Ltd Respondents* [1966] AC 451).

The three contracts set out above frequently need to be analysed in conjunction with each other, in order to ascertain the rights and liabilities of the various parties. For instance, the sale contract will determine when risk (and thus insurable interest) passes from vendor to purchaser. The contract of carriage will determine the obligations of the carrier to the owner in the event of loss or damage.

Goods in transit insurance eliminates any inability of cargo interests (eg, owners) to recover, in part or at all, the value of the goods from the carrier.

In the event of loss or damage, the cargo insurer will pay up to the full insured value of the goods. If the carrier has taken out the policy, it must, after deducting any sums due to it (eg, charges for carriage), account to the owner for the surplus. If the contract of carriage requires the carrier to effect insurance, it will hold those proceeds on trust, offering the owner a degree of protection in the event of the carrier's insolvency. No trust arises if there is no obligation on the carrier to insure (*Re Dibbens & Sons (In Liquidation)* [1990] BCL C 577).

Therefore, the distinction between goods in transit insurance and carrier's liability insurance is that in the latter case, the carrier may only recover to the extent of its own liability; whereas goods in transit insurance enables a carrier to use its insurable interest in the goods to insure them for their full value. This means that in the event of loss or damage to the goods, the full value of the goods can be recovered; but once the carrier has been indemnified for its own loss, it holds the remainder of the sum paid out as trustee for the owner of the goods (*Tomlinson v Hepburn* [1966] AC 451).

GOODS IN TRANSIT AND CARRIER'S LIABILITY DISTINGUISHED

33.02 Goods in transit insurance should be distinguished from whatever liability insurance the carrier may have; although when the carrier effects goods in transit insurance for the benefit of cargo interests (eg, owners), confusion can arise between the two policies. If the cargo insurer does indemnify cargo interests in respect of a loss during transit, the cargo insurer will (under most legal systems) be subrogated to the cargo interests' right to claim against the carrier.

The difference between the two situations is that, whereas the cargo insurer indemnifies the loss in full, its ability to recover from the carrier (or its insurer) will depend on establishing a legal liability. This may or may not be fault-based and can be important:

(a) In international air carriage subject to Montreal Additional Protocol No 4 1975 or the Montreal Convention 1999, the air carrier's liability is absolutely limited to 17 Special Drawing Rights per kilogram (unless the cargo interests have declared a higher value for carriage). In high-value cargo cases, the cargo insurer may only be able to recover a minute proportion of the claim.

(b) The claims by cargo interests against goods in transit insurers and the recourse claim against the carrier may be subject to different laws, which may lead to inconsistent results.

COVERAGE UNDER GOODS IN TRANSIT POLICIES

Commencement and termination

33.03 The policy starts when the carriage commences. The points at which carriage begins and terminates both depend on the construction of the policy:

(a) Goods in the carrier's custody awaiting loading were covered under a policy effective when the goods were 'in transit per [carrier's] vehicles' in *Crows Transport Ltd v Phoenix Assurance Co Ltd* [1965] 1 WLR 383, followed by the Court of Appeal in *Eurodale Manufacturing Ltd v Ecclesiastical Insurance Office plc* [2003] EWCA Civ 203 – even in relation to goods which were only held at a warehouse and not transported during the time in which the carrier had an insurable interest in the goods.

(b) Goods in the carrier's physical possession will be insured under a policy covering goods in the carrier's 'trust' – the term is not given its literal legal meaning. Goods in the possession of the carrier's agent will be in the carrier's 'trust' even if the agent intends to abscond with them (*John Rigby (Haulage) Ltd v Reliance Marine Insurance Co Ltd* [1956] 2 QB 468).

(c) Theft by a dishonest authorised carrier is usually covered: a clause excluding 'theft by a bogus subcontractor' is only effective where goods are entrusted to someone other than the genuine subcontracted carrier at the outset (*London Tobacco Co (Overseas) Ltd v DFDS Transport Ltd and Others and Sun Alliance and London Insurance plc (Third Party)* [1994] 1 Lloyd's Rep 394).

(d) Goods which have safely arrived at the carrier's warehouse at destination have been 'finally disposed of' by the carrier (even though the consignee has not collected them) (*Bartlett & Partners, Ltd v Meller* [1961] 1 Lloyd's Rep 487).

Transit

33.04 'Transit' refers to the passage of goods from one place to another. It does not stop because the vehicle is temporarily parked. The policy covered theft of goods while a van was parked and left unattended in *Sadler Bros Co v Meredith* [1963] 2 Lloyd's Rep 293. On the other hand, deviation may take the goods outside the scope of cover. In *S.CA (Freight) Ltd v Gibson* [1974] 2 Lloyd's Rep 533, goods were damaged during an unauthorised trip to the centre of Rome after loading for carriage to Manchester. The deviation was considered a joyride and not part of the 'transit', so the goods were not covered.

Storage

33.05 Specific provision may appear in a policy covering road haulage for overnight storage in a secure location. There are many authorities on this issue, such as:

(a) a yard enclosed by high walls but without a roof is not a 'garage' (*Barnett & Block v National Parcels Insurance Company, Ltd* (1942) 73 Ll L Rep 17);

(b) nor is it a warehouse (*Leo Rapp, Ltd v McClure* [1955] 1 Lloyd's Rep 292);

(c) but goods in an enclosed yard and covered by tarpaulins are 'in store' (*Wulfson v Switzerland General Insurance Company, Ltd* (1940) 67 Ll L Rep 190); and

(d) a railway arch is not a 'public warehouse' (*Firmin & Collins, Ltd v Allied Shippers, Ltd* [1967] 1 Lloyd's Rep 633).

In *Glencore International AG v Alpina Insurance Co Ltd (No 2)* [2004] 1 Lloyd's Rep 567, it was held that a request for open cover for transit and storage would not be limited by a 30-day premium-free period, as that clause could not be construed (as desired by the insurer) as a request for 30 days' cover only.

EXCLUSIONS AND CONDITIONS

33.06 Typically, goods in transit insurance will not cover goods while the vehicle has been 'left unattended'. Of the many decisions based on this test, the following circumstances amounted to a vehicle being left unattended:

(a) A driver walked 37 yards away from the vehicle in order to urinate. For part of that time, he had his back to the vehicle (*Starfire Diamond Rings, Ltd v Angel* [1962] 2 Lloyd's Rep 217). The Court of Appeal expressly sought to avoid a precise definition of the phrase 'left unattended', but it is clear from the judgments of Lord Denning MR and Upjohn LJ that the driver should be in a position to see the vehicle and/or hear anything taking place, and have a reasonable prospect of preventing any interference.

(b) A driver parked his vehicle outside a customer's premises, in his vision but not in his immediate proximity (*Ingleton of Ilford, Ltd v General Accident Fire and Life Assurance Corpn, Ltd* [1967] 2 Lloyd's Rep 179).

On the other hand, the insurance was still effective where:

(a) the driver was asleep in the cab (*Plaistow Transport, Ltd v Graham* [1966] 1 Lloyd's Rep 639);

(b) the vehicle was within a few feet of the carrier's representative but outside her line of vision (*Langford and Langford v Legal and General Assurance Society Ltd* [1986] 2 Lloyd's Rep 103); and

(c) the vehicle was parked at a petrol pump while the carrier's representative was paying for petrol (*T O'Donoghue Ltd v Brian Malcolm Harding and Edgar Hamilton & Carter Ltd* [1988] 2 Lloyd's Rep 281). Critically, the vehicle was parked as close as possible to the kiosk and the driver kept a close watch on it, only diverting his attention to sign the credit card slip.

Other conditions that may be imposed include the following requirements:

(a) There must be adequate locks on the vehicle. However, in *De Maurier (Jewels), Ltd v Bastion Insurance Co, Ltd and Coronet Insurance Company, Ltd* [1967] 2 Lloyd's Rep 550, it was held that compliance with such a clause was not a condition precedent to the insurer's liability.

(b) The vehicle must be locked when the loss occurred and there must have been forcible entry. In *Princette Models, Ltd v Reliance Fire and Accident Insurance Corporation, Ltd* [1960] 1 Lloyd's Rep 49, evidence that the vehicle was unlocked entitled the insurer to avoid the claim.

(c) The carrier must take reasonable care of the goods. This is interpreted narrowly and requires the carrier only to avoid acts of recklessness rather than mere negligence. A carrier's failure to check references of an employee who later absconded with the insured goods was not a failure to act with reasonable care in *W & J Lane v Spratt* [1970] 2 QB 480.

Loss

33.07 Whether a loss has occurred is a question of fact. Under an all risks policy, all that must be proved is loss or damage in transit. Knowledge of the whereabouts of the goods does not necessarily prevent a claim; for example, goods detained illegally by state authorities were 'lost' for the purposes of an all risks policy in *London and Provincial Leather Processes, Ltd v Hudson* [1939] 2 KB 724.

THE MARINE INSTITUTE CARGO CLAUSES

Commencement and duration of cover

33.08 Cargo insurance written in the London market is frequently governed by the Marine Institute Cargo Clauses. Separate forms have been drafted for marine and air carriage. The current form of each is the 2009 revised edition. The main structure is the same under each form; and each includes the transit clause (the 'warehouse-to-warehouse' clause), which determines the commencement, duration and termination of cover. The insurance:

(a) starts when the goods leave the warehouse or place of storage named in the policy – the requirement to name this point eliminated disputes as to whether insurers were on risk for land journeys prior to sea or air carriage;

(b) continues during the course of transit; and

(c) finishes on the first of the following events:

  (i) delivery to the warehouse or place of storage at destination;

  (ii) delivery to any other warehouse or place of storage which the carrier elects to use for storage other than in transit, or for allocation to individual purchasers;

  (iii) (in the marine clauses) the expiry of 60 days after completion of discharge of the goods from the vessel at the final port of discharge; or

  (iv) (in the air clauses) the expiry of 30 days after unloading from the aircraft at the final place of discharge.

Cover will remain in place despite delay due to circumstances beyond the control of the owner, such as war or strike at the point of discharge. The interaction of the various elements of the clause and the issue of which circumstances are within the control of the owner were examined (under an earlier form of the warehouse-to-warehouse clause) in *Safadi v Western*

Assurance Co [1933] 46 Ll L Rep 140. The owner consigned goods from Manchester to Damascus; the final port of discharge for the sea carriage was Beirut. It was said that the rail journey from Beirut to Damascus was too dangerous to convey the goods and they remained in Beirut for more than 30 days (the limiting period in the form at the time), but were then destroyed by fire. The judge found that the owner knew of the risks in Syria and had chosen to keep the goods in Beirut when they could have been conveyed to Damascus without undue danger. In those circumstances, the events were within the control of the owner, so the extended cover did not apply.

The point in time at which cover attaches can have an important impact on the insurer's liability. Conflicting legislative and contractual provisions for the attachment of cover were considered in *Nima SARL v The Deves Insurance Public Co Ltd (The 'Prestrioka')* [2002] EWCA Civ 1133. In that case it was argued that a warehouse-to-warehouse clause under the Institute Cargo Clauses overrode statutory provisions on attachment in the Marine Insurance Act 1906. That Act provides at s 44 that where the destination is specified in the policy and the ship, instead of sailing for that destination, sails for any other destination, the risk does not attach. It was held that this clause does not override s 44. If, on an assessment of the facts, the court holds that the ship never intended to head for the named destination at the time of departure, then it will have never embarked on the named voyage and cover will not have attached.

Scope of cover

33.09 The Marine Institute Cargo Clauses provide for three levels of cover:

(a) all risks (the 'A' clauses);

(b) marine and loading risks (the 'B' clauses); and

(c) marine risks only (the 'C' clauses).

The air clauses only provide for all risks cover. War risks are generally excluded, but there are separate institute war clauses available if required.

Under all risks cover, cargo interests only have to show that goods were in sound condition upon despatch but damaged on arrival (*Electro Motion, Ltd v Maritime Insurance Company, Ltd, and Bonner* [1956] 1 Lloyd's Rep 420) for the insurer to be *prima facie* liable. The insurer then has the burden of proving that the loss was due to an excepted peril (*Re National Benefit Insurance Co* [1933] 45 LI L Rep 147).

Change in the course of transit

33.10 If the goods fail to reach their destination due to an interruption in transit outside the owner's control, cover terminates unless a continuation is requested and additional premium paid if required. Cover will then continue until the first of two events occurs:

(a) sale at an intermediate port; or

(b) the expiry of 60 days after arrival at an intermediate port.

The provisions encompass the carrier failing to complete the carriage, with or without cause, which may include a voluntary change of destination or the effective frustration of the voyage. In such circumstances the owner is entitled to maintain cover on premium and at conditions to be agreed, so long as immediate notice is given to the insurer.

When goods are intended for transshipment, arrival of the goods in a warehouse or place of storage in the destination named in the policy does not normally end the cover. This is because the policy does not contemplate a final place of storage in the named destination and it would be impractical to require separate cover to be arranged from that point onwards (*Bayview Motors Ltd v Mitsui Marine and Fire Insurance Co Ltd* [2002] EWCA Civ 1605).

Chapter 34

Legal expenses insurance

- Forms of cover
- Regulation

FORMS OF COVER

Before the event insurance

34.01 Legal expenses insurance provides the insured with an indemnity, subject to financial limits under the policy, in the event that he becomes embroiled in legal proceedings as a litigant. Cover of this type is included in many forms of liability insurance, whereby the insurer agrees either to defend or to indemnify the insured in respect of the costs of any legal proceedings brought against him. In relation to motor and employers' liability policies, this cover may also extend to providing an indemnity for the cost of criminal proceedings brought against the insured (eg, driving offences and breaches of health and safety legislation). This insurance is provided before the event and so is known as before the event (BTE) insurance.

Pursuant to the Insurance Companies (Legal Expenses Insurance) Regulations 1990 (SI 1990/1159), such BTE insurance cover has developed so that it is now possible to obtain insurance against general litigation costs, whether such general litigation is anticipated or not. Cover is generally written on the basis of costs incurred during the year of cover granted by the policy, so that the insured is under a duty to disclose to the insurer all potential legal disputes at the date of the inception of the insurance.

Despite efforts by specialist brokers and insurers over the last 20 years, very little 'standalone' legal expenses insurance has been sold in the UK. Nearly all UK business is part of a more general package policy, normally sold as an add-on to a household or motor policy. There has been a significant amount of regulatory scrutiny in relation to the add-on market and issues such as value for money (see **34.03**).

After the event insurance

34.02 While it is possible for a litigant to purchase legal expenses insurance cover after the event that has given rise to his potential costs exposure, such insurance cover can be expensive. This is known as 'after the event' (ATE) insurance.

In purchasing ATE cover, the insured is obtaining cover in the event that he fails in his action against the third party and costs are awarded against him.

ATE cover is often sold alongside conditional fee arrangements offered by solicitors. The ATE insurer will have to indemnify the insured in such circumstances in relation to his opponent's costs and disbursements (eg, counsel's fees). Cover will only normally be offered based on counsel's opinion as to the likelihood of success. Should circumstances change, cover under the policy may effectively cease for future costs (eg, if the insured were to continue with a case after counsel has opined that the case is no longer likely to succeed).

Since 1 April 2013 (subject to certain limited exceptions), it has no longer been possible to recover the cost of ATE insurance from the insured's opponent should the insured win his case.

REGULATION

Regulatory requirements

34.03 Legal expenses insurance gives rise to potential conflicts of interest affecting the legal expenses insurer itself, where it is both the legal expenses insurer of party A and the property or liability insurer of party B, and A and B become involved in a dispute. The possibility that one or other of the parties may be pressurised to settle the dispute on disadvantageous terms has been recognised, and two sets of amendments were made to the regulation of insurance companies by the Insurance Companies (Legal Expenses Insurance) Regulations 1990 (SI 1990/1159) and the Insurance Companies (Legal Expenses Insurance) (Application for Authorisation) Regulations 1990 (SI 1990/1160). The Regulations were based on the European Community's Legal Expenses Directive 1987 (87/344/EEC). The combined effects of the Regulations are as follows:

(a) Legal expenses cover must be provided in the form of an independent policy or a separate section of the policy (SI 1990/1159, reg 4). There are some important exceptions to this – notably marine insurance, liability insurance and travel insurance sold with travel arrangements (SI 1990/1159, reg 3).

(b) An insurer offering legal expenses insurance must take steps to prevent claims under a legal expenses policy from being dealt with by a person that deals with claims under other policies. The simplest way of avoiding potential conflicts of interest is by use of an independent subsidiary (SI 1990/1159, reg 5).

(c) The insured under a legal expenses policy is entitled to instruct a lawyer of his choice; this right takes effect as a term of, and must be expressed in, the policy (SI 1990/1159, reg 6). There is an exception to this requirement for breakdown assistance insurance where neither that insurer nor the insurer providing the legal expenses cover in relation to use of a motor vehicle in the UK provides liability cover; and further provided that legal advice and representation are provided for each of them by completely independent lawyers.

(d) Legal expenses insurance is a distinct class of general insurance business and authorisation to carry on legal expenses insurance business must be obtained from the Prudential Regulation Authority under the Financial Services and Markets Act 2000 – it is not possible for such business to be written on an 'ancillary basis' to other classes of general insurance without such permission.

(e) Any dispute between the insured and the legal expenses insurer must be resolved by arbitration if the insured so wishes and the policy must mention this right (SI 1990/1159, reg 8).

Add-on insurance

34.04 As stated above, legal expenses insurance, and in particular BTE insurance, is commonly sold as an add-on to home or motor insurance policies. The add-on market has been the subject of significant regulatory attention and additional rules (eg, on cross-selling) added by the EU's Insurance Distribution Directive (2016/97).

The result of Financial Conduct Authority investigation and scrutiny (eg, of insurance value measures) has resulted in a more onerous regulatory regime relating to the sale of legal expenses insurance as an add-on. Product design and governance will be important to ensure that the product is appropriate for the target market and provides value for money. Similarly, it is necessary to ensure transparency in relation to pricing and the ability to cancel together with an active election of the product from the customer (for optional add-on products).

Chapter 35

Marine insurance

- 'Marine insurance' defined
- General principles
- Types of marine policy
- The premium
- Warranties
- Currency of the voyage
- Marine risks: hulls and freight policies
- Marine risks: cargo policies
- Exclusions from marine cover
- Marine losses
- Measure of indemnity
- Rights of insurers

'MARINE INSURANCE' DEFINED

The Marine Insurance Act 1906

35.01 Marine insurance is governed by a statutory code, the Marine Insurance Act 1906 (MIA 1906). The Act was not an attempt to change the law as it stood at the time, but rather sought to codify eighteenth and nineteenth century decisions on marine insurance. The rules of the common law, including the law merchant, are preserved, save insofar as they are inconsistent with the Act (MIA 1906, s 91(2)). When reading the Act's provisions, care should be taken, as much of the Act lays down presumptions which operate only if no contrary intention is shown in the contract of insurance. As has been explained elsewhere in this book, certain provisions in the Act have recently been amended by the Insurance Act 2015.

Marine insurance is generally written in London on the basis of standard conditions which are incorporated into the insurance contract. While London underwriters may agree to provide cover based on a number of different sets of conditions, the standard clauses are those now issued by the International Underwriting Association of London, known as 'Institute clauses'. Institute clauses exist for policies covering hull and machinery (time and voyage), freight (time and voyage), cargo, war and strikes (hulls, cargo and freight), and the interests of mortgagee banks. This is not an exhaustive list. The Institute clauses set out the risks covered together with other terms relevant to the scope of cover provided and the obligations on the insured. The clauses amend and supplement certain provisions in the Act.

This chapter looks at those aspects of insurance law unique to marine insurance.

Nature of marine insurance

35.02 A policy of marine insurance indemnifies the insured against 'marine losses, that is to say, the losses incident to a marine adventure' (MIA 1906, s 1). A marine adventure involves the exposure to 'maritime perils' of a vessel, cargo or freight earned by a vessel, as well as the risk that the owner of (or other person interested in or responsible for) insurable property may incur liability (MIA 1906, s 3). A 'maritime peril' means any peril consequent on or incidental to the navigation of the sea, including perils of the sea, fire, war and piracy (MIA 1906, s 3). 'Marine insurance' is widely defined and includes a policy taken out by the mortgagee of a vessel (*Continental Illinois National Bank & Trust Co of Chicago v Bathurst (The 'Captain Panagos DP')* [1985] 1 Lloyd's Rep 625).

Policies covering mixed sea and land risks

35.03 A contract of marine insurance may cover both land and sea risks (MIA 1906, s 2). The most common illustration of this is the standard cargo cover written in the London market (Institute Cargo Clauses A, B and C, cl 8) which provides cover on a 'warehouse-to-warehouse' basis.

A policy covering the construction of a vessel is also a marine policy (MIA 1906, s 2(2)). Such types of policy may be stated to terminate either when the vessel is delivered to the purchaser or when the vessel is launched. Port risks policies can be issued to cover the risks of a vessel laid up in port.

GENERAL PRINCIPLES

The duty of fair presentation

35.04 In the same way as for other contracts of insurance, marine insureds are obliged to make a fair presentation of the risk in accordance with the Insurance Act 2015, unless the parties opt to 'contract out' under Section 17.

Insurable interest

35.05 An insured must have an insurable interest in the subject matter of the insurance (as defined by MIA 1906, s 5). The insured need not have an insurable interest when it takes out the policy, but must have such an interest at the time of loss (MIA 1906, s 6). (See also MIA 1906, ss 7–14 and **Chapter 4**.)

Assignment

35.06 A marine policy is freely assignable, unless the policy itself provides otherwise (MIA 1906, s 50(1)). The ability to assign marine policies is commercially essential in respect of both hull and cargo insurance. Claims under hull policies are routinely assigned by owners of vessels to their mortgagee banks. Cargo policies are assigned by the seller to the buyer of goods under cost, insurance and freight and related sales. Where insured property is sold, there will not be an automatic assignment of rights under the insurance to the buyer and there needs to be a separate agreement to this effect (MIA 1906, s 15) (see **Chapter 3**).

The policy

35.07 A contract of marine insurance is deemed to be concluded when the proposal of the insured is accepted by the insurer, whether a policy is issued at the same time or not (MIA 1906, s 21). Where marine insurance is placed at Lloyd's, the contract is usually concluded when the slip is executed by the underwriter (see **Chapter 11**).

A contract of marine insurance is inadmissible in evidence unless it is embodied in a marine policy in accordance with the Act (MIA 1906, s 22). The only requirements for a marine policy are that the policy must contain the name of the insured or the person effecting the policy on his behalf (MIA 1906, s 23); must be signed by or on behalf of the insurer (MIA 1906, s 24); and must designate the subject matter insured with reasonable certainty (MIA 1906, s 26).

TYPES OF MARINE POLICY

Voyage and time policies

35.08 A marine policy may insure a particular voyage or it may last for a stated duration (MIA 1906, s 25). There can also be a 'mixed policy' covering both voyage and time elements. For example, a policy can be for a stated voyage, with the insured being covered for a period of days following the safe arrival of the vessel.

The distinction between time and voyage policies can be important because of the following differences:

(a) Under a voyage policy – whether on hull, cargo or freight – the insured warrants the seaworthiness of the vessel at various stages, including the commencement of the voyage (MIA 1906, s 39(1–4)) although the application of the warranty is generally limited for cargo insurance by cl 5 of the Institute clauses. Under a time policy, there is no implied warranty of seaworthiness (MIA 1906, s 39(5)). For unseaworthiness of the vessel to provide the insurer with a defence in respect of resulting loss or damage, it must prove that the vessel was sent to sea in an unseaworthy condition with the privity of the assured (MIA 1906, s 39(5)).

(b) There are strict rules in the MIA 1906, ss 42 to 49 concerning voyage policies which by definition do not apply to time policies. The insured voyage must commence within a reasonable time; otherwise the insurer may avoid the contract (MIA 1906, s 42). If the voyage commences from a different location to that agreed in the insurance contract or if the vessel sails for an alternative destination, the risk does not attach (MIA 1906, ss 43 and 44). Changes of voyage, deviation and delay may also discharge the insurer from liability (MIA 1906, ss 45, 46 and 48). Certain deviations and delays are excused, such as where caused by circumstances beyond the master's control or where necessary to save the vessel or human life (MIA 1906, s 49). In addition, the Institute clauses covering hull and cargo risks contain held covered clauses maintaining the cover under the insurance in the event of delay, provided that the insured gives notice immediately upon becoming aware of the change and amended terms and premium are agreed.

Valued and unvalued policies

35.09 Under s 27 of the MIA 1906, a policy of marine insurance may be either valued or unvalued. A policy is valued if it specifies the agreed value of the subject matter insured. All other types of policy are unvalued. The principal significance of the distinction relates to the amount recoverable following a loss:

(a) If a policy is valued, then in the absence of fraud, the value agreed by the parties is conclusive (MIA 1906, s 27(3)). The measure of indemnity will be either the agreed value in the event of total loss or a proportion of the agreed value in the event of partial loss.

(b) If a policy is unvalued, the measure of indemnity is determined by reference to the market value of the subject matter insured calculated at the date of commencement of the risk, plus certain charges and expenses (MIA 1906, s 16).

An insured may therefore insure marine property for a sum in excess of its true value; this is a departure from the true indemnity principle which underlines insurance. However, there are advantages for both sides. The insured is buying certainty and can take into account the costs of purchasing replacement property. For the insurer, the higher the agreed value, the higher the premium. Further, for hull insurers, a high agreed value reduces the prospect of a constructive total loss, as under the Institute clauses the cost of repairs must exceed the insured value, not the market value, for such a claim to arise. An agreed value may be set aside in the event of fraud.

It is therefore important to distinguish between an agreed value (denoting a valued policy) and a sum insured (denoting an unvalued policy), where the sum insured fixes the maximum indemnity of the insurer, leaving the insured to prove its loss by reference to the insurable value of the property (MIA 1906, s 16). This is a question of policy interpretation.

There have been a number of cases illustrating the principles that the courts will apply in considering whether a policy is valued or unvalued, including *Kyzuna Investments Ltdv Ocean Marine Insurance Association*

(Europe) [2000] Lloyd's Rep IR 513 (yacht insurance) and *Thor Navigation Inc v Ingosstrakh Insurance* [2005] 1 Lloyd's Rep 547 (hull insurance). While yacht and hull insurance is usually placed on an agreed value basis, and while both policies incorporated the Institute clauses which are drafted for use with valued policies, it was held that the use of the words 'sum insured' meant that both policies were unvalued.

Floating policies and open covers

35.10 A 'floating policy' describes cover provided by the insurer in general terms, leaving the name of the ship or ships and other particulars to be defined by subsequent declaration (MIA 1906, s 29(1)). The insured is obliged to declare all risks falling within the terms of the cover and the insurer is bound to accept all such declarations (MIA 1906, s 29(3)).

The maximum aggregate amount that can be insured in respect of all of the declarations will usually be set out in the floating policy. Each declaration will, therefore, reduce the amount of further cover available to the insured under the facility.

An open cover policy fulfils a similar function by allowing the insured to make declarations in respect of risks falling within the terms of the cover. In an open cover, however, there is generally no aggregate limit as found in a floating policy; rather, there is a limit for each declaration. Open covers may fall within the statutory definition of 'floating policies' – see the discussion in *Glencore International AG v Ryan (The 'Beursgracht') (No 2)* [2001] 2 Lloyd's Rep 608.

There are also covers used in the marine market which fall outside the definition of 'floating policies'. Under some facilities, the insured can elect whether to declare a particular risk; but if he does, the insurer is bound to accept. With this type of cover, the insurer runs the risk that the insured will be selective in the risks which are declared. Under other types of facility, each declaration must be agreed by the insurer.

THE PREMIUM

35.11 There are three important differences between the rules relating to marine and non-marine payment of premium (see **Chapter 5**):

(a) In marine insurance, there will frequently be a policy term allowing the insured to obtain additional cover subject to the payment of additional premium. There is a statutory mechanism allowing an additional premium to be fixed (MIA 1906, s 31).

(b) Unless otherwise agreed in the policy, where a marine policy has been arranged through a broker, the broker bears personal responsibility to the insurer for payment of the premium (MIA 1906, ss 52–54).

(c) Marine insurance law is marginally more generous than general insurance law as to when the insured is entitled to a return of his premium in the event that the risk fails to attach or terminates early (MIA 1906, ss 82–84). The Institute clauses and International Hull Clauses also permit a return of premium to the insured in certain circumstances.

WARRANTIES

What is a warranty?

35.12 A 'warranty' is a contractual promise by which the insured undertakes that some particular thing shall or shall not be done; that some particular condition will be fulfilled; or that a particular state of facts is or is not true. If the warranty is not complied with, the insurer's liability will be suspended from the time of the breach until the breach is remedied (Insurance Act 2015, s 10). A breach of warranty will also be actionable only if non-compliance with the warranty could have increased the risk of the loss occurring in the circumstances in which it occurred (Insurance Act 2015, s 11).

Marine insurance warranties

35.13 In addition to any express warranties contained in the policy, certain warranties are implied into contracts of marine insurance.

Implied warranty of seaworthiness for vessels

35.14 The implied terms relating to seaworthiness vary depending on whether the policy covers a voyage or is for a specified time (MIA 1906, s 39).

Voyage policies

35.15 There is an implied warranty that at the start of the voyage, the ship is seaworthy for the purpose of the particular voyage insured (MIA 1906, s 39(1)). A ship is seaworthy if she is reasonably fit to withstand the ordinary perils of the sea for the insured voyage (MIA 1906, s 39(4)). The requirement of seaworthiness embraces the condition of the vessel, the competence of the crew and the stowage of the cargo. Where the policy attaches while the ship is in port, the ship must also be reasonably fit to meet the 'ordinary perils' of the port (MIA 1906, s 39(2)).

If a voyage involves different stages, the ship must be seaworthy at the start of each stage for that particular stage (MIA 1906, s 39(3)). For example, if the voyage is first on a canal and then at sea, the ship must be seaworthy for the voyage through the canal at the commencement of the voyage through the canal, and then must be seaworthy for the voyage at sea at the commencement of the sea voyage, even if work is required to be done after the ship has transited the canal in order to make her seaworthy for the sea voyage.

Time policies

35.16 There is no implied warranty of seaworthiness at any stage in a time policy. Instead, the insurer is not liable for any loss attributable to unseaworthiness if the ship was sent to sea in an unseaworthy state with the 'privity' of the insured (MIA 1906, s 39(5)).

35.17 To be privy to unseaworthiness, the insured must have had knowledge of the defects in the ship and that these defects made the ship unseaworthy. 'Knowledge' for these purposes includes 'blind eye knowledge' (*Compania Maritima San Basilio SA v The Oceanus Mutual Underwriting Association (Bermuda) Ltd (The 'Eurysthenes')* [1976] 2 Lloyd's Rep 171; *Manifest Shipping & Co Ltd v Uni-Polaris Insurance Co Ltd and la Réunion Européene (The 'Star Sea')* [2003] 1 AC 469; [1997] 1 Lloyd's Rep 360).

Seaworthiness of goods

35.18 There is no warranty that the cargo must be seaworthy (MIA 1906, s 40(1)). However, for a voyage policy on goods, there is an implied warranty that at the commencement of the voyage, the ship is not only seaworthy as a ship, but is also reasonably fit to carry the cargo to the destination contemplated by the insurance (MIA 1906, s 40(2)).

Warranty of legality

35.19 There is an implied warranty that the adventure insured is a lawful one and that, so far as the insured can control the matter, the adventure shall be carried out in a lawful manner (MIA 1906, s41). The question of legality is determined as a matter of English law.

If the adventure is legal at the outset, but then becomes illegal, the insurer is discharged from the point of illegality. There is a distinction between an illegal venture and a venture which is legal but is performed unlawfully. The implied warranty of legality will usually apply only to the former.

Warranty of neutrality

35.20 In time of war, a term is sometimes included in the policy warranting that the ship or her cargo is neutral. This warranty is in an attempt to protect against the property being seized by belligerent countries.

If insurable property is expressly warranted neutral, then the insured property must have a neutral character at the commencement of the risk (MIA 1906, s 36(1)). In addition, so far as the insured can control it, the neutral character of the property must be preserved for the period of the policy. If a ship is expressly warranted neutral, s 36(2) of the MIA 1906 implies a further condition that the ship shall carry the necessary papers to establish her neutrality, so far as the insured can control this.

Warranty of nationality

35.21 There is no implied warranty as to the nationality of a ship, or that her nationality will not be changed during the period of the policy (MIA 1906, s 37).

Warranty of good safety

35.22 Where the subject matter insured is warranted 'well' or 'in good safety' on a particular day, it is sufficient if the property is safe at any time during that day (MIA 1906, s 38)).

CURRENCY OF THE VOYAGE

35.23 Under a voyage policy, the insured risk is defined by the voyage to be performed and any changes in the voyage may therefore fundamentally alter the risk. Under time policies on ships, there are fewer restrictions, as insurers have agreed to cover all voyages during the period in question. There are, however, some restrictions on voyages under time policies where, for example, the vessel sails outside Institute warranty or navigating limits (hull risks) or into additional premium areas (war risks).

The MIA 1906 lays down certain rules specific to voyage policies.

Commencement of risk

35.24 Voyage policies normally provide for the cover to start 'from' a particular port, or 'at and from' a particular port. If the voyage is insured 'at and from' a port, the cover commences as soon as the ship arrives at that port in good safety. It is not necessary for the ship to be at the port when the contract is concluded, but there is an implied condition that the insured adventure will commence within a reasonable time. If the voyage is insured 'from' a port, the cover commences as soon as the vessel sets sail from that port, again subject to an implied condition that the risk will commence within a reasonable time (MIA 1906, s 42(1)). A breach of this implied condition gives the insurer the right to avoid the insurance contract.

Breach of the implied condition concerning delay will not provide the insurer with a defence to claims if the delay was due to circumstances known to the insurer before the contract was concluded or if it waived the condition (MIA 1906, s 42(2)).

Where the place of departure is specified in the policy and the ship sails from somewhere else, the risk does not attach (MIA 1906, s 43). Similarly, where the destination is specified in the policy and the ship sails for another destination, again the risk does not attach (MIA 1906, s 44).

The performance of the voyage

35.25 After the insured risk has commenced, the insurer may have defences to claims where the voyage is not performed as agreed or there is a change of voyage, delay or deviation.

Change of voyage

35.26 If the insured voluntarily changes the destination of the vessel, then this constitutes a change of voyage and, unless the policy provides otherwise, the insurer is discharged from liability from the time of change (MIA 1906, s 45). The insurer comes off risk as soon as the decision to change the voyage is manifested. It does not matter whether the ship has in fact changed course (MIA 1906, s 45(2)). The change of voyage must be voluntary.

Delay and deviation

35.27 If, under a voyage policy, the insured does not prosecute the voyage with reasonable dispatch, the insurer is discharged from liability as from the time when the delay became unreasonable (MIA 1906, s 48).

A deviation occurs if the ship departs from the insured route, but still intends to sail to the agreed destination. The route to be followed can be agreed with the insurer. If there is no agreement, it will be the customary route for that particular voyage (MIA 1906, s 46). If there are several ports of discharge, the insured must follow the agreed order or, if there is no agreement, call at the ports in geographical order (MIA 1906, s 47). Once there has been an actual deviation, rather than the mere intention to deviate, the insurer is automatically discharged from liability (MIA 1906, s 46(1)(3)). It is immaterial that the ship may have regained the insured route before the loss occurs.

The insurer is still liable if there has been a lawful excuse for delaying or deviating. The possible lawful excuses are listed in s 49 of the MIA 1906 and are as follows:

(a) where authorised by the terms of the policy;

(b) where caused by circumstances beyond the control of the master or owners of the vessel (eg, bad weather, outbreak of war);

(c) where reasonably necessary to comply with a policy warranty (eg, re-equipping a vessel in order to make her seaworthy for the next stage of the voyage);

(d) where reasonably necessary for the safety of the ship or insured subject matter;

(e) in order to save human life or aid a ship in distress where human life may be in danger;

(f) where reasonably necessary to obtain medical or surgical aid for any person on board the vessel; and

(g) where caused by the barratrous conduct (see **35.36** below) of the master or crew, if barratry is an insured peril under the policy.

MARINE RISKS: HULLS AND FREIGHT POLICIES

General considerations

35.28 The Institute Hulls Clauses offer a standard form of cover against a wide range of marine perils. There are also a separate set of hull clauses, being the International Hull Clauses 2002 and 2003.

Clause 2 of the current Institute clauses divides the insured perils into two groups. The second group provides cover as long as the loss or damage has not resulted from want of due diligence by the insured.

In this context, 'the insured' includes owners, managers, superintendents and onshore management.

The Institute clauses also cover certain liability risks (collision, general average and salvage). Other liability risks facing owners are generally insured through membership of a mutual protection and indemnity club.

Summary of cover

35.29 Hulls and freight policies usually provide cover for:

(a) loss or damage caused by:

- (i) perils of the sea, rivers, lakes or other navigable waters (see **35.31** below);
- (ii) fire, explosion (see **Chapter 27**);
- (iii) violent theft by persons from outside the vessel (a degree of force is necessary, even if only against property, and theft by passengers or crew is not covered – MIA 1906, Sch 1, para 9);
- (iv) jettison;
- (v) piracy (see **35.34** below);
- (vi) contact with land conveyance, dock or harbour equipment or installation;
- (vii) earthquake, volcanic eruption or lightning; and
- (viii) accidents in loading, discharging or shifting cargo or fuel (previously subject to the due diligence provision);

(b) subject to the due diligence provision, loss or damage caused by:

- (i) bursting of boilers, breakage of shafts or any latent defect in the machinery or hull (see **35.35** below);
- (ii) negligence of master, officers, crew or pilots (see **35.37** below);
- (iii) negligence of repairers or charterers, provided that such repairers or charterers are not an insured under the policy;
- (iv) barratry of master, officers or crew (see **35.36** below); and
- (v) contact with aircraft, helicopters or similar objects or objects falling therefrom;

(c) pollution hazard:

- (i) loss of or damage to the vessel caused by a governmental authority acting to prevent or mitigate damage to the environment or a real or threatened pollution hazard; and
- (ii) loss resulting directly from damage to the vessel for which the insurer is liable under the insurance, provided that the actions of the governmental authority have not resulted from a want of due diligence by the insured;

(d) collision liability:

(i) 75 per cent of any sums payable by the insured to third parties in respect of legal liabilities arising from a collision;

(ii) excluding sums paid in respect of removal of wrecks; loss of life, personal injury or illness; and pollution, contamination or damage to the environment;

(e) salvage and general average; and

(f) sue and labour.

Perils of the sea

Definition

35.30 'Perils of the sea' refers only to fortuitous accidents or casualties of the sea, excluding the ordinary actions of the winds and waves (MIA 1906, Sch 1, para 7). It is not a peril of the sea where the vessel sinks simply due to old age or decay.

The most common peril of the sea is heavy weather. There is no need for the weather to be unforeseeable or exceptional to constitute a peril of the sea (see *J Lloyd Instruments Ltd v Northern Star Insurance Co Ltd (The 'Miss Jay Jay')* [1985] 1 Lloyd's Rep 264). On the other hand, a peril which is inevitable will not satisfy the requirement of fortuity.

A peril of the sea must be 'of the sea'. Machinery breakdown is excluded from cover under this heading, as the event must be one that can only happen at sea (*The Thames and Mersey Marine Insurance Co, Ltd v Hamilton, Fraser, & Co* (1887) LR 12 App Cas 484).

Burden of proof and causation

35.31 The burden of proving that a loss was fortuitous and caused by a peril of the sea is on the insured. So, if a vessel sinks in unexplained circumstances, there is no presumption that the loss was caused by an insured peril (*Rhesa Shipping Co SA v Herbert David Edmunds* [1985] 2 All ER 712; *National Justice Compania Naviera SA v Prudential Assurance Co Ltd ('The Ikarian Reefer')* [1993] 2 Lloyd's Rep 68). However, where the insured can prove that the vessel was seaworthy when she set out, there is no evidence from the crew as to the cause of loss and the vessel has never been seen again, there may be a presumption that the vessel sank due to perils of the sea (*Lamb Head Shipping Co Ltd v Jennings (The 'Marel')* [1992] 1 Lloyd's Rep 402; affirmed on appeal [1994] 1 Lloyd's Rep 624).

It is important to bear in mind that the entry of seawater into a vessel is not of itself a peril of the sea.

Unseaworthy vessels

35.32 If a loss results from a combination of unseaworthiness and adverse sea conditions, the position is as follows:

(a) Under a voyage policy, the insured has impliedly warranted the seaworthiness of the vessel for the particular voyage and the insurer can rely upon breach of warranty (MIA 1906, s 39(1)). The application of the warranty of seaworthiness is generally limited for cargo insurance by cl 5 of the Institute clauses.

(b) Under a time policy, there is no warranty of seaworthiness, but the insured cannot recover if he was privy to the unseaworthy state of the vessel when she set sail and the loss was attributable to unseaworthiness (MIA 1906, s 39(5)).

(c) If the insurer cannot rely upon the defences above (eg, because the insured under a time policy was not aware of the unseaworthiness), the insured will still need to demonstrate that a proximate cause of the loss was perils of the sea.

Piracy

35.33 'Piracy' includes passengers who mutiny and rioters who attack the ship from the shore (MIA 1906, Sch 1, para 8). Violence, or the threat of force, is necessary, as 'piracy is not committed by stealth' (*Athens Maritime Enterprises Corporation v Hellenic Mutual War Risks Association (Bermuda) Ltd (The 'Andreas Lemos')* [1982] 2 Lloyd's Rep 483). Piracy is not restricted to the high seas, but may occur in territorial waters. The pirates must be acting for personal gain and not for some wider public or political motive (*Republic of Bolivia v Indemnity Mutual Marine Assurance Co, Ltd* [1909] 1 KB 785). As long as it is possible to procure the release of cargo from pirates by lawful means, there will be no total loss entitling a cargo owner to recover under the policy absent express words (*Masefield AG v Amlin Corporate Member Ltd* [2011] EWCA Civ 24).

Machinery damage

35.34 Failure of machinery is not a peril of the sea, as machinery can fail whether or not a vessel is at sea. Lack of cover for this type of loss was remedied by the '*Inchmaree*' clause, which covers loss or damage caused by bursting of boilers, breaking of shafts or any latent defect in the machinery or hull of the vessel, subject to the insured complying with the due diligence provision. This clause does not, however, extend to the cost of repairing the defect itself (*Scindia Steamships (London) Ltd v London Assurance* [1937] 3 All ER 895; see also *Promet Engineering (Singapore) Pte Ltd v Sturge (The 'Nukila')* [1997] 2 Lloyd's Rep 146).

Barratry

35.35 'Barratry' includes 'every wrongful act wilfully committed by the master and crew to the prejudice of the owner' (MIA 1906, Sch 1, para 11). The essence of barratry is a breach of duty by the master or crew, which causes loss to the owner. It does not matter that the master or crew were in fact disobedient in an attempt to further the owner's interests, as in *Earle and others v Rowcroft* [1803-1813] All ER Rep 166, where the vessel was seized in an enemy port after the crew had entered the port in an attempt to obtain a higher price for the cargo. Other common examples of barratry include:

(a) smuggling by the crew, breach of customs regulations or illegal trading;

(b) deviation by the crew in order to use the vessel for their own purposes; and

(c) deliberate scuttling of the vessel by the crew, perhaps in an attempt to hide the fact that the cargo has been sold by the crew and the proceeds retained, as in the case of *Shell International Petroleum Co Ltd Appellants v Gibbs Respondent* [1983] 2 AC 375.

An owner can succeed in a plea of barratry only if he had no connection with the conduct of the master or crew, and the burden of proving that he was implicated so as to defeat a claim for barratry is borne by the insurer. Indications of an insured's involvement will include any motive which he may have had for sinking the vessel and whether there was good opportunity for communication between the insured and the crew (see *The Ikarian Reefer* at **35.32** above). Moreover, the insured must have exercised due diligence in his supervision of the crew. An insured who turns a blind eye to the crew's conduct or who is aware of previous breaches of instructions by them, but takes no steps to remedy the problem, may be unable to recover if the vessel is lost as a result of barratry (*Pipon v Cope* (1808) 1 Camp 434).

Negligence

35.36 Cover is provided for loss or damage caused by the negligence of the master or crew; the insurer remains on risk (cl 6.2 of the Institute clauses and MIA 1906, s 55(2)(a)). The cover for negligence is subject to the due diligence provision.

MARINE RISKS: CARGO POLICIES

Summary of cover

35.37

Standard form cover is provided by the Institute Cargo Clauses.

Three different classes of cover are available:

(a) all risks (Institute Cargo Clauses (A));

(b) limited risks, including fire or explosion, the vessel being stranded or sunk, overturning or derailment of land conveyance, collision, discharge of cargo at a port of distress, earthquake, jettison, washing overboard and entry of sea water; (Institute Cargo Clauses (B)); and

(c) more limited risks, covering the risks set out immediately above except excluding earthquake, washing overboard and entry of sea water (Institute Cargo Clauses (C)).

EXCLUSIONS FROM MARINE COVER

War and strikes risks

35.38 The Institute Hulls, Freight and Cargo Clauses covering marine risks all exclude losses caused by war, strikes and related risks. War and strikes cover can be obtained separately under the Institute War and Strikes Clauses (see **Chapter 24**).

Wilful misconduct

35.39 The insurer is not liable for any loss attributable to the wilful misconduct of the insured (MIA 1906, s 55(2)(a)). This reflects the common law principle that insurance covers fortuitous events, and not losses brought about by the insured's own deliberate conduct. There is, however, a fine line between deliberately caused losses and thoughtless conduct giving rise to an unintentional loss: only the former is excluded. An insured who fails to take reasonable care to avoid a loss is not, under this principle, debarred from recovering under the policy unless it provides to the contrary. The burden of proof is on the insurer to prove fraud.

Delay

35.40 The Institute Hulls and Cargo Clauses exclude loss or damage caused by delay, reflecting s 55(2)(c) of the MIA 1906. The 'time charter' clause of the Institute Freight Clauses excludes 'any claim consequent on the loss of time whether arising from a peril of the sea or otherwise', although there is no statutory exclusion similar to that relating to hulls and cargo policies.

Inherent vice and related perils

35.41 Unless the policy provides otherwise, loss or damage caused by 'ordinary wear and tear, ordinary leakage and breakage, inherent vice or nature of the subject matter insured' is excluded (MIA 1906, s 55(2)(c)). The Institute clauses reflect this and also exclude insufficiency of packing or preparation of the subject matter insured.

'Inherent vice' involves a loss arising due to the condition of the subject matter insured, without the operation of any external factors, such as where the natural sweating of leather gloves caused condensation which in turn caused damage to the gloves (*TM Noten BV v Paul Charles Harding* [1990] 2 Lloyd's Rep 283). The meaning of 'inherent vice' was considered in *Global Process Systems Inc and Anor v Syriakat Takaful Malaysia Berhad* [2011] UKSC 5).

Section 55(2)(c) of the MIA 1906 makes it clear that loss or damage caused by inherent vice can be covered. This is a question of construction of the policy, as in *Soya GMBH Mainz Kommanditgesellschaft v White* [1983] 1 Lloyd's Rep 122, where a policy on a cargo of soya beans, covering 'the risks of heat, sweat and spontaneous combustion', was held to cover natural sweating of the beans.

MARINE LOSSES

Forms of loss

35.42 Four forms of loss are recognised by marine insurance law:

(a) actual total loss;

(b) constructive total loss;

(c) partial loss (particular average); and

(d) general average.

An 'actual total loss' requires destruction of the subject matter insured or for the insured to be irretrievably deprived of possession of the subject matter. A 'partial loss' usually refers to damage. A 'constructive total loss' is an intermediate claim and is concerned with a loss which, while not amounting to an actual total loss, is in effect a total loss in an economic sense. General average arises where one party to a shared adventure incurs a loss, in the form of sacrifice or expenditure, to assist the other parties in time of general peril. General average losses are adjusted between the interested parties – for example, owners and cargo interests.

Policies may cover either partial loss and/or total loss (MIA 1906, s 56). A policy on total loss will be presumed to include both actual and constructive total loss (MIA 1906, s 56(3)). If total loss only is covered, the policy may be warranted to be 'free of particular average' (MIA 1906, s 76).

Actual total loss

35.43 An 'actual total loss' takes place where:

(a) the subject matter insured is destroyed or so damaged as to cease to be a thing of the kind insured, or the insured is irretrievably deprived of the subject matter (MIA 1906, s 57) (eg, see *Fraser Shipping Ltd v Colton* [1997] 1 Lloyd's Rep 586); or

(b) in the case of a ship, she has been missing for a reasonable time (MIA 1906, s 58).

Constructive total loss

Definition

35.44 A 'constructive total loss' is a loss which does not amount to an actual total loss but is, in effect, a total loss in the economic sense. Such a loss occurs in any one of six situations:

(a) The subject matter is reasonably abandoned on account of an actual total loss appearing to be inevitable (MIA 1906, s 60(1));

(b) The subject matter is reasonably abandoned because it could not be preserved without an expenditure which would exceed the value of the preserved subject matter (MIA 1906, s 60(1));

(c) The insured is deprived of the possession of his ship or goods by an insured peril and it is unlikely that he can recover them within a reasonable time (MIA 1906, s 60(2)(i)(a));

(d) The insured is deprived of the possession of his ship or goods by an insured peril and the cost of recovering them would exceed their value when recovered (MIA 1906, s 60(2)(i)(b));

(e) A ship is damaged and the cost of repair would exceed the repaired value (MIA 1906, s 60(2)(ii)). Under the Institute clauses, the test is whether the expenditure would exceed the insured value of the vessel; and

(f) Goods are damaged and the cost of repair and forwarding the goods to their destination would exceed their value on arrival (MIA 1906, s 60(2)(iii)).

Effect of constructive total loss

35.45 If there is a constructive total loss, the insured has the option to claim from the insurer an indemnity based either on a total loss or on a partial loss (MIA 1906, s 61). In most circumstances, the insured will wish to recover for a total loss, as the full insured value of the vessel is then payable and any increased value policy will be triggered.

Notice of abandonment

35.46 To recover for a constructive total loss, the insured must usually serve on the insurer a 'notice of abandonment' (MIA 1906, s 62(1)). Service of the notice does not alter the nature of the insured's loss, but merely the amount recoverable (*Bank of America National Trust and Savings Association v Chrismas (The 'Kyriaki')* [1993] 1 Lloyd's Rep 137). For service of the notice to be valid, it may be oral or written (MIA 1906, s 62(2)), and must be given with reasonable diligence after the insured has received reliable information or after a reasonable time for enquiries if the information is doubtful (MIA 1906, s 62(3)). If the notice is accepted – which can be done expressly or impliedly through conduct of the insurer, but not through mere silence (MIA 1906, s 62(5)) – it is binding on the insurer (MIA 1906, s 62(6)). This does not, however, deprive the insurer of the right to rely upon defences of which it was unaware when the notice was accepted (*Norwich Union Fire Insurance Society, Ltd Appellants v WMH Price, Ltd Respondents* [1934] AC 455, a case in which the loss had, unknown to the insurer, been caused by an uninsured peril).

Service of a notice of abandonment is unnecessary in the case of an actual total loss (MIA 1906, s 57(2)); the effect of service is merely to allow an insured who has suffered a constructive total loss to recover on the basis of a total loss rather than partial loss. A notice of abandonment can be dispensed with even in the case of constructive total loss where the insurer has waived service or where service would serve no useful purpose (MIA 1906, s 62(7)(8)). The insurer is not obliged to accept notice of abandonment.

The requirement for a notice of abandonment was considered in *Kastor Navigation Co Ltd v Axa Global Risks (UK) Ltd* [2004] 2 Lloyd's Rep 277.

Abandonment

35.47 If the insured has suffered an actual total loss, or a constructive total loss where a notice of abandonment has been served, then:

(a) the insured is entitled to be paid the full insured value of the insured subject matter; and

(b) the insurer has the right to take what remains of the insured subject matter by way of salvage (MIA 1906, s 63(1)). If a ship is abandoned, the insurer is entitled to take any freight which is in the course of being earned by the ship (MIA 1906, s 63(2)), although under the Institute clauses the hull insurer will waive the right to freight in favour of the freight insurer.

Partial loss

35.48 Marine policies cover 'particular average', which consists of two elements:

(a) partial loss, which arises where the subject matter has sustained damage which can be repaired at a cost less than the repaired value (MIA 1906, s 64); and

(b) salvage charges, which are charges payable by the insured under maritime law to a person who has attempted to avert the insured peril or minimise its consequences. (MIA 1906, s 65).

Charges incurred under contract with a salvor – 'particular charges' – do not fall within the definition of 'particular average', but may be recovered by the insured under a separate 'sue and labour' clause (see **35.56** below).

General average

35.49 A 'general average loss' is a loss caused by or directly consequential on a 'general average act'; it includes expenditure and sacrifice (MIA 1906, s 66(1)). There is a general average act where such expenditure or sacrifice is reasonably and voluntarily made at time of great peril by one person for the benefit of others (MIA 1906, s 61(2)). An illustration of a general average act is the jettisoning of cargo from a vessel which is shipping water in an attempt to preserve the vessel and the remaining cargo on board.

An insured who performs a general average act is entitled to recover from his insurer (MIA 1906, s 66(4)). He also has the common law right, which will vest in his insurer by way of subrogation, to claim a rateable contribution from the other persons interested in the adventure who have benefited from the general average act (MIA 1906, s 66(3)). General average contributions are insured under the Institute clauses (MIA 1906, ss 66(5), 73).

Normally, general average contributions are settled between the insurers of the various interests represented in the adventure. The situations in which a general average loss takes place and the principles governing the settlement between insurers are laid out in the York-Antwerp Rules.

MEASURE OF INDEMNITY

General introduction

35.50 The amount which the insured can recover under a marine policy – the 'measure of indemnity' (MIA 1906, s 67) – depends upon whether the policy is valued or unvalued (see **35.09** above):

(a) In the case of a valued policy, the value of the subject matter agreed by the parties at the outset is, in the absence of fraud by the insured, conclusive as between the parties (MIA 1906, s 27(3)). The amount which the insured recovers is therefore based upon the agreed value.

(b) If the policy is unvalued, which is comparatively rare in marine insurance, the basis of the measure of indemnity is the 'insurable value', calculated in accordance with s 16 of the MIA 1906. The insurable value is normally the value of the subject matter at the date of the commencement of the risk (compare non-marine insurance, where the insurable value is assessed at the time immediately prior to the loss). Unvalued marine policies are subject to average, the insured being deemed to be his own insurer for any uninsured sum (MIA 1906, s 81). Thus, if the insured is covered for 90 per cent of the actual value of the subject matter and suffers a partial loss of, say 50 per cent, the insurer and the insured will bear the loss in the proportions 90:10, so that the insured will recover only 45 per cent of the total insurable value from the insurer and must bear the remainder himself.

Loss of or damage to the vessel

35.51 If the vessel has been totally lost, the insured recovers:

(a) under a valued policy, the full sum agreed (MIA 1906, s 68(1)); and

(b) under an unvalued policy, the full insurable value, determined as of the date of the commencement of the risk (MIA 1906, s 68(2)).

If the vessel has been damaged, the agreed value is disregarded and the insured recovers under both a valued and an unvalued policy in accordance with the following principles:

(a) Where the vessel has been repaired, the insured recovers the reasonable cost of repairs (MIA 1906, s 69(1)) – under the Act, recovery is limited to two-thirds of this figure, but this restriction is ousted by the Institute clauses and the International Hull Clauses;

(b) Where the vessel has been only partially repaired, the insured recovers the reasonable cost of the repair effected plus depreciation (the diminution is value of the vessel due to her partially repaired state), subject to the ceiling of the reasonable cost of full repair (MIA 1906, s 69(2));

(c) Where the vessel has not been repaired and has not been sold, the insured recovers depreciation arising from the unrepaired damage, subject to a limit of the reasonable cost of repair (MIA 1906, s 69(3)); and

(d) Where the vessel has not been repaired and has been sold, the insured recovers the difference between the market value of the vessel immediately prior to the loss and the sum for which she was sold (*Pitman v The Universal Marine Insurance Co* (1881-82) LR 9 QBD 192).

Loss of or damage to cargo

35.52 If the cargo has been totally destroyed, the insured recovers:

(a) under a valued policy, the full sum agreed (MIA 1906, s 68(1)); and

(b) under an unvalued policy, the full insurable value, determined by the invoice price of the goods when purchased by the insured (MIA 1906, s 68(2)).

If the cargo is a partial loss, the insured recovers:

(a) under a valued policy, a proportion of the agreed value representing the degree of damage (MIA 1906, s 71(1)); and

(b) under an unvalued policy, a proportion of the insurable value representing the degree of damage (MIA 1906, s 71(2)).

If the cargo has been delivered to its port or final destination and is there found to be damaged, the insured recovers:

(a) under a valued policy, a proportion of the agreed value representing the diminution of the actual market price at the place of arrival (MIA 1906, s 71(3)); and

(b) under an unvalued policy, the difference between the undamaged and the damaged market price of the goods at the place of arrival (MIA 1906, s 71(4)).

Loss of freight

35.53 If an insured peril deprives the insured of his ability to recover the costs of carriage of cargo or of the hire of his vessel, the insured will recover:

(a) under a valued policy, the full agreed value or a proportion of the agreed value representing the degree of loss (MIA 1906, s 70); and

(b) under an unvalued policy, the full insurable value or a proportion of the insurable value representing the degree of loss (MIA 1906, s 70).

Suing and labouring

Nature

35.54 The suing and labouring clause is invariably found in English marine insurance policies on property. Where the policy contains such a clause, the sue and labour cover is deemed to be a separate agreement to the agreement found in the contract of insurance.

The duty

35.55 It is the duty of the insured, and his agents, under a marine policy to take all reasonable measures to avert or minimise a loss (MIA 1906, s 78(4)). Under the Institute Time Clauses, if such measures are taken by the insured, he can recover an additional sum up to the amount insured under the policy.

The duty to sue and labour is not absolute. The insured must take all reasonable measures to avert or minimise a loss. Therefore, an insured who fails to summon assistance in the belief that the vessel is in no immediate danger, and who also fails to take steps which would be known only to a skilled engineer, to stem an ingress of water, is not in breach of the duty (*AP Stephen v Scottish Boatowners Mutual Insurance Association (The 'Talisman')* [1989] 1 Lloyd's Rep 535). Further, an insured who fails to institute proceedings against a third party is not in breach of the duty if the proceedings are unlikely to result in a recovery from the third party (*Bayview Motors Ltd v Mitsui Marine and Fire Insurance Co Ltd* [2002] 1 Lloyd's Rep 652).

A failure on the part of the insured to sue and labour may provide the insurer with a defence to the claim on grounds that the loss has been caused by the insured's failure to act rather than an insured peril (*National Oilwell (UK) Ltd v Davy Offshore Ltd* [1993] 2 Lloyd's Rep 582; *State of the Netherlands (Represented by the Minister of Defence) v Youell and Hayward* [1997] 2 Lloyd's Rep 440, [1998] 1 Lloyd's Rep 236). If the insured fails to mitigate a loss – for example, by pursuing a recovery action – the insurer may have a claim in damages to the extent it has been prejudiced *(Noble Resources Ltd and Unirise Development Ltd v George Albert Greenwood (The 'Vasso')* [1993] 2 Lloyd's Rep 309*)*. The duty of the insured to sue and labour is reciprocated by the insurer's duty to indemnify the insured for the costs of suing and labouring, although this duty is contractual rather than statutory (MIA 1906, s 78(1)). Indemnification is required only if the insured's action has been taken to avoid a loss by a peril insured under the policy (MIA 1906, s 78(3)); although the Court of Appeal has held that the insured can make a claim on the insurer if the insured had good grounds for believing that the peril faced by his property was covered under the policy (*Integrated Container Service Inc v British Traders Insurance Co Ltd* [1984] 1 Lloyd's Rep 154*)*.

Costs recoverable

35.56 The costs recoverable are laid down by the Institute clauses and International Hull Clauses, which extend to:

(a) salvage charges incurred under contract (but not salvage charges incurred under maritime law, in the absence of contract – MIA 1906, ss 65 and 78(2)) – in practice, most salvage is conducted under contract; and

(b) other costs reasonably and properly incurred, which may include costs which are incurred in an unsuccessful attempt to avert the loss.

The insured can only recover reasonable expenditure – that is, those expenses that a reasonable person would incur to preserve his property if he had no insurance.

The amount recoverable under the suing and labouring clause is additional to the policy monies themselves, as the clause is regarded in law as a totally distinct contract. However, under the Institute clauses, the sue and labour indemnity is limited to the amount insured. Further, if the insured is under-insured and is only able to recover a proportion of his loss, then he may only recover the same proportion of his suing and labouring costs. Under the 2003 version of the International Hull Clauses, this reduction for under-insurance has been abolished.

RIGHTS OF INSURERS

35.57 The rules in the MIA 1906 relating to the rights of insurers following payment are identical to those applicable in non-marine insurance:

(a) ss 32 and 80 (see **Chapter 18**); and

(b) s 32 (see **Chapter 16**).

In addition, as discussed earlier, where an insurer pays a total loss, it is entitled to take over what remains of the insured property.

Chapter 36

Motor vehicle insurance

- Nature of motor vehicle insurance
- The contract
- First-party cover
- Compulsory insurance scheme
- Motor Insurers' Bureau
- Changes as a result of Brexit
- Financial Ombudsman Service

NATURE OF MOTOR VEHICLE INSURANCE

36.01 There is no class of insurance called 'motor insurance'. Like other forms of insurance, the cover available is made up of a mixture of different types of insurance, the main one being the liability to third parties for accidents (eg, damage to property and personal injury). This is the cover which is compulsorily required by law. Other forms of cover seek to indemnify the insured in relation to his own (ie, first-party) losses. Motor insurance can also result in long-tail liabilities as a result of serious personal injury claims. As a result of the Solvency II Directive, and to reflect their long-term nature, such liabilities giving rise to annuity-type payments must now be determined separately using life assurance techniques.

The types of cover available can therefore be broken down as follows:

(a) First-party motor vehicle insurance: The minimum cover is for fire and theft (normally combined with third-party cover), although comprehensive cover – including injury to the insured himself or damage to his property – is generally available.

(b) Third-party compulsory insurance: This covers the driver's liability to any third party, including any passenger, and includes personal injury and property damage inflicted by the insured on a third party. It should also cover the insured's own legal costs in defending such liability claims.

Where the third party suffers loss following the negligent driving of a person either who is uninsured or who cannot be identified, the third party is protected by the fall-back Motor Insurers' Bureau (MIB) scheme.

36.02 There have been significant changes to the law relevant to motor insurance following the entry into force of the Consumer Insurance (Disclosures and Representations) Act 2012 (CIDRA) and the Insurance Act 2015. These are mainly changes to the nature of the insured's obligation of disclosure and the effect of contractual provisions (eg, warranties and conditions precedent). Other significant changes have resulted from EU law in this area, consolidated in the Motor Insurance Directive (2009/103/EC), and from the effects of Brexit. These include practical changes such as the inability to pursue claims for EU compensation in the UK (see **36.32** below).

It should also be noted that new law in this area has already developed in relation to car sharing (eg, pre-planned where the arrangement covers costs of the driver) and automated vehicles (see the Automated and Electric Vehicles Act 2018, which establishes the compulsory insurer's liability for accidents caused by an automated vehicle when driving itself on a road or another public place in Great Britain). The market has also developed products to insure the liability to pay policy excesses, as well as gap insurance (eg, to cover outstanding financing if a car is written off) and additional legal expenses insurance. The sale of such products has been subject to intense scrutiny by the Financial Conduct Authority (FCA), which has conducted a number of reviews relating to the motor insurance market and the add-on products which often now accompany it. This has resulted in regulatory requirements applicable to the design of these products, the way in which they are sold (both initially and on renewal), and the way in which claims are managed.

THE CONTRACT

Form of the contract

36.03 Much consumer motor insurance is now sold online, either by insurers or by price comparison websites. The form of the contract may therefore vary significantly depending on the sales channel. Regulatory requirements also now how have a bearing on the design (including pricing or products) and the way in which they are sold. Similarly, the regulatory requirement to act in the best interests of customers and, for consumers, the requirements of the Consumer Rights Act 2015 will have an impact on the fairness (and the transparency to the customer) of terms included in such contracts. Specific rules apply in relation to pre-contractual disclosures (eg, the insurance product information document (IPID)) and renewal notices (see **Chapter 43**). At the time of writing, further requirements are likely to be imposed in relation to pricing and auto renewal of motor insurance contracts.

Non-disclosure and misrepresentation

36.04 As a result of CIDRA and the Insurance Act 2015, the law in relation to non-disclosure and misrepresentation has changed significantly (see **Chapter 6**), as has the position in relation to the effect of terms in a contract of insurance stated to be warranties or conditions precedent. Warranties are now required to be specific (and not created by basis of the contract clauses). Also, warranties and conditions precedent, where not delineating the scope of cover, can be relied on only to the extent that they are relevant and/or the relevant breach is continuing).

The proposer for a motor policy must still answer truthfully all questions put to him. CIDRA requires that consumer insureds (ie, individuals acting wholly or mainly outside of their business) are under a duty to take reasonable care not to make a misrepresentation. The insurer is therefore obliged to ask consumers clear questions in relation to matters it considers relevant. CIDRA retains the requirement that the insurer must have been induced by the misrepresentation. Therefore, the insurer will have to demonstrate that without the misrepresentation, it either would not have entered into the contract at all or would not have done so on the same terms. A misrepresentation for which the insurer has a remedy under CIDRA is called a 'qualifying misrepresentation'. Such a misrepresentation can be either deliberate or reckless on the one hand, or careless on the other. It is for the insurer to show that a misrepresentation was deliberate or reckless.

36.05 Where the misrepresentation was deliberate or reckless, the insurer's remedy is that it can refuse the claim and avoid the policy. A statement will be deliberate if the consumer knew that it was untrue or misleading. It will be reckless where the insured did not care whether or not the representation was untrue or misleading, and either knew that it was relevant to the insurer or did not care whether it was relevant to the insurer. Following a deliberate or reckless misrepresentation, the policy will be treated as if it had never existed and all claims by the insured can be refused. The insurer can retain any premium unless it would be unfair not to return the premium.

Where the misrepresentation is careless, CIDRA provides for a proportionate remedy to reflect the position that the insurer would have been in had the true facts been known. It is for the insurer to show that a misrepresentation was deliberate or reckless; otherwise it will be deemed careless. Where the insurer would have excluded a particular type of claim, it should not have to pay claims falling within that exclusion. Where a warranty or excess would have been imposed, the resulting claim should reflect a policy that included such a warranty or excess. Where the insurer, on knowing the true facts, would have charged a higher premium, a proportionate settlement should be given to the insured (eg, if the additional premium would have been 25 per cent of the correct premium, any claim will be reduced by 25 per cent). Finally, where the insurer would have declined the risk altogether, the policy may be avoided and the premium returned.

If the insurer becomes aware of a careless misrepresentation, at any time before a claim arises, it can notify the insured of proposed revised terms and any additional premium. The consumer receiving notice of revised terms may terminate the contract by giving reasonable notice to the insurer. On termination, the consumer will be entitled to a refund of premiums for the balance of the contract term.

The law can now be seen to be similar to the practice of the Financial Ombudsman Service (FOS) (see **36.33** below); although it should always be remembered that the FOS decides cases on the basis of what is fair and reasonable, and is not obliged to decide cases based on the law. This can still, therefore, lead to differences in cases decided by the FOS and cases decided by the courts.

36.06 The Insurance Act 2015 provides remedies which are very similar to those provided for consumers under CIDRA and similarly abolishes basis of the contract clauses. It also prevents warranties being relied upon where the breach of warranty is no longer continuing at the time of loss or where it is not relevant to the actual loss suffered. The main differences between the Insurance Act and CIDRA are that non-consumer insureds are under a duty to make a fair presentation of the risk to the insurer (rather than taking reasonable care not to make a misrepresentation); and that, provided that the specified transparency obligations are complied with, it is possible to effectively dis-apply most of the Insurance Act's provisions in relation to non-consumer contracts. However, it should be noted that it is not possible to contract out of the abolition of basis of the contract clauses (which converted statements into warranties). Because of this ability to contract out of the Insurance Act's provisions, previous law relating to utmost good faith in the context of misrepresentation and non-disclosure, warranties and fraudulent claims may in such cases continue to be relevant. In practice, such contracting out is not expected to occur in most motor insurance contracts.

Where the insured has deliberately not disclosed information or has acted recklessly, the Insurance Act provides that the insurer can avoid the contract and keep the premium. In all other cases, the Insurance Act provides a remedy proportionate to the insured's failure; and while this may still include avoiding the policy (eg, where the insurer would not have accepted the risk), the premium will need to be returned.

36.07 Previous case law relating to the duty not to make pre-contractual non-disclosures will no longer apply to consumers (eg, where it relates to a right to avoid for careless non-disclosure). It may be applied to commercial motor policies where the Insurance Act provisions have been excluded and a duty of utmost good faith has been imposed. However, it is useful to understand issues which have previously been held to be material facts in relation to motor policies, as these are likely to inform appropriate questions and the items to be included in a fair presentation of risk. These include:

(a) the age of the vehicle (*Santer v Poland* [1924] 19 LI L Rep 29);

(b) the price paid for the vehicle or its current market value;

(c) the nature of the insured's interest in the vehicle – for example, whether the insured is the owner or hirer of the vehicle (*Guardian Assurance Co Ltd v Sutherland* [1939] 63 Ll L Rep 220);

(d) the location of the vehicle and whether or not it is to be kept garaged;

(e) the age of the driver (*Broad v Waland* [1942] 73 LI L Rep 263);

(f) the driving experience of the driver (*Corcos v De Rougemont* [1925] 23 LI L Rep 164);

(*g*) the persons who will be driving the vehicle (*Magee v Pennine Insurance Co* [1969] 2 QB 507);

(*h*) the driving record of the insured, including criminal convictions (*Dent v Blackmore* [1927-1929] 29 LI L Rep 9); and

(*j*) the previous claims record of the insured (*Farra v Hetherington* [1931] 40 LI L Rep 132).

Policy conditions

36.08 It is usual for motor policies to contain a range of conditions which limit the insured's use of the insured vehicle and require its maintenance. Motor policies will also lay down conditions dealing with the making of claims and prohibiting the insured from admitting liability to any third person in the event of an accident. It should be noted that Section 2 of the Compensation Act 2006 provides that an apology, an offer of treatment or other redress shall not of itself amount to an admission of negligence or breach of statutory duty. This may therefore reduce the effect of breaching such a requirement. It is also normal for the policy to contain a 'reasonable care' clause, requiring the insured to take all reasonable steps to avoid loss (see *Hayward v Norwich Union Insurance Ltd* [2001] EWCA Civ 243). All of these obligations must now be considered in the context of the obligation to treat customers fairly and, in relation to consumer insureds, the provisions of the Consumer Rights Act 2015 which invalidate unfair contract terms. The FCA's Insurance Conduct of Business rules also impose requirements in relation to the design of products (eg, meeting the needs of the target market and selling products for which the insured is eligible to claim), and the need to be clear about exclusions, to provide appropriate pre-contractual information and to act fairly in dealing with claims.

36.09 In addition, in relation to compulsory third-party claims, insurers are prevented, under s 148 of the Road Traffic Act 1988 (RTA 1988), reflecting art 13 of the Motor Insurance Directive, from relying on the vast majority of policy conditions in order to defeat such third-party claims. Such condition may, however, be relied upon as regards any first-party claim (ie, by the insured). If the insurer is required to make payment under this provision in circumstances in which he would otherwise have had a defence, the insurer can seek an indemnity from the insured himself (RTA 1988, ss 148(3)–(4) and 148(6)).

The matters which cannot be relied upon by the insurer are as follows (RTA 1988, s 148(1)–(2)):

(a) the age or physical or mental condition of persons driving the vehicle. There are often clauses which limit cover where the insured is under the influence of alcohol or drugs. In *Criminal Proceedings against Bernaldez C-129/94* [1996] All ER (EC) 741, the European Court of Justice (ECJ) held that any contract term restricting the liability of the insurer to third parties in connection with an insured who caused an accident while intoxicated was void;

(b) the condition of the vehicle – for example, a term which requires the insured to maintain the vehicle in good condition or which requires the vehicle to be kept 'roadworthy';

(c) the number of persons that the vehicle carries;

(d) the weight or physical characteristics of the goods that the vehicle carries (eg, overloading);

(e) the time at which or the areas in which the vehicle is used. The most common clause restricting use – the 'social, domestic or pleasure' (SDP) limitation – would seem to fall outside this category (see further **36.10** below). Examples of SDP would not include commuting to work or driving an injured employee from his place of work to receive medical attention (*Passmore v Vulcan Boiler and General Insurance Co Ltd* [1936] 54 LI L Rep 92); although giving a lift to someone on the way home from work may not change the nature of the journey (*AXA Insurance UK Ltd v EUI Ltd (T/A Elephant Insurance)* [2020] EWHC 1207 (QB));

(f) the horsepower or cylinder capacity or value of the vehicle;

(g) the carrying on the vehicle of any particular apparatus;

(h) the carrying on the vehicle of any particular means of identification other than any means of identification required to be carried by or under the Vehicle Excise and Registration Act 1994; and

(j) any condition which removes the liability of the insurer in the event of some specified thing being done or omitted to be done by the insured after the happening of the insured event (s 148(5)) – for example, late claims and admissions of liability by the insured.

Section 148(7) of the RTA 1988 also provides that, notwithstanding anything in any enactment, an insurer issuing a compulsory insurance cover (ie, meeting the requirements of s 145 of the RTA 1988 (see below)) shall be liable to indemnify the persons or classes of persons specified in the policy in respect of any liability which the policy purports to cover them for.

36.10 Although the UK has implemented the EU requirement for compulsory insurance (now contained in the consolidated Motor Insurance Directive) in the RTA 1988, the relevant provisions should still be interpreted purposively, in a way which is consistent with the terms of the Directive. The lower courts (eg, not the Court of Appeal or the Supreme Court) are also bound by the pre-Brexit case law of the ECJ. Over time, certain inconsistencies between UK law (eg, the RTA 1988 provisions and historic domestic case law) and EU law have become apparent. Examples include the nature of the use of the vehicle as a means of transport; use on private land; provisions limiting the extent of cover; and conditions attaching to a third party's right of direct enforcement against the insurer. There are also potential inconsistencies in relation to English law rules which mean that the insured should not be able to deliberately bring about the insured event or to rely on something arising as a result of his own illegal act.

Some of the potential inconsistencies with EU law (eg, where they result in uninsured losses) are addressed by the terms of the UK compensation arrangements (via agreements with, and the constitution (articles of association) of, the MIB). One particular point to note is that it is possible, under English law, for insurance not to cover all uses of a car. Generally, motor insurance will cover liabilities as a result of an accident and will not cover damage which is deliberate. Similarly, there is a good deal of authority on limiting cover to SDP uses. A number of these issues (including whether it is possible to have limitations on cover such as SDP and deliberate damage) were considered in *Roadpeace v Secretary of State for Transport and MIB* [2017] EWHC 2725 (Admin). The judge decided that there was no incompatibility with the provisions of the Motor Insurance

Directive where insurance was subject to scope of use restrictions and uninsured losses would be covered by the MIB. The judge did, however, make a declaration that the UK position on limiting cover to use of a vehicle on the road or other public place was not compatible with EU law (based on the decision in *Vnuk, Case C-162/13, and Rodrigues de Andrade, C-514/16*). In *Colley v Shuker* [2020] EWHC 3433 (QB), it was held that the MIB, as an emanation of the state, had an obligation to remedy the UK failure in relation to s 152(2) of the RTA 1988 (which permitted an insurer to avoid a policy and therefore liability to third parties). This section has subsequently been limited to avoidance (or a declaration of the right to do so) prior to the relevant accident; but it is still arguably inconsistent with the Motor Insurance Directive. The UK government has announced that it intends to depart from this EU decision in *Vnuk*. It therefore seems that Brexit may well result in continued inconsistency and future differences (see further **36.32** below).

Driver extension clauses

Other drivers

36.11 Many policies permit the vehicle to be driven by other identified persons or by any person driving with the insured's consent. In the event that liability to a third party is incurred, any person who is authorised to drive the vehicle is given a direct cause of action against the insurer (RTA 1988, s 148(7)).

The question of what constitutes consent by the insured to another person is important for determining:

(a) whether the insurer is liable under the policy; and

(b) whether the driver has committed a criminal offence by driving the vehicle while uninsured (RTA 1988, s 143).

Other vehicles

36.12 It is also common for the policy to allow the insured to drive any other vehicle on a third-party basis. Such cover is, however, merely ancillary to the primary cover; and if the insured's own vehicle is sold, the policy lapses and the insured is no longer insured under his own policy to drive any other vehicle (*Rogerson v Scottish Automobile & General Insurance Co Ltd* [1931] 41 LI L Rep 1; *Tattersall v Drysdale* [1936] 52 LI L Rep 21).

FIRST-PARTY COVER

36.13 A motor policy covering first-party risks will normally extend to the following forms of protection:

(a) personal injury suffered by the insured. Cover may be restricted to 'accidental injury caused by violent, external and visible means'; and

(b) property damage inflicted upon the insured's property – in particular, his vehicle.

In addition, it may cover the loss of no claims bonus (known as protected no claims bonus). It is also common for add-on policies to be sold with motor insurance to cover legal expenses (eg, uninsured losses such as personal injury and any policy excess not covered by the first-party coverage), loss of keys, misfuelling and hire cars.

COMPULSORY INSURANCE SCHEME

Compulsory insurance requirement

36.14 Section 143 of the RTA 1988 lays down two criminal offences:

(a) using a motor vehicle on a road or other public place when there is not in force a policy covering statutory liability; and

(b) causing or permitting the use of a motor vehicle on the road or other public place when there is not in force a motor policy covering statutory liabilities.

A 'motor vehicle' is a mechanically propelled vehicle (other than an invalid carriage) intended or adapted for use on roads (whether or not fit to do so); and a 'road' is any highway to which the public has access (RTA 1988, ss 185, 192) (see *Cutter v Eagle Star Insurance Company Limited* [1998] 4 All ER 417; *Clarke v Kato* [1998] 4 All ER 417). This limitation has been held to be inconsistent with EU law (see *Colley v Shuker* [2020] EWHC 3433 (QB), but is now unlikely to be changed (see **36.10**).

There is also an offence under s 144A of the RTA 1988 of keeping a vehicle which does not meet insurance requirements (ie, by the person in whose name the vehicle is registered). This offence is committed where, subject to similar exemptions to the s 143 requirement to insure, a motor vehicle registered under the Vehicle Excise and Registration Act 1994 does not meet the insurance requirements under the RTA 1988.

Failure to insure

36.15 Failure to insure not only is a criminal offence, but also amounts to a civil wrong. The victim of an uninsured driver may, therefore, bring an action for breach of statutory duty against him and against a person who caused or permitted him to use the vehicle without insurance (*Monk v Warbey* [1936] 1 KB 75). This is likely to be of little significance for the victim himself, as he will have a remedy against the MIB in such a case (*Norman v Aziz* [2000] Lloyd's Rep IR 52). However, the MIB can, by use of subrogation, sue the tortfeasor and seek to recover its payment accordingly.

Using a motor vehicle

36.16 As can be seen from the requirements described in **36.14** above, compulsory insurance is defined in terms of 'use' of a vehicle. The 'user' of the vehicle is the person who has control over it at all times; this will generally be the driver. A passenger in a vehicle cannot normally be said to be using it (see *Hatton v Hall* [1997] RT R 212). However, a passenger may be regarded as a 'user' if he is the vehicle's owner (*Cobb v Williams* [1973] RT R 113); if he has helped to steal the vehicle (*Leathley v Tatton* [1980] RTR 21); or if he has allowed himself to be carried in pursuance of a joint enterprise (*O'Mahoney v Joliffe* [1999] RTR 245). A person in a parked car may be the user of it (eg, if he opens the door or does something consistent with the normal function of the vehicle – see *BTA Baltic Insurance Co AS v Baltijas Apdrosinasanas Nams AS* (C-648/17)).

Causing or permitting use

36.17 A criminal offence is permitted by the person in control of the vehicle (who is normally but not necessarily the insured) only where use by an uninsured person is authorised by him. If the insured allows another person to use his vehicle on condition that that person produces his own insurance, uninsured use by that person does not amount to an offence on the insured's part, as the condition is not satisfied (*Newbury v Davis* [1974] RTR 367). The position is otherwise if the insured simply takes the user's word that he is insured and does not make his permission conditional on it (*Baugh v Crago* [1975] RTR 453).

Exemptions

36.18 Exemption from the compulsory insurance requirement is given to various public service vehicles – for example, local authority, police, air force and health service.

Section 150 of the RTA 1988 provides, in relation to car sharing (as defined in that section),that conditions in compulsory insurance policies, such as those limiting cover to SDP or preventing use of the vehicle as a hire vehicle, shall not apply.

Scope of the compulsory insurance

36.19 The policy must be issued by a UK-authorised insurer (eg, under the Financial Services and Markets Act 2000 (FSMA 2000)) or an insurer authorised in Gibraltar that is authorised to sell into the UK. European Economic Area (EEA) insurers must have a UK authorised branch in order to write UK business (or be able to rely on a temporary permission post Brexit). In all cases, the insurer must belong to the MIB (RTA 1988, s 145(2), (5)–(6)).

The policy must (subject to specified exemptions) in relation to use of the vehicle provide cover in respect of the following:

(a) Death or personal injury: The policy must cover such persons specified in the policy in respect of liability for the death of or personal injury to any person caused by or arising out of the use of the vehicle on a road or other public place in Great Britain. In *Dunthorne v Bentley* [1996] PIQR P323, where the driver ran across the road into the path of an oncoming vehicle, her reason for being in the road was held to have arisen from the use of her vehicle. Liability for death or personal injury cannot be limited or excluded, and in the UK such cover is therefore unlimited.

The driver's liability for the cost of emergency treatment (under ss 157–159 of the RTA 1988, which covers in-patient and out-patient treatment) must also be covered.

(b) Property damage: The policy must cover the insured and such persons within the policy in respect of liability which may be incurred for damage to property (RTA 1988, s 145(3)(a)) up to a limit which is currently £1.2 million.

(c) EU risks: Where the vehicle is normally based (ie, registered) in Great Britain, the level of cover is that required in Great Britain (ie, unlimited in relation to personal injury or death and limited to £1.2 million in relation to damage to property) or, in relation to liability in Northern Ireland or the EU, such higher amount as would be required in such jurisdictions. Where the vehicle is normally based in the EU, the level of cover should be the local level if higher than that required in Great Britain (RTA 1988, s 143(3)).

(d) The protection of passengers: The compulsory insurance requirement extends to passengers in the insured's vehicle, including the insured when he is a passenger or person driving the vehicle with his consent. An agreement between the insured and the passenger seeking to exclude or restrict the insured's liability to the passenger is void under s 149 of the RTA 1988.

(e) Automated vehicles: In the case of an automated vehicle, the policy must also provide for the insurer's obligations to an insured person under s 2(1) of the Automated and Electric Vehicles Act 2018 (liability of insurers etc where an accident is caused by automated vehicle) to be obligations under the policy. For this purpose, 'insured person' means a person who is covered under the policy to use the vehicle on a road or public place in Great Britain.

As stated in **36.09** and **36.10** above, it is not possible, as regards compulsory third-party claims, to rely on provisions in the policy which exclude or reduce the insurer's liability if the loss is within the scope of the policy.

Obligation for insurer

Authorised drivers

36.20 A victim has the right to enforce a judgment obtained in relation to a liability covered by compulsory insurance against the insurer (RTA 1988, s 151).

A number of conditions must be met before the direct action may be brought:

(a) The victim must have obtained judgment against the driver (execution of which is not stayed or pending);

(b) The policy must not have been cancelled or the insurer must not have obtained a declaration that it was entitled to avoid the policy for non-disclosure or misrepresentation under CIDRA or the Insurance Act) *prior* to the event giving rise to the liability (RTA 1988, s 152(2)); and

(c) The victim must have given the insurer notice within seven days of commencement of proceedings (RTA 1988, s 152(1)(a)). No special form of words is required and the onus is on the insurer to prove that it did not have the necessary notice or warning (*Desouza v Waterlow* [1999] RTR 71).

Unauthorised drivers

36.21 Section 151(2)(b) of the RTA 1988 provides that if there is a motor policy in force covering the insured, the insurer under the policy will be liable to meet judgments against unauthorised drivers, including a thief. This implements EU requirements (eg the Motor Insurance Directive). The amount and the conditions for liability are the same as for insured or authorised drivers, subject to one exception: the insurer is not liable to a victim who has suffered physical injury or property damage while being carried in a stolen vehicle, unless the passenger either was unaware that the vehicle was stolen (in the RTA, stolen/unlawfully taken) or could not reasonably have been expected to alight from it (RTA 1988, s 151(4)). In *Covea Insurance plc v Greenaway* [2021] 3WLUK 379, the court had to consider whether 'stolen' in this context also encompassed the wider concept of 'taken without consent'. In that case, the insurer was seeking to establish that the claimants, who had travelled in a car belonging to another passenger's father, knew that it had been 'stolen' (as required by Article 13 of the Motor Insurance Directive). The court accepted, based on the practice of the ECJ, that expert evidence in relation to the terms used in other language versions of the Motor Insurance Directive could be adduced to aid construction of the English language version.

Provision of information

36.22 The driver of a motor vehicle who is involved in an accident which causes physical injury or damage to property is under a statutory duty to give his name and address and to produce his insurance documents. Failure to comply with this duty is a criminal offence (RTA 1988, s 170). In *DPP v McCarthy* [1999] RTR 323, the driver was permitted to give his name and the address of a third party (ie, his solicitor's address).

The victim's direct action against the insurer

36.23 Following the introduction of the European Communities (Rights against Insurers) Regulation 2002, there is a direct claim against insurers in relation to liabilities under compulsory insurance policies (eg, without a judgment against the insured). However, this direct right of action is expressed to apply to the extent that the insurer is liable to the insured person. This could allow the insurer to rely on contractual provisions that would not be available against a third party and may not therefore be consistent with the Motor Insurance Directive provisions, which the Regulation was supposed to have implemented.

MOTOR INSURERS' BUREAU

36.24 The statutory scheme for compulsory liability insurance for motor vehicles, which had existed in the UK from 1930, proved from its inception to have two weaknesses:

(a) The negligent driver may have been uninsured; and

(b) The negligent driver may not have been traceable ('hit and run' cases).

In both cases, there was no insurance fund against which the victim could claim. The MIB was established in 1946 to provide a fund. The MIB, which consisted of all authorised motor insurers, entered into an agreement with the government under which the MIB was to accept liability for the victims of uninsured drivers. In 1969, this was extended to cover victims of untraced drivers.

The MIB has entered into a series of Uninsured Drivers Agreements and Untraced Drivers Agreements with the Secretary of State. These are described further below. Both the current Uninsured Drivers Agreement and the Untraced Drivers Agreement can be terminated by either the Secretary of State or the MIB giving the other party not less than 12 months' notice in writing. This would, however, be without prejudice to the continued operation of the relevant agreement in respect of accidents occurring before the date of termination.

Compensation of victims of uninsured drivers

36.25 The current Uninsured Drivers Agreement is the 2015 Agreement, which applies in relation to accidents occurring on or after 1 August 2015 (the previous 1999 Agreement covered the period from 1 October 1999 to 1 August 2015). The role of the MIB under the agreement is to provide a safety net for innocent victims of drivers who have been identified but are uninsured.

MIB's obligation to satisfy compensation claims

36.26 The MIB's basic obligation is to satisfy judgments which fall within the terms of the agreement and which, because the defendant to the proceedings is not insured, are not satisfied. It is also possible that the MIB could cover a claim made against an insurer which the insurer has refused to pay (other than where the claimant's claim was not made within the policy's stipulated timeframe or the claimant has incurred a liability to any other person which could have been avoided by making a claim under and in accordance with the provisions of the insurance policy). In order to avoid unnecessary cost and delay, the MIB will often seek to settle before judgment is obtained. The MIB operates a complaints procedure, but is not subject to the FOS or any other formal ombudsman scrutiny of its decisions.

Exceptions

36.27 The MIB is not liable under the agreement in the case of a claim:

(a) in respect of loss or damage caused by the use of a vehicle owned by or in the possession of the Crown, unless the responsibility for motor insurance has been undertaken by someone else, or the vehicle is in fact insured;

(b) made against any person who is not required to insure, by virtue of s 144 of the RTA 1988, unless the vehicle is in fact insured;

(c) a claim (commonly called 'subrogated') made in the name of a person suffering damage or injury, which is in fact wholly or partly for the benefit of another who has indemnified or is liable to indemnify that person (eg, an insurer that has paid an insured loss);

(d) a claim in respect of damage to a motor vehicle or losses arising from such damage, where the use of the damaged vehicle was itself not covered by a contract of insurance, as is required by Part VI of the RTA 1988, and where the claimant knew or ought to have known that was the case; and

(e) a claim made by a passenger in a vehicle where the loss or damage has been caused by the user of the vehicle, if the user of the vehicle was not covered by a contract of insurance and the claimant knew or ought to have known that the vehicle was being used without insurance or had been stolen or unlawfully taken.

Conditions precedent to the MIB's obligation

36.28 The claimant must take reasonable steps to establish whether there is any insurance covering the use of the vehicle which caused the injury or damage (ie, using the MIB database). If enquiries show that there is an insurer, then even though the relevant liability may not be covered by the policy in question, the claim should be pursued with such insurer. The claim should be directed to the MIB if there is no insurance governing the use of the vehicle; if the insurer cannot be identified; if the insurer asserts that it is not obliged to handle the claim; or if for any other reason the insurer will not satisfy any judgment.

The MIB does not have to wait for judgment to be obtained before intervening and a claimant may apply to the MIB before the commencement of proceedings. Claims should be made as soon as possible, using the MIB's application form and accompanied by supporting documents. Claims can be made online or sent to the MIB's registered office. The claimant must give the MIB notice in writing within 14 days of commencement of legal proceedings.

Subject to which MIB agreement applies, different rules are then laid down by which the claimant must notify the MIB of procedural developments in his case.

Limitations on MIB's liability

36.29

(a) Property damage compensation: The MIB's maximum liability in respect of any one accident for property damage and losses flowing from such damage is limited to £1 million (or whatever figure is laid down by the Secretary of State in its agreement with the MIB from time to time).

(b) Compensation received from other sources: The MIB may deduct from the relevant sum an amount equal to any compensation from, for example, the Policyholder Protection Scheme or an insurer.

Untraced drivers

36.30 Where the owner or driver of a vehicle cannot be identified, application may be made to the MIB under the relevant Untraced Drivers Agreement. The date of the accident is relevant in order to determine which agreement is applicable. The current Untraced Drivers Agreement is the 2017 agreement and it covers accidents occurring on or after 1 March 2017. The 2003 Agreement continues in force in relation to accidents occurring on or after 14 February 2003 but before 1 March 2017.

The current agreement provides, subject to specified conditions, for the payment of compensation for death or personal injury. Damage in respect of damage to property caused by an identified vehicle is only covered subject to the same cap as applies to compulsory insurance (ie, in s 145(4)(b) of the RTA 1988), which is currently £1.2 million.

The agreement does not apply to a case in which:

(a) the death or bodily injury was caused or arose out of the use of a motor vehicle which was owned by or in the possession of the Crown; or

(b) at the time of the accident, the person suffering death or bodily injury was allowing himself to be carried in a vehicle and, either before or after the commencement of his journey, he could reasonably have been expected to have alighted from the vehicle if he knew or had reason to believe that the vehicle was stolen or unlawfully taken, or was being used without insurance.

The MIB will not be under any liability in respect of the relevant death or injury if the applicant is entitled to receive compensation from the MIB under the Uninsured Drivers Agreement. Where it is unclear whether the owner or driver of a vehicle has been correctly identified, it is sensible for the claimant to register a claim under both the Untraced Drivers Agreement and the Uninsured Drivers Agreement, following which the MIB will advise which agreement will, in its view, apply in the circumstances of a particular case.

Unlike the position under the Uninsured Drivers Agreement, where there may be a legal case or a judgment may have been obtained, for the Untraced Drivers Agreement the MIB has to come to a view about the amount that it considers a court would have awarded.

Article 75 insurers

36.31 Insurers will be liable to satisfy claims which would otherwise be covered by the MIB where they would be the relevant insurer (other than where the insured was driving another vehicle), but they are not liable as:

(a) they have avoided the policy (eg, for fraud, non-disclosure or misrepresentation);

(b) the cover has been backdated; or

(c) the liability is otherwise not covered by the scope of use under the policy.

This is as a result of art 75 of the MIB Constitution, which insurers – as members of the MIB (which is a requirement to write compulsory motor insurance) – are bound by. The liability that insurers incur under art 75 is therefore referred to as an 'Article 75' liability. The Article 75 liability is subject to the same conditions as the MIB's liability, but is treated as a liability of the insurer. Disputes as to who is the appropriate insurer will be determined by the MIB.

CHANGES AS A RESULT OF BREXIT

36.32 Motor insurance is one of the areas affected, from 1 January 2021, by Brexit. There are consequences which are particular to motor insurance, such as the loss of access to UK claims representatives for EEA insurers and the involvement of the MIB in respect of EEA claims. There are also a number of more general Brexit-related issues, including the following:

(a) Less choice: Insurers offering the required compulsory third-party insurance must now be authorised in the UK (as well as being members of the MIB).

(b) Less certainty in relation to the interpretation of the retained EU law (eg, the Motor Insurance Directive as implemented in the UK): As a result of Brexit, the lower courts (ie, not the Court of Appeal and the Supreme Court) are required to interpret such retained EU law in accordance with the decisions of the ECJ. The case of *Covea v Greenaway* referred to above also indicates the difficulty for UK courts seeking to determine ambiguity (eg, in language) in the way the ECJ would have done.

(c) As post-Brexit EU case law will no longer apply in the UK, there is scope for future divergence between the law in the UK and the EU. It also appears that changes will be made to the law in the UK to remove some of the existing conflicts with EU law in this area (eg, the proposal to remove the effect of the *Vnuk* case, which required compulsory insurance in relation to the use of vehicles on private land (see **36.10**)).

(d) Lack of clarity around rights due to uncertainty regarding the applicable law: Motor insurance can lead to cross-border claims involving people in the EU. While the law of the UK insurance policy may be a law of the UK, claims against drivers in the EU will be subject to the law in that country or the country of origin of the driver/car.

(e) The need to pursue overseas legal claims or compensation claims in the relevant jurisdiction rather than the UK: Motorists (or insurers) may need to pursue a claim in the EU. This will be the case even where the MIB has reciprocal agreements in place to make compensation available in EU countries. Such claims will need to be taken in the relevant EU courts and will be subject to the procedure and law of the relevant country. Even where there is a reciprocal agreement between the MIB and a compensation body in the EU in relation to uninsured or untraced drivers, the relevant claim for compensation will still need to be made in the relevant EU country.

(f) Enforcement of overseas judgments: Motorists (or insurers) are likely to need to enforce judgments in the EU.

FINANCIAL OMBUDSMAN SERVICE

36.33 The FOS is the informal dispute resolution mechanism established under the FSMA 2000 and which is free to use by those claiming against an insurer. UK authorised insurers are subject to the compulsory jurisdiction of the FOS, which applies to the regulated activities of FSMA authorised persons (including third-country branches of overseas insurers in relation to the activities of the branch). There is also a voluntary jurisdiction, which is effectively a contractual arrangement by which a person – the voluntary jurisdiction participant – agrees that the scheme will apply. The voluntary jurisdiction can only extend to activities which, although not regulated activities, could be regulated activities.

The FOS is not required to decide cases on ordinary legal principles and may impose a result it considers fair and reasonable in all the circumstances. The amount of compensation available is subject to a maximum as follows:

(a) £355,000 for complaints referred to the FOS on or after 1 April 2020 (relating to acts or omissions by firms on or after 1 April 2019);

(b) £350,000 for complaints referred to the FOS between 1 April 2019 and 31 March 2020 (relating to acts or omissions by firms on or after 1 April 2019);

(c) £160,000 for complaints relating to acts or omissions by firms before 1 April 2019, and which are referred to the FOS after that date: and

(d) £150,000 for complaints referred to the FOS before 1 April 2019.

The law of non-disclosure and misrepresentation following CIDRA and the Insurance Act is now much closer to the historic practice of the FOS in relation to claims made on that basis. The FOS also now publishes its cases in a way which is organised around particular issues and is easier to search. The main advantage for policyholders that are eligible to use the FOS is that the service is free to use and is not binding on them.

Chapter 37

Product liability insurance

- Introduction
- The risk insured
- Claims occurring or claims made
- Exclusions
- Conditions

INTRODUCTION

37.01 While product liability insurance is not compulsory – unlike, for example, motor insurance or certain types of professional indemnity insurance – it is vital protection for any company engaged in manufacturing or the supply of goods to a third party. The policy provides cover for legal liability in respect of personal injury or damage to property arising from the sale or supply of products specified in the policy. The policy customarily also covers legal costs. Damages awards and the costs of litigation can be both substantial and difficult to predict, and insurance against exposure to such risks is arguably essential for any business.

Product liability insurance can take the form of a specific policy, but it is more often included in a general liability policy which also covers public and sometimes employers' liability. However, for the purposes of this chapter, the product liability provisions will be dealt with in isolation.

THE RISK INSURED

37.02 The wording of the operative clause will vary, but in general terms the policy provides an indemnity for sums which the insured becomes legally liable to pay by way of compensation or damages, in respect of accidental bodily injury or loss of, or damage to, property caused by products sold or supplied by the insured.

The Consumer Protection Act 1987

37.03 The Consumer Protection Act 1987 (CPA 1987) introduced statutory liability for defective products. The CPA 1987 implemented the EU Product Liability Directive (EU Directive 85/374/EEC on liability for defective products). The strict liability created under Part I of the CPA 1987 operates alongside liability in negligence and will operate regardless of the provisions in any contract limiting liability.

The CPA 1987 imposes strict liability on a producer for damage caused by a defective product. A claimant does not have to establish fault on the part of the manufacturer; only that the product was defective, the claimant suffered damage and there is a sufficient causal link between the defect and the damage caused. The courts have added guidance on what will be considered a 'defect' under s 3 of the CPA 1987. A product has a defect where the safety of the product is not what a consumer would expect. This is an objective test. In *Wilkes v DePuy International Ltd* [2016] EWHC 3096 (QB) it was held that 'any assessment of [product] safety will necessarily require the risks involved in use of that product to be balanced against its potential benefits including its potential utility'.

Product liability is to be distinguished from any kind of manufacturer's guarantee. The defect in the product cannot be part of the design but must be an accidental defect.

The Consumer Rights Act 2015 imposes additional obligations on manufacturers and producers – namely that goods must be of satisfactory quality (s 9) and fit for purpose (s 10).

Compensation or damages

37.04 Policy wordings vary as to whether they refer to 'compensation' or 'damages'. For the most part, any such variation will not matter and there will be no difference in the level of cover available.

However, the distinction will be important in some instances. Some product liability policies exclude liability arising from litigation in the US because of the magnitude of damages awards and costs that can be awarded in some states. For those which do not contain such an exclusion, an award of punitive damages – which is not uncommon in the US – can vastly increase the amount payable under the policy. If the operative clause refers to 'damages', the policy will cover the full amount awarded (subject to any limits of liability). If, on the other hand, the operative clause provides an indemnity for 'compensation', the indemnity will not extend to any award of punitive damages, as such damages are not compensatory in nature. The punitive element will be excluded from the insurer's liability under the policy and will be solely for the account of the insured.

Financial loss

37.05 The cover is against sums awarded in respect of 'bodily injury' and 'loss of or damage to property'. It does not indemnify the insured against liability for pure financial loss which is not a direct consequence of the physical damage. For example, where sugar supplied by the insured to A for incorporation into mincemeat was contaminated, rendering the mincemeat unfit for use, the insured's liability for the cost of replacing the mincemeat was covered by its product liability policy; but A's loss of profits resulting from the loss of a contract with B and the enforced renegotiation of a contract with C was not a direct consequence of the damage to the mincemeat caused by the incorporation of contaminated sugar and was therefore not covered.

It is possible to obtain an extension to the policy to cover pure financial loss. However, such extensions of course require an additional premium and contain a number of exclusions.

Accidental injury and damage

37.06 In order to be covered under the policy, the injury and/or property damage must be 'accidental'. This may be dealt with by using 'accidental' in the operative clause, or by way of an exclusion which provides that there is no indemnity if the circumstances giving rise to the claim resulted from the deliberate act or omission of the insured. So, for example, if a car manufacturer knew there to be a dangerous defect arising from the manufacturing process for the car's braking system but continued selling the cars while investigating the position, any injury to a customer resulting from the failure of the braking system would not be covered by the policy, as such injury would not be accidental. However, if the existence of a defect in the braking system was not known to the manufacturer, any customer injuries which resulted would be covered.

Territorial and jurisdiction restrictions

37.07 The policy will specify the territory within which the injury or damage must occur in order to be covered. Although it is possible to restrict the geographical area in this way, many businesses are international and, even if they do not overtly have an overseas operation, it is perfectly feasible for their products to be sold or transported anywhere in the world without their knowledge or involvement. It is impossible for an insured to predict where its products might cause damage, and many policies therefore provide cover for injury or damage occurring anywhere in the world.

It is less common for the policy to contain a restriction as to the jurisdictions in relation to which the insurance will respond to a claim. However, such restrictions can be provided for. The insurer may, for example, wish to restrict its liability to claims brought within its resident jurisdiction – this would enable a more educated assessment as to the likely quantum of a claim, the amount of legal costs and the length of time litigation will take. Mindful of US damages levels, some policies exclude claims brought in North America. Forum shopping is not uncommon and a product liability insurance policy can take this into account by the use of jurisdictional restrictions.

However, the use of such jurisdictional restrictions is not particularly common. It is more usual for a policy to require that coverage disputes be dealt with in a specified jurisdiction.

CLAIMS OCCURRING OR CLAIMS MADE

37.08 There are two means of dealing with the question of which policy is the relevant one for the purpose of paying out on a claim: 'claims occurring' and 'claims made' forms. The 'claims made' policy is more common.

Claims occurring

37.09 Historically, this form was in general use. The insurer is on risk for claims in respect of injury or damage which occurred during the policy period. Policies are normally renewed every year, commonly with different underwriters on risk in each year. The policy against which the claim is to be applied is that which was current when the damage giving rise to the claim occurred. This can lead to uncertainty for insurers. For example, some forms of bodily injury, such as asbestosis, might have occurred many years before manifesting themselves and resulting in a claim under the product liability insurance. However, the insurer named on the policy year when the injury occurred, which could be decades earlier, would still be on risk. Claims occurring policies are still used, but their significant drawback is that the insurer can never know with confidence when it is no longer on risk.

Claims made

37.10 This form of policy fixes the insurer's exposure to claims made during the period of the policy. It represents a considerable improvement for insurers over the claims occurring policy, in that it provides certainty as to when they are on and off risk. It also avoids what can be an extremely difficult assessment, for which expert assistance may well be required, as to when an injury might have occurred. Claims relating to tobacco litigation and asbestosis, where the injury to a plaintiff might occur over a number of years with the cumulative effect of smoking or with each exposure to asbestos, are obvious examples of when it might be difficult to pinpoint when the injury occurred.

A disadvantage of the 'claims made' policy can be numerous claims being made in just one or a few policy years in respect of events occurring many years previously. This is the converse of the 'longtail' problems inherent in claims occurring policies, as illustrated by the asbestosis claims. That risk can be alleviated from the insurer's point of view by the use of liability limits which can set either a maximum liability for any policy year and/or a maximum aggregate per claim.

There could clearly be a risk of the insurer refusing renewal of a policy in circumstances where there has been an occurrence which has not yet resulted in claims. A hybrid claims made and occurrence provision can be included in the policy. If there has been an occurrence which has been notified within the policy period, the policy might provide that claims subsequently notified will be covered. Alternatively, it is possible for the insured to obtain an extension to the policy which affords the insured an additional specified period in which to make a claim, provided that the occurrence giving rise to the claim was during the policy period.

EXCLUSIONS

37.11 Exclusions will obviously vary from policy to policy, but the most common are dealt with below.

Injury to insured's employee and damage to insured's property

37.12 This reinforces the fact that the policy covers the liability of the insured to third parties, and not injury or damage suffered by the insured itself. There are other policies available by which the insured can protect itself from the risk of injury to its employees or damage to its property.

Contractual liability assumed by insured

37.13 The essence of this exclusion is that the insurer cannot know the full extent of the contractual relationships to which the insured is committed. The insured might enter into a contractual commitment which could significantly extend the insurer's liability. Such commitments are excluded, and the insurer will not pay out unless the insured would have been found liable in any event, even if the contract in question had not been entered into. This exclusion may be of limited application given that most additional contractual commitments assumed by the insured are likely, if breached, to result in liability for financial loss which is not in any event covered by the policy.

Damage to a product, lack of fitness for purpose, repair, replacement, recall and disposal of defective goods

37.14 The rationale for this exclusion is that the policy is intended to cover liability in respect of injury and property damage to third parties, and thus will not respond when the insured is found liable for claims which attach to the product itself. Some of these claims – such as those relating to fitness for purpose, product recall or disposal – are likely to comprise financial loss rather than property damage or bodily injury, and for that reason would generally not be covered by the policy in any event.

Disputes can arise if the policy does not make clear whether this exclusion applies to a product in its entirety or only to a defective component part. Generally, the insurer will intend to exclude liability for defects in the product as a whole. If this is not made expressly clear in the policy, the insured may attempt to limit the application of the exclusion to the particular component that has proved defective.

Although there are circumstances in which the insured will have both a statutory and common law obligation to recall a product in relation to which a defect is discovered, the expenses involved in that exercise are not covered by a product liability policy unless the insured has obtained an extension to the policy.

The giving of advice, design and specification for a fee

37.15 This exclusion normally applies where such services are supplied without a product resulting. Liability in connection with some of these activities, such as the giving of advice, is excluded, as insurance protection can be obtained by way of a professional indemnity policy.

It is possible for a slightly different and more problematic exclusion to apply where a product is supplied which excludes claims for liability arising from the failure of a product to perform the purpose for which it was supplied due to design or specification defects. Assessing whether the malfunctioning of a product is due to a design defect (which would not be covered) or some other cause, such as a fault in the manufacturing process (which would be covered), will not always be a straightforward assessment and may require a great deal of expensive expert analysis.

Other exclusions

37.16 A number of other exclusions are often found in policies: radioactive/nuclear contamination; war; pollution (particularly if there is a risk of claims being brought in the US or Canada); deliberate acts of the insured; products supplied for incorporation into aviation products; product tampering; contamination; and extortion (rare but, where required, the subject of a separate policy).

CONDITIONS

37.17 The conditions which appear in product liability policies are fairly standard and generally unremarkable.

The insured is normally required to give immediate written notice of circumstances which may give rise to a claim. The insured must not admit liability or enter into any negotiations without the insurer's consent. The insurer has full discretion in the conduct and settlement of claims. The policy will normally provide for cancellation on notice to the insured.

Reasonable precautions

37.18 Most policies will require the insured to take reasonable precautions at its own expense to prevent circumstances which might give rise to a claim under the policy and to rectify any defects which might give rise to a claim as soon as possible after they come to its notice. Compliance with this condition may well include instituting a product recall at its own expense. We have already seen that the cost of such an exercise will be excluded from the indemnity provided by the policy. This condition makes clear that failure to institute a recall could also allow the insurer to avoid liability entirely under the policy.

Chapter 38

Professional indemnity insurance

- Sources of professional liability
- Compulsion to insure
- Basis of cover
- Scope of cover
- Extensions to the basic insuring agreement
- Exclusions
- Conditions
- Dispute resolution

SOURCES OF PROFESSIONAL LIABILITY

38.01 Professionals' liability can arise from several sources: an undertaking to achieve a desired result; a contractual duty to exercise reasonable skill and care (either expressly provided for in the professional's terms of engagement or implied by law (Supply of Goods and Services Act 1982, ss 13, 16; Consumer Rights Act 2015, ss 49 and 57); a concurrent duty of care owed to the client in tort (*Henderson v Merrett* [1995] 2 AC 145); or a duty of care owed to a third party who is not a client (*Hedley Byrne & Co Ltd v Heller & Partners Ltd* [1964] AC 465; *Caparo v Dickman* [1990] 2 AC 605; *White v Jones* [1995] 2 AC 207).

COMPULSION TO INSURE

38.02 Certain professionals are required by statute or the rules of their professional bodies to provide satisfactory evidence of professional indemnity insurance cover before they are permitted to practise. The governing body of a profession or its regulators (eg, the Financial Conduct Authority (FCA) for UK insurance brokers and other authorised intermediaries – see Chapter 3 of the Prudential Sourcebook for Mortgage and Home Finance Firms, and Insurance Intermediaries in the FCA Handbook) may impose requirements as to minimum limits and terms of cover, and may stipulate an approved minimum wording. It may also designate approved insurers.

BASIS OF COVER

38.03 Professional indemnity policies written in the London market are generally 'claims made' policies, rather than 'occurrence basis' policies.

Under an occurrence basis policy, the insurer agrees to indemnify the insured for loss arising out of a defined event which must occur within the policy period, irrespective of when damage arises. A considerable period of time may elapse between the occurrence of the insured event and loss arising from it.

Under a claims made policy, the insurer agrees to provide indemnity for any claim made against the insured during the policy period, irrespective of when the event giving rise to the claim occurred. The insurer must be notified of claims prior to the expiry of the policy period. Problems can arise if proceedings are issued but the insured is not made aware of them until after the expiry of the policy period (*Robert Irving & Burns v Stone* [1998] Lloyd's Rep IR 258). The court will avoid 'excessive formality' in considering whether or not a claim has been made against the insured (see *J Rothschild Assurance plc v Collyear* [1999] Lloyd's Rep IR 6, where there were no actual claims as the liabilities were established as a part of the industry-wide pensions mis-selling review instigated by a regulatory body).

The insured may have the right (or obligation) to notify 'circumstances which may give rise to a claim'. If a claim is made after the end of a policy period during which circumstances were notified, cover may still be available, provided that the claim arises out of the circumstances notified.

SCOPE OF COVER

38.04 Although breaches of contract and acts of negligence may, in some cases, be illegal, illegality will not by itself deprive insured professionals of cover where they are in breach of duty, in spite of the *ex turpi causa* principle of public policy (ie, a person may not enforce rights under a contract of any kind if it is tainted by illegality). The courts now take a proportionate approach based on a range of factors which consider the public policy underlying the illegality (see *Patel v Mirza* 2016 UKSC 42 and *Stoffel and Co v Grondona* [2020] UKSC 42). However, it should be noted that the FCA Rules (General Provisions 6.1) prohibit insurance against financial penalties imposed by the FCA.

The operative clause of a professional indemnity insurance policy may restrict cover to negligent acts, errors or omissions. Alternatively, cover may be widely drawn in respect of 'any act, error, omission, breach of contract or duty, or allegation thereof'. In *Total Graphics Ltd v AGF Insurance Ltd* [1997] 1 Lloyd's Rep 599, a failure to place insurance as instructed was not proved to be a negligent act, error or omission within the terms of the policy; but see also *Simon v Warrender Proprietary Ltd v Swain* [1960] 2 Lloyd's Rep 111. Consideration may need to be given as to whether conduct is deliberate and as to whose conduct is covered.

Some professional indemnity policies define the nature of the insured's business and seek to limit the indemnity available by reference to the professional's business activities. Indemnity may nevertheless be available for work performed gratuitously.

Whatever the terms of the operative clause, it is necessary to look at the cause of a loss to determine whether indemnity will be available. A judgment of a court is likely to be determinative of indemnification. However, where a claim is compromised short of judgment, it is not enough to rely upon the manner in which the claim was formulated against the insured; it is necessary to ascertain the real basis on which the claim was compromised (*MDIS Ltd (formerly McDonnell Information Systems Ltd) v Swinbank* [1999] 2 All ER (Comm) 722, where a claim was compromised but turned out to be based on an employee's dishonesty; and *West Wake Price & Co v Ching* [1957] 1 WLR 45).

EXTENSIONS TO THE BASIC INSURING AGREEMENT

38.05 Indemnity will usually be available against the costs of defending any claim covered by the policy; it may extend to the costs of enquiries or investigations (eg, regulatory or disciplinary proceedings) which are connected to or arise out of covered claims or circumstances. Special provisions usually apply to the costs of defending criminal proceedings (see **38.06** below). Defence costs may be included within the limit of indemnity or be payable in addition. Indemnity may also be extended to cover the following:

(a) partners and employees who have left an insured firm but were with it at the date of the act or omission, or have performed work after retirement in the name of, or on behalf of, the insured firm;

(b) another firm where the insured firm acquires or merges with that other firm (eg, cover may be provided for predecessor or successor firms, such as partnerships); and

(c) partners or employees who act in various capacities in the course of their professional duties, but the insured firm itself has no legal liability arising out of an individual's appointment.

EXCLUSIONS

38.06 Indemnity will usually be excluded in respect of:

(a) claims for which the insured firm is entitled to indemnity under a previous policy or under other existing policies under which payment is actually made;

(b) any fines, penalties, punitive or exemplary damages;

(c) awards of multiple damages (save as to the compensatory amount);

(d) claims where there is adjudged to have been fraud or dishonesty by an insured, committed with actual fraudulent or dishonest purpose and intent (save that innocent partners may still be covered in respect of any liability and indemnity may be available for costs of defending criminal proceedings, if the accused is acquitted);

(e) trading losses or liabilities incurred by a business managed or carried on by the insured (although cover will generally be available for claims against receivers, liquidators or administrators acting in their normal capacity);

(f) losses arising from guarantees of investment performance or warranties or guarantees;

(g) claims made in specific jurisdictions (eg, the US and Canada), on the grounds that these can lead to higher awards of damages; and

(h) liabilities for personal injuries and property damage (though there may be indemnity in respect of loss of documents – for example, where solicitors hold important and valuable documents such as title deeds on behalf of clients).

CONDITIONS

38.07 Professional indemnity insurance policies commonly include the following conditions:

(a) a requirement of prompt written notice of any claim and provision of such information as the insurer may reasonably require;

(b) a specified limit to the insurer's liability and a retention of risk by the insured;

(c) aggregation of claims arising out of the same or related acts or omissions;

(d) a requirement that the insured not admit liability for or settle any claim, or incur any costs or expenses, without the insurer's written consent. This may be coupled with a right for the insurer to take over conduct of the defence or settlement of a claim, subject to a 'QC clause' (see **38.08** below); and

(e) where a professional governing body has imposed minimum terms of cover, a special condition providing that the insurer will waive its rights to avoid cover for non-disclosure or misrepresentation, late notification or breach of condition. Where the insurer suffers prejudice in consequence of such conduct, it may have rights against the individuals concerned.

DISPUTE RESOLUTION

38.08 Where the insurer is entitled to take over conduct of the defence or settlement of any claim in the name of an insured, the insured is usually protected against being required to contest proceedings by the inclusion of a 'QC clause'. This provides that insurer and insured shall agree upon counsel who shall advise whether proceedings should be contested or pursued. Solicitors and counsel instructed to advise in such circumstances must have regard to the insured's interests, among other matters (see also **Part 4**).

Chapter 39

Public liability insurance

- Nature of cover
- The insuring clauses
- Exclusions

NATURE OF COVER

39.01 Public liability insurance protects companies against legal liability for injury to third parties or damage to their property arising out of and in the course of business. While this core protection is not a statutory requirement in the same way as employers' liability insurance, it is nevertheless an important form of cover due to the range of personal injury and property damage claims which may be brought by clients, visitors or the general public, and the significant legal fees that can result. Public liability insurance is often purchased as a package with employers' liability insurance and sometimes also product liability insurance. It is also a core element in most commercial insurance products that aim to meet all of a business's insurance requirements under one policy.

39.02 At the outset, it is worth being clear about what public liability insurance does not cover. It does not cover injuries to employees, for which employers' liability insurance is needed. It does not cover claims against directors and officers, for which directors' and officers' liability insurance is needed. It does not cover claims against the company for negligent acts or omissions, for which professional indemnity insurance is needed; and in the majority of cases, product liability will also not be covered.

39.03 However, in addition to the core personal injury or property damage referred to above, nowadays policies can incorporate a number of valuable extensions. These are considered in more detail below.

THE INSURING CLAUSE

39.04 Public liability insuring clauses generally cover damages or compensation arising from three trigger events:

(a) accidental personal injury to any person;

(b) accidental damage to tangible property; or

(c) accidental nuisance, accidental trespass or accidental interference with any easement or right of air, light, water or way.

39.05 In each case, the trigger event must occur during the period of insurance and in the course of the insured's business. Also note that the trigger event must be accidental; deliberate or intentional acts are not insured. The insuring clause will also ordinarily cover defence costs and legal liability for claimants' costs and expenses in connection with claims arising from the trigger events.

EXCLUSIONS

39.06 The exclusions in a typical public liability insurance are aimed at excluding cover for losses that one would expect to be covered under another form of insurance, as described above. Standard exclusions therefore include employers' liability; liability arising from breach of the insured's professional duties; damage to the insured's own property; product liability; cyber; and pollution – the latter of which may be insured under an environmental insurance policy.

EXTENSIONS

39.07 It is commonplace for policies to have large numbers of extensions that are generally sub-limited. An exhaustive description of all of the potential extensions is beyond the scope of this chapter, but a representative sample is as follows:

(a) defence costs associated with defending criminal proceedings arising from breach of health and safety at work legislation;

(b) liability for compensation and defence costs arising from claims under relevant provisions of the Data Protection Act 2018 and the General Data Protection Regulation (EU) 2016/679;

(c) liability by virtue of s 3 of the Defective Premises Act 1972;

(d) personal liability of employees and directors incurred overseas;

(e) manslaughter defence costs;

(f) advertising liability, where the insured incurs liability for libel, slander, infringement of copyright or invasion of privacy rights arising from the insured's advertising activities; and

(g) crisis containment costs.

39.08 The wide range of possible extensions can be seen from this list. Of particular note, the availability of extensions for data protection claims may provide a degree of comfort to insureds who are not minded to purchase cyber insurance policies. While the data protection extension does not by any stretch accord insureds the same level of protection as a cyber insurance policy, it does give them (sub-limited) cover for third-party exposures arising from data breaches. In the presently very busy climate for such proceedings, this extension can therefore be particularly advantageous.

DEFENCE COSTS

39.09 Like most liability insurance policies, public liability insurance policies provide cover for costs that are incurred in defending claims brought by third parties. From the insured's perspective, the key practical point to be aware of is that it may be necessary to obtain the insurer's prior consent to the incurring of such costs. The requirement for prior consent enables the insurer to exert a degree of control over the selection of external lawyers and the incurring of costs. The inclusion of a claims cooperation (or control) clause also enables the insurer to participate in the defence of inward claims as the insurer deems appropriate; and it is also often a requirement that the insurer's prior consent to any settlement is obtained.

Chapter 40

Reinsurance

- Nature of reinsurance
- Formation of reinsurance agreements
- Reinsurance pools
- Misrepresentation and non-disclosure
- Terms of reinsurance agreements
- Qualifying requirements for solvency purposes

NATURE OF REINSURANCE

40.01 The importance and purpose of reinsurance lie in the ability of primary insurers to spread risk and so contribute to the function of the insurance market in distributing risk in a sustainable and economically efficient way. A reinsurer can reinsure its liability by way of 'retrocession', the reinsurer being termed the 'retrocessionaire' and the reinsured the 'retrocedant'. Multiple levels of reinsurance can cause confusion and, more importantly, serious practical complications. Occasionally, the same insurer appears at different levels of the reinsurance, with the result that an insurer is effectively reinsuring itself.

Although the principles discussed in this chapter apply to all forms of reinsurance, most of the problematic issues are taken from non-marine reinsurance for the simple reason that this is the class of business which seems to have given rise to most of the judicial consideration, particularly in the more modern cases. In a handbook of this nature, particularly when reinsurance is dealt with in a single chapter, there is hardly any room to mention, let alone discuss fully, disputes which can arise in particular sectors of the reinsurance market (eg, marine reinsurance placed on a 'total loss only' basis where the original policy provided cover against all risks). One particular specialist area which does not deserve complete omission, but which cannot be examined in any depth, is life reinsurance. This class of reinsurance is exceptional because, unlike every other form of reinsurance (see **40.02** below), it may include elements which are not, strictly speaking, indemnities against liability of the reinsured. With the exception of certain group life contracts, life reinsurance is generally written on a proportional basis (see **40.04** below), and will be written either on the same terms as the original policies or on what is known as a 'risk premium' basis. In the latter type of reinsurance, the only risk reinsured is that of premature death; the reinsurer does not reinsure any endowment element of the original policy.

Reinsurance is now regulated in a very similar way to insurance under the terms of the Financial Services and Markets Act 2000 (FSMA 2000) and subordinate legislation (see **Chapter 42**). Reinsurance business is not defined as a separate regulated activity requiring authorisation under the FSMA 2000; it is regulated by reference to the same activities as direct insurance (eg, effecting and carrying out a contract of insurance). There are, however, differences in regulation for 'pure reinsurers' (ie, those only carrying on reinsurance and not any direct insurance business). It is now also possible to pass underwriting risk through an insurance special purpose vehicle (ISPV) or other alternative risk transfer arrangements. These enable insurance companies to mitigate risks that they face or to optimise aspects of their capital management. A description of these structures is beyond the scope of this chapter; but, for example, ISPVs securitise the result of insurance profits and losses by issuing debt which funds the provision of reinsurance and where the return on the debt is dependent on the profitability of the reinsurance. A modified regulatory regime applies to such entities.

General definition

40.02 A 'contract of reinsurance' was defined by Mansfield CJ in *Delver v Barnes* (1807) 1 Taunt 48 as: '... a new insurance effected by a new policy on the same risk which was before insured in order to indemnify the underwriters from their previous subscriptions; and both policies are to be in existence at the same time.'

Reinsurance is a form of indemnity insurance taken out by an insurer to cover its own exposure to the underlying risk. It is a separate contract with terms which may – and often do – differ from those in the original insurance contract. The definition in *Delver v Barnes* indicates that a reinsurance contract is a fresh policy issued by the reinsurer on the original subject matter. Aspects of this definition (eg, that the original policy must have been issued prior to the reinsurance) are no longer considered to be a requirement for a contract of reinsurance. Because of the underlying concept of indemnity (acknowledged by Law Commission Insurance Contract Law Issues Paper No 4, p 3), there has been uncertainty as to whether reinsurance should be categorised as liability insurance (eg, an insurance of the original insurer's liability) or a reinsurance of the risk covered by the underlying contract. The point was considered by the House of Lords in *Wasa International Insurance Co Ltd and AGF Insurance Co Ltd v Lexington Insurance Co* [2010] 1 AC 180, which reaffirmed that the subject matter of a contract of reinsurance is the original subject matter insured (in respect of which the reinsured has an insurable interest by virtue of its policy of insurance), rather than an insurance of the reinsured's liability under the original policy of insurance.

Separate contract

40.03 The *Delver v Barnes* definition and the *Wasa* decision also make it clear that reinsurance is a separate contract with terms which may differ from those in the underlying insurance policy. There seems to be a general presumption in English law that facultative reinsurance (see **40.04** below) is to be construed as being 'back to back' with the underlying insurance, so that the insurer's liability is more or less mirrored in the reinsurance agreement (see *Forsikringsaktieselskapet Vesta First Respondents (Plaintiffs) v Butcher Appellant (First Defendant)* [1989] AC 852; *Groupama Navigation et Transports v Catatumbo CA Seguros* [2000] 2 Lloyd's Rep 350). The position is wholly different with a reinsurance treaty (see **40.08** below), which covers the whole of an insurer's risk or the whole of a particular type of risk of the reinsured (see *AXA Reinsurance (UK) plc v Field* [1996] 2 Lloyd's Rep 233, although that case was reversed on other issues). See further below in relation to incorporation of language from the underlying insurance contract).

The contract between the insured and the insurer is separate from the contract between the insurer and the reinsurer (*Meadows Indemnity Co Ltd v The Insurance Corporation of Ireland plc and International Commercial Bank plc* [1989] 2 Lloyd's Rep 298). Ordinarily, therefore, the operation of the principle of privity of contract means that the insured has no ability to claim against the reinsurer in the event that the insurer neglects to pay under the original policy. This point is affirmed by s 9(2) of the Marine Insurance Act 1906, which provides that the original insured has no right or interest in respect of any reinsurance arranged by the insurer. The insured's right of recourse, therefore, is against his own insurer alone; or, in the event of the insurer's insolvency, he may be entitled to compensation from the Financial Services Compensation Scheme, provided that the policy is provided by a 'relevant person' as defined by the FSMA 2000 (see **Chapter** 7).

Some reinsurance agreements nevertheless provide that, in the event of the reinsured's insolvency, the insured has a direct claim against the reinsurer for sums owing by the reinsurer to the reinsured in respect of the original insured's claim. Until the Contracts (Rights of Third Parties) Act 1999 came into force, any such 'cut-through' clause would have been ineffective as a matter of English law, as the insured was not a party to the reinsurance agreement and could not enforce the clause against the reinsurer. The Contracts (Rights of Third Parties) Act 1999 makes provision, however, for the possibility of a third party enforcing a term in a contract which expressly confers such a right upon the third party. If the Act is not excluded by the contract, it may allow the original insured to make a claim directly against the reinsurer. Whether such provisions will be effective against the liquidator of an insolvent reinsured may, however, be doubtful. If a reinsurer has direct policyholders, they will have priority over its reinsurance business; and even within its non-priority creditors, there may be issues with provisions triggered on insolvency and which diminish the assets available for distribution to the reinsured's other creditors so that its assets are not distributed *pari passu* (ie, in equal proportions) to creditors of the same class. Further discussion of this complex topic is beyond the scope of this book. It should also be noted that s 15 of the Third Parties (Rights Against Insurers) Act 2010 provides that it does not apply to rights against reinsurers.

Forms of reinsurance

40.04 Reinsurance may take one of two forms:

(a) facultative reinsurance, which is the reinsurance of a single risk by means of a specific reinsurance policy; or

(b) treaty reinsurance, by virtue of which the reinsurer makes a standing offer to the reinsured that all risks fitting a given description and within given financial limits accepted by the reinsured are covered by the treaty. Treaties are either obligatory (the usual form), in that the reinsurer has no right to refuse individual liabilities accepted by the reinsured; or facultative/obligatory, in which case the reinsured is permitted to pick and choose the risks to be ceded to the reinsurer.

Both facultative and treaty reinsurance may be either proportional or non-proportional.

Under a proportional reinsurance contract, the risk is shared between the reinsured and the reinsurer in fixed proportions. Such contracts may be either:

(a) quota share, in which the reinsurer participates in the reinsured's original business on substantively the same terms as the reinsured for its proportion of the risk; or

(b) surplus, in which the reinsured retains part of the original risk and cedes the surplus, generally in amounts representing exact multiples of the amount retained (called the reinsured's 'line').

Under a non-proportional reinsurance contract, the liability is layered: the reinsured bears a retention and the sum in excess of the retention is accepted by the reinsurer:

(a) Excess of loss reinsurance is the most common form of non-proportional reinsurance, under which the reinsurer covers part of each loss sustained by the reinsured in excess of the reinsured's retention and subject to the limit of indemnity of the reinsurance contract.

(b) Stop loss reinsurance is a variant under which the reinsurer's liability begins once the aggregate of the reinsured's losses reach a given financial limit.

Reinsurance is commonly arranged in excess layers, and it is possible to find more than one form of reinsurance involved in respect of a single risk. For example, the reinsured may bear the first £25,000 of loss itself, reinsure the next £100,000 under a quota share arrangement and arrange excess of loss cover with another reinsurer for all losses exceeding £125,000, but subject to a limit of £500,000.

Reinsurance treaties will often be evidenced by lengthy and complex documents. By contrast, facultative reinsurance may be created by a 'slip policy', which specifies the nature and basic terms of the contract; although the Market Reform Contract (see **1.15**) contains much more detailed policy wordings than was the case before a standard market contract was introduced.

One other issue which arises in relation to reinsurance contracts relates to the coverage and duration of the contract. Reinsurance contracts are often either annual contracts or expressed to cover a specified period. There are a number of different coverage options used in different lines of reinsurance business. In broad terms, these options are as follows:

(a) Claims made: In this case, cover is provided in respect of claims made during the stated period of the insurance, irrespective of when the cause of loss started.

(b) Losses occurring: In this case, the loss must occur during the stated period of insurance.

(c) Risks attaching/policies issued cover: In this case, cover is provided in respect of relevant risks that the cedant accepts during the stated period of the insurance.

FORMATION OF REINSURANCE AGREEMENTS

Reinsurance in advance of insurance

40.05 The definition of 'reinsurance' in *Delver v Barnes* (see **40.02** above) contemplates that the insurer will reinsure only after the underlying insurance policy is in place. Market practice, particularly in the case of large risks, is often to the contrary: frequently, a broker instructed to place insurance will seek reinsurance first, thereby making it easier to find original insurers prepared to accept the primary risk, since they will have the knowledge that a substantial proportion of their liability can be passed on to reinsurers. This practice can lead to legal difficulties in relation to the duty of care owed by the broker placing the reinsurance, since the reinsured – to whom that duty is normally owed – may not have been ascertained when the reinsurance was placed. The broker will need to take reasonable care and, importantly, inform the reinsured if there are differences in the cover (see *General Accident Fire and Life Assurance Corpn v Peter William Tanter v Peter William Tanter (The 'Zephyr')* [1985] 2 Lloyd's Rep 529; *Youell v Bland Welch & Co Ltd (The 'Superhulls Cover' Case) (No 2)* [1990] 2 Lloyd's Rep 431).

REINSURANCE POOLS

40.06 Large risks and treaties are generally underwritten by groups of reinsurers rather than by one reinsurer individually. Reinsurers may, for this purpose, enter into pooling arrangements whereby the pool members agree that each of them will accept a given proportion of the risks underwritten by the pool. A pool will often be represented by an underwriting agent, which may be given authority either to underwrite at its discretion or to receive and pass on risks for consideration by the pool members themselves (eg, where the pool member is dealing on a non-admitted basis). The pool will sometimes be represented by one of its number, acting as a 'fronting' company, which will accept the risk in its entirety. The fronting company will then enter into retrocession agreements (ie, reinsurance of reinsurance contracts) with the other pool members, with the result that the fronting company retains its agreed proportion of the risk, while the retrocessionaires (ie, the companies agreeing to the retrocession contract) have their individual agreed proportions of the risk ceded to them. Fronting may produce administrative savings and overcome problems where only the fronting company is authorised to carry on reinsurance business in the territory in which the pool is operating. Fronting can, however, also give rise to problems, particularly if one of the retrocessionaires becomes insolvent and cannot indemnify the fronting company for the retrocessionaire's agreed proportion of the original risk.

MISREPRESENTATION AND NON-DISCLOSURE

Facultative agreements

40.07 Facultative reinsurance agreements are contracts of liability insurance and are thus subject to the usual duty of utmost good faith (eg, to make a fair presentation of the risk). The reinsured may be in breach of its duty in one of two ways:

(a) if there is a false statement in, or a material omission from, the proposal form for the original policy and this has been incorporated by reference into the reinsurance agreement; or

(b) if there is a false statement or a material omission in the negotiations between the insurer and the reinsurer.

A deliberately false statement made to the insurer, but not repeated to the reinsurer, renders the original policy, but not the reinsurance agreement, voidable. If the insurer chooses not to rely upon a right not to pay and pays the claim, the reinsurer may have a defence to the reinsured's claim on the basis that the reinsured has not made a *bona fide* settlement of the underlying loss (see **40.21** below).

Treaties

40.08 Reinsurance by treaty normally has two distinct stages: the making of the treaty and the declaration of individual risks to the treaty. Although the treaty (especially if not obligatory) may not be, strictly speaking, a contract of reinsurance, but rather a framework agreement, it is nevertheless clear that a full duty of utmost good faith operates at the stage of placement of the treaty, requiring the reinsured to make a fair presentation of the risks which will be allotted to the treaty (see *Glasgow Assurance v Symondson* (1911) 104 LT 254). The position under a line slip (which is essentially a delegated authority allowing someone to bind risk on behalf of the reinsurer), which requires separate consideration of each risk bound, is different. A line slip is a contract *for* insurance, which is not itself a contract of utmost good faith; whereas individually, the declarations to the line slip are contracts *of* insurance and therefore of utmost good faith (see *HIH Casualty and General Insurance Ltd v Chase Manhattan Bank* [2001] Lloyd's Rep IR 191, confirmed by the Court of Appeal on this point at [2001] Lloyd's Rep IR 703 at 719).

Some difficulty surrounds the question of whether full disclosure is required when each individual risk accepted by the insurer is ceded to the reinsurer under the treaty. The reinsured may be under a contractual duty to submit particulars to the reinsurer by way of lists of risks, called '*bordereaux*'. Probably, however, no additional duty of disclosure arises at this stage. It is not the case that each individual cession under a treaty takes effect as a separate contract of reinsurance in its own right (*Citadel Insurance Co v Atlantic Union Insurance Co SA* [1982] 2 Lloyd's Rep 543). Many reinsurance agreements are expressed or construed as obligatory, so that the reinsurer cannot refuse to accept the ceded risk. Indeed, in some cases, the issuing of a policy by the insurer operates as an automatic cession of liability to the reinsurance treaty. A duty of disclosure would therefore appear to be superfluous.

For facultative obligatory or open cover arrangements, where the reinsured decides which risks to reinsure, the reinsurer's protection arguably stems not from the doctrine of utmost good faith, but from an implied term in the reinsurance contract under which the reinsured agrees to exercise reasonable care in the carrying on of its business. The implied duties were set out in *Phoenix General Insurance Co of Greece SA v Halvanon Insurance Co Ltd* [1985] 2 Lloyd's Rep 599 (although decided differently on appeal, but approved in this respect). Under the formulation adopted there, the reinsured is required to conduct its business in accordance with the ordinary practice of the market and to exercise due care and skill in the conduct of all business applicable to the treaty. In particular, the reinsured impliedly agrees to:

(a) keep full and proper records of all risks accepted, premiums received and claims against it;

(b) investigate all claims to ensure that they fall within the cover of the policy before paying them;

(c) properly investigate proposed risks before acceptance;

(d) keep full, proper and accurate accounts showing the amounts due and payable by the reinsurer to the reinsured;

(e) ensure that all amounts payable to the reinsured are collected promptly; and

(f) ensure that all documents are available for inspection by the reinsurer.

Although this case probably remains good law in relation to facultative/obligatory (or other proportional) contracts, the Court of Appeal in *Bonner v Cox* [2006] 2 Lloyd's Rep 152 held that a reinsured owes no such implied duty of care to a reinsurer in excess of loss business. Obiter statements extended this to other non-proportional treaties, but did not decide on proportional treaties.

What is 'material' for the duty of fair presentation?

40.09 The Insurance Act 2015 applies to new contracts and variations made after 12 August 2016 (eg, new treaties and risk placed under facultative obligatory treaties). The pre-Insurance Act law will therefore continue to apply to existing long-term treaties. Also, as the Insurance Act is a codification of much of the case law relating to the nature of disclosure (if not the remedies available), it may well be relevant in similar cases going forward to inform decisions such as what is material and whether or not the reinsurer was induced to enter into the contract. There are only a few cases in which the issue of what constituted a material fact for the purposes of a reinsurance agreement has arisen squarely for decision under the pre-Insurance Act law. The next section sets out some examples.

The amount of the reinsured's retention

40.10 The retention is the primary protection available to the reinsurer, so that any intention on the part of the reinsured to reinsure this retention elsewhere will be material (*Traill v Baring* (1864) 33 LJ Ch 521). This principle has, however, been diluted in more modern authorities:

(a) In *Société Anonyme d'Intermediaries Luxembourgeois v Farex Gie* [1995] LRLR 116, the court held that although it was accepted that the cedant's retention would be a matter of great concern to a reinsurer, nevertheless, unless a reinsurer is told – or is entitled to assume from a previous course of dealing – that there is or is not a significant retention on each risk which it is being asked to accept, it is up to the reinsurer to ask what the position is.

(b) In *Kingscroft Insurance Co Ltd v Nissan Fire & Marine Insurance Co Ltd* [1999] Lloyd's Rep IR 603, it was held that a whole account quota share reinsurer was not entitled to avoid its contract on the grounds that the reinsured had sought excess of loss reinsurance for its retained line under the quota share contract, since the obtaining of such reinsurance was a common practice in the London market, and the whole account quota share reinsurer ought to have known that the reinsured might choose to purchase excess of loss protection in respect of its retention.

The reinsured's previous losses and claims history

40.11 This is clearly an important factor which a reinsurer will wish to take into account (see *Pan Atlantic Insurance Co Ltd v Pine Top Insurance Co Ltd* [1994] 2 Lloyd's Rep 427). It should be noted, however, that claims experience in recent years may not always be a reliable guide, as losses may take some time to become manifest, particularly in relation to issues caused by natural disasters and third-party liability.

The extent of the reinsured's liability under the original policy

40.12 If the original policy commits the reinsured to liability in cases which the reinsurer would normally expect to find excluded, the reinsured must disclose the existence of the exceptional liability: see *Property Insurance v National Protector Insurance* [1913] 108 LT 104 (winter cover for marine risks on the Great Lakes); *Sumitomo Marine & Fire Insurance Company v Cologne Reinsurance Company* 552 NYS 2d 891 [1990] (acceptance of liability for risks of nuclear damage).

Remedies for misrepresentation or non-disclosure

40.13 A reinsurance contract is voidable for breach of the reinsured's duty of utmost good faith prior to placement. If the breach consists of a misrepresentation, the court will not excuse the misrepresentation by applying s 2(2) of the Misrepresentation Act 1967 and awarding damages to the reinsurer in lieu of its right to avoid (see *Highlands Insurance Co v Continental Insurance Co* [1987] 1 Lloyd's Rep 109). Many reinsurance treaties contain an 'errors and omissions' clause, which provides (in effect) that the reinsurer must meet any claim despite an error or omission by the reinsured in operating the agreement. A clause of this type is, however, intended only to rectify clerical errors in the supply of information during the currency of the agreement and was held, in *Pan Atlantic Insurance* (see **40.11** above), not to excuse any breach of the duty of utmost good faith on the part of the reinsured.

TERMS OF REINSURANCE AGREEMENTS

Duration

40.14 There is probably a presumption that a facultative reinsurance contract is to commence and terminate on the same days as the underlying policy, and ambiguous wording in the reinsurance contract will be construed accordingly (see *Commercial Union Assurance Co plc v Sun Alliance Insurance Group plc and Guardian Royal Exchange plc* [1992] 1 Lloyd's Rep 475); but such a back-to-back construction may not always be possible (see *Youell v Bland Welch & Co Ltd* at **40.05** above, where the reinsurance was held to include a 48-month cut-off for the cover). There is no presumption of symmetry of duration between the original policy and the reinsurance agreement in the case of treaty reinsurance. Indeed, it is quite common for a reinsurance treaty to be placed on a 'risks attaching' basis – that is, where the period of the reinsurance is (say) 1 January to 31 December 2021, it will cover losses under any original policies issued by the reinsured during that period. It is possible, in such circumstances, for the reinsured to issue a 12-month policy in November 2021 under which a loss occurs in October 2022. Notwithstanding that the period of the reinsurance contract will have expired some ten months earlier, this loss will still be covered by the reinsurance.

Incorporation by reference

40.15 Facultative reinsurances may consist of a slip policy referring to standard market terms and appended to the original policy. The reinsurance may attempt to incorporate the terms of the original policy by wordings such as 'all terms and conditions as original' or simply 'as original'. It is settled that this form of wording has an incorporating effect, but only in respect of such terms in the original policy as are appropriate to a contract of reinsurance (see *Home Insurance Company of New York v Victoria-Montreal Fire Insurance Company* [1907] AC 59; and *Pine Top Insurance Co Ltd v Unione Italiana Anglo Saxon Reinsurance Co Ltd* [1987] 1 Lloyd's Rep 476). Attempts at incorporation by reference have given rise to considerable uncertainty in a number of reported reinsurance cases, and were criticised by the House of Lords in *Forsikringsaktieselskapet Vesta* (see **40.03** above). The law of contractual interpretation has arguably taken a more literal turn in recent years, the basis on which provisions will be interpreted being what a reasonable person with the background information reasonably available would have understood, even if that produces a result which may not seem sensible from a commercial perspective.

Inspection of records clauses

40.16 Reinsurers may not be given detailed information about the underwriting of the original account which they have agreed to protect or about the claims arising under that account which are presented to them for settlement. In substitution for the provision of detailed information of this nature, the parties to reinsurance treaties usually agree to confer on the reinsurer a right to inspect the books and records of the reinsured. Data protection requirements for personal data may now also result in either that right being made clear to the policyholder or the consent of the policyholder to such disclosure being obtained. In some cases, data is also anonymised.

Even in the absence of an express clause such as this, a right of inspection will probably be necessarily implied into a reinsurance treaty. Such a term was agreed by the parties to be implied into the facultative/obligatory contact in *Phoenix General Insurance* (see **40.08** above). While *Bonner v Cox* disapproved the implication of some of these terms into excess of loss contracts (see **40.08** above), the issue of an implied right of inspection did not arise there. Some doubt has, however, been cast on a reinsurer's right of inspection in the absence of an express inspection of records clause by the following remarks of Hoffmann LJ in *SAIL v Farex Gie* (see **40.10** above):

> 'Reinsurers are free to stipulate for whatever rights of inspection they please ... If they are not entitled to inspection as a matter of contractual right and a dispute arises, English law gives them no procedural means of inspection unless they are first able to raise a triable issue on the material otherwise available to them. This may mean that reinsurers are unable to uncover defences which greater rights of inspection would have revealed, but this is a commercial risk which they accept at the time when the contract is made.'

It may be, however, that Hoffmann LJ's comments should be confined to cases where a reinsurer with no readily apparent defence to the reinsured's claims is attempting to embark upon a 'fishing expedition' in the hope that a viable defence will emerge from the inspection.

If a reinsurer is already in possession of information entitling it to avoid the contract, the exercise by the reinsurer of a contractual right of inspection may be disadvantageous, as the reinsured may be able to argue that the reinsurer has waived its right by asserting a contractual right such as inspection (see *Iron Trades Mutual Insurance Co Ltd v Companhia de Seguros Imperio* [1991] 1 Re LR 213). In *Strive Shipping Corpn v Hellenic Mutual War Risks Association (The 'Grecia Express')* [2002] 2 Lloyd's Rep 88, however, it was suggested that exercising a right to inspect should not be regarded as an affirmation of the contract because an inspection of records provision should be seen as an ancillary but independent provision in the reinsurance, similar in effect to an arbitration clause. In order to avoid any risk of suggestion that the reinsurer has affirmed the contract, however, an inspection in these circumstances should be carried out only under a clear reservation of rights.

If, on the other hand, a reinsurer does not have evidence which will entitle it to avoid the contract, but suspects that such evidence exists, inspection should be demanded without delay. In *Trinity Insurance Co Ltd v Overseas Union Insurance Ltd* [1996] LRLR 156, the reinsured applied for summary judgment against the reinsurer in respect of unpaid claims, and the reinsurer was refused leave to defend the action when its request for inspection of the reinsured's records was made only after the summary judgment application.

Arbitration clauses

40.17 Arbitration is the most common method of dispute resolution used in reinsurance contracts. From the parties' perspective, it has the advantage of privacy and confidentiality, and the ability to have the dispute resolved by arbitrators with expert knowledge of reinsurance, with a binding decision at the end of proceedings. Reinsurance is a highly specialised field with its own complexities, customs and practices. However, it should be borne in mind that arbitration can be as costly and time consuming as court proceedings, and some very large insurers will thus use mediation and expert determination instead.

Where arbitration is applicable, it is sometimes necessary to have first exhausted contractual dispute resolution procedures. Arbitration is likely to follow an agreed set of rules – for example, the ARIAS Arbitration Rules. An arbitrator is likely to be selected by each side, with a third arbitrator selected by the two party appointees. Arbitrators are likely to be required to be persons with insurance/reinsurance experience of at least ten years and to be lawyers or other professional advisers serving the industry. If the two arbitrators fail to appoint the third arbitrator, then ARIAS itself will do so. The place of arbitration will be stipulated and there is likely to be a time limit by which the decision of the arbitration must be issued together with any award. The usual rule is that the costs of the arbitration (including legal costs) are in the discretion of the tribunal, although the parties may make an agreement in this regard (eg, to share the costs except for their legal fees, which will remain the responsibility of the side incurring them), provided that they do so after the dispute has arisen; any antecedent agreement relating to costs is rendered invalid by s 60 of the Arbitration Act 1996. Importantly, the arbitration clause will normally survive any termination of the reinsurance agreement. Arbitration has the attraction of providing privacy in relation to a dispute unless there is an appeal to the courts in respect of lack of jurisdiction, serious irregularity in the proceedings award or a mistake of law.

Losses and claims

Accrual of reinsured's right to indemnity

40.18 In liability insurance, there is a general presumption that the insurer's obligation to indemnify the insured arises on proof of the insured's liability and not on discharge of that liability – that is, by actual payment to the third party by the insured. The same principle applies to reinsurance contracts. The point is likely to be of particular significance when the reinsured has become insolvent and is unable to make payment to its original insureds. The explanation for the decisions reached in some noteworthy reinsurance cases may be that this presumption is sufficiently strong to override what appears to be express language to the contrary. For example, in *Home & Overseas Insurance Company v Mentor Insurance Co* (UK) [1989] 3 All ER 74, the reinsurer's obligation, as expressed in the 'ultimate net loss' clause of the contract, was to indemnify the reinsured for losses which the reinsured 'actually paid'. The Court of Appeal held that the meaning of that phrase was sufficiently uncertain to merit an arbitration hearing as to whether the reinsurer came under any liability before actual payment had been made by the reinsured. The same approach was adopted *In Re A Company No 0013734 of 1991* [1992] 2 Lloyd's Rep 415; and in what is now the leading case on this issue, *Charter Reinsurance Co Ltd v Fagan* [1996] 2 Lloyd's Rep 113, the House of Lords held, in the context of a claim by an insurance company in provisional liquidation against its reinsurer for an indemnity, that the words 'actually paid' in the ultimate net loss clause in the relevant reinsurance contract had, in effect, to be construed as 'liable to be paid'.

Loss settlements clauses

40.19 A persistent difficulty in reinsurance law has proved to be the development of contract language under which the reinsurer is liable to indemnify the reinsured for genuine settlements reached with the original insured, even though it might subsequently prove to be the case that the reinsured was not liable to the original insured as a matter of law. In *Hill v Mercantile and General Reinsurance Co plc* [1996] 1 WLR 1239, Lord Mustill recognised that there is an inherent tension in reinsurance between, on the one hand, the need to avoid investigating the same issues twice; and on the other, the need to ensure that the integrity of the reinsurer's bargain is not eroded by a settlement over which it has no control. In the resolution of this conflict, there are only two rules, both of them obvious. The first is that the reinsurer cannot be held liable unless the loss falls both within the cover of the policy reinsured and within the cover created by the reinsurance. The second is that the parties are free to agree on ways of proving whether these requirements have been satisfied.

Early wordings

40.20 The earliest attempt to resolve this 'tension of reinsurance' was the phrase 'pay as may be paid thereon', which was used in the late nineteenth century. A line of cases, however, beginning with *Chippendale v Holt* [1895] 1 Com Cas 197, held that these words did not have the desired effect and meant instead that the reinsurer was liable to the reinsured only if the reinsured was actually liable to the original insured; a *bona fide* settlement of the original claim did not, therefore, suffice.

Follow the settlements

40.21 The setback (from the reinsured's point of view) of *Chippendale v Holt* (see **40.20** above) led to the adoption of a number of fresh formulations, including 'follow the settlements'. This wording was tested before the Court of Appeal in *The Insurance Co of Africa v SCOR (UK) Reinsurance Co Ltd* [1985] 1 Lloyd's Rep 312. The Court of Appeal held in this case that the 'follow the settlements' clause had the effect of reversing *Chippendale v Holt*, with the result that reinsurers which have agreed to follow their reinsured's settlements are obliged to indemnify reinsureds whose liability has been established by judgment or arbitration award, or who have 'acted honestly and … taken all proper and businesslike steps in making their settlement'. Reinsurers are not entitled to reopen a genuine settlement and seek to prove that there was no legal liability on the part of the reinsured. However, in that case, there was also a claims cooperation clause which meant that the settlements had to be approved by the reinsurer.

Pure *ex gratia* payments (in the sense of payments made in the absence of liability rather than judgment) are, however, probably not included in this formulation; neither should a term be implied that any costs incurred by the reinsured in defending the original insured's claim are to be indemnified by reinsurers.

It was subsequently held in *John Robert Charman v Guardian Royal Exchange Assurance plc* [1992] 2 Lloyd's Rep 607 that the burden of proving that the reinsured has not acted in a proper and businesslike fashion is borne by the reinsurer. This case also decided that a reinsured acts properly in investigating a loss by appointing a reputable loss adjuster, taking reasonable steps to ascertain that the loss adjuster's report has been fairly reached and negotiating with the insured in a businesslike fashion on receiving the report.

Alternative formulations

40.22 Some reinsurance wordings require reinsurers to follow the reinsured's settlements, including any *ex gratia* payments. The validity of such clauses has yet to be tested, but they are arguably binding on the basis that '*ex gratia*' should not be interpreted as meaning 'in the absence of liability', but only 'without admission of liability' (see *Edwards v Skyways Ltd* [1964] 1 WLR 349). *Ex gratia* can, however, also be construed in a wider sense as covering settlements which are made on the basis that there is no liability to indemnify: see *Assicurazioni Generali SpA v CGU International Insurance plc* [2003] Lloyd's Rep IR 725. This judgment was upheld by the Court of Appeal ([2004] EWCA Civ 429), but without further consideration of the meaning of '*ex gratia*'. In *Charman v Guardian Royal Exchange* (see **40.21** above), the clause in question obliged the reinsurer to follow the settlements of the reinsured 'liable or not liable'. The court held that these additional words did not extend the reinsurer's liability to *ex gratia* payments (in the sense of payments made in the knowledge that there was no liability); and that the words were, in effect, meaningless. Other clauses require that the settlement of the original claim fall within the terms of both the original policy and the reinsurance contract (see *Hill v Mercantile & General Reinsurance Co plc* [1996] 1 WLR 1239).

It should be noted that it is now quite common for reinsurance covering business subject to the jurisdiction of the Financial Ombudsman Service (FOS) to make clear that FOS awards are covered, even if they may contain elements which are strictly *ex gratia* because the FOS is not required to decide cases only on the basis of the strict legal position.

In the US, the formula 'follow the fortunes' has long been used and is generally regarded as having at least the same effect as 'follow the settlements', so that the reinsured is entitled to be indemnified for genuine settlements, but cannot seek recovery for *ex gratia* payments.

Claims cooperation and control provisions

40.23 The wide liability accepted by reinsurers under some 'follow the settlements' and 'follow the fortunes' clauses is restricted by other policy terms. Under a claims cooperation clause, the reinsured is obliged to keep the reinsurer informed of the progress of negotiations with the insured and not to reach any settlement unless the reinsurer has approved it. Under a claims control clause, the reinsured is obliged to relinquish to the reinsurer the control of all negotiations with the original insured.

It was decided in *Insurance Company of Africa v SCOR* (see **40.21** above) that the reinsurer's obligation to follow the reinsured's settlements is overridden by a claims cooperation or control clause. A claims cooperation clause in Insurance Company of Africa's reinsurance contract did not, however, affect the actual result in this case, as the reinsured was held to have proved its liability to the original insured, so that the reinsurer was obliged to provide an indemnity. It is important to note that if the claims cooperation or control clause is expressed as a condition precedent, any failure to cooperate will deprive the reinsured of the right to indemnity, notwithstanding the possibility of proof of the reinsured's underlying liability (*Gan Insurance Co Ltd v Tai Ping Insurance Co Ltd* [2001] Lloyd's Rep IR 291).

Aggregation

40.24 One issue that may arise in relation to reinsurance is the applicability of aggregation clauses. Aggregation clauses enable two or more separate losses to be treated as a single loss for certain purposes where they are linked in some way. This can be to the advantage of the reinsurer – for example, the reinsurer may not be liable where separate losses are held not to be capable of aggregation, or its loss will be limited where the aggregate total loss arising from an occurrence or event is over a certain monetary amount. Conversely, where there is a deductible, it can be to the advantage of the ceding insurer to aggregate issues that arise from the same cause. Aggregation can also benefit an insurer which has obtained insurance (eg, a professional indemnity) in relation to the operation of its business (eg, misselling; but see further below). Clearly, there will be occasions where what constitutes a single event or cause will be unclear, yet could have considerable implications for the reinsurer's liability.

The choice of language by which the parties describe the unifying factor in an aggregation clause is clearly of great importance and careful consideration of previous cases is required. The more general the description of the unifying factor, the wider the scope of the aggregation clause. Examples of unifying factors commonly used are an 'event' or 'occurrence', 'originating cause' and 'one source or original cause'. So, for example: 'An "event" is something which happens at a particular time, at a particular place and in a particular way ... a cause ... is something altogether less constricted. It can be a continuing state of affairs; it can be the absence of something happening.' 'Occurrence' usually has the same meaning as event, but can be wider. A state of affairs or an omission cannot constitute an 'event'. The 'unities' test was developed in relation to the question of what constitutes an event by Mr Michael Kerr QC, sitting as an arbitrator in *Dawson's Field Arbitration Award* in 1972. This arose out of the hijacking of four aircraft in 1970 by the Popular Front for the Liberation of Palestine. Three of the aircraft were destroyed at Dawson's Field and the question was whether this arose out of 'one event'. As the hijackings occurred at different locations and by different perpetrators, they could not be regarded as one event. However, their destruction on the ground in close proximity, more or less simultaneously, within a few minutes and as the result of a single decision was, the arbitrator decided, one event. In the absence of unity in time or place, unity of intent or central orchestration is probably not sufficient to constitute a single event or occurrence. A similar issue arose in relation to whether the 11 September 2001 attacks constituted one or more events and careful consideration of the individual cases is required.

Choice of law problems

40.25 One consequence of the fact that the contracts between the insured and insurer on the one hand, and the insurer and the reinsurer on the other, are separate contracts (see **40.02** above) is that each is capable of being governed by a different law (for more on choice of law see **Chapter 2**). This may entail that, even though the wordings of the insurance and reinsurance agreements are identical, different meanings are to be ascribed to the words used under their respective governing laws (see *St Paul Fire and Marine Insurance Co v Morice* (1906) 11 Com Cas 153, 22 TLR 449; *Forsikringsaktieselskapet Vesta; Groupama Navigation* (see **40.03** above) and *Lexington Insurance Co v Wasa International Insurance Co Ltd and AGF Insurance Co Ltd* [2009] UKHL 40).

QUALIFYING REQUIREMENTS FOR SOLVENCY PURPOSES

40.26 This section sets out some high-level requirements for reinsurance to be relied upon in calculating a cedant's solvency position. It is a high-level summary of some key points and does not provide a comprehensive summary of the key prudential requirements relating to the use of reinsurance in the UK.

As many EU countries did not regulate reinsurance, it was necessary for a separate directive – the Reinsurance Directive (2005/68/EC) – to be agreed to apply solvency and other requirements to pure reinsurers. The directive provided for harmonisation of the basis of authorisation/regulation; portfolio transfers; and the right to exercise a single market passport subject to home country supervision and for reinsurers to be included in insurance group and financial conglomerate group calculations. The Reinsurance Directive was implemented in the UK with effect from 31 December 2006 and was replaced by the Solvency II Directive (2009/138/EC) on 1 January 2016. The Solvency II Directive introduced rules relating to reinsurers that EU (and now, following Brexit, UK insurers) can use and additional conditions that reinsurance contracts must satisfy if the cedant is to take credit for the reinsurance for solvency purposes.

Which reinsurers can be used? Eligible counterparties

40.27 The treatment of reinsurance from the cedant's perspective can depend upon whether the reinsurer (or, where relevant, a special purpose vehicle (SPV)) is UK authorised (based on where it has its head office) and/or the status (credit rating) of the reinsurer. In order for a UK cedant to take reinsurance into account when calculating its solvency capital requirement (SCR) (required under Solvency II), reinsurers must:

(a) be authorised in the UK and in compliance with their SCR;

(b) have a credit rating of at least credit quality step 3 (Standard & Poor's) BBB;

(c) be a Solvency II compliant SPV (or meet equivalent requirements); or

(d) be authorised in a country that has been assessed as 'equivalent'. EU countries have been assessed as equivalent for the purposes of reinsurance; as have Switzerland and (other than in respect of limited scope companies) Bermuda.

The required status can also be achieved using Solvency II compliant collateral or guarantees to cover the reinsurer's maximum exposure.

Enforceability and risk transfers

40.28 The Solvency II Regulation (Commission Delegated Regulation (EU) 2015/35), onshored to the UK as at 31 December 2020, specifies different criteria to be applied for arrangements passing *underwriting risk* to those passing *financial* risk (see arts 211 and 212 respectively). However, it imposes qualitative requirements in both cases which limit the recognition to the amount of risk in respect of which there has been a legally enforceable and quantifiable risk transfer. These requirements also apply in relation to guarantees and collateral arrangements.

The Solvency II rules on risk transfer are similar to the requirements on risk transfer that applied pre-Solvency II, in that there needs to be legally effective and enforceable documentation in place. This documentation must clearly set out the scope of the risk transfer. The contractual arrangement should not be subject to any condition which could undermine the effective transfer of risk because fulfilment of the condition is outside the direct control of the cedant. So, for example, to enable full risk transfer, the arrangement should not terminate automatically on insolvency (or earlier financial deterioration, such as a rating downgrade) of the cedant. It is also a requirement that there are no connected transactions which could undermine the effective transfer of risk (eg cross-default or set-off).

Risk mitigating effect of reinsurance

40.29 As with other types of risk mitigation, reinsurance which satisfies the Solvency II requirements will have an effect on the cedant's solvency capital calculation. The amount of mitigation to be taken into account will be the difference between the capital required for the relevant underwriting risk with the reinsurance in place and that which would apply if the reinsurance were not in place. Where a counterparty to a reinsurance contract ceases to comply with the SCR after the reinsurance contract has been entered into, the protection offered by the reinsurance may be partially recognised, provided that the cedant can demonstrate that the counterparty has submitted a realistic recovery plan to its supervisory authorities and that compliance with the SCR will be restored within the timeframe defined in the recovery plan. The effect of the risk mitigation technique should be reduced by the percentage by which the SCR is breached. No equivalent relief applies where, for example, the reinsurance undertaking relies upon its credit rating being at least credit quality step 3 and it suffers a ratings downgrade.

Counterparty default risk

40.30 One of the most noticeable changes as a result of the implementation of the Solvency II Directive has been the focus on counterparty default risk. In calculating its SCR, a cedant now needs to specifically take into account the risk of a reinsurer failing to pay. However, this risk can be mitigated by collateral which satisfies the Solvency II collateral rules. It can also be improved by guarantees (eg, provided by parent companies with a higher rating), as long as the Solvency II requirements relating to guarantees are complied with.

Chapter 41

War risks and related perils

- The insurability of war risks
- Particular war risks
- Proximate cause
- Perils related to war risks
- Strikes
- Terrorism and political risks

THE INSURABILITY OF WAR RISKS

The market

41.01 Insurers have always been cautious in writing insurance against the perils of war, due to the potentially devastating consequences of war. In times of peace, insurance for mainland risks will generally include war cover. However, as far as transport policies are concerned – particularly those on vessels and aircraft – there is a heightened danger of the insured subject matter encountering war conditions in other regions; and the practice is for insurers to exclude liability for losses consequent upon war, but to provide separate cover at an increased premium.

PARTICULAR WAR RISKS

41.02 There are numerous possible exclusions for matters relating to war and other similar risks. It is, however, common to exclude liability for insurrection, riots, civil commotion, war and/or civil war. Exceptionally, the peril of piracy is treated as a marine peril rather than a war risks peril.

War

41.03 The word 'war' has been the subject of numerous court decisions. It has been held to include not just full war between nations, but also localised conflicts over the ownership of territory (*Kawasaki Kisen Kabushiki Kaisha of Kobe v Bantham Steamship Co, Ltd* [1939] 2 KB 544 – the Chino-Japanese dispute) and civil war (*Curtis & Sons v Mathews* [1918] 2 KB 825 – the Irish Easter Rising). In determining whether a war exists, the English courts are not concerned with formal declarations of war or even whether the British government has recognised, for diplomatic purposes, that a state of war exists.

In *IF P&C Insurance Ltd (Publ) v Silversea Cruises Ltd* [2004] Lloyd's Rep IR 696, there was an *obiter* view that the 11 September 2001 events at the World Trade Center did not amount to acts of war.

Civil war

41.04 In addition to being a subdivision of war, civil war is an insurable peril in its own right. The meaning of this phrase was considered at length by Mustill J in *Spinney's (1948) Ltd, Spinney's Centres SAL and Michel Doumet, Joseph Doumet and Distributors and Agencies SAL v Royal Insurance Co Ltd* [1980] 1 Lloyd's Rep 406, a case which concerned the destruction of commercial assets in Beirut in 1976 during fighting between various Lebanese religious groups. The judge held that the existence or otherwise of a civil war should be determined by reference to three matters:

(a) Are there identifiable opposing sides? This test excludes fighting between purely disparate groups, but the mere fact that each side is made up of factions does not prevent a finding of civil war. Some degree of polarisation is required.

(b) Do the opposing sides have coherent objectives? The most likely objective is territorial, although the obtaining of political concessions may be sufficient.

(c) Is the scale of the dispute sufficient to amount to civil war? Relevant factors include the number of combatants and casualties; the size of the territories occupied by the protagonists; the degree and duration of the conflict; and the extent to which ordinary life has been disrupted.

In the *Spinney's* case, Mustill J ruled that none of these elements of civil war had been satisfied on the facts.

Rebellion and revolution

41.05 A 'rebellion' was defined by Mustill J in the *Spinney's* case (see **41.04** above) as 'organised resistance to the ruler or government of a state, intended to supplant their authority over all or a part of the state'. As the *Spinney's* case itself demonstrates, if those responsible for the fighting do not have the coordinated intention of the overthrow of authority, there cannot be a rebellion. The word 'revolution' has never been defined in an insurance case, but would seem to bear much the same meaning as 'rebellion'.

Insurrection

41.06 An insurrection, like a rebellion, requires some intent on the part of those opposing authority to supplant that authority in all or a part of that state, but is satisfied by a lesser degree of coordination than that necessary for a rebellion. If the coordination is present, it is irrelevant that there has been coercion on the part of the insurrectionists to obtain popular support (*National Oil Co of Zimbabwe (Private) Ltd v Nicholas Collwyn Sturge* [1991]

2 Lloyd's Rep 281 – uprising in Mozambique). However, in the absence of any intention to overthrow the government, there cannot be insurrection (see the *Spinney's* case at **41.04** above). The necessary evidence of intention can be ascertained from literature issued by the opposing force, as in the *National Oil Company of Zimbabwe* case.

Civil commotion

41.07 'Civil commotion' is a state of affairs something short of civil war and consists of violent internal disorder which is coordinated, but not necessarily aimed at the overthrow of a government (see the *Spinney's* case at **41.04** above). The limits of civil commotion are illustrated by *London and Manchester Plate Glass Co, Ltd v Heath* [1913] 3 KB 411, where suffragette movement supporters simultaneously (and without threat of personal violence) broke shop windows in various parts of London. The Court of Appeal held that there was no civil commotion, as the acts were not sufficiently proximate to each other to amount to coordinated violence; and in any event, violence was not involved in the damage itself, but rather in protests following the arrest of the movement's supporters, such protests not having been coordinated.

Riot

41.08 The term 'riot' was given a statutory meaning by s 1 of the Public Order Act 1986. The criminal offence of riot (which applies equally to insurance contracts – Public Order Act 1986, s 10(2), amending the definitions in the Schedule to the Marine Insurance Act 1906) takes place, in accordance with s 1(1):

> '… where twelve or more persons who are present together use or threaten unlawful violence for a common purpose and the conduct of them (taken together) is such as would cause a person of reasonable firmness present at the scene to fear for his personal safety.'

Riot can be committed in private as well as in public; the 12 persons need not use or threaten violence simultaneously; and the common purpose can be inferred from the behaviour of the participants (Public Order Act 1986, s 1(2)–(5)). It is also perfectly possible to have riot by silence if the necessary threats are implicit by conduct. There cannot, however, be riot if violence is used not in furtherance of the participants' main objective, but rather in their attempts to effect an escape (*Athens Maritime Enterprises Corpn v Hellenic Mutual War Risks Association (Bermuda) Ltd (The 'Andreas Lemos')* [1983] 1 All ER 590, which involved escape from the scene of a robbery).

Hostile acts by or against a belligerent power

41.09 This phrase is found in marine policies and is aimed at the case in which a merchant vessel assisting in the war effort has been lost as a result of its activities. The wording indicates that the loss must be caused by either an attack by an enemy or an attack on an enemy.

Derelict weapons of war

41.10 Loss caused by abandoned or derelict weapons of war is treated as a war risk by the Institute Marine Cargo Clauses. The clauses were altered to this effect in 1982, following the decision of the High Court in *Costain-Blankevoort (UK) Dredging Co Ltd v Davenport (The 'Nassau Bay')* [1979] 1 Lloyd's Rep 395, in which it was held that a dredging vessel which was lost after having sucked up live shells abandoned after the Second World War had not been the victim of hostilities, on the ground that the dumping of ammunition was a peaceable and not a hostile act.

PROXIMATE CAUSE

41.11 Where damage to property results directly from conflict, the need for loss to be proximately caused by war is easily satisfied. More difficult issues arise where losses occur as an indirect result of war.

The relevant proximity will be efficiency, not time; so when a ship was torpedoed in the First World War but later sank due to damage sustained as a result of being towed and harboured, the proximate cause was still the torpedo (*Leyland Shipping Co Ltd v Norwich Union Fire Insurance Society td* [1918] AC 350).

PERILS RELATED TO WAR RISKS

41.12 Issues may arise which are related to war risks, such as the situations dealt with in the following cases:

(a) Loss has occurred in the course of preparation for war (eg, in the training of troops or in the course of evacuation): It is unlikely that such losses can be regarded as proximately caused by war. Nevertheless, there were cases in the first quarter of the twentieth century in which it was held that the theft of vehicles to be used in bombing and other terrorist raids were losses proximately caused by civil war (in Ireland). For example, *Thomas Boggan v The Motor Union Insurance Co* (1923) 16 Ll L Rep 64, in which a domestic car was hijacked apparently for terrorist use, illustrates this line of authority.

(b) The loss inflicted is of an economic rather than a military nature, with the intention of undermining the economy of the state: This was the case in *National Oil Company of Zimbabwe* (see **41.06** above), in which an oil pipeline was destroyed by rebels for this very purpose. The High Court ruled that the loss was one caused by insurrection.

Other causation tests

41.13 The doctrine of proximate cause is often excluded in relation to war risks and is replaced by other forms of wording. Where a policy excludes war risks, it may exclude all direct and indirect consequences of war. In contrast, a war policy may require that a loss have been caused solely by a war or allied peril risk before cover is provided.

STRIKES

41.14 Cover against loss caused by strikes is frequently excluded from policies on commercial goods and such an exclusion is standard in marine and aviation policies. In the marine market, strikes insurance is nevertheless available. It is important to distinguish direct losses from the financial consequences of delay flowing from strikes. Whether the strikes wording incorporates losses caused by delay is a matter of construction of the wording in question, but the general presumption is that loss by delay is not proximately caused by a strike.

TERRORISM AND POLITICAL RISKS

Political risks exclusions

41.15 Marine and aviation policies commonly exclude loss caused by terrorists and persons acting from a political motive. There is no English case law on the meaning of these terms, and one question which remains to be decided is whether the phrase 'political motive' has to be assessed in accordance with the intention of the person causing the loss or whether its meaning is objective. Similar, and largely unresolved, problems have been encountered in extradition law (the general effect of which is to prevent the extradition of persons for crimes of a political nature) and in relation to parole (see *R (on the application of Botmeh) v Parole Board for England and Wales* [2008] EWHC 1115 (Admin)) in relation to the difficulty of establishing such a motive.

There are a number of UK statutory definitions of 'terrorism', but it can generally be regarded as the use of violence for the purpose of putting the public or a section of the public in fear.

Terrorism risks and commercial buildings

41.16 At the end of 1992, the insurance market determined, in the light of the St Mary Axe bomb in April 1992, to withdraw terrorism cover from commercial and industrial properties – a move forced upon insurers by an earlier decision of the reinsurance market to withdraw reinsurance cover for such risks. Following expressions of concern, both by the operators of commercial buildings and by institutional investors, the government agreed to provide the necessary reinsurance cover itself in order to allow insurance to be reinstated. The reinsurance scheme subsequently agreed between the market and the government was given the force of law by the Reinsurance (Acts of Terrorism) Act 1993. In light of the events of 11 September 2001, terrorism cover has been significantly restricted for domestic premises in the UK.

Under the 1993 Act, insurers continue to withdraw insurance cover in excess of £100,000 (£2.5 million in respect of blocks of flats) for terrorist risks. Those insurers wishing to participate in the scheme reinstate terrorism cover for sums in excess of this figure, at premiums based on commercial rates. Reinsurance is provided by Pool Re, a company formed for this specific purpose by participating insurers which participate as its members (ie, it is a mutual company). Pool Re is funded by premiums, by investments and, if necessary, by a levy on its members. Pool Re's risk is retroceded to the government in consideration for a premium, and on usual reinsurance terms. By acting as insurer of last resort, the government has ensured the continuation of terrorism cover. The scheme does not prevent insurers from seeking reinsurance on the open market. It will be seen that the scheme does not provide insurance cover against terrorism to all operators of commercial buildings, but rather only to those operators which are prepared to pay a commercial premium for such cover.

The scheme covers 'acts of terrorism' – a phrase defined as meaning 'acts of persons acting on behalf of, or in connection with, any organisation which carries out activities directed towards the overthrowing or influencing, by force or violence, of Her Majesty's Government in the United Kingdom or any other government *de jure* or *de facto*' (Reinsurance (Acts of Terrorism) Act 1993, s 2(3)). This definition makes it clear that the scheme applies only to organised terrorism rather than to isolated acts of vandalism. Subtly different definitions are often employed in domestic motor or buildings and contents insurance.

Part 6

Regulatory Matters

Chapter 42

Regulation of insurance companies

- Authorisation requirement
- Regulated activities
- Defining what constitutes a contract of insurance
- UK regulators
- Consequences of conducting unauthorised insurance business
- Legal and procedural requirements for authorisation by the PRA and FCA
- Ongoing supervision
- Financial Ombudsman Service
- Brexit

AUTHORISATION REQUIREMENT

42.01 Section 19 of the Financial Services and Markets Act 2000 (FSMA 2000) provides that no person may carry on (or purport to carry on) a regulated activity in the UK by way of business unless he is an authorised person or an exempt person (what is defined in the FSMA 2000 as the 'general prohibition').

Contravention of the general prohibition is a criminal offence which, in the most serious cases, can result in an unlimited fine and/or imprisonment for up to two years. It is also an offence under s 24 of the FSMA 2000, for a person to describe himself (in whatever terms) as an authorised or exempt person; or to behave or otherwise hold himself out in a manner indicating, or which is reasonably likely to be understood to indicate, that he is authorised or exempt when he is not.

Section 31 of the FSMA 2000 provides that the following categories of people are authorised persons:

(a) a person who has a Part 4A permission to carry on one or more regulated activities; and

(b) a person who is otherwise authorised by a provision of, or made under, the FSMA 2000.

Exempt persons include appointed representatives of authorised persons who can be appointed to perform certain specified activities (eg, insurance distribution), but only to the extent that the authorised person has agreed in writing to accept responsibility for the activities of that representative. Also exempt are those specified in an exemption order pursuant to s 38 of the FSMA 2000. The Financial Services and Markets Act 2000 (Exemption) Order 2001 (SI 2001/1201) (as amended) provides for various exemptions (eg, trade unions providing provident benefits or strike benefits are exempt from the general prohibition against effecting or carrying out contracts of insurance).

Section 418 of the FSMA 2000 (as amended) contains three scenarios where a person is 'deemed' to carry on an activity in the UK even if, on the ordinary meaning of the words, he might not be carrying on such activity in the UK. One such scenario is where a company has a head office outside the UK, but a regulated activity is carried on from an establishment maintained by it in the UK.

Section 21 of the FSMA 2000 also prevents a person from 'communicating an offer or inducement to engage in an activity specified as a controlled activity', unless he is authorised under the FSMA 2000 or the communication is approved by an authorised person. This restriction – the financial promotion restriction – effectively enables rules to be applied to the approval of marketing and other materials issued as part of the process of selling insurance contracts. The main requirement is that they be clear, fair and not misleading.

REGULATED ACTIVITIES

42.02 Section 22(1) of the FSMA 2000 provides that a 'regulated activity' is an 'activity of a specified kind' which is 'carried on by way of business' and relates to an investment of a specified kind.

The Financial Services and Markets Act 2000 (Regulated Activities) Order 2001 (SI 2001/544) (as amended) (RAO) sets out the 'regulated activities' and the 'investments' in relation to which authorisation is required. For an activity to be a 'regulated activity', it must be carried on in relation to one of the specified investments. 'Rights under a contract of insurance' constitute a specified investment.

Effecting contracts of insurance as principal and carrying out contracts of insurance as principal are two of the regulated activities prescribed by the RAO. Insurers may also carry on the Insurance Distribution Directive (EU) 2016/97) (IDD) activities of arranging or making arrangement with a view to the sale of an insurance contract which are regulated under art 25 of the RAO and described in more detail in **Chapter 43.**

DEFINING WHAT CONSTITUTES A 'CONTRACT OF INSURANCE'

42.03 There is no exhaustive statutory definition of what constitutes a 'contract of insurance' for the purposes of the RAO. Somewhat unhelpfully, the RAO defines a 'contract of insurance' as any contract of insurance which is a contract of long-term insurance or a contract of general insurance. As required by the Insurance Directives and then the Solvency II Directive, UK regulation of insurance extends to some types of contracts which would not be regarded as contracts of insurance, such as fidelity bonds, performance bonds, administration bonds, bail bonds, customs bonds and similar contracts of guarantee. The list of both long-term and general insurance contracts applicable for regulatory purposes therefore includes categories which would not constitute contracts of insurance. This can cause confusion in trying to define a contract of insurance.

Part I of Sch 1 of the RAO sets out descriptions of 18 classes of contracts of general insurance for regulatory purposes; and Part II of Sch 1 sets out brief descriptions of nine classes of contracts of long-term insurance for regulatory purposes.

The headings are:

(a) General insurance:
   - (i) accident;
   - (ii) sickness;
   - (iii) land vehicles;
   - (iv) railway rolling stock;
   - (v) aircraft;
   - (vi) ships;
   - (vii) goods in transit;
   - (viii) fire and natural forces;
   - (ix) damage to property;
   - (x) motor vehicle liability;
   - (xi) aircraft liability;
   - (xii) liability of ships;
   - (xiii) general liability;
   - (xiv) credit;
   - (xv) suretyship;
   - (xvi) miscellaneous financial;
   - (xvii) legal expenses; and
   - (xviii) assistance.

(b) Long-term insurance:
   - (i) life and annuity;
   - (ii) marriage and birth;
   - (iii) linked long term;
   - (iv) permanent health;
   - (v) tontines;
   - (vi) capital redemption;
   - (vii) pension fund management;
   - (viii) collective insurance etc; and
   - (ix) social insurance.

Some of the descriptions under the headings are broad, while others are very narrow.

It is therefore necessary to consider case law to assist in trying to define a contract of insurance (see **42.04** below).

As a consequence of the lack of a clear statutory definition, the Prudential Regulatory Authority (PRA) and the Financial Conduct Authority (FCA) have considerable discretion as to whether a particular business is to be challenged on the ground that it is conducting an unlawful insurance business. The FCA provides guidance in its handbook (Perimeter Guidance Manual (PERG) 6) on how it approaches the issue of whether a particular contract is or is not a contract of insurance – including, for example, in relation to extended warranties offered by retailers. This guidance is helpful; but ultimately, this is subject to the decision of the courts.

Characteristics of an insurance contract

42.04 While there have been some reported decisions of UK courts addressing the issue of what does or does not constitute a contract of insurance, these are based on the particular facts of the case; the courts have been careful not to define conclusively what is and what is not a contract of insurance.

The most widely quoted definition of an 'insurance contract' is that of Channell J in *Prudential Insurance Company v Commissioners of Inland Revenue* [1904] 2 KB 658. In that case, three elements were identified which, if present in a contract, are likely to cause it to be construed as an insurance contract:

(a) It is a contract under which, in return for the making of a payment or payments (generally called premiums), the insured secures some benefit on the occurrence of an event;

(b) That event must be uncertain as to whether it will happen or not; or if the event is inevitable, there must be uncertainty as to when it will happen; and

(c) The event must be adverse to the insured (though it is to be noted that cases since have drawn a distinction between indemnity and contingency insurance – for example, the event triggering endowment and annuity policies and certain other forms of contingency insurance may not be adverse).

In many cases, if a claim can properly be made under the policy, the benefit receivable by the insured will be a money payment. However, 'payment' can take the form of services to the insured or the repair or replacement of damaged items.

For instance, in *Department of Trade and Industry v St Christopher Motorists' Association Ltd* [1974] 1 All ER 395, the High Court held that payment in the form of services to the insured (in this case the provision of transport if a driver was disqualified from driving) should be characterised as an insurance contract.

While household insurance policies might offer repair or replacement services, not all contracts offering services in relation to goods are insurance contracts. Contracts under which the provider undertakes to provide periodic services (but not a repair and replace service or coverage of accidental damage) in relation to goods may not be insurance contracts. Similarly, warranties given by manufacturers or retailers in connection with the sale of goods are not generally regarded as insurance contracts; if they were, then most manufacturers and retailers would need to be authorised as insurance companies. The regulators draw a distinction between such manufacturing and retailers' warranties which, if limited in time and scope to those obligations usually associated with the relevant goods or services, can form part of the package being sold. Where, however, the warranty is provided by a third party or after the point of sale, it is much more likely to be regarded as a contract of insurance. The FCA, in PERG 6.7, argues that a warranty given by a seller which is of the same nature as a seller's usual obligations as regards the quality of goods or services of that kind is not a contract of insurance; but that if, for instance, an extended warranty has to be paid for or is provided by third parties, then that is likely to be insurance (*Re Digital Satellite Warranty Cover Ltd* [2011] EWHC 122 (Ch)).

There are exemptions for certain organisations which confer only benefits in kind which may otherwise be regarded as insurance – for example, art 12 of the RAO exempts contracts when the primary benefit is the provision of motor vehicle breakdown services generally by employees of the provider.

The courts have also held that a where, for example, a benefit which would otherwise be provided as part of an insurance contract is provided only on a discretionary basis, this is not a contract of insurance (*Medical Defence Union Ltd v The Department of Trade* [1979] 2 All ER 421). This case considered whether the Medical Defence Union (MDU), which indemnifies doctors against claims alleging professional negligence, was carrying on an insurance business. If the MDU was carrying on insurance business, its members would have had to contribute a substantial capital sum to enable it to meet the capitalisation requirements of the legislation governing insurance companies. It was held that the contracts issued by the MDU were not insurance contracts because the MDU had a discretion, but not an obligation, to provide benefits to a member (although in practice the discretion was always exercised).

CONSEQUENCES OF CONDUCTING UNAUTHORISED INSURANCE BUSINESS

42.05 An agreement made by a person in the course of carrying on a regulated activity in breach of the general prohibition will generally be unenforceable against the other party (FSMA 2000, s 26). The other party (ie, the insured) is entitled to recover any money paid or transferred by him under the agreement, with compensation for any loss sustained by him as a result.

A person who is authorised with a Part 4A permission who carries on a regulated activity outside the scope of his permission is not guilty of an offence and the transaction is not void or voidable (FSMA 2000, s 20(2)).

UK REGULATORS

42.06 Since 1 April 2013, there have been two insurance regulators for authorised insurance companies: the PRA and the FCA. The Financial Services and Markets Act 2000 (PRA-Regulated Activities) Order 2013 specifies that the regulated activities of 'effecting' and 'carrying out' a contract of insurance are PRA-regulated activities. IDD activities (eg, introductions, advice, sales and arranging insurance contracts) (see **Chapter 43**) are regulated by the FCA. It should also be noted that the Financial Policy Committee (FPC) is responsible for protecting the stability of the UK financial system as a whole (ie, at the macro level). The FPC is situated within the Bank of England and aims to identify risks which have the potential to cause instability to the UK financial system. It has oversight, through governance arrangements, of the PRA and FCA; and it makes recommendations and offers advice. Ultimately, it also has the power to intervene to ensure action is taken to guard against risks to financial stability.

Both of the financial services regulators share responsibility for supervising insurance and reinsurance companies, but each has a different remit (statutory objectives). It is the PRA's responsibility to ensure that insurance companies meet required solvency and risk management standards. The FCA has responsibility for the conduct of business.

For insurance companies (other than those with premiums of less than €5 million and reserves of less than €25 million), the majority of the prudential regulation is undertaken under the Solvency II Directive provisions, as implemented in the PRA rules, various statutory instruments and the UK on-shored version of the Solvency II Regulation. Both of the regulators regulate through a mixture of high-level principles (Fundamental Rules in the PRA's case and Principles for Business in the FCA's case), detailed rules and guidance. This is supplemented from time to time by public statements and letters to insurance companies. Both regulators are subject to an obligation to consult before they change their rules and consultation papers, and the policy statements that follow them are often a very useful form of guidance as to the purpose and meaning of the rules.

Given that insurance companies are dual regulated, there is obvious scope for overlap in that regulation. The areas of potential overlap for insurers include regulation of individuals carrying on significant roles within regulated entities. Although governance is primarily a prudential issue, the PRA and FCA share some responsibilities in this area. The Senior Manager & Certification (SM&CR) regime – which requires prior approval of certain senior personnel in key roles and certification (on an annual basis by the insurer) of other senior personnel – is shared, so that there are both PRA and FCA SM&CR rules. The PRA and FCA entered into a Memorandum of Understanding (April 2013) to set out how each will operate and cooperate with the other in furtherance of their statutory duty to coordinate the exercise of their functions. In addition, the FSMA 2000 provides for cross-membership of boards and a veto mechanism for the PRA to reduce the risk of regulatory actions threatening financial stability or the disorderly failure of an insurance company. The chief executive of the FCA also sits on the governing body of the PRA and vice versa.

LEGAL AND PROCEDURAL REQUIREMENTS FOR AUTHORISATION

42.07 When a business wishes to be authorised to conduct insurance business in the UK, it must submit an application to the PRA for Part 4A permission under the FSMA 2000. The PRA must receive the consent of the FCA to grant authorisation. Both regulators will consent to the authorisation only where the applicant has been able to demonstrate that it meets certain threshold conditions. The threshold conditions for each regulator are set out in Sch 6 of the FSMA 2000. Guidance is also provided by the FCA in the Threshold Conditions Sourcebook (COND). Under s 41(2) of the FSMA 2000, the PRA must, in granting a Part 4A permission, ensure that the applicant will satisfy, and continue to satisfy, the threshold conditions in relation to all of the regulated activities for which permission is sought.

For an insurer or reinsurer to be authorised in the UK, it must have its head office and registered office in the UK. Alternatively, a third-country branch may be established and authorised in the UK.

Each of the regulators has a set of rules which is available online and divided into different sections. The PRA has a rulebook for Solvency II firms and a rulebook for non-Solvency II firms. (Solvency II is the EU-derived framework that sets the amount of capital insurers must hold as well as the risk management framework they must follow.) The FCA has a handbook of rules and guidance. Not all of the rules in the FCA Handbook apply to insurance companies, so it is important to consider the application of each rule to the set of circumstances being considered. The FCA rules cover different administrative and conduct obligations, including the insurance conduct of business rules; the code of conduct for staff in regulated firms; rules on how client money must be handled; and rules on dispute resolution (among many other areas). The FCA rules cover requirements for insurance distribution – as required by the UK version of the IDD as implemented in the UK (see **Chapter 43**).

The FCA's PERG provides guidance on where the perimeter of regulation is considered to lie. This is important guidance, as it sets out the regulator's views on what will and what will not be considered to be a regulated activity; but as stated above, it should be remembered that the court is the final arbiter on this point.

The PRA has six months to make its determination as to whether to authorise an applicant following submission of a completed application pack, although this may vary depending on the complexity of the application. The PRA will wish to discuss applications to authorise new insurance companies prior to their formal submission as applications.

The FSMA 2000 confers broad powers on the regulators to determine the procedure for applications and details relating to the granting of permissions. The PRA, on granting the permission, specifies the permitted regulated activity or activities, but may describe them in such manner as it thinks appropriate (FSMA 2000, s 55F). The permission granted will consist of three elements:

(a) a description of the activities, including any limitations;

(b) the specified investments involved; and

(c) any requirement to be imposed pursuant to s 55L or 55M of the FSMA 2000.

ONGOING SUPERVISION

42.08 Both the PRA and the FCA have ongoing responsibility for the supervision of insurance and reinsurance companies. The remit of supervision is limited by statutory objectives. The PRA has a general objective, which is to promote the safety and soundness of PRA-authorised firms. It also has an insurance objective, which is to contribute to securing an appropriate degree of protection to those who are, or may become, policyholders.

The PRA takes a forward-looking approach to supervision and undertakes stress tests in the insurance sector to identify potential harms to policyholders or the wider economy. The FCA's strategic objective is for the relevant markets to function well. To achieve this, the FCA has operational objectives of consumer protection, market integrity and competition. It is with these objectives in mind that it supervises insurance companies. The FCA undertakes thematic reviews into areas of concern in a market and publishes its findings. Depending on what harms are identified, it may then introduce changes in policy.

High-level 'Principles'

42.09 The PRA has eight fundamental rules that insurance and reinsurance companies must comply with. These require a PRA-authorised firm to:

(a) conduct its business with integrity;

(b) conduct its business with due skill, care and diligence;

(c) act in a prudent manner;

(d) at all times maintain adequate financial resources;

(e) have effective risk strategies and risk management systems;

(f) organise and control its affairs responsibly and effectively;

(g) deal with its regulators in an open and cooperative way, and disclose appropriately to the PRA anything relating to the firm of which the PRA would reasonably expect notice; and

(h) prepare for resolution so that, if the need arises, it can be resolved in an orderly manner with a minimum disruption of critical services.

The FCA has 11 Principles for Businesses. These require that an authorised firm:

(a) conduct its business with integrity;

(b) conduct its business with due skill, care and diligence;

(c) take reasonable care to organise and control its affairs responsibly and effectively with adequate risk management systems (the Senior

Management Arrangements, Systems and Controls section of the FCA Handbook sets out more guidance in relation to this);

(d) maintain adequate financial resources;

(e) show proper standards of market conduct;

(f) pay due regard to the interests of its customers and treat them fairly;

(g) pay due regard to the information needs of its customers and communicate in a way which is clear, fair and not misleading;

(h) manage conflicts of interest fairly;

(j) take reasonable care to ensure the suitability of its advice and discretionary decisions for any customer who is entitled to rely upon its judgement;

(k) arrange adequate protection for clients' assets when it is responsible for them; and

(l) deal with its regulators in an open and cooperative way, and disclose to the FCA appropriately anything relating to the organisation of which the FSA would reasonably expect notice.

Regulatory rules

42.10 The PRA's Rules for Solvency II firms and the on-shored UK Solvency II Regulation implement the main governance requirements applicable to insurers. In addition, the Supervision Manual of the FCA Handbook contains additional guidance on governance for insurers (eg, in relation to outsourcing). The regulators' rules and guidance cover areas including the use of auditors and actuaries; the use of appointed representatives; transfers of insurance business; the waiver and modification of rules; and the notification of changes in control of a company.

Senior Manager & Certification

42.11 Both regulators also include requirements for individuals in specified senior management roles (controlled functions) to be approved as 'fit and proper' for their position (as required by s 59ZA of the FSMA 2000). Broadly, a 'senior management function' (SMF) is a function that carries responsibility for managing (or taking or participating in decisions concerning) an aspect of a firm's affairs that involves, or might involve, a risk of serious consequences for the firm, or for business or other interests in the UK. Senior managers do not have to be in the UK.

Both the FCA and the PRA require that individuals in SMFs within the business be approved by the relevant regulator before taking up their post (each regulator specifies the roles for which approval must be sought). SMFs are subject to a duty of responsibility and should have a statement of responsibilities document so that it is clear what aspects of the business they are responsible for. SMFs are given certain prescribed responsibilities which ensure that individuals take ownership of aspects of the firm's governance.

Each of the two regulators determines which senior management functions within a business require approval. For example, the PRA designates the chief executive (SMF1), chief risk officer (SMF4) and chief finance officer (SMF2) roles as functions that require approval from the PRA; as well as a number of oversight functions, such as chair (SMF9) and the chairs of the risk committee (SMF10), the audit committee (SMF11) and the remuneration committee (SMF12).

The FCA designates executive directors (SMF3) as SMFs, in addition to other roles within the business, such as the money laundering reporting officer (SMF17), chair of the with-profits committee (SMF15) and the compliance oversight function (SMF16).

Other individuals, who are UK employees of the firm, who are not SMFs but who might cause harm to the firm or its customers or who are material risk takers, must be certified annually as fit and proper to perform their job. These people are in 'certified functions'.

All staff – excluding certain ancillary roles, such as catering and security staff, and receptionists – will be subject to the Individual Conduct Rules. SMFs will be subject to both the Individual Conduct Rules and the Senior Manager Conduct Rules.

Enforcement

42.12 Both regulators are given powers under the FSMA 2000 to take enforcement action against firms or individuals where this is necessary to advance their objectives. Among the powers granted to the regulators are the ability to withdraw authorisation; ban individuals from working in financial services; apply to court to freeze assets; secure the return of money to customers; issue financial penalties against firms or individuals; prosecute firms and individuals who undertake regulated activities without authorisation; and issue statements of public censure.

The FCA's position on enforcement is outlined in the Decision Procedure and Penalties Manual of the FCA's Handbook (DEPP). The FCA will consider all relevant facts and circumstances when deciding whether to take action against a person for a financial penalty under the relevant sections of the FSMA 2000 (and/or other appropriate enforcement action). Under s 206 of the FSMA 2000, the FCA may impose a penalty of such amount as it considers appropriate. The FCA's approach is set out in DEPP 6.5 and is based on a five-step framework. The steps are as follows:

(a) Step 1: Disgorgement (ie, the aim is to deprive the firm of any financial benefit of the breach);

(b) Step 2: Proportionate action (ie, to reflect the nature, impact and seriousness of the breach);

(c) Step 3: Adjustment for mitigating factors;

(d) Step 4: Adjustment for deterrence; and

(e) Step 5: Discount for settled cases.

The FCA must give the firm a warning notice that it proposes to impose a fine or make a public statement setting out the fine and/or the statement as appropriate. If the FCA decides to go ahead with the planned action, it must issue a decision notice. The authorised firm may then appeal the decision by referring it to the Upper Tribunal (Tax and Chancery).

FINANCIAL OMBUDSMAN SERVICE

42.13 The Financial Ombudsman Service (FOS) is the informal dispute resolution mechanism established under the FSMA 2000, which is free to use by those claiming against an insurer.

UK authorised insurers are subject to the compulsory jurisdiction of the FOS, which applies to the regulated activities of FSMA authorised persons (including third-country branches of overseas insurers in relation to the activities of the branch). There is also a voluntary jurisdiction, which is effectively a contractual arrangement by which a person – the voluntary jurisdiction participant – agrees that the scheme will apply. The voluntary jurisdiction can only extend to activities which, although not regulated activities, could be regulated activities.

The FOS is not required to decide cases on ordinary legal principles and may impose a result that it considers fair and reasonable in all the circumstances. It was confirmed in *Heather Moor & Edgecomb Ltd v UK* (2011) 53 EHRR SE18 that deciding cases on this ground, rather than in accordance with the law and without necessarily involving an actual hearing, is consistent with the European Convention on Human Rights.

Complainants are usually consumers who have purchased policies. However, the following are also eligible complainants under the FCA's Dispute Resolution Sourcebook (2.7.6):

> '(5) the complainant is a person for whose benefit a contract of insurance was taken out or was intended to be taken out with or through the respondent;
>
> (6) the complainant is a person on whom the legal right to benefit from a claim against the respondent under a contract of insurance has been devolved by contract, assignment, subrogation or legislation (save the European Community (Rights against Insurers) Regulations 2002)…'

Eligible complainants are:

(a) consumers;

(b) small businesses that employ fewer than 50 people and have a turnover that does not exceed £6.5 million and an annual balance sheet amount that does not exceed £5 million at the time the complaint is made to the firm;

(c) charities with an income of less than £6.5 million; and

(d) trusts with assets of less than £5 million

Amount of compensation

42.14 The amount of compensation available is subject to a maximum as follows:

(a) £355,000 for complaints referred to the FOS on or after 1 April 2020 (relating to acts or omissions by firms on or after 1 April 2019);

(b) £350,000 for complaints referred to the FOS between 1 April 2019 and 31 March 2020 (relating to acts or omissions by firms on or after 1 April 2019);

(c) £160,000 for complaints relating to acts or omissions by firms before 1 April 2019, and which are referred to the FOS after that date; and

(d) £150,000 for complaints referred to the FOS before 1 April 2019.

The FOS can also award interest on top of the maximum award limit. It has now been established that if a claimant accepts a determination of the FOS, it cannot then litigate the same complaint (*Clark v In Focus Asset Management & Tax Solutions Ltd* [2014] EWCA civ 118). If a claimant is not happy with the redress awarded, it can reject the FOS award and will then be free to litigate. It should also be noted that while the amount of redress awarded may be limited, firms can – and in practice, do – accept recommendations to pay higher amounts. Generally, as befits an informal dispute resolution procedure, the FOS does not award costs against the losing party (the complainant does not have to pay at all, as any case fee is borne by the insurer). It is, however, possible that an award of costs could be made.

The law of non-disclosure and misrepresentation following the Consumer Insurance (Disclosure and Representations) Act 2012 and the Insurance Act is now much closer to the historic practice of the FOS in relation to claims made on that basis. The FOS also now publishes its cases in a way which is organised around particular issues and is easier to search. The main advantage for policyholders that are eligible to use the FOS is that the service is free to use and is not binding on them.

BREXIT

42.15 The UK has now left the European Union and the transition period (also known as the 'implementation period') drew to a close on 31 December 2020. The free trade agreement entered into between the UK and the European Union did not expressly cover financial services (albeit that some general provisions may have some relevance). Consequently, for insurers and insurance distributors that previously used the passport under the EU single market directives, this right is no longer available to them. This means that UK insurers are no longer authorised in European Economic Area (EEA) states and, other than as set out below, EEA insurers are no longer authorised in the UK.

The UK has put in place a Temporary Permissions Regime (TRP) for those firms that applied or notified the appropriate regulator before the required date. This effectively treats the EEA firm as authorised for its pre-Brexit passporting activities and allows it to continue that business. In due course, such firms are expected to be authorised as UK third-country branches. The temporary Part 4A permission should last for a maximum of three years. While in the TPR, EEA firms will be subject to specified rules of the UK regulators. Transitional relief also applies in relation to certain aspects of the rules.

For firms that do not wish to move towards UK authorisation, the UK has also created a Financial Services Contracts Regime (FSCR) which allows pre-Brexit business to be run off without entering the TPR or applying for full authorisation of a UK branch. Entities which passported into the UK on a freedom of establishment basis (and those that leave the TPR after the end of the transitional period without a UK authorisation) are subject to a form of deemed authorisation, 'supervised run-off', which will make them subject to a certain amount of UK regulation. For entities which passported on a freedom of services basis, the FSCR, in the form of the Contractual Run-Off Regime, provides an exemption from the requirement for authorisation in relation to regulated activities required to run off pre-Brexit policies (ie, from the end of the transition period). The FSCR applies for a period of 15 years.

Various conditions apply to the continuation of the FSCR regime, including retaining home state authorisation.

Chapter 43

Regulation of sales of insurance products

- Regulation of insurance intermediaries
- What insurance mediation activities are regulated?
- Authorisation and ongoing supervision
- Insurance: Conduct of Business Sourcebook
- Further provisions of the FCA Handbook

REGULATION OF INSURANCE INTERMEDIARIES

43.01 The sale of insurance contracts in the UK is regulated by the Financial Conduct Authority (FCA). The FCA is responsible for the authorisation and supervision of firms involved in the sale of insurance products – namely insurance companies that sell directly to their customers, insurance intermediaries (including price comparison websites), companies with delegated authority and insurance brokers. Policies sold to consumers have many more restrictions applied than do sales to commercial customers. The regulatory regime applicable to the sale of non-investment insurance contracts is less onerous than that which applies to those involved in the sale of qualifying contracts of insurance (see **43.07** below for definition). See **42.03** for a description of the classification of contracts of general insurance and contracts of long-term insurance.

Many of the rules that are applied to the sale of insurance policies derive from EU legislation now implemented into UK law. The main EU-derived laws relevant to the sale of insurance policies are the Insurance Distribution Directive ((EU) 2016/97) (IDD); the Distance Marketing Directive (2002/65/EC); and the E-commerce Directive (2000/31/EC). The UK's approach to implementing the IDD and its predecessor (the Insurance Mediation Directive, which came into effect in 2005) was through domestic legislation – in part, through secondary legislation amending the Financial Services and Markets Acts 2000 (Regulated Activities) Order 2001 (SI 2001/544) (RAO), which describes the activities that are regulated and through conduct of business rules of what is now the FCA.

The Insurance Distribution Directive

43.02 The IDD amended and repealed the Insurance Mediation Directive. The aim of the IDD was to provide common minimum standards for the regulation of insurance intermediaries and to create a single market for sales of insurance policies within the EU. In the IDD, insurance mediation activities are referred to as 'insurance distribution' and both insurance intermediaries and insurers can be insurance distributors.

The main requirements of the IDD are as follows:

(a) All distributors of reinsurance or insurance policies should be registered with a competent authority. This means that anyone in the UK that undertakes an insurance distribution activity must be authorised to do so by the FCA and appear on the UK Financial Services Register.

(b) Insurance or reinsurance companies that sell directly to their customers as well as price comparison websites must be registered.

(c) An insurance distributor (but not reinsurance distributor) should act 'honestly, fairly and professionally in accordance with the best interests of its customers'. This requirement imposes a high standard upon all distributors (including direct sellers and those distributing to professional customers) to consider the interests of customers in their business.

(d) Anyone distributing insurance or reinsurance policies must have appropriate knowledge and competence to do so.

(e) Anyone distributing insurance or reinsurance policies should be of good repute.

(f) Distributors must have professional indemnity insurance of at least €1.25 million applying to any one claim and €1.85 million in aggregate.

(g) Insurance intermediaries must disclose certain pre-contractual information to the policyholder before the contract is concluded. This includes the intermediary's identity and address, whether it provides advice about the product being sold and how a customer can register a complaint.

(h) Intermediaries must provide the customer with information that helps them to determine whether the intermediary is independent and how it is being paid for the services it provides to the customer.

(i) Before the contract is concluded with the customer, the intermediary must, on the basis of information provided to it, identify the demands and needs of the customer and provide objective information about the product. For sales to consumers, an insurance product information document (IPID) must be provided that shows clearly what the product does and does not cover. Life products which are pure protection contracts are sold with a different document, called a policy summary; and life investment products which are packaged retail investments are sold with a key information document.

(j) Where the intermediary provides advice to the customer on a whole of market (eg, unrestricted) basis, it must provide a personalised recommendation to him based on a fair analysis of the market.

(k) When a non-insurance product is sold alongside an insurance product as part of a package, the distributor must inform the customer whether the insurance product can be bought separately and give details (eg, costs and charges) for each component of the package. Such a product can be mandatory. Where it is not, an active election to take out the non-insurance product should be obtained.

(l) When an insurance product is sold alongside another product and is not the primary product, it should not be mandatory (eg, the customer must be given the option to buy the items separately and an active election to take out the insurance product should be obtained). Certain exemptions apply to this requirement (eg, for certain packaged bank accounts).

(m) Insurance companies or intermediaries that design and distribute insurance products must have in place governance arrangements that enable the company to identify a target market for the product and monitor whether or not that product continues to remain suitable for the target market over the lifetime of the product.

WHAT INSURANCE INTERMEDIATION ACTIVITIES ARE REGULATED?

43.03 Insurance distribution activities (contained in the RAO), if carried on by way of business in the UK, will require authorisation from the FCA unless the person conducting such activities is an appointed representative (see **43.06**) or falls within an exclusion. The relevant activities are as follows:

(a) Making arrangements for the purchase of contracts of insurance, whether in respect of a specific policy (RAO, art 25(1)) or more general distribution arrangements for insurance policies (RAO, art 25(2)): This covers a range of activities, including negotiating the terms of the contract on behalf of the insured or insurer; or helping a customer to fill in an application form and sending the form to the insurer. Importantly, art 25(1) requires that the arrangement being undertaken have the direct effect of bringing about a contract of insurance. Essentially, it is a 'but for' test. In contrast, art 25(2) covers those actions undertaken to bring about a contract of insurance – it is not necessary that this is in fact the result (the intention is key). This activity will extend to any arrangements of an ongoing nature whose aim is to facilitate parties entering into transactions.

Note that an exclusion in art 33B of the RAO excludes from the scope of regulation for simple introductions and the mere provision of information about the policyholder to the intermediary or insurer. This is unlikely to extend beyond basic contact information such as name, address and contact details.

(b) Advising a person on a contract of insurance: This includes recommending a specific insurance policy to a customer.

(c) Dealing in contracts of insurance as an agent: This includes entering into a contract of insurance with a customer on behalf of an insurer or an insured. This will include situations where an intermediary has the authority to bind a principal (either the insured or an insurer), even if the power is restricted within parameters.

(d) Assisting in the administration and performance of a contract of insurance: This includes activities post-contract – for example, notifying an insurance claim to the insurer and negotiating settlement of the claim on behalf of the customer.

Agreeing to carry on such activities is also regulated.

Claims management on behalf of a UK authorised insurer or any reinsurer is not a regulated activity, but negotiating and settling claims on behalf of an overseas insurer or reinsurer is likely to necessitate that the insurer or reinsurer be authorised in the UK. Simply providing information to a claimant or insurer in connection with the assessment of a claim is also not a regulated activity. Expert appraisal and loss adjusting (insofar as loss adjusting is carried out on behalf of an UK authorised insurer or any reinsurer) are not regarded as activities which require regulation insofar as they amount to assisting in the administration and performance of a contract of insurance.

By way of business

43.04 The insurance mediation activity must be carried on by way of business for it to be subject to regulation. Activities carried on otherwise than for remuneration cannot be 'by way of business'. For example, an employer that offers a health insurance package to its employees but does not receive a commission or any other commercial benefit as a result of this activity will not generally be carrying on insurance mediation by way of business. However, the remuneration test for this purpose is to be construed widely. 'Remuneration' covers monetary and non-monetary payments and does not have to be provided separately from remuneration for other services. For example, an intermediary may not be paid to sell insurance to its customers, but still needs to consider whether it is carrying on regulated activities by way of business, since its business may still be receiving a financial benefit from selling the insurance.

Exclusions

43.05 If a person is carrying on a regulated activity as set out above, there are some exclusions which may be applicable. For example, four important exclusions are as follows:

(a) 'Connected contracts of insurance' (RAO, art 72B): This exclusion is relevant to retailers of goods (other than motor vehicles) or travel agents selling insurance policies or helping customers make claims under them. Retailers and travel agents can benefit from this exclusion where their activities are limited to general insurance policies relating to non-motor goods ('connected contracts of insurance') which:

   (i) have an annual premium of €600 or less or, where the insurance is complementary to a service being provided by the provider whose duration is less than three months, €200 or less;

   (ii) cover the risk of breakdown, loss of, or damage to the goods supplied by the retailer; or, in the case of travel, cover the risk of damage to, or loss of baggage and other risks limited to events management (for customers who are not individuals or small businesses) or vehicle hire (without accommodation);

(iii) cover the non-use of services (eg, the cancellation of a ticket);

(iv) do not cover liability risks (ie, liability of the insured to third parties) except, in the case of travel risks, where this cover is ancillary to the main cover provided by the contract; and,

(v) are complementary to the non-motor goods or the services supplied by the retailer.

This exclusion allows an authorised person to distribute insurance products through an unauthorised person (Insurance Conduct of Business Sourcebook (ICOBS) 2.6).

The relevant authorised person (eg, the insurer) must, however, also ensure that the unauthorised person complies with many of the IDD requirements relating to insurance distribution (eg, as a matter of contract rather than as a regulated entity).

(b) Provision of information on an incidental basis (RAO, s 72C): This exclusion is available (in relation to the activities of arranging and assisting in the administration and performance of a contract), as long as the provision of information is in relation to a contract of insurance and is incidental to the profession or business carried on by the information provider, whose business does not otherwise carry on any regulated activities. For example, a dentist would be able to rely on this exclusion to provide information about specific kinds of dental insurance to his customers or give his customers the details of providers of dental insurance without needing to become authorised. However, this exclusion would not be applicable if the person does more than introduce the customers to insurers or brokers – for example, by providing advice in the form of a recommendation to buy a specific policy or filling out an application form on behalf of a customer.

(c) Large risks (RAO, art 72D): Distribution activities in relation to certain classes of general insurance business (so-called 'large risks'), which includes cover for trains, aircraft and ships and financial loss insurance for larger insureds, are exempt, provided that the risk or commitment covered by the contract is not situated in the UK.

(d) The provision of limited information (RAO, art 33B): The art 33B exclusion exists to regulate activities under either art 25(1) or 25(2) (arranging deals in contracts of insurance) where the activity consists of the 'mere' provision of limited information about a policyholder to the insurer or information about the insurer to the policyholder. This will exclude basic introductory information from the scope of regulation. The exclusion can only be relied upon where the provider of the information takes no other step to assist the conclusion of the contract. Article 33B requires that the information be limited to information about a potential policyholder and does not extend to information about the risk. This will mean that the scope is limited to names, addresses, emails and so on, and information that is gathered as part of the day-to-day business of the person making the introduction.

Appointed representatives

43.06 A person who is carrying on insurance distribution activities can avoid the need to become regulated by the FCA (ie, is exempt from regulation) if he can persuade one or more authorised insurers or insurance intermediaries to appoint him as their appointed representative. Appointed representatives are not directly regulated by the FCA; instead, the person appointing them takes regulatory responsibility as principal for their activities. A written contract must be in place, as any principal must accept responsibility in writing for the activities of the appointed representative (the required terms of which are set out in the FCA Handbook in Supervision Manual 12.5).

AUTHORISATION AND ONGOING SUPERVISION

43.07

Overview

In the UK, insurance intermediaries are only subject to supervision by the FCA and are not dual-regulated firms.

To be authorised under Part 4A of the Financial Services and Markets Act (FSMA 2000), intermediaries must submit an application to the FCA. The FCA will determine whether or not the applicant meets the 'Threshold Conditions' for authorisation. The Threshold Conditions are set out by the FCA in Sch 6 of the FSMA 2000. Guidance is also provided by the FCA in the Threshold Conditions Sourcebook. Many of the provisions and regulatory powers referred to in **42.06** and **42.07** in the context of insurance companies are also relevant to insurance intermediaries that become authorised by the FCA.

Insurance intermediaries will be subject to the FCA Principles for Business (see **42.09**) and many of the rules contained in the FCA Handbook, including those relating to the prior approval by the FCA of those carrying on 'senior management functions' and the need for the intermediary to assess and certify individuals carrying on 'certified functions ' (see **42.11**). The FCA Handbook applies a different set of conduct requirements to insurance distribution activities depending upon the nature of the contract. Essentially, general insurance business and pure protection contracts are sold under simpler rules than life insurance policies with an investment element.

For regulatory purposes life insurance business is broadly divided between investment (known as 'qualifying insurance') contracts and non-investment (known as 'pure protection') contracts. A qualifying insurance contract is a long-term contract which is neither a pure protection contract nor a reinsurance contract. A pure protection contract is one which only provides insurance cover in the event of death or incapacity due to illness, sickness or infirmity, with any surrender value capped at the amount of premiums paid.

Different conduct of business rules apply to each such category. For investment business which also includes long-term care insurance contacts and annuity contracts, the FCA's Conduct of Business Sourcebook (COBS) applies; whereas for non-investment business (unless the firm elects to use COBS), ICOBS applies. In this chapter, only ICOBS rules are considered.

All authorised intermediaries must hold a minimum level of capital and professional indemnity insurance (see **43.19**). They are also subject to rules relating to the identification and management of client money and client mandates in the FCA Client Assets Sourcebook (CASS (see **43.18**)).

Insurance: Conduct of Business Sourcebook

43.08 The ICOBS rules apply to:

(a) insurance intermediaries carrying on insurance distribution activities in relation to non-investment insurance contracts;

(b) insurers when selling directly in relation to non-investment insurance contracts;

(c) firms which manage the underwriting capacity of a Lloyd's syndicate as a managing agent at Lloyd's in relation to a non-investment insurance contract; and

(d) firms which communicate or approve a non-investment financial promotion.

ICOBS rules do not apply to reinsurance contracts or transactions involving large risks where the risk is located outside the UK. The rules applicable to the sale to commercial customers of contract covering large risks located in the UK are also limited (eg, the customer's best interests rule and rules on cross-selling). There are exemptions from many of the rules for authorised professional firms and for service companies.

Different rules apply depending on whether the firm is dealing with a consumer (a policyholder acting outside his business or profession) or a commercial customer. All chapters are relevant where a firm deals with a consumer. The rules are less stringent in relation to dealings with a commercial customer. If it is not clear whether a person is a consumer or not, he must be treated as a consumer.

In part, ICOBS implements provisions contained in a number of EU Directives: the IDD (in respect of non-investment insurance contracts); the Distance Marketing Directive (in respect of non-investment insurance contracts and distance non-investment mediation contracts); and Solvency II (in respect of cancellation rights and information requirements).

It should be noted that even where firms are not subject to ICOBS, they are still subject to the FCA Principles of Business, which include the requirement to treat customers fairly (see **42.09**).

General rules

43.09 ICOBS 2 sets out rules relating to communication, unfair inducements and record keeping. Any communication with customers must be clear, fair and not misleading. ICOBS 2 includes requirements for the communication and approval of financial promotions – for example, product brochures, advertising by email, in magazines, websites or television. There are certain exemptions; but any firm needs to show that it has taken reasonable steps to ensure that every promotion is clear, fair and not misleading.

The rules on inducements provide that a firm should not offer or accept an inducement if it is likely to conflict with a duty that it, or the recipient firm, owes to its customers. An 'inducement' is a benefit offered to a firm, or any person acting on its behalf, with a view to that firm or person adopting a particular course of action. This can include, but is not limited to, cash, cash equivalents, commission, goods, hospitality or training programmes.

The IDD introduced a requirement, contained in ICOBS 2.5, to act honestly, fairly and professionally in the best interests of its customer. This is known as the 'customer's best interests' rule and will apply to all aspects of the insurance distribution chain, including the design of products, how intermediaries are remunerated and the terms of the policy. Unlike many other provisions in ICOBS, this rule also applies to intermediaries that do not deal directly with the customer.

Distance communications

43.10 ICOBS 3 contains rules on distance marketing and communications and online sales. Intermediaries and insurers selling directly must provide consumers with certain information in good time before the conclusion of a distance contract (in other words, a sale without simultaneous physical presence). Additional rules (in ICOBS 6) set out the responsibility of insurance companies and intermediaries to produce and provide this information. The information must be provided in a clear and comprehensible manner. When a customer is telephoned by a firm, the identity of the firm and the purpose of the call must be made clear.

The firm must communicate all the contractual terms and conditions of the contract as well as the information required by the distance contract rules to the customer in good time before the conclusion of the contract. Abbreviated distance communications rules apply to telephone sales, although the full information must still be provided to the customer after the conclusion of the contract.

Distance marketing information includes the name and main business address of the firm; the name and address of any representative office in the UK; a statement of regulatory status disclosure; a description of the services to be provided; the price to be paid; and information on how to cancel the contract and how to make a complaint.

A firm must not seek to enforce any obligations under a distance contract against a consumer in the event of an unsolicited supply of services, the absence of reply not constituting consent. ICOBS 3.1.12 does, however, provide an exception for successive operations.

Disclosures

43.11 ICOBS 4 covers various disclosures to customers. For a firm to comply with the general requirements to act in the customer's best interests, it needs to consider what information customers will need in order to make an informed decision about the products that they are looking to buy.

A firm must provide a customer with its address and identity, and disclose whether or not it will provide a personal recommendation to the customer. Insurance intermediaries must explain to the customer that they appear on the Financial Services Register. They must also disclose whether or not they have a 10 per cent or greater direct or indirect voting or capital holding in any insurance company or whether any insurance company (or its parent) has such a holding in the intermediary. The intermediary must also explain whether it acts as agent for the insurance company or for the insured. Intermediaries must explain whether or not, if they are providing a personal recommendation, that recommendation is given on the basis of a fair analysis of the market; and whether they are under an obligation to conduct distribution exclusively with one or more insurance companies.

The format of communications is considered in ICOBS 4. The FCA limits the means of communication to paper, other durable media other than paper (eg, PDFs) and websites. Information must be delivered in a clear and accurate manner, and must be in one of the official languages of the UK (where the risk is located within the UK).

Additional measures are imposed on the sale of pure protection policies and payment protection insurance. Where a firm is not responsible for making a personal recommendation about the suitability of the pure protection or payment protection product, it must take reasonable steps to ensure that customers understand that they are responsible for deciding whether the product will meet their demands and needs.

When the IDD came into effect on 1 October 2018, it introduced enhanced requirements for the disclosure by intermediaries of remuneration. Accordingly, intermediaries must disclose to the customer the nature and basis of the remuneration they receive for distributing the policy. They must disclose whether the customer must pay a fee or whether they receive commission included in the premium. This will require the intermediary to disclose whether it receives any other form of benefit in kind for distributing the product. Insurance companies that sell directly must disclose the nature of any remuneration paid to staff in relation to the sale. This may include remuneration paid by another party in the distribution chain or in the form of bonuses aligned to sales targets.

Where a commercial customer asks how much commission is being paid in relation to the contract it is buying, intermediaries must disclose the amount in cash terms where possible. If the intermediary is unable to disclose the amount, it must at least disclose the means by which the amount can be calculated.

The rules on the disclosure of remuneration are additional to the fiduciary duties that agents owe to their principal. These include the obligation not to make a secret profit. They are also in addition to the need to treat the customer fairly.

There are additional rules for the sale of pure protection products sold alongside retail investment products.

Appropriateness and suitability

43.12 ICOBS 5 contains rules concerning the suitability for customers in line with their demands and needs. Guidance in the chapter reinforces the FCA's Principle 6 (a firm must pay due regard to the interests of its customers and treat them fairly), in that firms should take reasonable steps to ensure that customers only buy policies under which they are able to make a claim. In the case of payment protection policies, firms are obliged to ensure that customers only buy policies under which they are eligible to claim.

Where insurance is offered as part of a packaged bank account, the firm must ensure that the customer can claim each of the benefits under each policy offered in the package. This will require the firm to check whether the customer meets the qualifying requirements for making a claim. The customer must receive an eligibility statement each year, recommending that the customer review the suitability of the product.

Before the conclusion of any contract, distributors must specify, on the basis of information that they have obtained from the customer, what the demands and needs of the customer are. A statement of demands and needs must be communicated to the customer prior to the conclusion of the contract. When proposing a policy, the firm must ensure that it is consistent with the customer's demands and needs.

When an insurance policy is sold with advice, the firm must take reasonable care to ensure that the advice is suitable. Where an intermediary informs the customer that it gives advice on the basis of a fair analysis, it must give that advice on the basis of analysis of a sufficiently large number of insurance policies available on the market.

The FCA has, over a number of years since 2014, been reviewing a number of issues in relation to value in the insurance industry and in particular the pricing of products offered to consumers. This has resulted in a number of obligations (eg, product governance requirements) designed to ensure that customers are treated fairly. At the time of writing, the FCA has introduced an obligation for certain products for firms to provide data known as insurance value measures. It also intends to make further changes to its rules relevant to pricing of home and motor insurance contracts.

Product information

43.13 ICOBS 6 concerns product information. This will include all the documents that must be given to the customer before the conclusion of the contract. Firms are obliged to provide customers with appropriate information before and after the conclusion of the contract, when there are mid-term changes and at renewal. The level of information provided must take into account the complexity of the policy and the type of customer.

When the IDD came into effect a new document – the IPID – became mandatory for all sales to consumers. The IPID is highly standardised and fits a template that is pre-designed in terms of the format, font size and symbols used. It is produced by the 'manufacturer' (ie, an insurance company or intermediary that designs the terms, conditions and pricing) of the product. The IPID provides appropriate information, but there is likely to be information that needs to be provided in addition to the IPID.

Insurance companies are responsible for producing, and intermediaries for providing to the customer, information about the insurance product. Where an insurance company sells directly to customers, it must both produce the relevant information and provide it to the customer.

The firm must provide the customer with details of the law applicable to the contract, as well as the arrangements for handling policyholder complaints. It must also provide consumers with information about the right to cancel the policy. For protection products, price information must be provided in a way that helps the customer to relate the price to a regular budget. Price information should include at least the total premium.

Rules determine the information that must be provided at policy renewals. This will include the amount of premium; the impact of mid-term changes; a reminder to shop around after the fourth renewal; and a statement that the customer should check to see whether the policy remains appropriate.

ICOBS 6 also contains product-specific rules on guaranteed asset protection products, optional additional products, cross-selling and travel insurance and medical conditions. These mean that an active election is required where add-on products are offered with insurance and where insurance is an add-on to a non-insurance product. Firms offering travel insurance to consumers must also now include a signpost of the details of a medical cover firm directory that may be able to help where the consumer has been unable to obtain cover or where the cover is too expensive.

Cancellation

43.14 ICOBS 7 sets out prescribed periods of cancellation for different types of contracts – generally 30 days for pure protection contracts and 14 days for general insurance contracts subject to stated exceptions (eg, travel insurance for 30 days or less).

Specified information must be disclosed to the customer relating to how to cancel, any conditions and the duration of the cancellation period. If the customer requested coverage to commence before the cancellation period ends, then the insurer can generally retain a proportionate part of the premium and certain related expenses (eg, in relation to setting up the contract and payments to intermediaries).

Claims handling

43.15 Rules (in ICOBS 8) relating to claims handling require fair and prompt handling of claims by insurers. Insurers must not unreasonably reject a claim and must settle claims promptly and fairly.

ICOBS 8 sets out the circumstances in which it will be unreasonable to reject a policyholder's claim. Different rules apply depending upon whether the contract was subject to the Insurance Act 2015 and the Consumer

Insurance (Disclosure and Representations) Act 2012 or the previous law (see **Chapter 6**).

Extensive requirements have been introduced for the tracing of historic employer's liability policies. This is to enable policyholders who have contracted industrial diseases to trace the provider of compulsory employer's liability cover at the time that they were exposed to injury. The rules in ICOBS 8.4 require that insurers produce an employer's liability register and carry out historical searches of policies underwritten to ensure that the register can be searched by policyholders, employers or other insurance companies looking to identify who underwrote a risk in a particular year.

FURTHER PROVISIONS OF THE FCA HANDBOOK

Complaints handling

43.16 Insurance distributors are subject to the compulsory jurisdiction of the Financial Ombudsman Service (FOS) in relation to eligible complainants. All businesses covered by the FOS pay a general levy to contribute to its costs. For businesses regulated by the FCA, to help simplify administration, the FCA collects the levy at the same time that it collects both its own regulatory fees and the levy for the Financial Services Compensation Scheme. The maximum amount that the FOS can award has increased significantly and as from 1 April 2020 is £355,000. This is likely to result in more claims going to the FOS.

The rules for complaints handling for eligible complainants are contained in the FCA's Dispute Resolution: Complaints Sourcebook. 'Eligible complainants' include:

(a) consumers;

(b) micro-enterprises (ie, enterprises that employ fewer than 10 persons and have a turnover or annual balance sheet of not more than €2 million);

(c) charities which have an annual income of less than £6.5 million;

(d) trustees of a trust which has a net asset value of less than £5 million;

(e) small businesses (ie, enterprises with an annual turnover of less than £6.5 million and fewer than 50 employees or a balance-sheet total of less than £5 million); and

(f) guarantors.

The main provisions relate to insurance distributors acknowledging and settling complaints within set time limits and informing the complainant that he may refer the matter to the FOS. Insurance distributors must also have appropriate and effective procedures for registering complaints for persons who are not 'eligible complainants'.

Training and competence

43.17 The rules on training and competence are contained in the FCA's Training and Competence Sourcebook (TC). For all staff carrying out insurance distribution activities (and potentially those managing them), insurance distributors will need to comply with the TC rules. Although the FCA does not impose any examination requirements, insurance brokers will need to ensure that their employees are and remain competent for the work they do and are appropriately supervised; and that their competence is regularly reviewed. Post the IDD, there is now a minimum Continuing Professional Development requirement of 15 hours a year.

For staff giving advice to consumers, the more detailed rules in the TC will apply.

Client Asset Sourcebook

43.18 The client money rules relating to insurance distribution are set out in CASS 5. The rules requiring records and controls to prevent misuse of client mandates (eg, direct debits and other authorities over monies which are not client monies) are set out in CASS 8.The aim of CASS is to protect client money in the event that an intermediary becomes insolvent. There are two different means by which an intermediary can hold client money: through a risk transfer arrangement with the insurance company which agrees to be responsible for premium and claims money received by the intermediary; and by the intermediary holding client money in a trust account on behalf of the client. Risk transfer arrangements are mandatory where an intermediary is operating under a delegated authority from the insurer.

The requirements of CASS 5 will generally mean that monies held in connection with an UK regulated insurance distribution business must be held on trust for the client or in an approved bank until they are paid to the insurer. Alternatively, an intermediary may hold money on a risk transfer basis agreed with the insurer and disclosed to the client. This will mean that the insurer is liable for the money held by the intermediary (ie, it is deemed to be the insurer's money and premium will deemed to have been paid).Where the intermediary issuing a policy acts as agent of the insurer under a delegated authority, it must collect and hold premiums under a risk transfer arrangement. Risk transfer arrangements may also be agreed between an insurer and an intermediary in other scenarios, and may include monies paid by the insurer in relation to claims. CASS 5.2 sets out requirements in relation to such a risk transfer arrangement which may be summarised as follows:

(a) The intermediary should not receive money as agent of an insurer, unless:

   (i) it has entered into a written agreement with the insurer which expressly provides that it is to act as the insurer's agent in receiving premiums and/or holding other monies to be paid to the client (eg, refunds and claims monies) on behalf of the insurer; and

   (ii) it retains a copy of the agreement for at least six years from the date on which it is terminated;

(b) The intermediary must ensure that it informs those of its clients which are not insurance undertakings and whose transactions may be affected by the arrangement (whether in its terms of business, client agreements or otherwise), in writing, that it will hold their money as agent of the insurance undertaking and, if necessary, the extent of such agency (ie, whether it includes all items of client money or is restricted – for example, to the receipt of premiums); and

(c) The intermediary must be satisfied on reasonable grounds that the terms of the policies issued by the insurance undertaking to its clients are likely to be compatible with the risk transfer arrangement.

CASS 5.1.5A also provides that if the terms of a risk transfer arrangement permit the distributor to co-mingle risk transfer monies with client monies, the monies will effectively become client monies and the insurer's interests must be expressly subordinated to the interests of the clients. Care is therefore needed to ensure that risk transfer arrangements do not, unless intending to apply the client money rules, permit co-mingling, as otherwise the money would become subject to the client money rules.

Capital and professional Indemnity insurance

43.19 The FCA's Prudential Sourcebook for Mortgage and Home Finance Firms, and Insurance Intermediaries (MIPRU) sets out requirements in relation to regulatory capital and the minimum amount of professional indemnity insurance required (in accordance with the IDD). Capital requirements are set out in MIPRU 4 and 5, and insurance requirements are set out in MIPRU 3. MIPRU 3 requires insurance intermediaries to have a professional indemnity policy that provides a minimum annual indemnity of €1.25 million per claim and, in aggregate, the higher of €1.85 million and an amount equivalent to 10 per cent of annual income. Where a firm wishes to have an excess under the policy that is higher than the minimum level of indemnity, it must hold additional capital (calculated in accordance with a table set out in MIPRU).

Chapter 44

Insurance business transfers under the Financial Services and Markets Act 2000

- Introduction
- Use of insurance business transfers
- Law and practice
- Meaning of 'transfer'
- Court's jurisdiction
- Procedure
- Role of regulators
- Independent expert and scheme report
- Notification to policyholders and others, and access to documentation
- Court application
- Final hearing
- Effect of court's order

INTRODUCTION

44.01 Where parties wish to transfer the assets and liabilities of a general or life insurance business to another party, subject to limited exceptions, a court-approved insurance business transfer (a 'Part VII transfer') under Part VII of the Financial Services and Markets Act 2000 (FMSA 2000) is the only means of doing so in the UK.

A Part VII transfer permits the transfer of insurance business without the need for individual novations of insurance policies (and, accordingly, without policyholder consent). The process also provides a number of protections for policyholders, including:

(a) the appointment of an independent expert to review and report on the transfer;

(b) the approval of the court, which considers whether it is appropriate, in all the circumstances of the Part VII transfer, to sanction the scheme; and

(c) the right of any person who may be adversely affected by the Part VII transfer to object at the final court hearing.

The Prudential Regulatory Authority (PRA) and the Financial Conduct Authority (FCA) will also review the Part VII transfer and each has the right to attend and to be heard on the scheme in court.

Schemes will generally take nine to 18 months to put together and obtain court approval. The process requires coordination between the PRA, the FCA, the firms and their advisers (legal, actuarial and tax).

USE OF INSURANCE BUSINESS TRANSFERS

44.02 Subject to the limits of s 105 of the FSMA 2000 (see **44.05** below), a Part VII transfer can be used by life and general insurers in a wide variety of ways. The potential uses include:

(a) intra-group reorganisations;

(b) the sale of an insurance business (including discontinued lines of business);

(c) the demutualisation of a mutual insurance company; and

(d) fund restructuring, including the reattribution of the inherited estate of a life company.

The Part VII process can be used to transfer insurance assets and liabilities and other related assets and liabilities. For example, in addition to the reserves supporting the transferring insurance business, under s 112 of the FSMA 2000, the court can order the transfer of the benefit of other parts of the transferor's business, including contracts which the transferor would be unable to transfer unilaterally; and make orders in relation to other incidental, consequential and supplementary matters which it considers necessary to secure that the scheme is fully and effectively carried out.

LAW AND PRACTICE

44.03 Insurance business transfers were previously governed by Sch 2C to the Insurance Companies Act 1982, which set out different requirements for general and long-term business transfers. Very broadly, long-term business transfers required an order of the court and the production of a report by an independent actuary on the effect of the scheme, as well as the notification of policyholders. General business transfers required only the approval of the regulator (the Department of Trade and Industry, the Treasury and then the Financial Services Authority).

The procedure for life and general insurance business transfers is now unified under Part VII of the FSMA 2000, and both types of transfer require court approval and the production of an independent expert's report. The specific provisions relevant to Part VII Transfers are:

(a) Part VII of and Sch 12 to the FSMA 2000;

(b) the Financial Services and Markets Act 2000 (Control of Business Transfers) (Requirements on Applicants) Regulations 2001 (SI 2001/3625) (2001 Regulations);

(c) the Financial Services and Markets Act 2000 (Control of Transfers of Business Done at Lloyd's) Order 2001 (SI 2001/3626) in relation to transfers at Lloyd's;

(d) Chapter 18 of the FCA's Supervision Manual, forming part of the FCA Handbook (SUP 18);

(e) the PRA's policy statement, 'The Prudential Regulation Authority's approach to insurance business transfers', published in April 2015 (the PRA Statement); and

(f) the FCA's finalised guidance, 'The FCA's approach to the review of Part VII insurance business transfers', which was published in May 2018 (FG18/4).

MEANING OF 'TRANSFER'

44.04 The starting point, when looking at any proposed 'transfer' from the legal point of view, is that the general position under English law is that while it is possible to transfer contractual *rights* without the consent of the counterparty, it is not possible to transfer contractual *obligations* without consent. A novation, which is effectively a new contract between the transferee and the policyholder, will be required.

Insurance business transfer schemes are effectively statutory novations which do not require the consent of the policyholder or other counterparties of the transferor. The terms of the scheme will specify what is to transfer and may result in some historic liabilities remaining with the transferor.

A transfer is therefore to be distinguished from reinsurance; even though reinsurance can, as between transferor and transferee, pass economic responsibility in relation to the underlying contracts, legal liability to the policyholder remains with the transferor. In practice, an insurance business transfer will often follow, and therefore replace, an initial economic transfer of risk between the parties effected by way of reinsurance.

The PRA's Policy Statement and SUP 18 of the FCA Handbook contain regulatory guidance on what may constitute a transfer. First, the regulators take the view that a novation or series of novations (ie, individual agreements under which the policyholder agrees to the contract moving to the new insurer) can be capable of constituting a Part VII transfer if their number or value is equivalent to a transfer of part of a company's insurance business. This can be the case even if the parties have all consented to the arrangements. By contrast, neither the 'reinsurance-to-close' process at Lloyd's nor a mere transfer of renewal rights constitutes a transfer for the purposes of the legislation, as in those cases legal liability to a policyholder under an existing contract does not pass to the other party.

It is important for the applicants to clearly specify and define the transferring business (see paragraph 5.4 of FG18/4 and *PA(GI) Ltd v GICL 2013 Ltd* [2015] EWHC 1556 (Ch), in which case a dispute arose as to whether misselling liabilities had transferred).

COURT'S JURISDICTION

44.05 Section 105 of the FSMA 2000 limits the application of Part VII transfers in broad terms to the following:

(a) insurance and reinsurance business carried on in the UK by UK persons that have permission to carry on insurance business in the UK; and

(b) insurance and reinsurance business carried on in the UK by persons with permission to carry on insurance business in the UK that are not UK persons (ie, an overseas insurer in respect of its UK-authorised branch).

Additionally, a Part VII transfer must result in the transferred business being carried on from the transferee's establishment in the UK or Gibraltar. The scope of the insurance business transfer regime in the FSMA 2000 regime has narrowed following the UK's exit from the EU. This chapter only considers the position for Part VII transfers commencing on or after 1 January 2021 (the scope of the insurance business transfer regime in the FSMA 2000 has narrowed following the UK's exit from the EU).

Section 105(3) of the FSMA 2000 excludes certain types of schemes and so should be consulted by any parties considering undertaking a Part VII transfer.

The meaning of 'carrying on insurance business in the UK' is not straightforward and has been the subject of considerable judicial interpretation. In broad terms, however, issues such as where underwriting decisions are made, where policy administration is undertaken and where decisions on claims are made will be relevant. Section 418 of the FSMA 2000 makes clear that regulated activities carried on from a UK office by a firm with its head office outside the UK will still be regulated activities for the purposes of UK regulation.

PROCEDURE

44.06 The court procedure that is described below applies in England and Wales. There is a slightly different procedure in Scotland.

As an overriding comment on process, it is worth bearing in mind when planning an insurance business transfer that, even for a straightforward scheme, the Part VII transfer is likely to take at least nine to 12 months from start to finish. The reasons for this include:

(a) that the PRA (in consultation with the FCA) will assess the proposed independent expert prior to his appointment;

(b) that the PRA and the FCA in their regulatory guidance state that they expect it will take at least six to eight weeks to consider the draft documentation for the scheme, including the independent expert's report. In practice, they will often consider and comment on more than one draft of these documents;

(c) that the FCA expects firms to give policyholders, reinsurers and other interested persons a period of not less than six weeks to review the notices of the transfer prior to the final court hearing;

(d) if applicable, the need for the transferee to obtain PRA authorisation or vary its Part 4A permission under the FSMA 2000; and

(e) due diligence, which will need to focus on the transferring policies and related outwards contracts, other material contracts, foreign law governed contracts (following the decision in *Sompo v Transfercom* [2007] EWHC 146 (Ch) (*Sompo*) – see **44.12**) and contracts with subsidiaries of the transferor.

ROLE OF REGULATORS

44.07 The PRA and the FCA have assumed the functions previously held by the Financial Services Authority. The PRA and the FCA have agreed in a memorandum of understanding that the PRA is the lead regulator in relation to Part VII transfers. However, both regulators will consider Part VII transfers in line with their statutory objectives. The PRA has set out its expectations in the PRA Statement. The FCA's guidance is set out in SUP 18 and FG18/4.

Early engagement with the regulators is required as part of the process. The regulators will expect the parties to share a practical timetable and highlight any known key issues so that they may efficiently allocate resources. Any changes to this timetable should be notified to the regulators in advance. For larger and more complex transactions, an initial meeting between the applicants and the PRA and FCA is likely to be appropriate.

The applicants will need to pay the applicable regulatory fees to the FCA.

During the process, the PRA and the FCA will review key documents such as the scheme; the witness statements of the transferor and transferee explaining the terms of the transfer and the approach to policyholder notification; the policyholder notices; and the report of the independent expert. For transfers of long-term business, a report from the chief actuary of the transferor will be expected. Where such a transfer involves with-profits business, a report from the transferee's chief actuary will also be expected (see SUP 18). The regulators expect the applicants to provide them with near-final drafts and the timetable should allow the regulators at least six to eight weeks to complete their review. In practice, the regulators may review more than one iteration of these documents.

The PRA must also provide the required certificate as to the solvency of the transferee (Part I of, and Sch 12 to, the FSMA 2000).

The transferor is required by reg 3(5) and reg 4(1)(b) of the 2001 Regulations to provide the PRA and the FCA with copies of the application to court, the independent expert's report and the statement to policyholders at least 21 days before the final court hearing.

Although the PRA and the FCA do not need to approve a transfer scheme formally, in practice, the parties are highly unlikely to proceed with a Part VII transfer without the support of the PRA and the FCA. The PRA and the FCA each have a statutory right to attend the court hearing and make representations about the transfer (FSMA 2000, s 110). The practice has developed of the PRA and the FCA issuing reports to the court prior to each court hearing which are described further below.

INDEPENDENT EXPERT AND SCHEME REPORT

44.08 Under the Part VII regime, for both long-term and general business, there must be an independent expert appointed. The independent expert must make a report on the terms of the scheme. Section 109 of the FSMA 2000 specifies that the PRA must (in consultation with the FCA) approve both the identity of the independent expert and the form of his report. The PRA's agreement to the identity of the independent expert should be sought at an early stage of the process.

The PRA's guidance indicates that the expert should be an actuary for transfers of long-term business. While the independent expert need not necessarily be an actuary in relation to a transfer of general business, this is generally the case in practice. The suitability of a particular individual will depend on the nature of the scheme, the business being transferred and the companies concerned. The PRA will also assess the expert's independence from the companies involved.

The PRA and the FCA's guidance also sets out the matters with which a scheme report should deal. In broad terms, the independent expert will need to consider the impact of the Part VII transfer on the policyholders of each applicant, in terms of, *inter alia*, financial security and policy administration. The regulators will also draw any transaction-specific areas they expect the scheme report to cover to the independent expert's attention as part of their review process.

In practice, the independent expert's report is one of the most important documents that will be prepared, and will be relied upon heavily by the court (see **44.11**). Indeed, the court may well look to the expert for assistance in understanding some of the provisions of the scheme. For this reason, he should always attend the final court hearing.

A summary of the report for policyholders and other interested parties will also need to be prepared. The 2001 Regulations also provide that any person may obtain a copy of the report, together with a summary of the terms of the scheme, free of charge on request.

The PRA will also generally expect the independent expert to prepare a supplementary report before the final hearing to confirm whether his original conclusions remain unchanged, based on more recent financial information and any other relevant events since the date of the scheme report. The FCA states in FG18/4 that it expects this supplementary report to be made available to policyholders online no later than two weeks prior to the final hearing or longer if there is substantive new material.

NOTIFICATION TO POLICYHOLDERS AND OTHERS, AND ACCESS TO DOCUMENTATION

44.09 Applicants must comply with reg 3 of the 2001 Regulations, which sets out the following notification requirements:

(a) A notice stating that an application for a Part VII transfer has been made must be sent to every policyholder of the transferor and transferee and every reinsurer of the transferor whose contract of reinsurance is transferring (or the relevant reinsurance broker or lead reinsurer);

(b) The notice must also be advertised in the London, Belfast and Edinburgh Gazettes and two UK newspapers; and

(c) A copy of the independent expert's report, a statement setting out the terms of the scheme and a summary of the independent expert's report must be made available to policyholders.

In FG18/4, the FCA confirms that it interprets the term 'policyholder' very broadly. This can include employees under an employer's liability policy, third-party claimants under a motor insurance policy or any potential claimant, regardless of whether the possibility is remote. In light of this, compliance with the notification requirement in (a) can be difficult, particularly given the reliance on policyholder records of the transferor and transferee.

However, the 2001 Regulations permit the court to waive these requirements (in whole or part). The applicants will therefore typically formulate a plan for the notification's exercise setting out the proposed approach to communicating the Part VII transfer to policyholders, reinsurers and other interested parties (eg, distributors of white-labelled products, brokers, coverholders and claims administrators).

The courts and regulators have set out guidance as to factors that will be considered in assessing any waiver requests from the applicants. In *Re Aviva International Insurance Ltd* [2011] EWHC 1901 (Ch), Norris J set out several factors that the court will consider – for example, impossibility (eg, where historic records are incomplete) or proportionality (eg, where the costs of notifying the policyholder are disproportionate to any benefit of the notification; this might be particularly relevant on an intra-group transfer where the servicing arrangements will not change and the transferee is a strongly capitalised entity). These factors should be consulted but are not exhaustive and the applicants' proposals will need to be tailored to the facts of the Part VII transfer in question.

The scrutiny of the notification plan and the proposed documentation will predominantly be carried out by the FCA prior to the initial court hearing. The FCA will assess the proposals in light of the guidance and expectations set out in FG18/4. The applicants will be expected to justify their proposals in the witness statement in light of this guidance and set out any mitigating steps being undertaken where policyholders are not proposed to be notified directly (eg, advertising more widely than the 2001 Regulations require).

The FCA will also review the documentation to be provided to policyholders. The FCA's expectations are set out in FG18/4. In broad terms, the FCA will expect the documentation to be clear and concise, and will inform policyholders of how the scheme is likely to affect them and their rights to object, make representations to the court and obtain copies of the relevant documentation, along with the time and date of the hearing. Often, the FCA will also expect the parties to prepare a form of 'questions and answers' booklet covering frequently asked questions and likely areas of concern for policyholders. The FCA now expects the parties to make this documentation available on their website, in the manner set out in FG18/4.

In preparing the documentation, consideration should also be given to whether any other legal requirements might apply and local law requirements in other jurisdictions to which the documentation is being sent.

The applicants will need to keep a record of all responses received from policyholders and provide details of any objections to the regulators and the court prior to the final court hearing. Any person who alleges that he would be adversely affected by the carrying out of the scheme is entitled to appear at court.

COURT APPLICATION

44.10 Once the proposal is agreed between the parties and with the regulators, and is fully documented, the court process is started by an application to the Companies Court of the Chancery Division, submitting a Part 8 claim form together with a fee.

The first court hearing on the application takes place before an Insolvency and Companies Court judge. The hearing will cover whether the jurisdictional requirements are satisfied and the parties' proposals for the notification of policyholders and others, including any waivers requested from the 2001 Regulations' requirements.

A witness statement in support of the application and claim form will detail the company's authority to transfer the business; the reasons for the transfer; and – importantly – the proposals that the parties are making to notify transferring policyholders, the policyholders of the transferee company, reinsurers and other interested parties, or the relevant dispensations sought from the court in respect of these requirements.

As a Part VII transfer is an *ex parte* application, there is an obligation on the applicant to disclose all facts which reasonably could or would be taken into account by the judge in deciding whether to grant the application, and the applicants should consider this when preparing their witness statements.

As set out in **44.07** above, the PRA and FCA will in most cases deliver reports to the court. The reports issued to the court at the first court hearing will set out the relevant regulator's understanding of the scheme and any regulatory or supervisory issues within its remit that are relevant to the Part VII transfer. In particular, the FCA's report will typically set out its views in relation to the communication proposals and whether it objects to the waivers sought. Having reviewed the applicants' submissions and the regulatory reports, the court will give directions.

Following this hearing, the companies will implement the communications plan referred to above in line with the court's directions.

FINAL HEARING

44.11 Following implementation of the communications plan, a full hearing will be held before a judge at which he is asked to sanction the scheme.

The PRA and the FCA will customarily provide further reports to the court setting out their views on the transfer in the context of the applicants' evidence and the independent expert's reports, and will highlight any regulatory issues identified and proposed or required mitigations that should be brought to the court's attention. The FCA's report will focus on the notifications exercise and any objections received from policyholders.

The PRA and FCA each have a right to attend this hearing, as does any person who alleges that he would be adversely affected by the carrying out of the scheme.

The leading decision on whether anyone would be 'adversely affected' was made by Hoffmann J in the unreported case of *Re London Life Association* in 1989. Hoffmann J's key principles were summarised by Evans Lombe J in his decision in *Axa Equity & Law Life Assurance Society PLC v AXA Sun Life plc* [2001] 1 All ER (Comm) 1010. They are as follows:

(a) First, statute confers an absolute discretion on the court as to whether or not to sanction a scheme, but this is a discretion that must be exercised by giving due recognition to the commercial judgement entrusted by the company's constitution to its directors.

(b) The court is concerned with whether a policyholder, employee or other interested person, or any group of them, will be adversely affected by the scheme.

(c) This is primarily a matter of actuarial judgement involving a comparison of the security and reasonable expectations of policyholders without the scheme with what would be the result if the scheme were implemented. For the purpose of this comparison, statute assigns an important role to the independent expert, to whose report the court pays close attention.

(d) The regulators, by reason of their regulatory powers, can also be expected to have the necessary material and expertise to express an informed opinion on whether policyholders are likely to be adversely affected. Again, the court will pay close attention to any views expressed by the regulators.

(e) The fact that individual policyholders, or groups of policyholders, may be adversely affected does not mean that the scheme has to be rejected by the court. The fundamental question is whether the scheme as a whole is fair as between the interests of the different classes of persons affected.

(f) It is not the function of the court to produce what, in its view, is the best possible scheme. As between different schemes, all of which the court may deem fair, it is the company's directors' choice which to pursue.

(g) Under the same principle, the details of the scheme are not a matter for the court, provided that the scheme as a whole is found to be fair. Thus, the court will not amend the scheme because it thinks that individual provisions could be improved upon.

(h) The court, in arriving at its conclusion, should first determine what the contractual rights and reasonable expectations of policyholders were before the scheme was promulgated and then compare those with the likely effect on the rights and expectations of the policyholders if the scheme were implemented.

There are further principles that can be extrapolated from the cases as follows:

(a) When considering the question set out at (e) above, it is acceptable to take into account the advantages and disadvantages which would be secured by particular classes of persons by the implementation of the scheme. A balancing exercise is required, and this was made clear in the decision in *Re Refuge Assurance plc* (10 December 2000, unreported).

(b) In relation to (g) above, in *Re London Life Association* Hoffman J suggested that if the court viewed that the scheme was unfair, it could opine that the unfairness lay in a particular term and that a fresh scheme not containing the offending term would be likely to be acceptable.

(c) Although the judge in *Axa Equity & Law* referred to policyholders, the court will apply the same tests to objections raised by any other category of objector claiming to be adversely affected.

(d) In *Axa Equity & Law* it was stated that in any actuarial matter which is in dispute, the court's approach should be to accept the views of the independent expert and the regulator over those of the companies and any objectors. If the views of the independent expert conflict with those of the regulator, the court is likely to prefer those of the regulator.

These principles are a helpful summary. However, in *Re Prudential Assurance Company Ltd and Rothesay Life plc* [2020] EWCA Civ 1626, the Court of Appeal noted with disapproval the citation of the above factors as if they were applicable to transfers of every type of insurance business. The Court of Appeal was clear that the judge will always need to consider what factors are relevant based on the particular business and circumstances in question.

Furthermore, the principles above were established in respect of transfers of long-term business. The court in *Re Royal Sun Alliance Insurance plc* [2008] EWHC 3436 (Ch) set out how these principles should be adapted in respect of transfers of general insurance business. In particular, the reasonable expectations of policyholders of general insurance policies will, in most cases, be in respect of servicing level and the ability of the transferee to pay policyholders' valid claims. Richards J further set out that the court will be concerned to address 'real, as opposed to fanciful' risks to the position of policyholders.

The factors to which the court should have regard were further considered in *Re Prudential Assurance*. The Court of Appeal confirmed that the court's discretion is unfettered and is not exercised as a 'rubber stamp'. Indeed, the court should seek to identify any errors, omissions or instances of inadequate or defective reasoning. However, the court should always accord full weight to the opinions of the independent expert and the regulators, and should not depart from the independent expert's conclusions or the regulators' non-objections without significant and appropriate reasons.

In addition to the exercise of its discretion, the court will need to be satisfied that the jurisdictional requirements are met. Under s 111 of the FSMA 2000, the court will need to be provided with the certificate of solvency from the PRA in respect of the transferee; and the court must be satisfied that the transferee has the necessary authorisations to carry on the transferred business. The applicants will need to demonstrate that the requirements in the 2001 Regulations, as waived or varied by the directions order, have been met. Accordingly, the applicants will need to provide detailed evidence of the implementation of their communications plan to the court.

EFFECT OF COURT'S ORDER

44.12 The scope within which a court order may be given is set out in s 112 of the FSMA 2000. Typically, it will have the following effects:

(a) First, policy rights and liabilities will transfer without any requirement for consent by the relevant policyholder so that the transferee becomes directly liable to the policyholder and the transferor ceases to be liable for them – this is of course the principal objective of the order. The court also has the power to order the transfer of part of an insurance contract or reinsurance contract (see *Re AIG Europe Ltd* [2018] EWHC 2818 (Ch) and other schemes related to the UK's exit from the EU in particular).

(b) All other assets, rights, contracts and liabilities within the terms of the order will also transfer. The court also has the power to override contractual rights, such as prohibitions on the assignment of contracts, in connection with a transfer of insurance business. This is expressly set out in s 112(2A) of the FSMA 2000, but in practice parties may seek counterparty consent (eg, the consent of a key reinsurer) for commercial reasons.

(c) The court order is the only instrument needed to effect the transfer; although where registration is needed to perfect a transfer – for example, for real property and shares – the registration requirement is not dispensed with.

(d) The transaction is a transfer by operation of law of the assets and liabilities within the scope of the court order.

(e) Because the authority is given by statute, it does not extend to foreign law governed assets or liabilities that an order of a UK court cannot transfer as it has no jurisdiction – foreign law governed assets or liabilities will need to be transferred by separate documents in accordance with local laws. This will not, however, limit the effectiveness of the Part VII transfer in the UK (eg, if a policyholder brought proceedings in the UK against the transferor; see *Royal & Sun Alliance v British Engine* [2006] EWHC 2947 (Ch)). Per the decision in *Sompo* referred to above, if there were a material number of non-English law governed contracts within the scope of the transfer, the court would require evidence of its effectiveness in the relevant jurisdictions as part of its consideration of whether the order would serve a substantial purpose. The court stated in *Sompo* that it would not act in vain.

Where sanctioned, the court's order will specify the effective date of the Part VII transfer. Once the court has approved the Part VII transfer, the transferee must provide office copies of the court order to the PRA.

Index